EXPELLING PUBLIC SCHOOLS

Expelling Public Schools

HOW ANTIRACIST POLITICS ENABLE
SCHOOL PRIVATIZATION IN NEWARK

John Arena

University of Minnesota Press
Minneapolis
London

Copyright 2023 by the Regents of the University of Minnesota

All rights reserved. No part of this publication may be reproduced, stored in a retrieval system, or transmitted, in any form or by any means, electronic, mechanical, photocopying, recording, or otherwise, without the prior written permission of the publisher.

Published by the University of Minnesota Press
111 Third Avenue South, Suite 290
Minneapolis, MN 55401-2520
http://www.upress.umn.edu

ISBN 978-1-5179-1367-0 (hc)
ISBN 978-1-5179-1368-7 (pb)

Library of Congress record available at https://lccn.loc.gov/2022052888

Printed on acid-free paper

The University of Minnesota is an equal-opportunity educator and employer.

To my mother, Jean Marie Guidone Arena (1942–2013), who taught me compassion and commitment

Contents

Abbreviations		ix
Introduction. Whip Them Back into Line: The Class Politics of Antiracism		1
Part I. Movement Foundations		
1	Whose Schools, Whose City? Reading Newark through Social Movements	31
Part II. The Movement from Above		
2	Regime Change: Cory Booker, Philanthrocapitalism, and the New Civil Rights Movement of Our Day, 1996–2006	63
3	Booker in Power: Reconstructing the State and the Limits of Neoliberal Antiracism, 2006–2012	87
Part III. The Movement from Below		
4	Rebel City? Newark's Education Movement from Below, 2010–2013	115
5	The Clash of Disruptors: Who Would Prevail? 2013–2014	145

Part IV. Containing the Movement

6 Ras Baraka's Self-Determination Politics: 177
The First Time as Tragedy, Second Time as Farce,
Summer–Fall 2014

7 We All Become Mayor? Movement Reinvention   203
and the Ousting of Cami Anderson,
Spring–Summer 2015

8 Making Newark Governable Again: 231
Merging Movements through Racial Democracy,
2015–2018

Conclusion: Tell No Lies, Claim No Easy Victories   257

Acknowledgments   275

Appendix: Research Methods   277

Notes   283

Index   351

Abbreviations

ACORN	Association of Community Organizations for Reform Now
AFT	American Federation of Teachers
ALI	Abbot Leadership Institute
ANPS	Alliance for Newark Public Schools
AROS	Alliance to Reclaim Our Schools
BAEO	Black Alliance for Educational Options
BCEE	Business Coalition for Educational Excellence
BLM	Black Lives Matter
BPE	black political entrepreneur
BPMC	black professional managerial class
BUR	black urban regime
CDC	community development corporation
CFUN	Committee for a Unified Newark
CIO	Congress of Industrial Organizations
CPD	Center for Popular Democracy
CWA	Communication Workers of America
DFER	Democrats for Education Reform
E3	Excellent Education for Everyone
EDA	Economic Development Authority
ELC	Education Law Center
EWA	extended work agreement
FHA	Federal Housing Administration
FNF	Foundation for Newark's Future
GVZ	Global Village Zone
HUAC	House Un-American Activities Committee
ICC	Ironbound Community Corporation
ILA	International Longshoremen's Association

ix

x || ABBREVIATIONS

NAN	National Action Network
NCC	New Community Corporation
NCDN	Newark Community Development Network
NCSF	Newark Charter School Fund
NCUP	Newark Community Union Project
NEA	National Education Association
NESB	Newark Educational Success Board
NEW	Newark Education Workers
NJCU	New Jersey Communities United
NJEA	New Jersey Education Association
NJPAC	New Jersey Preforming Arts Center
NPS	Newark Public Schools
NSU	Newark Students Union
NTA	Newark Teachers Association
NTE	Newark Trust for Education
NTU	Newark Teachers Union
ONE	Organization of Negro Educators
PC2E	Parent Coalition for Excellent Education
POP	People's Organization for Progress
PULSE	Parents United for Local School Education
QSCB	Qualified School Construction Bond
RD	racial democracy
SD	social democracy
SDA	School Development Authority
SDS	Students for a Democratic Society
SSA	social structure of accumulation
TaLiN	Teachers as Leaders in Newark
TFA	Teach for America
UCC	United Community Corporation
UCORE	United Caucuses of Rank-and-File Educators
WPB	War Production Board

Introduction

Whip Them Back into Line

THE CLASS POLITICS OF ANTIRACISM

> The race line *is* a class line. It is rooted in the commitment to a politics of racial elite brokerage or racial representation that, as indicated in the increasingly torturous and convoluted formulations required to argue for funneling any problem or issue affecting black Americans into the discourse of racism and racial disparity, is ever more contradictory and inadequate the farther we get from the Jim Crow era in which it was born and evolved. . . . It is anchored within a political economy of race relations that delivers material and symbolic benefits disproportionally to members of the professional-managerial strata who occupy the status of brokers or representatives *and who insist on it as the default language of black political aspirations.*
>
> —Adolph Reed Jr., "The 'Color Line' Then and Now: *The Souls of Black Folk* and the Changing Context of Black American Politics" (emphasis in original)

Newark as an urban success story? In September 2010, two years after I became involved in local political organizing in Newark, New Jersey, Oprah Winfrey placed my newly adopted city in the national spotlight on her widely watched show. But this was not for the usual disparaging depiction of crime, poverty, derelict high-rise public housing, fiscal crises, racial strife, and other elements of the so-called urban crisis with which Newark has for decades been synonymous in the American imaginary. Rather, the billionaire TV host presented New Jersey's largest city as a model for the country. In an age of "red states and blue states, of everybody being so partisan about everything," as Winfrey lamented, Newark now stood out as a beacon of bipartisan cooperation to tackle the most vexing of urban problems—public schools.

|| 1

2 || INTRODUCTION

Gathering onstage Newark's star mayor Cory Booker, the newly installed Republican governor Chris Christie, and Facebook founder Mark Zuckerberg, Winfrey breathlessly announced that the powerful trio were "putting politics aside to help turn around the failing public schools in Newark, New Jersey." Booker—the forty-one-year-old Stanford-, Oxford-, and Yale-educated lawyer—explained that he and his allies had "been talking . . . for some time about creating a bold new paradigm for educational excellence." His Republican partner, Christie, chimed in announcing that Booker could now realize that vison because he, as head of the state-controlled school district, was "empowering" the mayor to carry out an "entirely new plan," one that would provide parents the choice to select high-performing charter schools over failing public ones. "So, Mr. Zuckerberg," Winfrey slyly asked as she turned to her fellow billionaire, "what role are *you* playing in all of this?" The Silicon Valley mogul announced, to a standing ovation, that he was making a $100 million "challenge grant" to transform Newark's failing school system into a "symbol of educational excellence for the whole nation." The entire endeavor—as Christie made clear by his earnest recounting of an exchange with a Newark mother desperately trying to place her son in a charter school to save him from the streets—was "all about the children."[1] It was, as the charter movement emphasized, "the civil rights movement of our day."[2]

Yet, confounding the hopes of Winfrey, Booker, Christie, Zuckerberg, and other parts of the elite-driven charter school movement, Newark instead became a symbol of popular opposition to corporate school reform. Spearheaded by students operating under the banner of the Newark Students Union (NSU), and joined by dissident teacher union activists, parents, and assorted community activists, mass protests emerged opposing the school reforms being carried out by Booker and Christie's handpicked superintendent, Cami Anderson. Fiery denunciations at school board meetings, student sit-ins of the superintendent's office, and mass walkouts of thousands of students shook the city during the first half of the 2010s.

In the face of this growing opposition, Booker exited to the U.S. Senate before his second term expired and realizing his signature school reform agenda. In the ensuing mayoral race, city councilman Ras Baraka, the son of famed poet and Black radical activist Amiri Baraka, handily defeated his hedge fund–backed opponent by riding the opposition to corporate school reform to victory in May 2014.

INTRODUCTION || 3

In his first year in office, protests escalated, culminating in massive student walkouts during spring 2015, demanding the resignation of Anderson, a return to local control, and an end to the corporate reform agenda. In June, Governor Christie signed—just weeks before announcing his 2016 presidential bid—an agreement with Baraka to remove school superintendent Cami Anderson and committed to an eventual return to local control. Then, with Baraka's assent, Christie replaced Anderson with Christopher Cerf, an even more influential figure in the charter school movement.

In office, Baraka trumpeted progress toward, and the eventual regaining of, "self-determination" by a return to local control of Newark's public schools. At the same time, the self-proclaimed "radical mayor" collaborated with his erstwhile opponents in advancing their privatization agenda, with the portion of Newark students in charter schools reaching one-third by the end of his first term and continuing to climb during his second.[3] This cooperation has included the mayor giving the green light to zoning changes for expanding charter schools to running a slate of school board candidates in alliance with pro–charter school forces funded by the Bill and Melinda Gates Foundation and other powerful foundations promoting privatization. Yet, despite the departure from his campaign rhetoric, Baraka's popular base in the public school movement has not publicly objected. It was a movement that, as Newark education blogger Bob Braun noted, was "building and unified" in opposition to state control and the privatization agenda, but then became splintered and quiescent following the accord.[4]

The purpose of this book is to address how and why this political transformation took place and, more broadly, to shed light on the mechanisms that reproduce, deepen, and manage inequality within the context of post–civil rights black and urban politics. Struggles over public schools, because of their centrality to ongoing efforts to transform urban political economies, provide an ideal window into the heart of contemporary black and urban politics. To carry out this study, I employed an extended case study methodology that examines the relationships among and between elite reformers and the teachers, unions, students, parents, and community members with whom they were engaged in the struggle over the fate of the city's schools.[5] This combined top-down and bottom-up analysis is used to address the paradox we confront in Newark: Why were Cory Booker and his powerful corporate school reform allies unsuccessful in generating consent to their agenda in Newark, New Jersey? How did a powerful movement emerge to defend public schools in the face of such formidable opponents? Conversely, how and why has Booker's successor, Baraka, been far more effective in generating consent to an agenda that does not differ markedly from that of the corporate reformers against whom he railed in his campaign? How did he win over student, teacher, and community activists, and why was that so important? What lessons can be drawn from this case study? Is there an alternative to school privatization and other core elements of the revanchist agenda now sweeping over working-class communities in Newark and cities across the country?

I argue that the answer to this conundrum lies in the power of a "black urban regime" (BUR) headed by Baraka and his deft wielding of a radical-sounding version of antiracist politics. In this study, I define antiracist politics, following political scientist Preston Smith II, as "racial democracy" (RD). At the center of RD ideology and its attendant political practice, be it in radical or neoliberal garb, is the construction of a unified "Black community," at times, as we see in the case of Newark, enlarged to include "people of color" or "Black and Brown communities"—of a unitary subject—that obscures real class divisions, interests, and ideological diversity. The central aim of this "unitary subject," per the ideology, is striving for "equal treatment in the marketplace as well as by government."[6] At its radical edge, RD ideology appears as an "anti-disparitarian" one that aims for an equal distribution of the "goods and the bads" of capitalism, ranging from wealth to exposure to environmental toxins to access to desirable neighborhoods and schools.[7]

Smith contrasts RD with the political norm of "social democracy" (SD)—which historically has enjoyed broad support among the black working class—that attacks "the broad inequality of U.S. society that stem[s] from [the] distribution of goods and services to a privileged few at the expense of a poor working majority." A central policy goal of a social democratic–informed agenda is the state-guaranteed right for *all* to quality housing, health care, education, jobs, and other basic needs. These rights are guaranteed regardless of race, gender, sexual orientation, and other "ascriptive hierarchies," *as well as*, which RD ideology leaves outside its bounds, ability to pay.[8] Smith demonstrates in his study that in practice, an RD-informed political agenda, particularly when decoupled from a SD-informed one, allows the "class interests" of affluent black Americans to remain hidden behind what is projected as the "race interests" of all African Americans.[9]

Cory Booker and the forces with which he was allied in advocating for the commodification of public education advanced their movement by deploying a RD-informed ideology that framed their efforts as "the civil rights movement of our day." Providing "school choice," as Booker argued in a 2000 interview with the *New York Times,* through vouchers or charters, was crucial for achieving "equal opportunity in America" for African Americans. This form of RD ideology is exemplary of what Michael Dumas, drawing from Jodi Melamed, calls "neoliberal multiculturalism," in which "neoliberal economic policies and ideological formations," rather than state action, are projected as central "to resolv[ing] the problem of racism."[10] Yet, while "choice policies privilege those already positioned to take advantage of the market," they simultaneously, as Julia Rubin, Ryan Good, and Michelle Fine argue, "disadvantage those unable to do so." That is, the RD advanced by Booker and his allies stood in contradiction to a SD agenda of good schools for all. To address that contradiction, market advocates ignore structural barriers and indict the black poor for a "culture of poverty" that allegedly prevents them from taking advantage of the opportunities "school choice" provides.[11] As black politics has increasingly taken what political scientist Lester Spence terms a "neoliberal turn," a culture of poverty ideology is increasingly invoked to manage the deepening contradictions between RD and SD agendas.[12]

In contrast, Baraka, who rose to prominence as an opponent of Booker and the corporate school reform movement, countered with a radical-sounding version of RD. For Baraka, the central issue was not principally opposing the privatization of public education but rather "self-determination" by regaining local control over Newark's school district from the state. The racial injustice was that while predominately white suburban school districts were able to run their affairs, Newark, a "Black and Brown" city, was instead subject to a form of "neocolonial" tutelage. Therefore, the primary struggle, as Baraka projected, was for RD in the administration of local schools. It was *not,* though, a SD class struggle over maintaining local schools in the public sphere for the benefit of *all* in the face of a billionaire-backed effort to privatize and harness them to a profit-making agenda. For his supporters, the most optimistic interpretation was that Baraka was advancing a two-stage struggle in which the RD contradiction had to

6 || INTRODUCTION

be solved before the SD plan could be tackled at some later, unknown date—that, to their consternation, never came.

Of course, the RD and SD agendas did not necessarily have to be separated. Indeed, state takeovers in Newark and around the country have been part of the corporate reform tool box to promote charters and destabilize and defund public schools. But, for Baraka, separating the two—indeed, focusing on RD *to avoid* addressing the class issues at stake—was crucial for managing the contradictions of his political project. Denouncing "neocolonialism" and demanding "local control" and "self-determination" for "Black and Brown communities" allowed Baraka and his allies to walk a political tightrope. On one side, he could appear as an antiracist movement ally by railing against a white Republican governor for holding in bondage a local district of Black and Brown students. At the same time, this ideology allowed him to avoid coming into conflict with, or at times harmonizing with, the political economy of state-backed, rent-intensifying real estate development of which public school privatization and other forms of "accumulation by dispossession" are integral components.[13]

The BUR headed by Baraka, just as with his predecessor Booker, was essentially what geographer Sam Stein calls a "real estate state," dedicated to—indeed, obsessed with—raising property values.[14] As Pauline Lipman has demonstrated in her study of Chicago, neoliberal education reforms, particularly shuttering public schools and expanding charters, are one of the key ways local and other levels of the "real estate state" advance rent-intensifying redevelopment, also known as gentrification. Contemporary neoliberal "educational policy," she argues, "is constitutive of urban restructuring."[15] Closing public schools displaces low-income, vulnerable families by destroying one of the chief, and often only, anchoring institutions serving distressed neighborhoods, or those newly targeted for upscaling. In contrast, the new charters, particularly what sociologists Molly Vollman and Elizabeth Brown call the "prestige" variety, are promoted by real estate developers as an important "amenity" to attract, serve, and retain the incoming gentry while further driving up land values. In addition, the clustering of charters in zones targeted for upscaling, including in new-build, "mixed-use" construction that combines upscale housing, retail, and charters, as exemplified in Newark's downtown Teachers Village complex, are part of the rent-intensification repertoire deployed by finance, insurance, and real estate (FIRE) with the crucial assistance of local state allies. The residents, be they owners or renters, of the mixed-use buildings, combined with parents of the charter students, assist in the "cross pollination of customers from various commercial spaces and amenities."[16] "The whole idea," as one New Jersey developer explained, "is that a parent can drop off their kid at the preschool, go upstairs, take a spin studio or yoga or dance, and go straight to work or do that before picking up their child."[17]

Baraka, who courted real estate and other investors during his campaign, embraced this hegemonic definition of urban development that rests on using state power and resources to increase land values. Thus the self-styled "radical mayor," who rose to power on the tide of a mass movement, had to engage in what historian Touré Reed calls "race reductionism." This entails abstracting "racial disparities" and oppressions—in this case, the absence of "local control" over the school district—"from the political economic forces that generate them."[18] Therefore Baraka deployed a race-reductionist RD politics that, in the name of defending "the community," has successfully, for now, derailed a "rebel city" movement challenging the displacement and dispossession at the heart of the capitalist urban process.[19] In the end, a politics focused on group oppression is, as political scientist Cedric Johnson argues, "a move that avoids facing the *class contradictions within black life,* and the tough political challenge of organizing a viable social movement suited to our own times."[20]

ANTIRACISM AS A PROTECTIVE LAYER OF CAPITALISM

An antiracist, RD-centered "black agenda" divorced from black politics' historic championing of an SD-centered one has, ironically, strengthened in the post–civil rights era. Undergirding RD's hegemonic status in the post-1970s era has been the growth of what black politics scholar Adolph Reed Jr. terms the "black professional managerial class" (BPMC), including a whole layer of black urban Democratic Party officeholders. This ideology has proved indispensable for the influential urban BPMC in performing their anti-SD duties of overseeing public housing demolition, school privatization, and other key elements of the neoliberal urban project that have wreaked havoc, in particular, on the lives of black working-class and poor communities. The widening inequality in terms of wealth and income over the last forty years within the "Black community," which is even more

8 || INTRODUCTION

pronounced than the class structure as a whole, further undergirds the utility of RD ideology and political practice.[21]

Now, in the face of emerging challenges to what political economist Les Leopold calls "runaway inequality," an ostensibly "antiracist" politics is deployed with added vigor by black elites and their class allies.[22] Their fire, ironically, is aimed at delegitimizing demands and derailing working-class struggles that could seriously challenge entrenched racial inequalities they purport to be against. The role that contemporary antiracist politics plays in opposing and undermining a social democratic or socialist agenda has led Willie Legette and Adolph Reed Jr. to reformulate the insight of fellow political scientist V. O. Key. In his 1949 study of Jim Crow's political dynamics, Key argued that "over offices there is conflict aplenty, but the race question muffles conflict over issues latent in the economy of South Carolina." White racial unity, based on keeping the "Negro . . . out of politics," operated as a capitalist class–protecting circuit breaker. Therefore, when "a glimmer of informed political self-interest begins to well up from the masses," Key observed, "the issue of white supremacy may be raised to whip them back into line." *Now*, "preoccupation with race," rather than "the Negro," Legette and Reed argue, "stifles political conflict . . . over issues latent in the economy."[23]

The injection of race to derail "informed political self-interest" among working-class people is deployed, Legette and Reed emphasize, across the United States' narrow Democratic–Republican political spectrum. "Today," they underscore, "race performs the function of suppressing working-class politics in the interests of both white and black political elites who are equally committed to capitalist class priorities as defining the boundary of political possibility."[24] A prime example is the rise of Donald Trump, whose open and thinly veiled racist appeals continue to be used to "whip," or at least channel, class discontent away from capital to more easily impose "capitalist-class priorities," ranging from tax cuts to deregulation. Yet, far from being pioneered by the forty-fifth president, displacing class concerns by mobilizing white racial resentment has been the modus operandi of the modern U.S. Right. Ronald Reagan, who "launched a racialized assault on the American welfare state" in the 1980s, wielded these politics with particular skill. The former Hollywood actor, as historian Reed argues, spun a narrative that indicted permissive liberal social policies of the 1960s for creating a parasitical class of black "welfare queens" who were bankrupting the country. Reagan, therefore, was able—with the assistance of a rightward moving Democratic Party abandoning the New Deal—to successfully bind "racial animus to economic anxiety in a narrative intended to nurture antistatist sensibilities among working-class and middle-class white Americans, whose prosperity was," as Reed points out the irony, "itself the product of the American welfare state."[25]

Likewise, Pauline Lipman argues that racializing the concepts of "public" and "private," with the former equated with "bad" and "black" and the latter with "good" and "white," has been a key ideological weapon for imposing the "neoliberal project." "Racism," she holds, "is the ideological soil for appeals to individual responsibility and ending 'dependency' on the state."[26] But what about *antiracism*? How might antiracism, in the context of a majority black city and government like as in Newark, in which a mass movement has emerged against a core component of the local governing regime's neoliberal public policy agenda, also whip a movement back into line?

UNDERSTANDING SCHOOL PRIVATIZATION THROUGH THE LENSES OF BLACK POLITICS AND SOCIAL MOVEMENTS

Majority or near-majority black cities, such as Newark, New Orleans, Detroit, Baltimore, Washington, D.C., Philadelphia, and Chicago, have been among the leading battlegrounds of school privatization over the last quarter century. Thus understanding the commodification of public education requires serious engagement with black politics and its class dynamics. But the "antiracist," "critical race," "racial capitalism," and other such frameworks that inform much of the scholarship on school privatization obscure the conflicting material interests, actors, agendas, and ideologies operating within black politics both in the contemporary period and historically. Indeed, these works, consistent with RD ideology, take race as the "primary political unit" and presuppose the existence of a "unitary black agency"—captured in the often invoked "black freedom struggle" neologism—fighting to win their common antiracist demands in the face of an all-encompassing "white supremacy." This approach, conversely, homogenizes whites and obscures the powerful class forces driving school privatization. In the end, the RD paradigm legitimates an antidemocratic racial brokerage politics in which an imputed common identity, interests, and enemy

10 || INTRODUCTION

"necessitate[ ]," Preston Smith argues in his critique, "that all blacks act as one under an elite leadership."[27]

A leading example of this approach is Kristen Buras's study of the mass privatization of public schools in post-Katrina New Orleans. Apart from a passing mention of "black allies" assisting "white entrepreneurs" in the post-Katrina charterization, Buras fails to engage at all the crucial role played by the local black political class and larger BPMC. This blind spot is a product of Buras's critical race theoretical and conceptual model that simplistically indicts an all-encompassing "white supremacy" aimed at "restoring white control over the city's largely black public school system," while eviscerating the crucial role played by, and the agency of, the BPMC and the larger political economy from which they benefit and which they defend.[28] Buras's study, and the theoretical framework that informs it, is representative of what Cedric Johnson terms "black organicism," one that "elides the differing and conflicting material interests and ideological positions that animate black political life in real time and space."[29]

The edited collection *What's Race Got to Do with It? How Current School Reform Policy Maintains Racial and Economic Inequality* employs what editors Picower and Mayorga term "a racial economic analytical framework, where racial hierarchies and class exploitation occur in symbiotic relationship." Yet the study, which emerged out of a Ford Foundation–funded project—the Ford Secondary Educational Racial Justice Collaborative—operates, as the crucially important funding instrument indicates, from a racial justice framework as well. The overwhelming focus of the study is on "structural racism," "racial capitalism," "white supremacy," "whiteness" and the way "White dominance over people of Color . . . is protected and maintained by current racial ideology and policies."[30] Yet, as Howard Ryan argues in his critique of Picower and Mayorga's edited work,

> while whites as a group, without doubt, reap educational and other privileges relative to people of color, most whites are far from being "at the top of the hierarchy of power" in a class society ruled by corporate elites. Moreover, some blacks (such as Obama) enjoy class power far beyond that of working class whites. Any analysis of corporate reforms, or what Picower and Mayorga call "racial capitalism," would be woefully inadequate without addressing issues of class power and how that impacts educational policymaking.[31]

Thus, what Picower and Mayorga call the "notion of racial capitalism," drawn from the work of the late Black studies scholar Cedric Robinson, presents real limitations for analyzing the concrete dynamics of school privatization, particularly in the context of the BUR. While the editors present their work as a "race and class synthesis," the study fails to address—like most "analyses pitched under the banner of racial capitalism," as Cedric Johnson argues in his critique—"with any seriousness the capitalist class relations that permeate the black population." Indeed, following Robinson, most racial capitalism–informed works are based on the assumption that "the black population constitutes an organic political community, with widely-shared experiences and interests."[32] How, then, does Picower and Mayorga's work, which identifies "protecting . . . the supremacy of Whiteness" as an overriding aim of school reform, help us understand the role of Booker, let alone the son of Amiri Baraka, in that process? Or, for that matter, how does it help us distinguish the multiracial group of teacher activists who spearheaded a union reform caucus to aggressively oppose privatization from of their well-funded and compensated white and black corporate opponents?[33]

Following a similar racial justice framework, Domingo Morel's recent study holds that state takeovers of local school districts were a product of white conservative backlash aimed at the "systematic political disempowerment of black communities."[34] Echoing the argument of Michelle Alexander with regard to the rise of the carceral state, Morel asserts that state takeovers reflect how "periods of democratic gains among historically marginalized groups are also traditionally followed by responses that restrict democratic advancements." Morel's singular focus on state takeovers was amenable to a RD, racial justice–informed framework, but it came at the expense of ignoring school privatization, to which it is intimately connected. In a telling omission, Morel's work, which included Newark as the primary case, failed to engage the privatization of schools and the intraracial and class conflict it generated.[35]

The approaches in these three studies are unable to capture the contradictory picture of really existing black politics, in which an apparently unitary subject—"the Black community"—is arrayed on different sides of the barricades over public schools. Indeed, as political scientist Lester Spence emphasizes in his study of school privatization in Philadelphia, Detroit, New Orleans, Chicago, and Oakland, all with large black populations, "blacks are not only victimized by the transformations in urban education."

> Black elites are partially responsible for the transformations. More specifically, black political officials have often assisted in the takeover moves and have reproduced language blaming black parents and school children for poor educational outcomes. Blacks have often created public schools and managed failing school systems, and black intellectuals have themselves touted neoliberal solutions.[36]

Expelling Public Schools echoes Spence's insistence that to understand neoliberal school reform, we need a serious engagement with black politics, or what Cedric Johnson terms "black political life—the heterogeneous, complex totality of shifting positions, competing interests, contradictory actions and behaviors that constitute black political engagement historically."[37] To really grasp school privatization, we must bust open, as Reed entitled his classic collection of essays, the "jug" of black politics and seriously examine its "stirrings."[38]

The other indispensable theoretical lens through which to examine school privatization, and other elements of the corporate agenda for public schools, is that of social movements. Mass teacher strikes in Democratic Party strongholds of Chicago and Los Angeles, "Red State Revolts" of teachers in Republican-dominated governments in the South and Southwest, the rise of the Union Caucuses of Rank-and-File Educators (UCORE) rank-and-file union reform insurgency, and the mass student walkouts against privatization and the testing regime, most dramatically seen in Newark, all underscore how popular social movements have been at the center of the struggle over public schools.[39] At the same time, efforts in support of commodifying public education have forged an impressive organizational network, mounted collective actions, and entered into battle armed with their own progressive ideologies. Thus, an adequate understanding of the conflicts over the fate of public schools, particularly in Newark, necessitates a critical social movement framework that captures the relationships of movements from above and below. To comprehend the complex dynamics encompassing school privatization, I turn to the rich fountain provided by BUR and social movement theories.

NEWARK AND THE BLACK URBAN REGIME

Newark's public school insurgency and its containment emerged under what political scientist Reed has termed a "black urban regime" form of the local state. The structural origins of the regime are found in the mechanization of southern agriculture that "pushed" and "pulled" displaced black peasants to the city, deindustrialization fueled by manufacturers' search for cheaper land and more tractable labor outside urban confines, and postwar racialized federal government housing policies crafted by the real estate, construction, and banking industries. The cities most detrimentally affected by deindustrialization, government-subsidized white relocation efforts, and redlining—with northeastern cities like Newark being particularly hard hit—began to face, by the 1960s, chronic fiscal problems fueled by declining jobs, population, and tax revenue. These trends, combined with the political empowerment and élan generated by the civil rights and Black Power movements, set the demographic, economic, social, and political context that gave rise, beginning in the 1970s, to a number of BURs— majority or near- majority black cities, with a predominately black city governments whose mass political bases are rooted in the cities' black working classes.[40]

Despite the excitement and great expectations that followed their elections, Reed underscored how deeply constrained these leaders, and the regimes they headed, were in delivering material gains for their black working-class electoral bases. The same long-term demographic and economic transformation that laid the basis for the BUR's emergence, combined with federal government retrenchment that took root in the 1970s, constrained the measures they could undertake. A further constraint were the class origins of the new black political leadership—drawn, as they were, from the BPMC, and often incorporated into urban politics in the 1960s through foundation- and federal government–funded Great Society programs. This background helped to favorably predispose this social layer to the pro-growth, counter-Keynesian, trickle-down development agenda advocated by the local corporate elite.[41] The new black political elite that managed the local state embraced the agenda of their corporate governing partners as simply "common sense."

Thus, for Reed, the BUR is a deeply contradictory formation, "caught between the expectations of its principally black electoral

14 || INTRODUCTION

constituency, which implies downward redistribution, and those of its governing coalition, which converge around the use of public policy as a mechanism for upward redistribution."[42] While this class contradiction is a structural feature of all forms of capitalist politics, the strain between the governing and electoral coalitions is particularly sharp under the BUR. This "tension is greater" under the BUR because

> (1) they govern in cities whose populations include relatively greater proportion of citizens most likely to be adversely affected by pro-growth politics, (2) those citizens are most likely to be black or Hispanic and (3) the regimes tend to validate themselves to minority electoral constituencies by invoking an image of progressive redistribution, whereas pro-growth politics is grounded in a more regressive principle.[43]

The BUR arises precisely at the time these pro-growth, regressive principles deepen in the post-1970s transition from what David Harvey terms the "managerialist" city of the Keynesian era to the successor "neoliberal entrepreneurial" regimes. Under the former, "urban governance [was rendered] less consistent with rules of capital accumulation," while under the latter, governing principles have "moved more rather than less into line" with capital's "naked requirements."[44]

Reed argues that the key to managing the central contradiction of the BUR, at least in the early years, has been the use of a RD discourse in which symbolic gains of the race stand in for material ones. That is, black mayors attempt to move

> policy debate away from substantive [material] concerns with potential outcomes and toward protection of racial image and status, as embodied in the idiosyncratic agenda of the black officials. In this way it becomes possible for black officials to maintain support from both their black constituents and the development elites that systematically disadvantage them.[45]

Therefore, the central contradiction of the regime was managed by projecting the interests of the black head of state and broader black professional managerial elite as isomorphic with those of an undifferentiated "Black community." But, Reed and political scientist Cedric Johnson point out, as black popular mobilization "has fragmented and waned" since the 1980s, the pressure to "harmonize contradictory imperatives of governing and electoral coalitions" of the BUR has been eased.[46] Thus the second wave of black mayors—from, approximately, the mid-1980s through the 1990s, covering such mayoral reigns as Sidney Barthelemy in New Orleans, Sharon Pratt Kelley in Washington, D.C., Sharpe James in Newark, and Andrew Young in Atlanta—witnessed a deepening of the neoliberal agenda and distancing from the "gestural racial populism" that characterized the first wave.[47] Consistent with this analysis, in my study on the destruction of public housing in New Orleans, I identified the increasingly important outsourcing role nongovernmental organizations played in managing the class contradictions involved in the BUR's deepening of the neoliberal agenda in the 1990s and 2000s.[48]

The most recent "third wave" of BUR mayors since the millennium, such as Ray Nagin in New Orleans, Stephanie Rawlings-Blake in Baltimore, Adrian Fenty in Washington, D.C., Michael Nutter in Philadelphia, and maybe most prominently Cory Booker in Newark, have been—reflecting a broader shift to the right in American politics—an "even more technocratic, Ivy-league pedigreed and staunchly market-oriented lot than their predecessors."[49] The assault on public education, which went into high gear in the 2000s, has been a defining feature of the policy agenda of the latest crop of black mayors. This turn also coincides, as sociologist Derek Hyra points out in his recent study, with the increasing return of capital to cities, including long-disinvested, majority black cities like New Orleans, Newark, and Washington, D.C.[50]

Reed argues that the neoliberal consensus has reached a level where the BUR itself has been transformed from an "uneasy biracial governing arrangement whose internal tensions were likely to surface around issues related to racial redistribution . . . [to] a more coherent interracial governing class."[51] That is, there is agreement among the governing class—and their investor partners—not only on the neoliberal development agenda but, consistent with the neoliberal ideal of social justice, on the equitable inclusion of professional managerial blacks, women, and other people of color in the division of political offices and contracts that had been a point of conflict in the past. This neoliberal diversity agenda from above is combined, of course, with a continued elite, multiracial assault on the standard of living of the largely black, Latinx, and immigrant urban working class of these cities. But the class nature of these attacks is obscured by an underclass ideology, embraced by these same political elites, that points to a dysfunctional culture among the black poor in particular, rather than political economy, as the key source of poverty and inequality.[52]

Aaron Schneider's detailed study of a new multiracial governing elite in post-Katrina New Orleans who act, along with various elements of local capital, as intermediaries for global-oriented capital in tourism, services, and construction provides further support for Reed's thesis.[53] Likewise, in Newark, the rise of the Booker-led regime represented a political formation more closely connected to global capital in real estate, hedge funds, and other investors intent on opening public education to the market. Where the Newark case departs from the experience of the last several decades is in the mass movement that emerged against school privatization. This movement disrupted the political quiescence upon which the BUR and its attendant neoliberal agenda have been predicated. How and why, then, did popular opposition emerge after decades of successful elite management of neoliberal restructuring? How do the elite respond when the old ways of managing and suppressing the class contradiction at the heart of this formation no longer work? To answer these questions, we need to combine the insights of the BUR conceptual model with the "powers" of social movement theory.[54]

DISRUPTIVE POWER AND THE BLACK URBAN REGIME

Power, defined by political scientist Michael Parenti as "the ability to get what one wants," is at the center of social movements.[55] Control over large amounts of wealth and the means of coercion are primary sources of power. The minority in societies who control these resources are well positioned to exercise power at the level of decision-making, agenda setting, and hegemony, which Parenti defines as "the ability of A to get others to act or think in ways that they would not ordinarily act or think, specifically in a way that maximizes A's interests."[56] But, social movement theorist Frances Fox Piven emphasizes, while control over vast amounts of wealth and force is an important source of power, there is also an alternative form, much more widely available, which she terms "disruptive power." The font of this power is rooted in "the interdependent relations," the "networks of cooperation," often intertwined, that bind modern complex capitalist societies together and are critical to their functioning.

In capitalist societies, the defining "interdependent relation" is between the minority (capitalists), who control the means of production and the majority (the working class), who have nothing but their labor power to sell. While the working class is compelled to labor for capitalists to obtain the necessities of life, capitalists are similarly dependent on the workers to obtain their own wealth through the extraction of surplus value. Examples of the labor–employer and other interdependent relations from the Newark case include teachers and other education workers and the school systems that employ them, students and school administrators, union officials and rank-and-file members, and the mayor and other elected officials "who depend on the acquiescence if not approval of enfranchised publics."[57]

Piven emphasizes that although these relations are interdependent, that is, each party needs the other, "they also inevitably give rise to contention, to conflict, as people bound together by social life try to use each other to further their often distinctive interests and outlooks."[58] Thus "disruptive power" is the latent power embedded in interdependent relationships, while "disruption" involves the activation of this power through the *withdrawal of cooperation.* That is, disruption is the leverage, the power, that is generated "from the breakdown of institutionally regulated cooperation."[59] The most dramatic example of this in Newark has been students walking out en masse from classes to press their demands.

MOVEMENTS FROM ABOVE AND BELOW

Although Piven's focus is on the deployment of disruption "from below," she does recognize that it can also be exercised by the dominant participant in cooperative relationships, such as capitalists disinvesting and closing down plants "plagued" by combative, disruption-prone workers.[60] Sociologists Alf Gunvald Nilsen and Laurence Cox develop this point further in their Marxist theorization of social movements, as they identify both "movements from above," which would capture the elite-led push for charters in Newark, and "movements from below," such as the popular challenge to the privatization of Newark's schools. Therefore, in this study, I define social movements broadly, "as a process in which a specific social group develops a collective project of skilled activities centered on a rationality—a particular way of making sense of and relating to the social world—that tries to change or maintain a dominant structure of entrenched needs and capacities, in part or whole."[61] Disruption, of both the elite and mass varieties, is at the center of the "skilled activities" movements deploy to advance structural change.

The elite "movement from above" variant is a "collective project" crafted by dominant groups "to reproduce and/or extend their hegemonic position . . . within a given social formation."[62] Struggles for hegemony occur, they add, at both horizontal and vertical levels in society. In the former, elite movements attempt to forge unity among different capitalist groupings and collaborators for their larger objectives and strategies to win them. At the vertical level, social movements from above struggle to gain the consent and incorporate sections of the working class, oftentimes by granting concessions to movements from below. Movements from above are played out, Nilsen and Cox emphasize, within various terrains and institutional forms, including "corporations, states, political parties, armed forces, religion, the law, public opinion," and, we can add, BURs.[63]

The dominant class uses its superior control over economic, political, and cultural sources of power to advance its agenda or, as sociologist Goran Therborne terms it, "the direction of society."[64] In the Newark case, the movement deployed these sources of power to advance the marketization of public education and the disciplining of education workers, all of which was legitimated as a progressive, inevitable, and "commonsensical" initiative. The ideological component of movements from above, which are of particular importance, deploy "rationalities," concretized in ideological offensives, to cultivate both unity among the dominant group and popular consent to their restructuring agenda: hegemony.[65]

Neoliberalism as a Social Movement

In this study, I conceive of efforts by the ascendant sectors of capital in finance, high tech, and real estate, and their political partners in the BUR and other political formations, to commodify public education in Newark and nationally as a social movement from above.[66] Furthermore, I conceptualize the school privatization drive as an integral component of advancing the larger capitalist collective project: the neoliberal social structure of accumulation (SSA). The SSA school, as developed by David Kotz and his collaborators, conceives of capitalism as operating through historically distinct constellations "of economic and political institutions, as well as dominant ideas"—SSAs—to promote profit making and a stable accumulation process.[67]

The neoliberal SSA emerged out of the 1970s crisis—most immediately in terms of profits and accumulation—of the preceding Keynesian/regulated capitalist SSA that was dominant from the late 1940s through the early 1970s. The rise and consolidation of the neoliberal SSA involved displacing Keynesian economic theory, which argued that capitalist economies were not self-regulating mechanisms. Capitalism needed, Keynesians argued, government intervention to guarantee full employment, prevent depressions, and provide "an expanding supply of such public goods as education and infrastructure" to advance profits and investments. In contrast, neoliberal economic ideology is rooted in the nostrum of "individual freedom of choice . . . as the fundamental basis of human welfare, with market relations understood as the institution that allows individual choice to drive the economy." On this basis, neoliberal ideologues indict states, and state intervention more broadly in society, "as the enemy of individual liberty," inefficient compared to the private sector, and simply "a parasite living off the hard work of individuals."[68]

Kotz also emphasizes that a variety of "neoliberal ideas," which flow from the economic theory, are deployed to legitimate and advance various components of the neoliberal project. For example, the Reaganite Right, later joined by most of the bipartisan neoliberal elite, peddled tales that "welfare programs destroy work incentives and make people dependent on handouts"—which had thinly veiled antiblack messaging—to legitimate the assault on the welfare state and public services. But, in a sign of its dynamism, which Kotz overlooks, the neoliberal ideological brew has expanded, over time, beyond right-wing nostrums to incorporate antiracist ideas as well. The clearest example has been their deployment to advance the charter movement in the late 1990s and 2000s. This antiracist, left-wing ideological arm—what Reed terms as one component of "neoliberalism's critical self-consciousness"—further strengthened after the 2008 economic crisis as it generalized a critique of the racial inequities of New Deal programs to one of public services and state intervention more broadly.[69]

This antistatist tale, drawing from Afropessimism thought, includes dismissal of multiracial social movements advocating their expansion since they inevitably betray black people.[70] More broadly, a "multicultural neoliberalism" ideal of social justice has congealed around an equal distribution of positions along the axes of race, gender, and other ascriptive categories, particularly at the upper echelons of society. This formulation of justice is one, as Dylan Riley argues, "entirely compatible with maintaining, and indeed worsening," which neoliberalism has dramatically intensified, "inequality in economic terms."[71]

The structural aim of the neoliberal SSA social movement, armed with its ideology, is to "transform the institutions of regulated capitalism into the institutions of neoliberal capitalism," with the state being a central arena of struggle. Kotz groups the main institutions transformed under neoliberalism into four categories: global economy, the role of the government in the economy, labor–capital relations, and the corporate sector.[72] In the realm of public education, the central institutional battlegrounds include the privatization and contracting out of public goods, public services, and tax cuts for business and the rich (the role of government); marginalization of collective bargaining and casualization of jobs (labor relations); and penetration of market principles inside schools and hiring of administrators/CEOs from outside the public school system (the corporate sector). I theorize the struggle in and against the Newark BUR from the 1990s through the 2010s as one over whether it would become a neoliberal-implementing local mechanism of school reform.

Contentious movements from below challenged the old postwar Keynesian SSA in the United States and globally at the economic, military, political, and ideological levels. This cumulative "crisis of democracy" led political and economic elites to search out, beginning in the 1970s, a new SSA "to reestablish," David Harvey emphasizes in his study on neoliberalism, "the conditions for capital accumulation and to restore the power of economic elites."[73] While the offensive began in the 1970s and has progressed through different phases since then, critical scholars emphasize the "geographically and historically contingent forms" that neoliberalism has taken.[74] Neoliberalism, they hold, is best conceived as a process, what Peck and Tickwell term "neoliberalization," which is "neither monolithic in form nor universal in effect."[75]

The contingent and uneven nature is due, in large part, to the resistance that these class attacks generate. As Alan Sears argues, the transformation from the Keynesian welfare state to the neoliberal "lean" version is not predetermined; rather, "the extent to which the transition occurs is mediated by the class struggle and the overall ideological climate."[76] The centrality of struggle underscores the value of using the Marxist conception of social movements, which couples movements from above—captured in such conceptions as "rollback" and "rollout"—with their corresponding movements from below. Yet, in many Marxist analyses, including those operating from the SSA school, and especially its sister, regulation theory, neoliberalism is presented as an all-encompassing, unmovable structure. These works make it appear that new "social structures" or "modes of regulation" unproblematically emerge to facilitate the new model of accumulation.[77] The danger of "keeping neoliberalism at the center of critical analysis," argues Helga Leitner and her colleagues, is that it "can reify its ubiquity and power, even when the intent is critique."[78]

An example of this problem is Jason Hackworth's otherwise very valuable study on the restructuring of cities along neoliberal lines, but which is bereft of challenges beyond a few journalistic accounts tacked on at the end—a pattern evinced in other works as well. The author, drawing from geographers Brenner and Theodore, conceptualizes the rollback and rollout stages—also referred to as the "destruction" and "creation" moments of the transition from Keynesian to neoliberal urbanism—being played out at the level of artifacts, policies, institutions, and agreements.[79] Yet, resistance is left out of the model. The possibility of sections of the working class not only being incorporated into the neoliberal rollout (the default position) but successfully defending the Keynesian position, or forging a pro–working class alternative that transcends the contradictory Keynesian class compromises, is not entertained.

My study, in contrast, places movements from above and below struggling over the transformation of Newark's public schools at the center of the analysis. This approach is crucial to provide organizers with useful lessons for future struggles, a central goal of this study. Therefore, to achieve these aims, we must, as Cox and Nilsen insist, "*engage with the reality of popular collective action.*"[80] "Bird's-eye view[s] of global resistance . . . ," in contrast, "that miss out on the complexities and dilemmas of actual mobilization and strategic lessons that flow

22 || INTRODUCTION

from these," fail to deliver on that challenge. Rather, we need studies that demonstrate

> how people come to take action, how they make alliances and convince other people to take a broader perspective, how they resolve strategic dilemmas or assess their chance of winning.[81]

The Newark case, and other contemporary popular challenges to the school privatization movement, highlights the importance of centering resistance. This is crucial both to better understanding the process of neoliberalization in the context of a BUR and for "imagin[ing] and creat[ing] alternative urban futures."[82] I now turn to highlighting the tools for bringing popular resistance, "movements from below," into the study of neoliberalism.

Neoliberal School Reform and the Social Movement from Below

Social movements from below are collective projects developed by the working class, and at times in alliance with other oppressed classes, who deploy a variety of "skilled activities," organized around a rationality or ideology, to defend or challenge existing social structures.[83] Sociologists Nilsen and Cox have developed a useful "movement-process" model to analyze movements from below and their potential—not inevitable—development. Like Frances Fox Piven and Richard Cloward, they recognize that social movements begin when working-class people "experience deprivation and oppression," which take place "within a concrete setting not as the end result of large and abstract processes." Therefore, as the authors of the classic *Poor People's Movements: Why They Succeed, How They Fail* hold, "it is the daily experience of people that shapes their grievances, establishes the measure of their demands, and points out the targets of their anger."[84]

Nilsen and Cox add, as a corollary to the Piven–Cloward thesis, that these quotidian experiences are not isolated examples of injustice but rather deeply rooted in the social structure. The troubles are simply the "clues to the underlying structures and relationships which are not observable."[85] The challenge for social movements, therefore, is to collectively develop a "sociological imagination" to make the connection between the "personal troubles" of milieu and the "public issues of social structures."[86] When these connections are made, movements expand and escalate their grievances, demands, targets, and actions. In the following paragraphs, I outline a five-stage process, drawn from Nilsen and Cox, as well as from Rosa Luxemburg's theory of the mass strike, of *potential* movement development involving a progressive "widening and deepening of the scope of collective action."[87]

The first stage of a movement from below, whether it be of an offensive or defensive variety, involves—similar to James Scott's concept of "infrapolitics" and further developed by Robin Kelley—challenges to the "common sense" that informs everyday activity. The dominant common sense represents, Gramsci emphasizes, a "contradictory consciousness" that includes elements rooted in the hegemonic project and "good sense" that represents, in kernel form, the workers' "own conception of the world."[88] Nilsen and Cox term these incipient challenges to dominant ideologies as "local rationalities." These are the basic building blocks of a movement from below in which new "ways of being, doing and thinking" emerge that challenge "the everyday routines and received wisdoms" of the hegemonic element of common sense.[89] These rationalities could be defensive in nature—deployed, for example, in the face of the charter movement attempting to roll back tenure protections—or offensive, as when new rights are demanded.

The second stage, or component, of movement processes, drawn from the work of David Harvey, is termed "militant particularism." This refers to situations—often under conditions where "local rationalities [become] increasingly articulated"—where "open confrontation with a dominant group in a particular time, in a particular place, in a particular conflict over a particular issue" takes place.[90] This conception is similar to David Camfield's "historical formations" approach to the study of working classes and class struggles, "as groups of people in particular times and places . . . as historical collectivities." Their struggles can take place not only in the workplace but in a variety of terrains, such as "social reproduction," including health, education, and housing. As Camfield emphasizes, "people do not stop belonging to classes when they leave their workplaces. Class relations [and struggle] pervade all aspects of social life."[91]

The "campaign" stage of resistance emerges when activists are able to extend localized struggles across social and spatial divides into a "generalized challenge" to the project being promoted by the dominant

24 || INTRODUCTION

group. A prime example is the mass challenge between 2012 and 2015 in Newark to the school privatization agenda. The fourth stage of a collective challenge under the Nilsen–Cox model comes in the form of a "social movement project" in which a campaign, or various combined campaigns, demand and mobilize for a deeper structural change in society. In the case of Newark, this would mean advancing from a particular front of the neoliberal movement from above to mounting a challenge to the broader SSA of which school privatization is an important component. Finally, the fifth level is a "potentially revolutionary situation" where movements from above and below struggle over "historicity," over the very organization of society, of which class will rule. The 1968–73 period, before the successful capitalist counterattack, represented on a global level such a conjuncture.[92]

Nilsen and Cox's processual model parallels what the German Polish revolutionary socialist Luxemburg termed the "mass strike" process. The mass strike is different from conventional strikes called by trade unions or even general strikes organized and led by trade union federations, often for one or two days over a specific measure, such as an austerity package dictated by the International Monetary Fund. The mass strike, Luxemburg emphasized, cannot "be decided at pleasure ... a kind of pocket knife that can be kept in the pocket and clasped 'ready for any emergency'" by trade union or leaders of other movements. Nor, Luxemburg went on, can it "be called at will even when the decision to do so comes from the highest committee of the strongest social democratic party."[93]

A mass strike emerges when a single strike—disruption—erupts in one locale and then spreads, seemingly spontaneously, into a growing strike movement. These strikes waves, which Luxemburg described as the "phenomenal form of the proletarian struggle," involve larger and larger layers of both organized and unorganized workers and students, out of which emerge new and stronger organizations. These mass upsurges, which can engulf whole industries or general strikes of cities or entire nations, can last for months or even years and invariably raise both political and economic demands. They tend to emerge when capital is unwilling or unable to concede concessions to workers and is often demanding concessions, while the ordinary forms of struggle have become ineffective.

An example of this process was the 1934 mass strike wave in the

United States, when, over a three-month period, general strikes broke out in three major cities. These strikes—in Minneapolis, Toledo, and San Francisco—raised economic demands and laid the groundwork for the legalization of strikes and labor unions under the 1935 Wagner Act. Out of this strike wave emerged the new Congress of Industrial Organizations, which brought together all workers in a plant and industry, including auto, rubber, and steel, as well as the Workers Alliance of America, which united unemployed and employed workers and fought around workplace and community struggles. In a short period, from 1934 to 1936, millions of previously unorganized—and seemingly unorganizable—workers were brought into the new mass industrial unions. This mass strike wave, and the organized working-class power that emerged from it, while not ending class rule, played the central role in gaining important concessions—coupled with major defeats and concessions—that congealed in the form of the Fordist–Keynesian SSA class compromise.

Intraclass Struggle

Though Luxemburg emphasized that a mass strike process could not be "called," socialist activists could help prepare the ground through educational work that "convinced workers of their common interests in a program that united political and economic demands."[94] When they do emerge, organizers can advance the mass strike process, she argued, by intervening with "lively agitation for the extension of demands."[95] The combination of escalating demands and larger and larger layers incorporated into the strike wave is the source of its power. The threat of continually expanding working-class unity instills fear among employers and the state, resulting in concessions in order to stop the process.

The importance of these interventions underscores that movement development, at every stage, is affected not only by struggles with the opposing dominant group, but also, maybe most crucially, by internal ones. As sociologist Colin Barker emphasizes, movements—the various ideologies, organizations, tendencies, activists, and ideas that make them up—are not only sites of cooperation but also "fields of argument," or what Maurice Zeitlin and Judith Stepan-Norris term the "intraclass struggle." Crucial questions that movements confront include the following:

26 || INTRODUCTION

> What is the movement's meaning and purpose? What is it seeking to defend and change? How are its boundaries defined? Who are its opponents? How should it define . . . and pursue its objectives? What strategies, tactics, repertoires of collective activity should it deploy? How should it respond to specific events and crises?[96]

But, Barker points out, of crucial importance for the Newark case, a movement's opponents also try to influence internal movement debates on how to advance their struggle in which activists engage. "The class struggle," he emphasizes,

> occurs not only between movements and their antagonists but also *within* them: *their ideas,* forms of organization and repertoires of contention are all within their opponents' "strategic sights."[97]

How and why Booker and Baraka attempted to influence the movement from below, particularly by advancing competing antiracist ideologies, is the central focus of this book.

ORGANIZATION OF THE BOOK

The chapters that follow, divided into four parts, examine Newark and the struggles over the city and public schools through the lens of social movements from above and below, along with the role of antiracist ideologies in these movements. Part I (chapter 1) uses social movements as a window to analyze and interpret Newark's development and transformation from European settlement in the 1660s through the emergence and consolidation of the BUR in the 1970s and 1980s. Part II (chapters 2 and 3) examines the rise and consolidation of power by the movement from above. Chapter 2 takes up the transition from the Sharpe James– to Cory Booker–led urban regimes in the early 2000s. I examine why James and other parts of the city's post–civil rights leadership, who had dutifully and skillfully advanced the neoliberal agenda for two decades, were now seen as obstacles to opening the new frontier of public education. I then turn to how elites in finance and high tech, operating through philanthrocapitalist organizational vehicles, consolidated support around Booker and a new generation of the BPMC, as well as some older elements, to gain local state power and advance the movement. I highlight the Black Power roots of the neoliberal form of antiracist ideology the movement from above deployed to legitimate its ascent. Chapter 3 analyzes Booker in power and how he and his movement were able to exploit favorable changes at the state government level to advance movement objectives, while failing to generate much popular consent to their agenda.

Part III (chapters 4 and 5) examines the challenge from below. Chapter 4 analyzes the various sources of the movement from below among students, teachers, and community activists and the first collective actions they mounted against their opponents. Chapter 5 turns to the crucial 2013–14 academic year as conflict escalated between superintendent Cami Anderson's attempts to impose a "shock therapy" privatization plan and the growing student-led movement to defend public schools. The year ended with a strengthened popular movement that forced Anderson to retreat on her reforms, led former allies to turn against her, and catapulted Ras Baraka, a leading critic of her reign, to City Hall.

Part IV (chapters 6, 7, and 8) examines the rise and consolidation of the Ras Baraka–led regime, the source of its contradictions, and the role of antiracism in masking them. Chapter 6 begins by tracing the ideological roots of Baraka's self-determination ideology and how it was wielded to delegitimize Booker and neoliberal school reform. At the same time, Baraka was deeply committed to a rent-intensification development agenda, one that intertwined with school privatization. After providing this context, I turn to how Baraka, during his crucial first six months in power, employed an antiracist ideology to reassure his elite governing coalition while simultaneously not alienating his most vocal, mobilized, and high-profile supporters in the movement defending public schools. Chapter 7 analyzes how Baraka was able to promote the spring 2015 mobilizations that forced out the school superintendent while gaining movement acquiescence to an equally pro-privatization replacement. Chapter 8 analyzes Baraka's increasing accommodation to charter schools, the winding down of the movement from below, and the crucial role antiracism played over the remainder of his first term in office.

In the book's Conclusion, I identify the lessons that can be drawn from the Newark case for advancing an effective class challenge to the deepening attacks faced by urban working classes across the United States and the growing authoritarian turn.

PART I

Movement Foundations

1

Whose Schools, Whose City?

READING NEWARK THROUGH SOCIAL MOVEMENTS

> Investment capital is sensitive—it still retains the legal right
> to seek a favorable atmosphere—it will continue to avoid
> unfriendly or harsh municipal policies.
> —Newark Chamber of Commerce, 1937

> We shouldn't even be fighting with the Italians. We're as stupid
> as they are. The business community takes out 3 billion a year
> from Newark, and we're fighting over crumbs.
> —Amiri Baraka, interview during the 1971
> Newark Teachers' Strike

Kenneth Gibson, Newark's first black mayor, often opined that "wherever America's cities are going, Newark will get there first."[1] But the confidence with which Gibson invoked his thesis belies the many questions it raises. How and why did Newark and other cities move in a particular direction? Who set the course, and who benefited? Was everyone in agreement on the road map? If not, how were conflicts over diverging destinations settled? Was there an alternative? In this chapter, I address these questions by analyzing Newark's contested political, economic, and spatial trajectory through the conceptual lens of social movements from above and below. While providing a historical overview from the city's founding in the 1660s to the state takeover of Newark's public schools in the 1990s, I place particular attention on the key turning points of the post–World War II era. The resolution of these periods of intense conflict, in which the contending ideologies and choices made by popular movements played a crucial role, provides not only answers to "How Newark Became Newark," as a historian entitled his work on the city, but lessons on how popular movements might construct "another Newark" as part of an egalitarian urban and global future.

FROM PURITANS TO PROLETARIANS

Dissident Puritan settlers from Connecticut uprooted the Lenni Lenape Indigenous community and established Newark in 1666, just after England, the new global hegemon, had ousted the Dutch as the colonial power in the Mid-Atlantic region. Under the mercantile capitalist stage of development that reigned through the colonial and early independence era, Newark, located on the Passaic River, and wedged between the Hudson and Delaware Rivers, as well as Philadelphia and New York, became an important transport and trading hub.[2]

The emergence of industrial capitalism in the United States, beginning in the early nineteenth century, transformed Newark into a center of manufacturing and the destination of successive waves of immigrants. The new economic elite, composed of representatives of industrial, finance, and merchant capital, moved to restructure the city government, as it would do periodically, to create a more favorable governing arrangement for its profit-making ventures. Thus, in 1836, "Newark became a charted municipality, abandoning the town-meeting form of government in favor of a mayor-council charter." Unsurprisingly, the first elected officials under this new, democracy-reducing, capital-friendly political structure "consisted mainly of wealthy men who had come to prominence in an industrialized Newark."[3]

By the eve of the Civil War, Newark had a population of more than seventy thousand, making it the eleventh largest city in the country and, according to historian Susan Hirsch, "the leading industrial city in the nation."[4] While the war over slavery initially disrupted the city's economy, the ensuing "bounty of government orders" helped produce "Newark's most spectacular era of industrial growth."[5] The city continued to expand as a manufacturing center throughout the late nineteenth and early twentieth centuries, as Italians, Jews, and Slavs, and, later, African Americans, joined the earlier waves of German and Irish immigrants who had settled in Newark. By 1910, Newark had nearly 350,000 inhabitants, making it the fourteenth largest city in the country, though its ranking and population would begin a long decline, first in relative and then in absolute numbers, in the ensuing decades.

One factor in the decline in population growth was state-imposed constraints on the city's geographic expansion. Beginning in the early twentieth century, rural and elite-dominated state legislatures in New

WHOSE SCHOOLS, WHOSE CITY? || 33

Jersey and other states passed incorporation laws that allowed suburbs, which cities previously had absorbed as they developed, to avoid annexation. The last suburb Newark annexed was Vailsburg in 1905, which brought the city to only twenty-four square miles, where it remains today.[6] In the first decades of the century, and especially in the 1920s, as historian Paul Stellhorn documents in his detailed study of class relations in Newark, capitalists themselves, and, later, other prosperous elements, began decamping from Newark while continuing to maintain, for now, their investments in the city. At the same time, while increasingly residing outside Newark, these capitalists worked to maintain their political dominance over the city. One example of this class power strategy was the effort by "progressive business and reform elements" to end the aldermanic ward system of government that had created numerous elected offices and boards dominated by German and Irish, and, later, Italian and Jewish, immigrants and their descendants, with its decentralized nature seen as an obstacle to developing the city "as they envisaged." In its place, elite reformers in Newark and around the country imposed in 1917 the businesslike commission form of city government designed to drastically reduce the number of elected offices and centralize power.[7]

By the 1920s, and the consolidation of the monopoly capitalist phase of development, industrial capital began moving out of older industrial cities. The concentration of manufacturing in urban centers, and the social movements this arrangement facilitated, resulted in capital no longer considering urban industrial agglomeration, as the late political economist David Gordon argued, "qualitatively efficient." While quantitatively efficient in producing output, this arrangement was now simultaneously undermining the ability of the "ruling class to reproduce its domination . . . [and] minimize producers' resistance."[8]

In the case of Newark, after the World War I–produced boom, older industries in leather, jewelry, and fertilizers went into decline, as did blue-collar employment. At the same time, new investments in electronics and chemicals advanced, while the city grew as an insurance and banking center, building on a foundation created by Prudential Insurance in the 1870s. In addition, as historian Paul Stellhorn emphasizes, while the exodus of Newark's business titans for suburban residences accelerated in the 1920s, they simultaneously underwent a revival of "civic boosterism," as they lent their political and financial support for an expansion of "transportation systems . . .

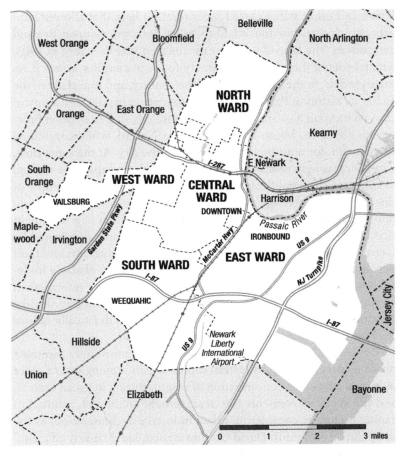

MAP 1. Map of Newark, New Jersey, and surrounding suburbs.

libraries, museums, cultural programs and better schools."[9] Further buttressing the progressive image of the decade were the governing methods of the Republican mayor Thomas Raymond. The politically astute Raymond made appeals to the city's post-1880 immigrant wave, particularly Jews and Italians, mainly through low-cost, largely symbolic overtures, such as a few high-level patronage positions for the upwardly mobile elements of these "races"—as they were referred to at the time. Additionally, in a departure from his Republican and progressive allies, he opposed prohibition, arguing that it was rooted in anti-immigrant "bigotry and provincialism." These measures, which required little or no material concessions, allowed the patrician Raymond, as they would for his BUR successors decades later, to appear progressive to his ethnic electoral base while still being "in perfect accord with most of the city's business elite."[10]

THE STRUGGLE FOR THE CITY: THE 1930S

The magnanimity of Newark's ruling elite, and the capitalist prosperity and successful containment of the postwar strike wave and radicalization that undergirded it, was upended at the end of the decade in the face of U.S. capitalism's most serious economic downturn to date. Even before the October 1929 stock market crash, Newark's economy had been weakening, particularly in construction, which had boomed during the 1920s. In the subsequent months, conditions worsened for Newark's working class as employment in the city's industries declined by 25 percent between January and November 1930. But, as in other parts of the country, workers resisted and radicalized. The decade witnessed, therefore, a three-way struggle between a strengthening Left—Newark saw a major mobilization for the 1930 Communist Party called "International Unemployment Day"—the New Deal mayor Ellenstein elected in 1933, and business interests grouped in various local and statewide organizations.

The central social movement strategy of the business elite was a disruptive one of blocking the ability of municipal governments to raise "matching funds" for Works Progress Administration public-sector jobs and service initiatives, particularly in public schools. This included not only refusing to buy city bonds unless relief spending for workers was cut but also orchestrating passage at the state level of a raft of legislation, known collectively as the Princeton bills, to constrain "irresponsible" local government borrowing and spending powers.[11] Possibly strengthening capitalist intransigence to Ellenstein's reforms was the Communist Party's new Popular Front strategy, which took hold in 1936. This now placed the Communist Party activists in alliance with the Roosevelt administration and his New Deal allies at the local level, such as Ellenstein, whom they had previously challenged electorally. This cross-class alliance undercut the movement, spurred on by the national mass strike wave of 1934, for establishing a labor party and, therefore, forging a political threat to the left of the Democrats' New Deal.[12]

36 || WHOSE SCHOOLS, WHOSE CITY?

Just as with Word War I, the looming prospect of another global capitalist conflagration at the end of the decade lifted the spirits of the local business elite. On September 1, 1939, as the Nazis unleashed their *Blitzkrieg* of Poland, prompting Britain and France to declare war on Germany, a leading chamber official observed, with much satisfaction, that "Newark can confidently look for a boom in business in its manufactured products." Indeed, the city's factories were soon operating at or near capacity, helping slash unemployment as the number of families on relief plummeted from more than ten thousand in September 1939 to six thousand by the end of 1940.[13]

NEWARK AND THE POSTWAR COUNTEROFFENSIVE

Postwar suburbanization, as David Harvey argues, was crucial for solving the "capital surplus disposal problem" of finding profitable outlets for surplus capital that had bedeviled the ruling class in the 1930s and which the mobilization of World War II had solved temporarily.[14] But, just as significantly, suburbanization solved the *political* crisis facing U.S. and—considering its new hegemonic role—global capitalism in the war's aftermath. "For a broad range of commentators," political scientist Michael Goldfield notes in his study of this crucial historical juncture, "the most striking feature of working class people during the 1930s and 1940s was their broad class consciousness and strong solidarity across ethnic, religious, and racial lines" that was rooted in the cities.[15] The demographic basis, renowned political analyst Samuel Lubell argued, were the children of 13 million immigrants that had come to the United States, mainly settling in urban centers, in the early twentieth century and entered adulthood in the 1930s. This was combined with 6.5 million internal migrants, black and white, who left the rural South and North for industrial cities like Newark. The class struggles of the 1930s, led by socialists of various stripes who forged new class organizations like the Congress of Industrial Organizations (CIO) and the Workers Alliance, fused the interests of urban immigrant and native-stock workers. The result, Lubell argues, was

the rise of a common class consciousness among all workers. The depression, in making all workers more aware of their economic interests, suppressed their racial and religious antagonism. Put

crudely, the hatred of bankers among the native American workers has become greater than their hatred of the Pope or even of
the Negro. . . . This rise in class consciousness . . . was a nationwide
phenomenon.[16]

As Lubell and other observers have noted, the struggle for black equality during this period was seen by many of this new working class,
particularly the children of immigrants, as a struggle for equality for
all Americans.

The disruption—withdrawal of support—of the neighborhoods
and places of employment of urban workers undermined the structural context that nurtured a "solidaristic culture" in the 1930s and
1940s. Suburbanization, in contrast, reinforced the dominant values of
individualism and "the sanctity of private property rights and wealth
over all other values."[17] Furthermore, by tying property values to racial exclusivity, postwar suburbanization provided an economic rationality or "common sense" to racism that deepened the geographic,
economic, and political divide between black and "white" workers.
Indeed, for the "in-between" Southern and Eastern European ethnics,
suburbanization played a central role in their construction as white.[18]

The federal government's real estate– and banking-crafted Federal
Housing Administration (FHA), and its cornerstone home mortgage
insurance program, was central to the disruption efforts. The FHA
loan requirements furthered uneven development between the city
and suburbs by instituting rules that favored new construction in
the new suburban subdivisions over rehabilitation of older inner-
city homes and of single-family detached homes over multifamily
dwellings. The uneven development was racialized as well, with the
FHA employing a racist, four-level loan rating system that was based
on discriminatory "best practices" previously established by the
real estate and banking industries. Under this lending regime, entire
neighborhoods—including the new suburban subdivisions—had to
be racially homogeneous, that is, all white, to qualify for FHA-insured
loans. Meanwhile the FHA cutoff loans—redlined—racially integrated
or largely black neighborhoods in the central cities, except for a few,
new middle-class black enclaves. Newark, which historian Kenneth
Jackson uses as one of his primary case studies in his classic *Crab Grass
Frontier,* was particularly hard hit by these policies. None of the city's

38 || WHOSE SCHOOLS, WHOSE CITY?

neighborhoods received the FHA's highest A rating (color green), while large sections were designated at the lowest D rating (color red) and denied loans altogether.[19]

The New Deal public housing program, while an important victory in the face of intense hostility from real estate interests, received much less funding than provided by tax expenditures in the form of home mortgage interest income tax deductions. Furthermore, as a "means-tested" rather than universal program like Social Security, public housing was vulnerable to political attacks, which intensified during the right-wing postwar turn. With passage of the 1949 Housing Act, public housing became increasingly the handmaiden of the federal government's "urban renewal" program, with the amount of public housing created for those displaced by "slum clearance" never coming close to meeting the need. Finally, in another assault on inner-city affordable housing, the federal highway program facilitated the exodus to the suburbs from cities like Newark, while wiping out wide swaths of urban housing and contaminating urban neighborhoods with lead-laden car exhaust.

Federal government policies further battered the urban working class by encouraging the exodus of manufacturing, with the blueprints, as with housing, crafted by industry. During World War II, the Roosevelt administration created the War Production Board (WPB) to take "control—though not ownership—of the nation's major manufacturing industries in order to mobilize resources for the war effort." But FDR's corporate appointees who led the WPB did not retool the existing plants, which were, despite earlier trends toward decentralization, still mainly located in cities. Instead, the WPB had the new federally financed plants built mainly in suburban areas. The site selection was driven by what Gordon would term "qualitative efficiency" in reproducing ruling-class domination. "Suburban locations were desirable," urbanists Peter Dreier, John Mollenkopf, and Todd Swanstrom note, "'because they were largely beyond the reach of unions,' which had a strong presence in the existing factories, and were not governed by big-city mayors, who were often sympathetic to unions."[20] The Pentagon's support for aerospace and electronics in the postwar decades continued these manufacturing—and population—shifts from urban to suburban as well as from the Northeast and Midwest to the Sunbelt. In addition, tax policies, such as those introduced by the Kennedy administration in 1962, that allowed for dollar-for-dollar tax credits for

WHOSE SCHOOLS, WHOSE CITY? || 39

new plants and construction, but not renovations, provided more fuel for urban capital flight.[21]

These federal housing and industrial policies fueled an exodus of manufacturing jobs and middle- and working-class whites from Newark in the postwar era. Between 1947 and 1967, the number of manufacturing establishments in Newark declined by 26 percent, from 1,847 to 1,413, and the number of workers dropped by an even more precipitous 35 percent, from 73,605 to 47,500. As seen in Table 1, the city's populations peaked in 1930, dipped during the Depression decade, enjoyed a small recovery during the war boom of the 1940s, and then began a swift decline. Between 1950 and 1960, 115,000 whites left the city, with only one outlying section of the city gaining white population. By 1956, "half of Newark's teachers and administrators lived outside the city."[22] During the crucial two decades spanning 1950 to 1970, the overall population declined from 438,776 to 382,417, a 14 percent drop. Among those joining this exodus was four-year-old Chris Christie, whose family departed in 1967, weeks before the Newark rebellion.[23] Despite never attending his hometown's public schools, he would, four decades later as governor, oversee their dramatic makeover in collaboration with the suburban-born mayor Cory Booker.

The Christie family, with little Chris in tow, headed for the federally subsidized suburban, green Essex County pastures of Livingston, New Jersey, whose overwhelmingly white population quadrupled between 1940 and 1970, from 5,972 to 30,127. Newark, in contrast, as a result of the mechanization of cotton production, U.S. underdevelopment policies in Puerto Rico, and discriminatory housing policies, had a majority black and Puerto Rican school district by 1960 and population by the late 1960s. The city would continue hemorrhaging population, including African Americans, who began exiting to inner-ring suburbs that also become majority black. Whitney Houston's family was among these transplants; they moved to neighboring East Orange in 1967. By the 1990s and 2000s, Newark's population began stabilizing at about 275,000 and is now again inching upward.

The structural violence of suburbanization and factory closures was combined with McCarthyite political repression against the Left in the unions and throughout American life. In Newark, a major target was the Newark Teachers Union (NTU), which had formed in 1936 as a chapter of the American Federation of Labor–affiliated American

Table 1. Newark population and racial composition, 1870–2020

YEAR	WHITE %	BLACK %	LATINO %	TOTAL POPULATION
1870				105,059
1880				136,508
1890				181,330
1900				246,070
1910		2.7		347,469
1920		4		414,524
1930	91	8.8		442,337
1940	90.3	10.7		429,760
1950	82.8	17.2		438,776
1960	65.6	34.4		405,220
1970	34	54.2	12	382,417
1980	22	58.2	18.6	329,248
1990	16	58.5	26.1	275,221
2000	14	52.9	29.5	273,546
2010	12	50.1	32.6	277,140
2020	11	50.1	36.3	311,549

Federation of Teachers (AFT). In contrast to the conservative and administrator-dominated Newark Teachers Association, the NTU attracted, historian Steve Golin argues in his in-depth study of the union, "members of marginalized groups just breaking into teaching," particularly African Americans, Italians, and especially Jews. Indeed, the base of the union was Weequahic High School in the heavily Jewish South Ward. This Left-led union was a central part of the "leftwing culture of the 1930s and 1940s that drew strength from the CIO, and encouraged office workers, government employees, and teachers to identify their struggles with those of industrial workers." The NTU's social movement brand of unionism united teachers, students, and the broader working class in common struggles, refusing to pit one against the other. The NTU activists fought for smaller class sizes to enhance teaching and learning, pressured the city to create a food program for many undernourished children, and denounced the national AFT for using a racist insurance company that refused to sell to blacks.[24]

The leading NTU activist was Bob Lowenstein, a renowned teacher who taught language classes at Weequahic High School and counted among his students the author Philip Roth, who studied there in the late 1940s. Lowenstein, who had a major influence on Roth and became the basis of a leading character in the award-winning author's 1998 book *I Married a Communist,* on the McCarthy era, was called, along with two other teachers and several left-wing activists, before a hearing held in Newark in 1955 by the notorious, Inquisition-like House Un-American Activities Committee (HUAC). After refusing to "name names," the Newark School Board fired Lowenstein despite two decades of service, a PhD from Johns Hopkins in French literature, and being one of the most respected teachers in the district. Because of the firing, and the general atmosphere of anti-Communist repression, the numbers in the NTU, which embodied the radical traditions of the 1930s, plummeted from 425 at the beginning of the 1950s to 125 at the end of the decade.[25]

STRUGGLING FOR NEWARK'S PUBLIC SCHOOLS ON THE POSTWAR TERRAIN

"Education," historian Jon Shelton argues in his study of the significant role of teacher strikes in the turn toward neoliberalism during the long 1970s, "became, in the post-war years, perhaps the primary battleground over race, gender, poverty and inequality."[26] Indeed, the struggle over Newark's public schools, most explosively expressed in the 1970 and 1971 teacher strikes, provides a window into the broader fight for the city, particularly during the pivotal period of the late 1960s and early 1970s. But, as Shelton emphasizes, to understand the battle for the city's schools, we need to examine the preexisting social terrain on which they took place. This terrain, shaped by the class struggles of the 1930s and the corresponding movement from above to contain them, structured, though did not determine, the unfolding and outcome of the struggle over Newark's public schools and the city more broadly.

First, as discussed earlier, the racially discriminatory suburbanization model produced a rapid white exodus as African Americans and Puerto Ricans became the majority in the public schools by 1960, and in the city by the mid- to late 1960s. Only Washington, D.C., and Gary, Indiana, witnessed as swift a transition as Newark to a majority nonwhite city. Yet, while Newark became a majority black and Puerto Rican city, public employees—teachers, police, welfare workers—as well as downtown white-collar employees, remained overwhelmingly white. The police, whose brutality provided the immediate spark for the 1967 rebellion, engendered widespread hatred—"the police were simply Devils to us, Beasts," as Amiri Baraka described the relationship—among the local nonwhite majority who were disproportionately recipients of their abuse. But even teachers, whose ranks included many second- and third-generation Italians and Jews, generated conflict with the students and parents they served because of their actual and perceived hostility and unconcern. Further contributing to the divide, a growing percentage of city employees no longer resided in the city. By the mid-1950s, half of Newark's public school teachers resided outside the city, a figure that would only increase in the subsequent decade.[27]

This dynamic, as Francis Fox Piven argues, was a feature of other older industrial cities experiencing similar demographic and political changes. Therefore it was not a surprise that "the keenest struggle," as Piven observed regarding public-sector militancy of the 1960s, "is with residents of central city ghettos. . . . Policemen, fire fighters, teachers and public-welfare workers increasingly complain about 'harassment' in the ghettos. For their part, growing numbers of the black poor view police, firemen, teachers, public-welfare workers and other city employees as their oppressors."[28] Contributing to this conflict was the decimation, as a result of McCarthyite repression, of the Left social movement unionism tendency among teachers, represented by activists like Bob Lowenstein in the Newark case, that could have put forward a program to challenge, or mend, this divide. Though Lowenstein had won his job back by the early 1960s, his social movement brand of unionism clashed with a narrower version "on the scope of demands and the relations of the Union to society" that increasingly took hold in the 1950s and 1960s.[29] All of this, in turn, strengthened Black Power activists, particularly after 1965, who advocated for Black "community control" of the city, especially schools. Thus the growing division between these natural allies, who were enmeshed in an interdependent relationship, weakened the collective disruptive power capabilities of teachers, students, and parents.

A second major factor impacting the struggle over the schools was the failure of the earlier labor upsurge to win the right of public workers to collective bargaining and, especially, to strike. In fact, after the postwar strike wave, which swept up public-sector workers as well, private-sector workers witnessed a retrenchment of the rights they had won under the 1935 Wagner Act. The 1947 Taft–Hartley law made illegal various forms of disruptive power and barred Communist Party members, who had, for the most part, been some of the strongest and most effective strike organizers and leaders, from elected leadership positions. In 1947, New York State, following strikes of city employees in Rochester and Buffalo and threats by New York City transit workers, passed the draconian Condon–Wadlin Act, which explicitly made public-sector strikes illegal and strikers subject to being fired.[30] In contrast, New Jersey, which experienced a 1945 strike by Paterson teachers, relied on court-ordered injunctions, drawing on past rulings barring public-sector strikes or even collective bargaining, to provide the legal machinery to contain disruption from below. With the postwar expansion of the public sector, many states passed legislation providing for collective bargaining rights, but very rarely rights to strike, a pattern New Jersey followed.[31] Thus the regime regulating New Jersey's public-sector workers contained the same "contradiction" as other states' regimes. It allowed public employees to join unions and collectively bargain, but simultaneously barred—in New Jersey's case through court injunctions—"from using the major weapon at their disposal for exacting leverage in those negotiations."[32]

A third key actor shaping the struggle over the schools was the suburbanization-fueled fiscal crisis that Newark and other cities confronted. The loss of businesses and residences—including through arson, which destroyed tens of thousands of homes—reduced the tax base to support schools, while the highways that ripped through neighborhoods slashed the value of the homes that survived. A city study found that between 1959 and 1974, Newark's property tax base declined by 21 percent. In addition, state legislation in the postwar period lowered taxes on the businesses that remained in the city. Funding for schools, as a result, took a major hit. In a study of sixteen large school systems, Newark ranked fourth in 1950 in per capita

44 || WHOSE SCHOOLS, WHOSE CITY?

pupil spending but dropped to last by the end of the decade. The declining capacity of Newark's tax base to adequately support public schools was not compensated by sufficient aid from the state. By the late 1960s, New Jersey ranked last in per capita direct aid to education.[33] One measure of the impact of the fiscal crisis, and the uneven suburban development model, is that by 1969, Newark had the lowest starting teacher salaries in Essex County. This marked a stark reversal from when Newark had historically been "the New Jersey leader in teacher salaries."[34]

THE NEWARK REBELLION AND INTRAMOVEMENT STRUGGLE

In addition to the three broad structural factors, the Newark rebellion impacted the late 1960s and early 1970s struggle over the schools. Between just 1965 and 1968, 329 urban rebellions—"Civil Disorders" in the obfuscatory language of the federal government's 1967 Kerner Commission—took place in 257 cities, involving 300 deaths, 60,000 arrests, and hundreds of millions of dollars in property losses.[35] Measured along these lines, the Newark rebellion of July 12–17, 1967, was, along with Detroit's, which followed a week later, among the largest and most iconic of the period. Over the course of five days, some fifteen hundred people were arrested, of whom 95 percent were black, and twenty-six people—all black civilians, except for one white cop and a fireman, most likely killed by friendly fire—were shot and killed by the Newark police, along with National Guardsmen and State Troopers dispatched by the governor. The state response was, as local civil rights activist Robert Curvin called it, "an orgy of violent, brutal retaliation against black citizens and businesses." The state's armed bodies also added to the $10 million in property damage by shooting out the windows and robbing previously spared black-owned businesses decked out with "SOUL BROTHER" or other such signs.[36]

The Newark uprising generated a number of concessions to local movements. One was the federal and state governments forcing Louis Danzig, the longtime urban renewal czar who ruled through his perch as head of the Newark Housing Authority, to negotiate with local activists over a planned 150-acre medical school. With this leverage, local activists negotiated several concessions, including a two-thirds reduction in the school's original footprint, sixty acres set aside for affordable housing, state funds for upgrading the municipal hospital, and affirmative action efforts to include minority contractors and workers in the construction of the hospital and recruitment of black and Latinx students.[37] More broadly, the urban uprisings around the country placed issues driving them, such as police brutality, rundown housing, poor schools, and unemployment, on the political agenda and generated a number of material concessions. These included the creation of a cabinet-level agency—the Department of Housing and Urban Development—while "public spending on housing and other urban issues went from $600 million at the beginning of the decade to more than $3 billion by the decade's end." At the same time, as Christian Parenti documents, the uprising prompted an expansion of the state's coercive arms, with the federal government, through the Law Enforcement Assistance Administration, pouring billions into beefing up local police forces and stepped-up repression against activists.[38]

Thus, in contrast to the dominant narrative that argues that the "riots" simply deepened or, as some absurdly claimed, produced urban decline, real material gains were in fact extracted. But, at the same time, the uprisings, while a response to oppressive conditions, were by no means conscious, strategic interventions.[39] No organizational forces either directed—despite the best efforts of HUAC and other conservative forces to pin the blame on various "subversives"—or emerged out of them.[40] Rather, they reflected, as Bayard Rustin argued at the time, frustration in the civil rights movement's failure, despite its important gains, in "addressing structural unemployment, racial injustice, and concentrated inequality in inner cities" besetting, in particular, working-class black Americans. Therefore the most important consequence of the revolts was how they were harnessed by contending forces within the civil rights movement's "fields of argument" to justify where the movement needed to go.[41]

One tendency, represented by A. Philip Randolph and Bayard Rustin, the key movers behind the 1963 March for Jobs and Freedom, had long advocated for the movement "to expand its vision beyond race relations to economic relations." In the context of the post-1965 crossroads of the movement following passage of the landmark Civil Rights (1964) and Voting Rights (1965) Acts, and the emerging ghetto revolts, they advocated, in a 1966 manifesto, reorienting the movement behind a "Freedom Budget" demand for a mass, federal government–sponsored public works and public services program.

To win this radical agenda required, they argued, a broad, multiracial working-class coalition with the political vehicle, consistent with the "realignment" strategy of their cothinkers Max Shachtman and Michael Harrington, being a transformed Democratic Party. In practice, Rustin's strategy meant not simply the movement's alignment with but its subordination and incorporation into the United States' "consensus Party," including its militarism that undermined his social democratic aspirations. This contrasted with Dr. Martin Luther King Jr.'s embrace of a similar multiracial class agenda, though one that was increasingly challenging the Democratic Party and the incompatibility of its wars abroad with jobs and equal rights at home.[42]

In contrast, a contending Black Power tendency, first enunciated by then Stokely Carmichael at the 1966 Meredith march, interpreted Newark and other uprisings as a vindication of their racial unity politics. Newark, and other "rebellions [that] popped like deadly firecrackers in city after city that summer," had a particularly transformative impact on LeRoi Jones—soon to be Amiri Baraka—who returned to his hometown in 1965 and would become the most important theoretician and organizer, in Newark and nationally, of a radical version of Black Power. For Baraka, the rebellions demonstrated that the oppressed, multiclass Black Nation was at war with its white supremacist oppressor from Newark to Namibia, North America to South Africa. "The Black Liberation movement," Baraka argued, "was rising up full out. It was a war, for us, a war of liberation."[43] Others, such as the aspiring crop of black politicians groomed by the city's Great Society antipoverty agencies, including future mayor Kenneth Gibson—who sat on the board of the United Community Corporation (UCC), the local War on Poverty Agency—had a less grandiose, more parochial, ethnic politics version of Black Power. Nonetheless, they embraced, like Baraka, a cross-class, racial unity politics, with the operationalization of Black Power understood as "taking City Hall"—administering the local state, including, indeed especially so, the public schools. As with Rustin, the vehicle would be the Democratic Party, though Baraka, in his national efforts, did try unsuccessfully to mount a national Black political party.[44]

The hegemony of the Black Power–ethnic politics paradigm, which ended up prevailing in the intramovement struggle, was both reflected and reinforced in Newark and nationally by four factors. One was the exodus after the rebellion of the largely white activists involved in

WHOSE SCHOOLS, WHOSE CITY? || **47**

a Students for a Democratic Society (SDS) community organizing operation—Newark Community Union Project (NCUP). Strategically informed by the Shachtman realignment strategy of reviving the New Deal coalition, NCUP had worked in the largely black Lower Clinton Hill neighborhood since 1964 undertaking various initiatives, from fighting slum lords to combating police brutality, while taking control over one of the area boards of the local community action program. But, "after the riots," as NCUP veteran Carol Glassman observed, "it changed. . . . Everything became much more self-conscious because there was a lot more tension around our role, our white role."[45] A second impulse was the Kerner Commission report, whose "most meaningful and lasting impact on American politics" was its indictment of a generic "white racism" as "the ultimate source of the manifold inequalities and disparities" its authors cataloged. Thus, despite the social democratic recommendations—which were by and large discarded—the main takeaway was not a radical economic restructuring but rather the need, indeed the urgency, for black political incorporation and "empowerment."[46]

A third factor was a flood, as occurred in other urban centers, of foundation-funded community development corporations (CDCs) beginning in the late 1960s. In Newark, this included the New Community Corporation, the Ironbound Community Corporation, Tri-City Citizens Union for Progress, the North Ward Education and Cultural Center, La Casa de Don Pedro, the FOCUS-Hispanic Center for Community Development, and even Amiri Baraka and his Kawaida Inc. housing-focused initiative, which entered the field, at least for a time.[47] In contrast to the Rustin tendency's goal of building a national, multiracial movement to confront the national state, CDCs' focus was localist and aimed at achieving "self-determination" and "local control." While the Freedom Budget called for a massive expansion of the public sector, the CDCs aimed to replace the cold, distant, racist, bureaucratic state in the delivery of social services and engage in other entrepreneurial activities, all of which dovetailed with Black Power and other forms of ethnic empowerment. In the end, the "fixers," as historian Julia Rabig referred to the CDCs in her sympathetic account, had no strategy to build an alternative power. The result, therefore, was a political habitus combining a mixture of grant writing to local and national foundations and government agencies, conversion into a neoliberal machine politics hybrid operation in the case of the Northward Center, or, particularly in the early years of these out-fits, "mau-mauing" liberal establishment elements for concessions.[48]

On the other side of the political spectrum, the post-1967 emergence of a mobilized White nationalist politics among the city's remaining white ethnics, particularly Italians, who still resided in large numbers in the North Ward, gave a further impulse to Black Power. The most significant leader of this movement was Anthony Imperiale. He ran and was elected to an at-large city council seat in 1968, organized vigilante patrols under the banner of the North Ward Citizens Committee, helped form branches in the East and West Wards, and gained national fame as a symbol of white "backlash" politics. Taking a page from his opponents, he invoked the language of "local control" and "insensitivity to the community" to justify his backing for a thinly veiled antiblack "law and order politics."[49]

THE RISE OF THE BLACK URBAN REGIME

Newark's elite had turned to the commission form of city government in the early twentieth century to better ensure their interests, but by the late 1930s, they had soured on this model, at least in the hands of Meyer Ellenstein.[50] After a failed earlier attempt, in 1954, following passage of enabling state legislation in 1950, voters approved a mayor-council system, with one councilperson for each of the five wards and four at-large—under which Irvine Turner, from the Central (formerly Third) Ward, became the first African American elected to city government. Leo Carlin, an Irish American Teamster union official, served two terms as mayor, 1954–62, under the new system. He, in turn, was ousted by the Italian American congressman Hugh Addonizio, thanks in part to significant support from African American voters who had largely been ignored by Carlin's "Irish Democratic establishment." Though "city hall became racially integrated like never before" under Addonizio, once in office, he betrayed his promises to oppose urban renewal projects in the Clinton Hill neighborhood, failed to take even minimal measures to rein in the police, dragged his feet on implementing antidiscrimination measures at the Barringer High School construction project, and, reflecting concerns of the emerging BPMC, failed to appoint the expected number of black administrators.[51]

In the 1966 election, Kenneth Gibson, a city engineer and vice president of the local antipoverty program, ran for mayor and obtained a surprising sixteen thousand votes, forcing Addonizio into a runoff against Carlin. After the 1967 rebellion, Baraka began holding weekly Sunday political discussions at his Spirit House cultural center with Gibson and a dozen or so other activists and aspiring politicians involved with the UCC. The all-male gathering, whose aim was taking local political power, dubbed themselves the "United Brothers." In 1968, under Baraka's leadership, the United Brothers, and the Committee for a Unified Newark (CFUN), which combined various Baraka-allied groups, held a Black Convention to select two candidates to run in a special city council election.[52] The following year, Baraka was the prime mover behind the 1969 Black and Puerto Rican Political Convention that chose Gibson as their mayoral candidate, and a list of seven candidates for council, collectively dubbed the "Community Choice" slate.[53] In the May 1970 primary, Gibson ran away with 40 percent of the vote, while Addonizio was far behind at 20 percent, as he edged out Imperiale for a spot in the June runoff. With Addonizio beginning trial for federal corruption charges while trying to campaign, and focusing his attacks on Baraka (tauntingly referred to as LeRoi Jones) as he embraced Imperiale's rhetoric, Gibson garnered 56 percent of the vote. Three other members of Gibson's slate—James, Westbrook, and Harris—won council seats, while six Italians garnered the remaining positions on the nine-member council.[54]

BLACK POWER VERSUS TEACHER POWER

In the early 1960s, the NTU, as teachers and other public employees began mobilizing in New York City and nationally, launched a major effort to win a collective bargaining contract. In 1964, the union circulated a petition demanding the school board hold an election to decide whether the NTU or the Newark Teachers Association (NTA), the local affiliate of the National Education Association, the formerly administrator-dominated grouping, would be the collective bargaining representative of teachers and threatened to strike if they did not follow through. The board conceded, and in a December 1964 vote, the NTA edged out the NTU, although the subsequent NTA-negotiated contract did not make many gains. Over the winter of 1965–66, both the NTU and the NTA, after the first one-year contract expired, went on strike. While the NTA crossed picket lines in the NTU-called December 1965 strike, both unions supported the

50 || WHOSE SCHOOLS, WHOSE CITY?

February 1966 NTA-called strike, which the school board suppressed with a court injunction. Out of this duel, the NTA won another representational election and ended up singing three-year contract ending January 31, 1970, although the key issue around binding arbitration for all grievances was not won.[55]

In 1968, after years of wrangling, the state legislature passed the New Jersey Employer–Employee Relations Act, which provided for collective bargaining, including state supervision of elections and mediation services provided by the governor-appointed Public Employees Relations Commission. But, importantly, while not explicitly barring strikes, like New York State's repressive 1967 Taylor Law, neither did the act guarantee the right. Indeed, the law's explicit aim was to avoid strikes by "promot[ing] harmonious resolution of public labor disputes," with the state authorities still being able to turn to the courts to contain teacher-led disruption.[56] Thanks to continued unhappiness with the contract, NTA leadership, and Addonizio's veto of a previously promised raise, the NTU, using the 1968 act, collected sufficient signatures to hold another representational election in November 1969. This time, the NTU won convincingly. More than three thousand of the thirty-four hundred teachers and substitutes turned out for the vote, with NTU garnering 2,020 votes and the NTA far behind at 571. The Organization of Negro Educators (ONE), "which was geared to the nationalist mood of the late 1960s," garnered 428 votes, from about half of the approximately 850 black teachers at the time. Consistent with black unity politics, "ONE attempted to cut across class lines and unite all Black teachers, aides, and administrators around their common racial identity," as it emphasized that it was bargaining for the teachers, students, and community. For its part, the NTU had various political tendencies, though the dominant one was a "bread-and-butter" unionism, composed largely, but by no means exclusively, of second- and third-generation Italian American men, many coming from blue-collar and union backgrounds. Although some of the teachers, particularly the younger ones, were inspired by the NTU's historic social movement unionism, the dominant tendency's central issues revolved around pay; exemption from "nonprofessional" responsibilities, such as cafeteria duty; and, especially, a strong grievance procedure. Thus, as historian Steve Golin argues in his account of the strikes, NTU and ONE both "grew out of strong nationwide

WHOSE SCHOOLS, WHOSE CITY? || 51

movements of the 1960s: the movement for teacher power and the movement for Black Power."[57]

Immediately after winning the jurisdictional election, the NTU and the AFT central office began preparing for a strike. The union had more than three hundred demands, but the key ones were a $1,300 pay increase for the starting salary ($6,700 to $8,000), lower class sizes, teachers freed from nonprofessional duties, and transfers and reassignments done by seniority. But the burning issue was a robust grievance procedure culminating in a final step of binding arbitration overseen by an independent third party. This would be the guarantor, from the teachers' perspective, that individual members or the union could file grievances to ensure that the contract was enforced without facing retaliation, particularly from imperious, vindictive principles. But, as Golin points out, the grievance procedure and arbitration, which could only be won by a strike, contradictorily "encouraged teachers to put their trust in experts and lawyers rather than in their own strength." Over the long term, this apparent victory would simultaneously draw teachers away from their real source of power.[58]

The Addonizio-appointed board, while conceding on the salary issue, refused to budge on binding arbitration, and therefore, at a mass meeting on Sunday, February 1, 1970, NTU members enthusiastically voted to go on strike. The board, after the union rejected their "final" offer and walked out of negotiations, immediately obtained a court injunction, and over the course of the seventeen-day strike, city police and county sheriffs arrested nearly two hundred teachers and jailed scores of others. While not supporting the Addonizio-appointed board, Baraka, CFUN, and their allied New Ark Community Coalition also opposed the strike, arguing that the "suburban" teachers could not comprehend the conditions faced by, nor were they concerned about the interests of, black students, who now composed the overwhelming majority.[59] Thus it was not surprising that in the predominantly black South, West, and Central Wards, parents, organizing with Baraka and the New Ark Community Coalition, kept many of the schools open as "they counterpicketed the striking teachers ... charging that they had betrayed the students." Despite the lack of black community support, two-thirds of the teachers consistently stayed out over the course of the seventeen-day strike. In the face of the teachers' combativeness, Addonizio, who was gearing up for a reelection race while facing a

52 || WHOSE SCHOOLS, WHOSE CITY?

federal indictment, pressured the board for a settlement, with teachers winning the salary increase; a class size capped at thirty; exemption from nonprofessional duties; and, above all, a "comprehensive grievance procedure with binding arbitration" in their one-year contract. But, reflecting the divisions the strike exposed and deepened, all three black members of the nine-person mayorally appointed board voted against approving the deal, with many black parents and community activists denouncing the board for capitulating to the union.[60]

A few months after the strike's conclusion, Gibson was elected as the city's first black mayor. He appointed three new members to the school board, most prominently Jesse Jacob, the Newark PTA president and virulent opponent of the union who had worked with authorities "to pass out injunctions, help arrest striking teachers, and testify against them in court."[61] Jacob, heavily influenced by the racially divisive 1968 Ocean Hill–Brownsville AFT-led strike in New York, identified teachers unions as being in direct opposition to the interests of black students and communities. To demonstrate that unbridgeable divide, Jacob, along with former school board member Dr. Wyman Garrett, incited a parent boycott of an elementary school after the NTU enforced a contract provision exempting teachers from nonteaching duties and blocking forced transfers. In their divide-and-conquer efforts, the ascending BPMC received invaluable assistance from narrow, white trade union leaders like Pete Petino and Vic Cascella, who identified community concerns as either inconsequential or in opposition to teacher interests and power.[62] The narrow approach to teacher unionism, a departure from NTU's origins, provided fodder for union critics like *Star-Ledger* reporter Bob Braun, who bemoaned their "distinct lack of civic mindedness." In his 1972 book *Teachers and Power,* he portrayed the NTU and other teachers unions mobilizing at the time as simply "special interests" concerned with accumulating as much power as possible at the expense of the children and democratic control of public education.[63] This narrative, of teachers unions having no concern for children, would be the ideological centerpiece of the neoliberal attack on them, and on public education more broadly.

For his part, Baraka, as the first step toward Black Power had been achieved with Gibson's election, saw the teachers union as an obstacle to the movement's self-determinationist project of "nationaliz[ing] the city's institutions as if it were liberated territory in Zimbabwe or Angola." Gaining control of the schools and the central role they would play in "Black Nationality Formation" were of primary importance in Baraka's nationalist project. Gibson, who had the responsibility of managing the city's long-standing and deepening fiscal crisis, all of which became more difficult following the state legislature's veto of his commuter tax plan, surely realized the benefits of Baraka and Jacob's RD politics. They could be used to rein in the wage and other demands of the teachers, even as Gibson's conventional capitalist politics clashed with the more grandiose ambitions of the nationalist firebrand.[64]

Jacob, whom the new black majority board selected as president, made it clear that his goal "was not to negotiate with the union, but to destroy it." Jacob and his chief negotiator, Don Saunders, with full backing from Baraka, stalled on negotiations over fall and winter 1970 as they simultaneously mobilized black community groups against the union. It was clear that the NTU would have to strike even to maintain a collective bargaining agreement, let alone preserve the gains made in the last contract. In contrast to the previous year, the 1971 strike, which began February 1 and did not end until mid-April, explicitly and brutally pitted whites, particularly Italians, against African Americans. The NTU president, as in 1970, was Carol Graves, a black woman who had in fact solidified her leadership in the most recent union election. But in the 1971 strike, ONE and other Black Power advocates attacked Graves and other black union leaders as inauthentic "colored lackeys," as the number of striking black teachers participating in the strike shrank significantly compared to the previous year. In the predominantly white and Italian East and North Wards, parents and other community members rallied to the strike, while in the largely black South, West, and Central Wards, striking teachers and opponents engaged in frequent street battles. For added muscle, the NTU turned to Anthony Imperiale and his vigilantes for assistance in attacking black activists opposing the strike, further deepening the racial divide.[65] The Newark Student Federation, as the conflict intensified, began to "embrace a nationalist program of Black power in school curriculum and staffing" and therefore "urged the board to reject a settlement with the teachers."[66] In the end, as the fratricidal conflict intensified, Gibson intervened and helped broker an agreement that preserved binding arbitration and modified slightly the "nonprofessional chores" provision. Nonetheless, the bitterness continued after the settlement, as black parents literally blocked teachers who had participated in the strike from entering schools, while white parents did

54 || WHOSE SCHOOLS, WHOSE CITY?

the same for teachers who had crossed picket lines during the strike. The courts also sought retribution for teachers striking in defiance of injunctions as scores served time in the county jail.[67]

Was there an alternative? Could the NTU have garnered the support of parents, students, and community members to facilitate rather than thwart the strike? As Piven has argued, mobilizing the support of insurgents' other interdependent relationships is crucial for the successful exercise of disruptive power.[68] Amiri Baraka, even at the height of his nationalist phase, did recognize the class basis of an alliance as exemplified by the epigraph that introduced the chapter. But to forge this alliance would have required the movement "jumping scales" by targeting not simply the fiscally constrained new BUR but the regional and national state, and the corporate interests, like Prudential, behind them, which had for decades strangled Newark and other urban centers from desperately needed revenue. The movement needed to advance from the "militant particularist" and "campaign" levels to a "social movement project" involving transformed organizational forms incorporating students and parents, broadened demands, and geographical and scalar expansion of the struggle that increasingly challenged the "social totality."[69] The NTU and AFT, saddled by a narrow "bread-and-butter" unionism, and their natural allies immersed in nationalism, of both the progressive and reactionary varieties—developments all nurtured by the postwar economic, political, and spatial structural changes—were not up to the task.

FOUNDATIONS FILL THE VACUUM

The narrowness of the unions opened the door to the foundations and their nonprofits to address underfunded urban schools and the gross disparities—rooted in the property tax–based school funding structure—in per-pupil education spending between cities and suburbs. In 1973, as the social movement upsurges of the 1960s were increasingly defanged, with the incorporating role of the BURs playing a part, the U.S. Supreme Court ruled in *San Antonio v. Rodriquez* that unequal school funding was *not* a violation of the Constitution's equal protection guarantee. Therefore, after *Rodriquez,* school funding litigants turned to the "education clauses of state constitutions" to argue that equitable funding of education was a right, with the Ford Foundation playing a central role in these efforts.[70] Indeed, Paul Tractenberg, a Rutgers Law professor and graduate of Newark's Weequahic High School, who would become the leading school equity litigator in New Jersey and beyond, argued that "Ford almost single-handedly started this national school funding equalization movement"—albeit a non-disruptive, legalist-focused "movement." "*Rodriguez,*" Tractenberg explains, "basically closed the federal courthouse door to this litigation and so it became this arduous state-by-state thing, and Ford was in there funding."[71]

In 1973, with encouragement and generous, sustained financial support from Ford, Tractenberg set up the Newark-based Education Law Center (ELC), through which he, and his collaborators and successors, litigated school funding cases from the 1970s onward. The ELC litigants, first under *Robinson v. Cahill* and later, beginning in 1981, under *Abbot v. Burke,* used the "thorough and efficient" education clause of the state constitution to challenge the state's inequitable education funding formula that disadvantaged New Jersey's older industrial cities. In 1990, the New Jersey Supreme Court, after years of litigation, ordered the Garden State to provide Newark and twenty-seven other poor urban districts "'greater than equal' resources, compared to their already advantaged peers in the state's wealthiest suburbs." After several years of wrangling with the New Jersey Supreme Court, and the issuing of new judicial mandates, by the 1997–98 school year, a formula for "parity funding was finally achieved," though New Jersey schools continued to be among the most racially and economically segregated in the country.[72]

THE COUNTEROFFENSIVE

While the state was pressed to provide more funding for education, it simultaneously began demanding more control and oversight of Newark and other "Abbott districts," as the cities in the suit were named. The pretexts for the intervention were "declining standards" and the damage these were doing to children. This growing elite consensus that began swirling around public education by the early 1980s was reflected and reinforced by the assertion of Terrel Bell, the Reagan administration's secretary of education, that there was a "widespread public perception that something is seriously remiss in our public school system." In 1981, as the new Republican president was breaking the air traffic controllers strike and Philadelphia's Democratic mayor

56 || WHOSE SCHOOLS, WHOSE CITY?

was crushing a teacher strike that helped end the long wave of public-sector militancy, Bell authorized the creation of a National Commission on Excellence in Education. The commission's 1983 report, *A Nation at Risk: The Imperative for Education Reform*, couched the crisis as threatening the country's global competitiveness, with the opening pages ominously announcing that "the educational foundations of our society are presently being eroded by a rising tide of mediocrity that threatens our very future as a Nation and a people." The report, along with the deepening of the neoliberal turn over the next decade, helped legitimate privatization as *the* reform imperative.[73]

In 1989, six years after the release of *A Nation at Risk*, the Business Roundtable (BRT) joined the crusade. The BRT, a powerful business federation composed of CEOs of major U.S. corporations whose formation in 1972 was a central part of the neoliberal capital offensive to roll back the Keynesian regulatory state, "took the bull by the horns" and united around a "systematic organizing posture" to advance corporate school reforms.[74] Underscoring its importance, the BRT's 1989 summer gathering focused for the first time solely on one policy issue: education reform. In another departure from past practice, the BRT invited "outside experts" to address the gathering, most prominently President George H. W. Bush and then Arkansas governor William Clinton. The BRT coalesced around the key priorities of establishing "state standards, state-mandated tests, and," crucially important for opening the way for charters, "rewards and sanctions." Three months later, President Bush—after what the *New York Times* reported as "discreet pressure" applied by BRT titans to "show more leadership in school improvement"—convoked, for only the third time in U.S. history, a president–governors summit to address education policy. The bipartisan gathering, with Bush's future presidential opponent Bill Clinton playing a prominent role, agreed on a set of "national education goals" that echoed the "standards-based accountability" philosophy on which the BRT had agreed at its June gathering.[75]

With the backing of the White House and governors, the BRT and its affiliates launched its ten-year, fifty-state offensive to advance its standards/testing/sanctions agenda through state houses across the country. Central to this strategy was forming state-level reform organizations, headed by a leading BRT member in the state. In New Jersey, this took the form of the Business Coalition for Educational Excellence (BCEE), established formally in 1996, which was led by the CEO of

WHOSE SCHOOLS, WHOSE CITY? || **57**

Prudential, headquartered in Newark, and included other corporate giants, such as Johnson and Johnson and Merck. The BCEE and its agenda were warmly received by the state political leadership, with Republican governor Christine Whitman joining the BCEE at its inaugural November 1996 New Jersey Business–Education Summit. At the gathering, she trumpeted that her administration had "developed . . . standards," adding that "they have to be implemented," which would "require profound change" that she was committed to carrying out.[76]

Even before the BCEE's formation, state officials were taking initiatives, such as takeovers of local school districts ostensibly in the name of improving student performance, that would become a central tactic to introduce neoliberal education reform. New Jersey was among the national leaders, with the state, in 1988, becoming the first in the county to "pass a 'takeover' law, which allowed the state's Department of Education to take over a school district for failure to demonstrate improvement."[77] The state conducted various audits of Newark's school system throughout the late 1980s and early 1990s, which culminated in a 1993 Comprehensive Compliance Investigation, the final step prior to a state takeover. Citing poor test scores, classrooms that were "filthy and in disrepair," and various cases of corruption, Whitman's administration ordered a state takeover of Newark's public schools in 1995. The takeover in Newark was part of a growing state and national trend, as public education became increasingly targeted and stigmatized by "reformers."[78]

The state intervention was vigorously opposed by the school board, which had become an elected body in 1982, and by the superintendent, Eugene Campbell, a former ONE official. Amiri Baraka and other community activists and organizations rallied under the banner of the Coalition for Voting Rights to oppose the takeover, while the Urban League and parent activist Maryam Bey applauded the decision. The union was divided, with NTU president Carol Graves, who was still at the helm after a quarter century, opposing it. In contrast, Joe Del Grosso, a former ally from the 1971 strike who successfully deposed her as president in May 1995, was on the other side, or at best neutral. Despite the "soon-to-be-fired Superintendent Eugene Campbell['s]" earlier combative stance, he refused to increase the political costs of the state takeover by engaging in disruption. Instead, he and fellow administrators cooperated with the Whitman administration in a smooth handover of the central offices on July 12, 1995—the twenty-eighth anniversary of the Newark rebellion. The state then installed Beverly Hall, an African American former deputy chancellor of New York City schools, as superintendent and abolished the elected board.[79]

In 1996, the year after Whitman oversaw the takeover of New Jersey's largest school district, she signed, with BCEE backing, legislation for authorizing the state's first so-called charter schools—privately run, but publicly funded. Approval for opening these schools would reside with the state's Department of Education, though funding would come from the local school budget (along with generous foundation and other private support), with the districts required to fork over 90 percent of per-pupil district spending for every student enrolled by the charters. In January 1997, Governor Whitman, in a celebratory gathering, champagne and all, announced that seventeen groups "had been granted charters to open new public schools and participate in the state's newest educational experiment."[80] Of the fifteen, two were from Newark, both of whom would become mainstays of the city's charter movement. One was awarded to the North Ward Center, run by homegrown neoliberal "fixer" Stephen Adubato Sr., and the other established the North Star Academy Charter School, which became the first school opened by what would become the national "Uncommon Schools" charter chain. Starting with only 172 students in a district of more than 47,000, this development did not create nearly as much response as the local control decision, though it would leave a much more lasting impact.[81]

PRIVATIZING NEWARK'S SCHOOLS: GETTING THERE WITH THE BLACK URBAN REGIME?

The brutal postwar assault by capital's movement from above on working-class power in older industrial cities left a devastating impact, particularly in Newark. Nonetheless, despite the obstacles of suburbanization and decentralization of industry, a powerful national (and global) revival of popular struggles emerged in the 1960s. This included, by the late 1960s and early 1970s, as Jefferson Cowie argues in *Stayin' Alive: The 1970s and the Last Days of the Working Class,* the emergence of rank-and-file labor insurgencies among mining, steel, auto, garment, agriculture, and, as we have seen, public-sector workers, particularly teachers. But, Cowie argues, despite their energy, [the labor insurgencies] rarely found a place in the national discourse, achieved little lasting institutional presence in the labor movement, left almost no legacy in American politics, and, most significantly, failed to become an enduring part of the class awareness of the nation's workers. . . . When the hammer of the sixties struck the labor institutions of the thirties, the sparks flew in the 1970s but few caught fire.[82]

While the teachers did leave an institutional, albeit contradictory, legacy, Cowie is correct that by the mid-1970s, the movements of the 1960s, which had spurred the ruling class to abandon the Keynesian SSA, as Kotz argued, had run out of steam.[83] Seen from the lens of social movement theory, the movements in Newark and beyond were unable to congeal into an anticapitalist challenge and alternative to the crisis-ridden Fordist–Keynesian model of capitalist accumulation, which, in turn, had emerged in response to the earlier 1930s upsurge. By the mid-1970s, as the movements in Newark and elsewhere stalled, the ruling class went on the offensive to impose their own solution to the twin crises of power and profit. The austerity solution to the 1975 banker-induced fiscal crisis in New York was an important watershed event in the emerging neoliberal movement from above. But BURs consolidating in Newark and across the country at the time were an integral part of the emerging neoliberal state machinery as well. This included Atlanta's first black mayor, Maynard Jackson, whose use of permanent replacements against striking municipal sanitation workers helped pave the way for Ronald Reagan's application on a national scale against striking air traffic controllers.[84] The antiracist legitimacy of the BPMC-led regimes provided invaluable assistance for imposing the neoliberal agenda of austerity, deregulation, privatization, and an expanded carceral state that hit the black working class with particular ferocity.

But, as we have seen across Newark's history, ruling elites have regularly reconfigured the local state to better serve their profit-making needs. By the 1990s, the opening of the "emerging market" of public education was a high priority for the neoliberal movement from above. Would Newark's black urban regime, now headed by the city's second black mayor, Sharpe James, be up to the task? Or would "reform," as in the 1830s, 1920s, 1950s, and 1970s, be necessary?

PART II

The Movement from Above

2

Regime Change

CORY BOOKER, PHILANTHROCAPITALISM, AND THE NEW
CIVIL RIGHTS MOVEMENT OF OUR DAY, 1996–2006

> We see social structures and social formations as the
> sediment of movement struggles, and as a kind of truce line
> continually probed for weaknesses and repudiated as this seems
> worthwhile—by social movements from above and social
> movements from below.
>
> —Alf Gunvald Nilsen and Laurence Cox, "What Would a
> Marxist Theory of Social Movements Look Like?"

"Ain't No Stopping Us Now!," the 1979 black anthem hit, was the
backdrop sound as Newark mayor Sharpe James savored his convincing May 1998 first-round reelection victory with his supporters at the
city's downtown Robert Treat Hotel. As he ascended to the stage and
led the crowd in a chant of "Dumped Crump, Fried Rice"—referencing
his two deposed African American challengers, Mildred Crump and
Ronald Rice Sr.—James must have felt invincible.[1] He had now won
his fourth consecutive election as mayor—and eighth municipal victory overall, including his four terms as the South Ward and at-large
councilman. The end of his fourth term would mark more than four
decades of uninterrupted black political leadership of the city, which
began with the election of Kenneth Gibson in 1970.

Further adding to James's confidence was his success in the face
of, as the lyrics went, "so many things that's held us down"—with "us"
synonymous with "me" in the class obfuscatory language deployed
by the black political elite. The then sixty-two-year-old James was,
like his predecessor, a product of the Great Migration that brought
some six million African Americans from the South to cities in the
North, Midwest, and West between World War I and 1970. Born in
1936 in Jacksonville, Florida, James's mother escaped with her two

|| 63

sons one night in 1944 from an abusive husband and stepfather of her children. Eventually settling in Newark, James was educated in local public schools. He later graduated with an education degree from New Jersey's Montclair State University and, after a stint in the army, received a master's from Springfield College. He began teaching in the Newark public school district in the mid-1960s and, like many of the first-generation post–civil rights black elected officials, first got involved in city politics through the federal government's Great Society antipoverty programs.[2] In 1970, James was part of the historic "Community Choice" slate that brought himself and two other African Americans to city council, made Kenneth Gibson the first black mayor of a major northeastern city, and marked the rise of the BUR in Newark and across the country.[3]

Despite the high expectations at the time, the first two decades of black rule witnessed a continued economic and demographic decline and further stigmatization of the city.[4] "But now," as the McFadden and Whitehead lyrics heralded and revelers grooved to on election night in Newark, "it looks like things are finally comin' around." Well, at least for some. During the 1990s, James oversaw an elite-defined "revitalization" of the city's downtown demanded by corporate interests—a directive epitomized by New Jersey's paper of record, the *Star-Ledger*, which exhorted in 1998 that James "must draw development into the city."[5] His biggest success in this regard was the construction, in partnership with the state and county, of the downtown New Jersey Performing Arts Center (NJPAC) and, later, a light rail that connected the facility to Penn Station, the city's intermetropolitan transit hub. In addition, James oversaw, with generous government subsidies, the construction of a downtown baseball stadium and, later, the Sports Arena to house two professional sport teams, replacing a failed, partially constructed shopping mall project.[6] Capital's renewed interest in Newark was also signified by the creation, in 1998, of the Newark Alliance, an entity that grouped the city's top corporate chief executives and leading state and local government officials to oversee a downtown revival.[7] That same year, "Newark's largest businesses," which had "long pushed for the creation of a special improvement district downtown," got their wish after the council passed enabling legislation to create the city's first such entity—and de rigueur for any downtown renaissance.[8]

The downtown revitalization was coupled with massive demolition of high-rise public housing in the city's working-class neighborhoods, with more than seven thousand units destroyed during the 1990s. James embraced the Clinton administration's so-called HOPE VI initiative that produced little hope, but lots of despair, for tenants, and lawsuits from advocates, as the new low-rise complexes included a drastically reduced number of public housing units. Nonetheless, James celebrated the demolitions, such as the 2002 implosion of the Stella Wright Homes—the site of the "longest, largest and most expensive rent strike in US public housing history"—where he, along with other officials, pulled the lever that detonated the towers.[9]

While rolling back "big government" in the form of public housing, James enthusiastically backed President William Clinton's rollout of a more punitive state.[10] In advocating for an "urban agenda" in Washington, James, as the *Star-Ledger* explained, "stressed," above all, "the need for more police funding, more jails, [and] incarceration for 'habitual offenders.'"[11] Clinton delivered on this wish list with James's assistance. As president of the National League of Cities, James played a central role in passing Clinton's 1994 Crime Bill, which expanded the death penalty and provided more than $16 billion for expanding state prisons and local police forces. As he proudly recounts in his autobiography, Newark's second black mayor "traveled across the country" with Clinton promoting the bill. He felt especially honored by the former Arkansas governor for choosing him "to speak in the White House Rose Garden to lobby Congress to pass the 100,000 New Cops Bill."[12] Consistent with the Clinton administration's neoliberal "reinventing government" initiative, the "upsizing of its penal arm" would be financed by reducing federal public employment from the "social-welfare sector of the state."[13] The crime bill contributed to hundreds of thousands more poor people, disproportionately black, being shuttled into the carceral state's expanded form of public housing. At the same time, his backing for the measure allowed James and his wife to be escorted, by their now close friends William and Hillary Clinton, for an overnight stay at the country's most luxurious public housing—the Lincoln Bedroom at the White House.[14]

Despite delivering on core components of the neoliberal agenda, the strengthening school privatization movement saw the James-led BUR—and similar political arrangements around the country—as an obstacle. Seen through the lens of SSA theory, the BUR emerges in the 1970s as a local state regulatory mechanism of the ascendant neoliberal capitalist accumulation model. But, despite the useful role it played, by the late 1990s and 2000s, it was in need of its own restructuring to pave the way for new profit-making opportunities. Some of the practices used by James and other BUR heads of state, such as accommodations to, and alliances with, teacher unions, were now obstacles to opening up the emerging education market.[15]

DRIVERS SEARCHING FOR NEW IMPLEMENTERS

Like *Expelling Public Schools,* Howard Ryan's study conceptualizes the corporate school movement as "an extension of the neoliberal bosses revolt" that took hold in the 1970s amid the crisis of Keynesianism. Within this elite-led insurgency, Ryan distinguishes between the movement's "drivers" and "implementers." The drivers consist of the movement's "major funders along with the key institutions they control" and are divided into three sectors—organized business, edubusiness, and philanthropic sectors. The implementers, in contrast, are the "politicians, think tank directors, school district superintendents, and other influential actors who carry out the drivers' wishes and may provide them with strategic advice."[16]

As discussed in the preceding chapter, the organized business sector, most prominently in the form of the BRT, played a central role in the late 1980s, the 1990s, and into the 2000s promoting corporate school reform, particularly in the form of imposing the standards, high-stakes testing, and sanctions regime. But following the movement's crowning achievement, the No Child Left Behind legislation, passed in 2001 under the George W. Bush administration, "the onus of national leadership for corporate schooling," Ryan argues, "shifted from the BRT to the edu-philanthropists and edubusiness."[17] With the standards and testing regime firmly implanted—though contested—the movement began to center its efforts on promoting private management of public schools.

In this study, drawing from the work of Kenneth Saltman and Linsey McGoey, respectively, I refer to the eduphilanthropic movement drivers as *venture philanthropy* or *philanthrocapitalism.* Educational philanthropy during the Keynesian era and the first half of the twentieth century also played a conservative role by "supporting public institutions in ways that were compatible with the ideological perspectives and material interests of the captains of industry." Furthermore, like their neoliberal-era counterparts, the exploitation of labor was the foundation from which the Rockefellers, Carnegies, Fords, and others gleaned their "endowments" and bestowed their "grants." But, under what Saltman calls the "scientific philanthropy" of this earlier era, grantees enjoyed some autonomy on how grants were used, and their "giving" was "marked by a spirit of public obligation and deeply embedded in a liberal democratic ethos." In contrast, philanthrocapitalism exercises close oversight of their grants—"social investments"—to ensure implementation of neoliberal objectives, such as privatization, weakening/eliminating collective bargaining and casualizing labor, and penetration of market principals in the operation of schools. Discarding the public service rhetoric of an earlier era, venture philanthropy draws on business terms, as "donors become 'investors,' impact is renamed 'social return,' evaluation becomes 'performance measurement,' grant reviewing turns into 'due diligence,' [and] the grant list is renamed an 'investment portfolio.'"[18]

The new focus, led by venture philanthropy and the real estate and finance wing of the edubusiness sector, required the movement to "jump scales" from the regional to the local, from state legislatures to urban regimes. Because of the way public education has been structured historically in the United States, the drive for privatization would make the local state apparatuses a central focus of movement activists. But the BUR form of the local state became among the first, if not the primary one, to be "probed for weaknesses," as Nilsen and Cox describe capitalist offensives in the epigraph of this chapter. The BUR's vulnerability was due to the racial and class inequities of the U.S. public education system under the previous Keynesian SSA, which the social movements of the 1960s challenged but were not successful in significantly remaking in an egalitarian direction. BURs were therefore, from the perspective of the movement from above, the weak link in the United States' Keynesian public school chain. In addition, further contributing to the targeting of BURs and other cities by the charter movements was the increasing return of capital to long-disinvested cities, such as Newark. But, even at the debilitated level of the BUR, a movement—a conscious political intervention—would be required to sunder the statist shackles.

Thus, in this and the subsequent chapter, I analyze the rise, abetted and backed by movement drivers, of a new cadre of "implementers" within Newark's BUR and how they worked to advance the movement's goal of commodifying public education. While analyzing a

68 || REGIME CHANGE

variety of implementers, I place primary attention on Cory Booker, who was the most influential among a new rising layer of the BPMC not only in Newark but nationally, championing school privatization. In particular, I examine Booker's relationship to philanthrocapitalism and other corporate interests, his early championing of "school choice," and the roots and centrality of an antiracist ideology for legitimating the entire privatization effort.

MR. BOOKER GOES TO NEWARK

Born in 1969, over a generation after James and Gibson, Cory Booker grew up in Harrington Park, New Jersey, an affluent, predominantly white suburb twenty-five miles north of Newark. His parents, both raised in the South, were executives at IBM and benefited from the civil rights victories that, among many changes, opened up the management ranks of Corporate America and housing options in the suburbs for upwardly mobile African Americans. Educated in the local low-poverty, well-resourced public schools, Booker did his undergraduate studies and master's in sociology at the elite Stanford University. He then received a prestigious Rhodes Scholarship to study at Oxford University and followed that up with a law degree from Yale University in 1997, before relocating to Newark.[19]

The rise to political prominence of Cory Booker in Newark signaled not only a generational change from Sharpe James but also a deeper structural transformation wrought by the end of the de jure system of racial segregation. The changes in American society that produced a Cory Booker have led, despite continuing deep racial disparities, to a more diversified, multiracial economic and political elite. One outcome, political scientist Adolph Reed Jr. argues, has been the emergence of a "coherent interracial governing class" in many cities, including black majority formations. This increasingly close alliance is the result, in part, of a "straightforward sociological dynamic" produced by

> black and white elites [who] increasingly live in the same
> neighborhoods, interact socially as individuals and families,
> attend the same schools and functions, consume the same
> class-defining commodities and pastimes, and participate in
> the same civic and voluntary associations, [and as a result] they

increasingly share a common sense not only about frameworks of public policy but also about the proper order of things in general. They share a sensibility and worldview and a reservoir of their class's cultural experiences, aspirations, quotidian habits and values, as well as the material interests that unite them as a stratum.[20]

Booker, of course, is an exemplar of this broader "sociological dynamic." Further cementing Booker into an elite form of "common sense" around public policy, particularly with regard to public education, has been his immersion in the philanthropic world. Booker, much like Barack Obama, with whom he is often compared, came to Newark under the aegis of philanthropy.[21] He permanently relocated to New Jersey's largest city in 1996, as he was finishing his law degree at Yale, and, upon graduation, received a two-year Skadden Foundation fellowship to provide legal representation to public housing and other low-income tenants.[22] But, well before graduating from law school, he was eyeing Newark, with which he was familiar from his youth, because, as he explained in a 2000 interview, "I always knew I wanted to work in inner-city Newark since college." In 1994, while at Oxford, he flew to Newark at the invitation of the Catholic-affiliated nonprofit New Community Corporation (NCC) to speak at a Dr. Martin Luther King Jr. holiday commemoration. The NCC was one of the leading nonprofit community development corporation "fixers" that emerged in the aftermath of the 1967 rebellion. The longtime NCC director and founder, Reverend William Linder, who, as part of his outfit's own privatized social welfare "shadow state," opened two charter schools, was impressed with Booker's "idealism" and encouraged him to relocate to the city, arguing that "we need fresh faces."[23] While at Yale, Booker made regular trips to Newark as he further developed relationships, particularly among investors, nonprofits, and philanthropists, who encouraged his plans.

After settling permanently in Newark, he moved next door to and later into Brick Towers, a federal government–subsidized high-rise apartment complex in the city's Central Ward. There he quickly developed a name for himself as a community activist advocating for the impoverished.[24] At the same time as he was building a base among low-income tenants and grabbing media attention, the then twenty-eight-year-old Stanford-, Oxford-, and Yale Law School–educated lawyer was also making contact and being welcomed by leading figures in Newark. Of particular importance was Raymond Chambers, a wealthy white investor and philanthropist with significant business interests in Newark and who was then in the midst of organizing the Newark Alliance—the peak business organization that grouped the city's leading executives and local and state officials.[25] Another important figure was Richard Roper, an influential black civic leader and private consultant who had served important advisory and executive roles in the Gibson administration and state government since the 1970s.

Roper, as he explained to me while we met in his comfortable home in the leafy suburb of Maplewood, first met Booker while the Skadden fellow was conducting a study "on things that needed to happen to begin to move Newark in a more successful direction." If you wanted the perspective of Newark's multiracial elite "on things that needed to happen," Roper was certainly the right person to interview. In the late 1990s, Roper was head of the Newark in the 21st Century task force, made up of twenty-two "academics, corporate executives, and philanthropists who have ties to Newark." As capital's return to the city accelerated, with old industrial New Jersey cities like Hoboken and Jersey City going through revivals, and Manhattan only a twenty-minute train ride away, the local elite saw increasing opportunities for the long-beleaguered city. "The successful launch of NJPAC" that occurred under James's leadership, Roper argued, was of particular significance with respect to reviving the city. The project showed that "a combination of private-sector engagement with the strong support of the state could produce a viable economic stimulus in the city." Nonetheless, Roper and other elites, like Raymond Chambers, who was a major financial contributor to the task force, still saw "apprehension of the private sector to invest in Newark." Undermining business confidence, according to Roper, was a city government that "was not sufficiently business friendly, that was inefficient, clumsy, unable to respond to the needs of the private sector . . . for efficiency."[26]

Thus, although James had been eager to deliver for developers by providing subsidies and overseeing the mass rollback of "Keynesian artifacts," such as the city's public housing, he was still seen as an obstacle to the regeneration the elite wanted to see. As Roper emphasized to the *Star-Ledger* during the 1998 election, "we're at a time where a group of politicians contributed what they could contribute, and it is time to bring a new set of actors to strut their stuff."[27] Cory Booker was clearly the type of politician Roper, Chambers, and other elites had in mind to create that business-friendly environment.[28]

It did not take long for Booker to decide to run for local office, a decision that received clear encouragement from Roper, Chambers, and other local elites. In spring 1998, less than two years after his arrival in Newark, he was elected to the city council for the Central Ward, which, for many years, had been the heart of Newark's black community. The backing he received from Stephen Adubato Sr., an influential Italian American political operator from the city's predominately Latinx North Ward, was important in several respects beyond the immediate race. First, the alliance with Adubato provided Booker with a locally based, politically powerful operator of one of the first charter schools in the city, which complemented his budding partnership with the national forces backing school privatization. Second, through Adubato, Booker forged political bonds with the city's Puerto Rican political elite—the largest Latinx group in the city—who were incorporated into Adubato's get-out-the-vote political machine, with some directly employed by his charter school and other parts of his privatized social service operation. Adubato's power, and by extension Booker's, increased in 2002 when Joseph DiVincenzo, a protégé and integral part of Adubato's operation, was elected county executive, further increasing their statewide influence.[29]

The other key factor in his victory was the unprecedented $150,000 he raised for the race drawn from "campaign . . . donations from a network of friends who are bankers, lawyers and stockbrokers from as far away as California, Puerto Rico and Florida and near-by New York City." Central among this network were wealthy members of the "Chabad-Lubavitchers," who investigative journalist Yasha Levine described as "a rabidly rightwing Hasidic cult." Booker became intimately connected to the group while at Oxford, a relationship he—and the cult leaders—further cultivated at Yale and in New Jersey. With this help, he defeated the James-backed, sixteen-year incumbent, George Branch.[30]

CORY BOOKER, HOWARD FULLER, AND THE MOVEMENT FROM ABOVE

Booker used his new platform to proffer some criticisms of James's dual development model that focused on downtown development

72 || REGIME CHANGE

at the expense of the city's working-class neighborhoods and residents.[31] But, as he began receiving extensive national media coverage, including a segment on the famed *60 Minutes* news show and in *Time* magazine, the primary public policy issue in which he immersed himself was public school reform—a major concern of the Newark in the 21st Century task force report and of the Newark Alliance.[32] His solution came straight out of the neoliberal policy handbook: provide parents of low-income children "choice" through school vouchers or charter schools. He brought this message to the right-wing Manhattan Institute in 2000, which was a national coming-out of sorts for the rising political star. Following standard talking points of the charter school lobby, he maligned the "old paradigm" of public schools as an "entitlement paradigm" not designed to serve children but rather for "large (especially black) big city mayors" to operate "race-based machines" of patronage. In contrast, Booker outlined to his well-heeled audience,

> I define public education not as a publicly guaranteed space and a publicly run, publicly funded building where our children are sent based on their Zip Code. Public education is the use of public dollars to educate our children at the schools that are best equipped to do so—public schools, magnet schools, charter schools, Baptist schools, Jewish schools.[33]

In 1999, the year before the Manhattan Institute address, Booker worked with the former Wall Street executive and Republican mayor of Jersey City Brent Schundler and wealthy New Jersey businessman Peter Denton to found the nonprofit E3—Excellent Education for Everyone—to promote vouchers to attend religious schools. The three went on a trip to Milwaukee, a center for voucher and charters, hosted by the Bradley Foundation, which had played a dubious role promoting Charles Murray's eugenics tract *The Bell Curve*.[34] Booker was also able to attract young black professionals to the privatization movement, such as Dana Rone, who was brought on as a well-compensated employee and later as a consultant for E3. She won a seat on the Newark Public Schools Advisory Board in 2000, a perch she used to promote neoliberal education reform.[35]

In the late 1990s, Booker also became a founding board member of the Black Alliance for Educational Opportunities (BAEO). The

Milwaukee-based Bradley Foundation played a central political and financial role in the BAEO's formation, while the BAEO also enjoyed generous funding from the Walton Family Foundation and the foundation of future Trump education secretary Betsy Devos—the Dick and Betsy Devos Foundation.[36] DeVos also formed in 1999 her own well-funded nonprofit "pro-choice" group—the Alliance for School Choice—which worked closely with the BAEO.[37]

The BAEO's founder and driving force was Howard Fuller, a former Black Nationalist and, later, a pro-voucher superintendent of Milwaukee's public schools in the early 1990s. Born in 1941 and formerly known as Owusu Sadaukai, Fuller was, as Cedric Johnson described him in his masterful account of the Black Power movement, "a skilled orator, resourceful and experienced community organizer, and erudite intellectual" who cut his political teeth in mid-1960s North Carolina with "a statewide organization committed to fostering political activism among the poor."[38] With the "mid-1960s sea change in black public discourse from liberal integrationism to Black Power militancy," he helped found, in the late 1960s and early 1970s, the Malcolm X Liberation University in Durham, North Carolina, and the national African Liberation Day Coordinating Committee. In the latter capacity, he worked to forge a broad, popular, black working class–rooted anti-imperialist politics in support of the then raging anticolonial struggles in Africa. Thus the seasoned organizer, who had now embraced an elite-driven movement, knew the importance of this neoliberal brand of "self-determination" education politics developing a popular base. He must have shared this counsel with his new, quarter-century younger comrade in the movement. Though Booker enjoyed similar oratorical skills, he did not have anywhere near the same political organizing acumen as the veteran 1960s activist. Therefore Booker would have undoubtedly benefited from, and been greatly influenced by, Fuller's strategic vision for advancing the Newark front of their national movement.

To help forge an indispensable, grassroots movement base, Booker and Fuller organized, in the early 2000s, several paid trips of Newark activists to see how various "school choice" initiatives operated in Milwaukee. As a good organizer, Fuller targeted for recruitment existing grassroots leaders who, if won to the movement, could help build the movement's ranks and generate popular consent to privatization. Among those targeted was Wilhelmina Holder, a Newark native and mother of several children in the public schools, who regularly attended school board meetings and headed various volunteer initiatives to assist students. "Dr. Fuller and his wife . . . were the lead people," she explains of the first trip she took in the early 2000s, while Booker was a councilman.

> A number of people went on the trip, a number of community people, a number of parents, the activists went, educators went . . . Dana Rone went . . . the late Ted Johnson, Dr. Johnson, when he was the lead black vice president at NJIT [local university], he went . . . a guidance counselor at Barringer [High School] at the time. . . . So there were a number of people. . . . The ministers didn't go this time but later on things were organized and they went. . . . I guess we were the pilot delegation, the first ones out of the gate and we were a mixed crew, a motley crew.

As Holder's account of the targeted grassroots and civic leaders underscores, Fuller and Booker, as leading intellectuals of the movement from above, were clearly engaged in a Gramscian "war of position" to forge popular consent in Newark to privatization. Of course, not all embraced the new "common sense." Holder, who "flew out there a number of times to look at these supposedly innovative schools," was intrigued by certain aspects of the voucher program but, in the end, was not won over.

> The thing was to look for innovation and hope. . . . And there was only one school I was interested in and that was the Harambee school, it was right in the middle of the projects, and obviously I can relate to projects, and it was Afrocentric and obviously I can relate to that. The children seemed to be really engaged and enjoyed the school and they had technology and I can relate to that. But I wasn't impressed with some of them because some of them were run by the Lutherans and this one, in that group, everybody is running their own little thing, no uniformity in terms of accountability. We found later that there was a man convicted of child molestation or something that ran the school out in Milwaukee. And then there was another one that ran off with the money, and the children were hurt by that.[39]

In contrast, others, particularly those drawn from the black ministerial ranks, were much more favorably disposed to the movement's ideological and material overtures. Fuller, who was shuttling back and forth to Newark and other New Jersey cities with significant black communities during these years, helped build that base. Highlighting the fruits of Fuller and Booker's organizing was the warm reception the movement's ideas and leaders received at the 2001 convention of the powerful Black Ministers Council of New Jersey. The gathering, which brought together more than one thousand ministers, embraced "school choice" and the Bush administration's broader "faith-based initiatives . . . to channel taxpayer money to religious organization for social work." Underscoring the alignment of the ministers with the school privatization movement—or, as the *Star-Ledger* put it, "the African American pastors are ready to play ball"—was that Fuller, Republican Jersey City mayor and E3 cofounder Bret Schundler, and Bush secretary of education Rod Paige addressed the minsters during a full day dedicated to "its top issue of improving education." Fuller, as part of the movement's ideological offensive to normalize privatization and provide talking points to many of his new or potential epigones, emphasized in his remarks that while some "go berserk" at any "mention [of] the V-word," vouchers were simply "a way to get money to the people." Reverend Reginald Jackson, the longtime president of the group and an African Methodist Episcopal pastor in nearby Orange, New Jersey, echoed the Gramscian "common sense" cultivated by the movement, declaring, "For us, it's not an issue of Democrats or Republican. It's a matter of productivity. Where schools are failing, parents should take charge. Parents ought to have choice."[40] Jackson became a vocal voucher supporter and later had his church sponsor its own charter school while assisting other churches in following the same path.[41]

Fuller's efforts were coupled with the grassroots organizing and lobbying of E3, which opened an office in Newark and brought on another young black professional, Derrell Bradford, to head the outfit after Dana Rone's departure. Highlighting the growing bipartisan consensus on neoliberal school reform—at least for "inner-city" schools—was E3's 2001 annual awards dinner. The gala was cochaired by former Republican governor Tom Kean, former Democratic governor Brendan Byrne, and sitting Democratic U.S. senator Robert Torricelli.[42]

"THE CIVIL RIGHTS MOVEMENT OF MY GENERATION"

Like Fuller and the BAEO, Booker portrayed the demand for vouchers and charters as a civil rights struggle that, consistent with the neoliberal agenda, required government to "get out of the way." In a 2000 *New York Times* profile titled "Young Blacks Turn to School Vouchers as Civil Rights Issue," the author described Booker as the most prominent of "a growing cadre of young blacks who have embraced vouchers, and school choice more broadly, as a central civil rights issue for their generation." Booker, who often invoked Malcolm X's famous "by any means necessary" call to arms in his evangelizing for neoliberal school reform, outlined to the *Times* reporter the connection between school privatization, consumer choice, and RD:

> It's one of the last remaining major barriers to equality of opportunity in America, the fact that we have inequality of education. I don't necessarily want to depend on the government to educate my children—they haven't done a good job in doing that. Only if we return power to the parents can we find a way to fix the system.[43]

Thus, in contrast to the Keynesian era, breaking down racist barriers to equal opportunity required unleashing, rather than constraining, market forces. The framing of privatization as a noble antiracist initiative that provided real choice was by no means peculiar to Booker but was the dominant ideology among "pro-choice" militants of all races and ethnicities in the elite-driven movement. Hedge fund capitalists, who, as a 2009 *New York Times* exposé pointed out, were "at the movement's epicenter," particularly in New York, embraced the antiracist ideology with particular zeal. For example, Goldman Sachs's African American vice president for private equity Robert Reffkin championed charter schools as "the civil rights movement of my generation."[44] Wendy Kopp, the white founder of Teach for America (TFA), a key organizational arm of the movement that helped achieve the neoliberal aim of casualizing academic labor by providing uncertified teachers for distressed urban and rural schools, wrote a book whose title—*One Day, All Children*—invokes words drawn from Martin Luther King Jr.'s famous "I Have a Dream" speech. The TFA alumni magazine is titled, likewise, *One Day*. The North Star charter school established in Newark in 1997, which later developed into the national chain Uncommon Schools, took its name from the newspaper published by the former slave and leading abolitionist Frederick Douglass.[45]

It might seem strange that the movement for "school choice," backed as it was by the Charles Murray–supporting groups, such as the Bradley Foundation, and one which, as Nancy Maclean's acclaimed study documents, first emerged in the 1950s as a right-wing strategy to oppose the desegregation of public schools, would be repackaged as an antiracist one.[46] Yet, another version of "choice" emanated from the Black Power movement of the late 1960s and early 1970s. As Russell Rickford explains in his meticulously documented study *We Are an African People: Independent Education, Black Power and the Radical Imagination*, "the black independent schools movement" was a leading component of Black Power activists' larger agenda of obtaining "community control" and "self-determination" and of forging a new "African personality."[47] Indeed, Newark, under the leadership of Amiri Baraka, who, Rickford correctly argues, "embodied the Pan African nationalist quest," became a leading laboratory for private alternatives to public schools. The African Free School established by Baraka's organization, the CFUN, and run by his wife, Amina Baraka—and attended by their son and future mayor, Ras—inspired similar initiatives around the country. Initially organized in the late 1960s as an after-school tutoring program, by 1972, Newark's African Free School had become a tax-exempt nonprofit corporation and a free-standing, alternative private school financed by "tithes of CFUN" members, volunteer labor, and foundation and government grants.[48]

There were other ideological and programmatic affinities between Black Power's and the neoliberal movement from above's versions of school choice. While Baraka and other Black Power militants worked to gain black control over the public schools—which led him to be a resolute opponent of the 1971 Newark teachers strike—they saw all public institutions, particularly public schools, as deeply flawed and destructive of black people. Baraka described Newark public schools and teachers "as mind distortion specialists" who extracted "hunks of black matter" from the minds of black children while replacing "living tissue with cancerous growths."[49] This mirrored the contemporary school choice movement's condemnation of ineffective teachers and "failing" public schools as also deeply racist. Public schools practice, as George W. Bush famously pronounced during a 2000 campaign address to the NAACP, "another form of bias," one that comes in the form of the "soft bigotry of low expectations." But, thanks to "a great movement of education reform," there was hope, the then Republican nominee reassured his black middle-class audience. This "great movement" would "provide," Bush explained in his typical ineloquent phrasing, "parents with options to increase their option, like charters and choice," to combat the insidious racism of low-performing public schools.[50]

Another parallel between the Black Power and neoliberal school reform movements is that both identified a deeply defective black populace, particularly the black working class, in need of reeducation to reclaim "captive minds" deformed by white racism.[51] Baraka, for example, pointed to the psychological damage to blacks immersed in "chaos," "degenerated situation," and pervasive racism. Haki Madhubuti, Baraka's Chicago-based comrade and fellow accomplished author, who founded Third World Press and later the CFUN-like Institute for Political Education, evinced particular "disdain" for "African American folkways," which he characterized as a "filthy invention" of an all-pervasive white racist system. "We sick," Madhubuti concluded, "because we don't know *who we are.*"[52] The cure was a new educational system to "purge alien value systems" and "construct the disciplined sons and daughters an embryonic nation requires." To do that, as Rickford points out, the African Free School and other Afrocentric schools of the period employed "a highly regimented" instruction, with emphasis placed on "catechisms . . . rote method . . . discipline and collective response" to create the new African personality.[53] While the contemporary reformers aim to create, instead, the "new neoliberal personality," charter schools are also characterized by authoritarian teaching methods, such as denying bathroom breaks, silent lunches, and monetary rewards for "good behavior," to instill discipline into a defective "underclass."[54] Just as the Black Power militants emphasized subjective will to change material conditions, likewise the charters emphasize a "no-excuses" philosophy regarding the capacity of low-income black students to succeed.

As social movement theorists Laurence Cox and Alf Gunwald Nils emphasize, "the projects of social movements from above involve rationalities expressed in ideological offensives . . . for which elites seek to gain popular consent."[55] Likewise, David Harvey, in his influential study of neoliberalism, has argued that "neoliberalization," of which school privatization is a key component, "requires politically and economically the construction of a neoliberal-based populist culture of differential consumerism and individual libertarianism." To help construct this culture, this new "common sense," neoliberals, Harvey argues, have drawn selectively from the progressive ideological streams of the 1960s that had united causes of individual freedom and social justice against powerful corporations, indeed even capitalism, all backed by an interventionist state. In contrast, under the new ideological formulation, neoliberals have embraced the "ideals of individual freedom" strain of 1960s thought, which they have used as an ideological battering ram "against the interventionist and regulatory practices of the [welfare] state." Indeed, under this new ideology, "capitalist corporations, business, and the market" are no longer identified as part of the problem, as in the past, but instead are recast as the vehicles for individual choice and emancipation. Likewise, Kotz argues that neoliberal ideology drew principally "upon long-established values embedded in American culture, such as individual freedom and autonomy and limited government."[56]

But, as I have demonstrated here, there is an added ingredient to the neoliberal ideological brew in the case of the movement to privatize public schools. The "skilled activities" of movement activists like Booker, Fuller, and new adherents like Reverend Jackson have also harnessed the antiracist and self-determinationist variants of 1960s liberatory thinking. Despite their radical veneer, ideas drawn from Black Power provided legitimation for neoliberal privatization initiatives of the early twenty-first century. In the past, the black elite demanded an expansion of, or at least inclusion in, the public sector to achieve the full participation of African Americans in American life. In contrast, under the new "antiracist" neoliberal ideology, that same public sector is indicted for denying opportunity and must be rolled back to achieve the aims of the "civil rights movement of our day."[57]

VYING FOR STATE POWER

Booker's movement work and his favorable and regular media coverage, along with his perch on the city council, positioned him well for his 2002 electoral challenge to longtime mayor Sharpe James. Highlighting Booker's and the broader movement's success in cementing a "postpartisan," neoliberal common sense around "school choice," he picked up endorsements across the political spectrum, from former New Jersey Democratic U.S. senator Bill Bradley to former Republican congressman and tax-cut proponent Jack Kemp.[58] Wall Street, importantly, was clearly excited. Hedge Fund investors backing the charter schools and voucher movement became increasingly, Booker himself argued, "motivated" to support him because they now had "an African American urban Democrat telling the truth about education."[59] Attesting to this support was Booker raising more than $3 million for the race as he surpassed the four-term incumbent in the cash sweepstakes. Of Booker's $3 million war chest, $565,000 came from Wall Street investors like Ravenel Boykin Curry IV, a philanthropist and head of a family-owned hedge fund, Eagle Capital Management, and Bain Capital investors. Booker would later vigorously defend the latter—founded by 2012 Republican presidential nominee Mitt Romney—after President Barack Obama leveled mild criticism at the firm during his 2012 reelection campaign.[60] Curry not only brought other investors on board in support of Booker's campaign but also financed a promotional film—*Street Fight*—on the 2002 race, which was written and directed by his brother, Marshall. The story line was a crusading Booker confronting the incumbent's corrupt, violent urban machine that lorded over an oppressed, cowed population—the same script that Booker parroted in his Manhattan Institute speech.

Underscoring how enfeebled the BUR had become under James, the incumbent's campaign centered on attacking Booker for his lack of racial authenticity rather than on any substantive policy differences. Reverends Jesse Jackson and Al Sharpton, members of the advocacy wing of the old "black leadership family," joined James on the campaign trail and leveled similar, but subtler, attacks on Booker's lack of authenticity.[61] The failure to attack on substantive grounds was because there weren't any. James's corporate-centered, state-subsidized development model exemplified what geographer Gordon MacLeod calls a "political economy of place rather than territory," in which "the benefits of flagship projects like convention centers and festivals are often more readily experienced by those, like tourists and place mobile capitalists, who live beyond the immediate locality."[62] A prime expression of this duality was the downtown Prudential Center sports complex, developed under his watch, which lacked an entrance, having simply a concrete wall on the side of the center that fronted a major transit and shopping thoroughfare for local working-class residents.[63]

The flip side of the downtown development model was James's role, in collaboration with the Clinton and Bush administrations, in "clearing the way" of "Keynesian artifacts" by "demolishing high-rise public housing and increasing the number of units for homeownership."[64] Yet, although promoted as a market panacea, the American homeownership dream in Newark turned into a nightmare for many as the city became a major target of "reverse redlining," with low-income, mostly black and Latinx homeowners victimized by various forms of predatory lending. By 2013, Newark had the second highest percentage of homes with underwater mortgages and one of the highest foreclosure rates in the United States.[65]

THE BLACK POLITICAL ENTREPRENEUR: FOR WHAT ENTREPRENEURIAL ENDS?

Political scientist Andra Gillespie, in her book *The New Black Politician: Cory Booker, Newark and Post-Racial America,* described Booker and his electoral ascent as a paragon of the "black political entrepreneur" (BPE) who challenges old-line, post–civil rights black Democrats by looking "beyond the black community for support, *particularly financial support.*"[66] While this was certainly true, what Gillespie's concept and analysis miss is where this money was coming from and for what ends. Booker, the quintessential BPE, was an avatar of the Wall Street–driven movement focused on opening up public education to the capitalist market. The old-line BUR leaders, like James, although dutifully delivering for capitalist urban regeneration efforts, were not considered up to the new tasks. His accommodations with organized labor, or at least the union bureaucracy, and his reliance, in part, on old, machine-style electoral financing through city employees meant that he was not suitable for leading a stepped-up assault on the public sector.[67] Therefore, by the late 1990s and early 2000s, movement activists on Wall Street, in Silicon Valley, in real estate, and in other capitalist sectors intent on further prying open the "emerging markets" of public education *and* central city real estate increasingly began turning to and cultivating BPEs, of which Booker was the most talented of a growing crop.

Although James managed to engineer a victory in the 2002 race, it was clear that the five-term incumbent's days were numbered.[68] Booker's impressive performance emboldened the funders of the growing pro–charter school reform movements by proving that their allied

82 || REGIME CHANGE

black Democratic political entrepreneurs could take power in cities and help open up the public education market. Reflecting the movement's optimism, hedge fund philanthrocapitalists, in the wake of the election, formed Democrats for Education Reform (DFER), with Booker as a founding board member, to promote, in particular, black Democrats in support of school privatization. The formation of DFER clearly showed that the hedge funders had established themselves as the most "significant political counterweight to the powerful teachers unions" in the battle to privatize public education.[69]

The reform movement found Newark to be a rich recruiting ground for new militants, such as Dana Rone, discussed earlier. Shavar Jeffries, a Newark native and graduate of Duke University and Columbia Law School, was a particularly prized recruit. Raised under humble circumstances in Newark by his grandparents, his class origins added to his racial authority. He marshaled this authenticity to weigh in on the failure of public schools for poor black youth—although he attended a private, suburban Catholic high school thanks to a Boy's Club scholarship—and the need for the no-nonsense, discipline-imposing, unbureaucratically constrained charter schools.

In 2001, Ryan Hill, a former TFA teacher in East Harlem, was following the entrepreneurial steps of other TFA alums by opening up the New Jersey market for the fledgling KIPP charter chain. Their first school in the Garden State would be in Newark—TEAM Academy, which opened up in 2002 in the city's mainly black South Ward. Jeffries, who had returned to his hometown a few years after law school, worked with Hill in getting the initiative off the ground as he became a founding board member of KIPP New Jersey and a leading champion of charters—what he termed, echoing movement ideology, "the civil rights issue of our day." This movement work included penning numerus editorials in the *Star-Ledger* in favor of school choice, being elected to the Newark Public Schools Advisory Board, later running as the movement's standard-bearer for the 2014 mayoral race, and, finally, taking the reins of DFER after his electoral loss to Baraka.[70]

Further exemplifying the headway the movement was making against the old guard was that many of their offspring were sensing the political winds—and financial flows—and joining the growing ranks of black pro-charter Democrats. A prime example is Ronald Rice Jr., whose father, Ronald Rice Sr., was the first African American elected from the city's West Ward and challenged Booker in the 2006 mayoral race. Underscoring that money is at times thicker than blood, Rice Jr. ran on the *opposing* "Booker team," both in 2002, unsuccessfully, and then again in 2006, when he was elected as the West Ward councilman and Booker's challenger was his own father.[71] After two terms on the city council, the Seton Hall Law School graduate became the chief lobbyist for the National Alliance for Public Charter Schools, an outfit bankrolled by the Walton and Gates Foundations, leading funders of the movement. The Rice Jr. case—who, unlike Booker, was not a BPE outsider but literally a child of the "Black leadership family"— underscores the power of the movement's superior financial resources to incorporate broader layers of the BPMC. It was not only Booker, the archetypal BPE, who increasingly sought out support "beyond the black community . . . particularly financial support."[72]

TAKING STATE POWER

To stay in the spotlight and challenge the "inauthentic," "outsider" tag, Booker founded a nonprofit, Newark Now. The outfit espoused an antistatist, self-help ideology and practice that would demonstrate, in the words of the rising star himself, that "we don't have to wait for government to do things."[73] As he promised, Booker ran and soundly defeated Ronald Rice Sr. in May 2006 to become Newark's third black mayor, after James dropped out only a few weeks before the election. Booker's victory, in a majority black city, inspired the movement. A core group of militants ensconced in the Michael Bloomberg regime across the Hudson River in New York City were particularly excited and expecting major changes from this historic movement breakthrough. They now had in power the "black man to put out there as a voice for choice, charters, and vouchers"—as Chris Cerf, a key player in the Bloomberg circle, who resided in the affluent Newark suburb of Montclair, put it. They had big expectations and were eager to help.[74]

Conversely, Booker's victory was a major blow to the old regime, including its national backers, who continued their attacks on the new mayor's lack of authenticity. In the immediate aftermath of Booker's inauguration, young and older members of the regime, including Rice Sr., Councilman Donald Payne Jr., Ras Baraka, and Al Sharpton, gathered to honor James, who would soon face an indictment from the U.S. attorney—and future ally of Booker—Chris Christie. Sharpton, in his address to the gathering and in a clear swipe at Booker, remarked "that as far as leadership goes he'd 'rather have an old freedom fighter' than 'laboratory-created Negroes,' whose politics have been imposed on the African-American community." Sharpton added, in a further dig at the new mayor, "We have leadership that does not come out of the continuity of struggle that preceded it."[75]

Yet, soon even some of the "old freedom fighters" would defect to the opposition and eagerly sign up to impose the privatization agenda. Chief among these was the always adaptable Sharpton himself, who found that the rewards for joining the movement from above were just too good to turn down. In June 2008, less than two years after disparaging Booker for his political associations, he joined a press conference with movement luminaries, most prominently D.C. school superintendent Michelle Rhee and her New York City counterpart, Joel Klein, to launch their Education Equity Project. The movement's new organizational initiative was, unsurprisingly, to promote a RD problematic and agenda for education: define the "achievement gap" between white and black students as the "overriding civil rights issue of the 21st century" and force the presumptive presidential nominees—McCain and Obama—to address the issue. In a fine example of Preston Smith's argument that the BPMC's class interests often hide behind what are presented as racial ones, Sharpton made clear that the solution to racially inequitable student outcomes would be of the corporate reform variety. The "traditional civil rights coalition needs to seek 'a new paradigm,'" the newly reinvented Sharpton argued, to confront teacher unions and force them to become "more accountable to student performance."[76]

The alliance deepened after Obama, a fellow backer of school choice, took office. In early 2009, Sharpton met President Obama and Republican Newt Gingrich at the White House, where the president urged the two "to go on tour to promote school innovation," that is, privatization. Sharpton eagerly accepted the invitation as he accompanied the former Republican House speaker and presidential candidate on a highly publicized national tour. Gingrich, espousing movement ideology, declared that "education has to be the No. 1 civil rights issue of the 21st century" as he emphasized how "passionate" he was about "reforming," that is, privatizing, "education."[77] Sharpton was handsomely rewarded for his embrace of the movement, as the revenue stream to his National Action Network (NAN) 501(c)4 skyrocketed from just over $1 million in 2006 to nearly $4 million in 2008, the year he joined forces with Klein, to $5.8 million in 2016. His annual salary from NAN jumped from zero in 2006 to $181,000 in 2008 to a respectable $688,000 by 2016.[78]

ASSESSING MOVEMENT ADVANCES

"Social movements from above," explain theorists Alf Gunvald Nilsen and Laurence Cox, "create and pursue their projects for the construction, reproduction and extension of hegemony on the basis of superior access of dominant social groups to economic, political and cultural power resources." In this case, capitalist forces, mainly from finance, real estate, technology, and retail, along with a talented new layer of the BPMC, with class power often mobilized through philanthrocapitalist foundations and nonprofits, were intent on extending their power by capturing local state apparatuses seen as crucial to advancing movement goals of commodifying public education. The old post–civil rights black political class had served capital well in demobilizing the struggles of the 1960s and managing downtown regeneration strategies. But now, some of the very mechanisms these officials had deployed to manage the contradictions of racialized, uneven urban capitalist development, such as accommodations to teacher unions and public employees, had become an obstacle to the new round of neoliberal restructuring targeting public education.

Crucial to the offensive was the construction of new "rationalities expressed in ideological offensives" to gain consent, as Nilsen and Cox emphasize, at both the vertical and horizontal levels. This chapter focused on the latter level by demonstrating how central an antiracist ideology was to binding the BPMC with its fellow white professionals and the philanthrocapitalists in the struggle to open up public education to the market. Yet, in contrast to a pure market ideology proffered in SSA theory, the central legitimating ideology in the drive to commodify public education was a hybrid, neoliberalized, antiracist one—"the civil rights movement of our day"—achieved through market "choice." This ideology, of course, was not drawn up from whole cloth but drew inspiration from the self-determinationist rhetoric, and private educational experiments, of the Black Power movement.

Thus the rise of the "implementer in chief," Cory Booker, and the movement from above upon which he rose, was far from "postracial," as political scientists Jonathan Wharton and Andra Gillespie portray him in their respective works. The form of the antiracist ideology the movement deployed, and the cultivation and advance of a new layer of the BPMC into the movement ranks, underscores the importance of race to this class offensive. The emphasis on incorporating the BPMC provides further support for the arguments made by Adolph Reed Jr. and Cedric Johnson regarding the hegemonic role this layer has historically played in defining "black interests" and the crucial role they play, as Johnson puts it, in "legitimating the processes of neoliberalization."[79]

The black political leadership of the 1930s and subsequent Keynesian era, and to a lesser extent the immediate post–civil rights years, had defined black interests as necessitating an expansion—or at least defense—of the public sector. In contrast, the new black elite defines public education and other sections of the public sector, such as public housing, as an obstacle to black advancement, that is, *their* class advancement. The material interests and political careers of a whole new layer, from Cory Booker to Shavar Jeffries and Ron Rice Jr., as well as lesser-known names—along with their white professional counterparts—are tied to advancing the commodification of public education. On the ground, Booker and his cohorts, and accompanied by defectors from an earlier generation, like Fuller and, later, Sharpton, cultivated popular consent to the movement from above's agenda. Cedric Johnson elaborates on the crucial role the "black political and business elites," such as Booker, play in the advance of urban neoliberalism:

> Their leadership can soften potential opposition among black neighborhoods and activist constituencies, and harness popular concerns about black advancement to pro-growth initiatives that may have little shared economic benefit for black residents. Hence, black political elites perform a powerful managerial function within the neoliberal city, one of assimilating pressures for systemic redress emanating from various black popular constituencies, while giving concrete form to liberal anti-racism through nominal racial integration, minority contracting and other symbolic benefits that do not disrupt the capitalist growth trajectory supported by the city's commercial and investor classes.[80]

Now, Booker had the opportunity to "perform a powerful managerial function" in the service of the movement as the local head of state. What would he do with it?

3

Booker in Power

RECONSTRUCTING THE STATE AND THE LIMITS OF NEOLIBERAL ANTIRACISM, 2006–2012

> We've been talking for quite some time about creating a bold new paradigm for educational excellence in the country, to show the way, to put the people of Newark in the driver's seat and the focal point, and to work to get all the assets and resources we need to give to them to succeed.
>
> —Cory Booker, speaking at the announcement of the $100 million award by Mark Zuckerberg on *The Oprah Winfrey Show,* August 24, 2010

> They're trying to make Newark a bedroom community for Newark middle management. . . . They're trying to run you out of this community.
>
> —Amiri Baraka, speaking at the packed February 2011 Newark Public Schools Advisory Board meeting

The election of Cory Booker as mayor of Newark electrified the school privatization movement. They now had, apparently, addressed their racial legitimacy deficit by placing a black privatization advocate as the chief executive of not just any majority black city but one that was a symbol of urban black America. This excitement was particularly evident among a layer of corporate school reform militants grouped across the Hudson River in the administration of billionaire New York City mayor Michael Bloomberg and his pro-privatization school chancellor, Joel Klein. One leading figure was Cami Anderson, a former head of New York City's TFA, an administrator under Klein, and "director of policy and strategy" in Booker's first mayoral run. Another key operator was Chris Cerf, who, like Klein, was a lawyer, not an educator. Before joining Bloomberg's school chief, Cerf had served with

|| 87

Klein in the Clinton administration's White House counsel office and later went on to head the for-profit Edison Schools operation.

Cerf first met Booker at a fundraiser in Montclair, New Jersey—a swanky Newark suburb where he and several other movement activists resided—where he swooned at Booker's "blistering critique of Newark schools and enthusiasm for charters." Both Cerf, who became an unofficial education advisor after their 2002 meeting, and Anderson, another confidante, expected the new mayor to use his power to take bold moves.[1] In particular, Cerf urged Booker to follow the "best practices" of other reformers, such as Bloomberg and mayors in several other cities, and push to obtain mayoral control of the public schools.[2]

But, at least for the first few years of his reign, Booker disappointed white allies, such as Cerf, who bemoaned that the new mayor refused to touch "this billion-dollar district."[3] The state, which had taken over the district in 1995, was then led by Democratic governor, and former Goldman Sachs executive, Jon Corzine. Although Corzine had angered teacher union officials by continuing to underfund the teacher pension fund and permitted the continued expansion of charters, he was not about to allow the state's largest school district to be turned over to a leading movement reformer. Booker, for his part, was not prepared to lead what he perceived as a losing battle. Thus, just as Colin Barker has argued about movements from below, the movement for privatizing education, in the key battleground of Newark, comprised "fields of argument ... [on] how should it pursue its objectives ... what strategies, tactics, repertories ... should it deploy? ... How should [it] respond to specific events?" As Barker emphasizes, and the Newark case highlights, "all these and other matters are open to ongoing contestation among a movement's varied adherents."[4]

Thus, in this chapter, I analyze how, within the changing constraints he faced, Booker chartered a course to advance the movement's privatization goals. In the first section, I address how and why, in the first few years of his administration, Booker pursued an elite form of disruption by working around rather than through the public school system. With the district still dominated by old BUR elements, Booker and his team forged deeper relations with philanthropic foundations and nonprofits, including by reconfiguring the local state, to disrupt the public schools and advance the movement. I then turn to the significant shift in movement strategy produced by the 2009 gubernatorial victory of

BOOKER IN POWER || 89

Republican Chris Christie, an ardent backer of charter schools and an advocate of fast-tracking reforms. I address how Booker and his movement allies exploited the favorable turn in the political opportunity structure to launch a direct assault on the public school system and the gains they made. I conclude with the movement's growing legitimacy deficit and the emergence of a movement from below.

ASSEMBLING THE TEAM, BUILDING THE INFRASTRUCTURE

Booker drew heavily for advice and personnel from the administration of Michael Bloomberg, who had long been a friend and backer of the rising Newark star. For example, he named Garry McCarthy, a high-level New York Police Department official schooled under the zero-tolerance, broken windows policing of Raymond Kelley and William Bratton, as his new police chief. For his other top priority of education, he tapped from the circle around Cerf. This grouping included Amy Rosen, another Montclair resident, a national reform leader in her own right, and business partner of Cerf in their Public Private Strategy Group, through which they contracted with the Klein-led New York City school regime.[5] Rosen encouraged her colleague De'Shawn Wright, an African American professional, to offer his services to Booker. Wright, after a two-year TFA stint in New York City in the late 1990s, experienced a meteoric career ascent that has risen in tandem with the fortunes of the school reform movement. Following his TFA movement apprenticeship, where he met Cami Anderson, who was heading up TFA's New York City operation at the time, he went to work as a policy analyst for Mayor Bloomberg's Office of Operations and then, in 2003, moved over to Joel Klein's Office of the Chancellor. There he worked with Rosen and Cerf to manage "key aspects of the Department's comprehensive reform initiative," including the breakup of large, comprehensive high schools into smaller "academies" and the expansion of charters.[6]

His transition to Newark began, Wright explains, after Rosen, his "friend," told him that Booker "admired a lot of what was happening in New York City and I was working there overseeing a lot of the work for Joel Klein." Based on an introduction by Rosen, another member of Booker's kitchen cabinet, Wright "came over [to Newark] just . . . to

90 || BOOKER IN POWER

give him some advice on the [inauguration] speech. But," he added, "I ended up getting offered a job and . . . joined him August 1st [2006] as his education advisor, then became his chief policy advisor."[7]

The veterans of the Joel Klein regime had big expectations now that their dream candidate was taking power. But, as explained earlier, taking direct control over the district was not possible while Democratic governor Jon Corzine was in office. According to journalist Dale Russakoff, a disappointed Cerf then "let the relationship atrophy," but by no means did Booker and his top school reform advisor give up on their privatization plans. Rather, the question for Booker and Wright was *how* they would proceed. That is, how, considering the existing political arrangements in the city and state, could they best advance the movement goals of dismantling the old Keynesian public school system and implementing their neoliberal privatized model? While jammed at the state level, the local leadership of Newark Public Schools (NPS) also presented obstacles. As Wright, Booker's chief educational advisor, explains, "the philosophical and ideological perspectives" of Booker and the superintendent of NPS at the time, Marion Bolden, "were not aligned . . . [with] what it would take to really improve educational outcomes in the city."[8]

Although Booker and Wright did "end up doing a number of small but important things" with Bolden, it was not the transformative changes they, and their political and ideological allies like Cerf and Rosen, wanted. The thinking of Booker and Wright, these leading African American strategists for implementing neoliberal reform, was that

> to change outcomes for kids and families you really have two options: you can continue to sort of dance around the edges for the rest of your first term or you can go to a space where you can actually have influence and that was the charter sector. Newark then had a small but vibrant charter sector . . . but because the state generally had been very stingy with their granting of charter approvals particularly under Democrats it was a pretty small pool.[9]

At the beginning of Booker's first term in 2006, and nine years after the state had approved the first charter schools, just under 7 percent, or approximately thirty-one hundred of the forty-five thousand students attending tax dollar–supported schools in Newark, were enrolled in charters. The "big three" at the time in the city were KIPP and North

Star/Uncommon, two large national chains, and the homegrown Robert Treat Academy, run by Stephen Adubato Sr.[10] Wright and Booker wanted to continue the rollback of the traditional public schools, but that route was closed off because they did not have a "partner." Therefore they decided to maneuver around the NPS behemoth and work to increase the number of, what Wright termed, high-performing "quality [i.e., charter] seats."[11]

To help expand the charter market and break the political logjam at the state, they turned to the large national foundations. Serendipitously, the Walton, Fisher, Jobs, Gates, and Robertson Foundations—all major players among the philanthrocapitalists promoting school privatization—were then just deciding to collaborate for a "collective impact" on several cities.[12] Their thinking was, according to Wright, "you know we're all out here sprinkling a little money here a little money there, if we come together and support a handful of cities we can probably do something much more significant and much more vibrant."

Wright's analysis of philanthropy's new collaborative approach is corroborated by education researchers Jeffrey Snyder and Sarah Reckhow in their study of foundation funding of K–12 education between 2000 and 2010. Furthermore, they found that after 2005, "districts most aligned with major education policy reforms"—charter school expansion and use of "alternative pathways to teacher certification," particularly TFA—"increasingly attracted philanthropic funding."[13] Philanthropy, the primary "drivers" of the privatization movement, were clearly emboldened not only by Booker's 2006 election but by the state takeover, just six months earlier, of New Orleans public schools by Louisiana's Democratic governor Kathleen Blanco in the wake of Hurricane Katrina. Blanco then oversaw a mass closure of the public schools and conversion of almost the entire district to charters.

The big five philanthrocapitalists chose Stig Leschly, described by the head of a local foundation as "a charming and exceedingly bright rising star in the charter arena," as their point man for their national expansion initiative. Formerly a lecturer at Harvard, where his "teaching and research focused on entrepreneurship and education reform," the consortium commissioned Leschly "to envision what a coordinated investment would look like."[14] He conducted a review of the one hundred largest cities and identified three, predominantly black, school districts—New Orleans, Washington, D.C., and Newark, all of whose local school boards had been, or were about to be, stripped of their powers—as offering the greatest opportunity for a return on their investment in terms of charter expansion. The five foundations put in a combined $20 million, with local foundations—Prudential, MCJ Amelior (Raymond Chambers), and Victoria—pledging an additional $1 million each, to form the Newark Charter School Fund (NCSF), incorporated as a 501(c)3 in 2008.[15] Consistent with the corporate logic and language of venture philanthropy, the funders had "measurable outcomes" they expected from their investment: an increase from 9.6 percent of district students in charters in 2008 (thirteen charter schools, forty-three hundred students) to 40 percent of all students by 2016–17.[16]

The NCSF was initially led by Leschly and then by Wright himself, until his first choice for director, Mashea Ashton, could take the reins in 2010.[17] Wright and Booker's other New York City education advisors both knew Ashton, a veteran of both the public and private arms of the movement, quite well. Her impressive résumé included serving as director of the charter school department in Joel Klein's New York City Department of Education, heading recruitment for KIPP, and finally, in 2007, joining Cami Anderson at New Leaders for New Schools. The latter operation, established to train a new neoliberal leadership cadre to administer charter and public schools, was cofounded by Jon Schnur, who would go on to craft the Obama administration's Race to the Top initiative to further federal support for the neoliberal rollback of public schools and rollout of charters.[18] Ashton later brought on a fellow member of the BPMC, Kimberly McLain, as NCSF's vice president of finance and operation. Helping make McLain a "good fit" is that she had previously been the managing director of planning for TFA, another Anderson employer.[19]

The forging of the diverse "Booker team" in Newark highlights the strengths of this elite movement. Through generous funding from philanthropy and personnel from Bloomberg's billionaire-philanthropist New York City regime, movement drivers forged a talented, well-compensated layer of implementers. This highly motivated, multiracial cadre eagerly volunteered for the Newark theater of the war against public education. In addition to the shared material interests, a common antiracist ideology was crucial for their class bonding and the élan they brought to their work. "There is a powerful need to believe," as Kotz argued with regard to the role of ideology for SSA implementers, "that one's actions are just and not merely self-seeking.

Coherent sets of ideas have a reality of their own. *They motivate and justify a program of action.*"[20]

PHILANTHROPY AND RESTRUCTURING THE LOCAL STATE

Not only was the national foundation–nonprofit complex enthused over Booker's election, but their less endowed cousins at the local and regional levels were as well. Before Booker, local foundations carried out their work without any real coordination with City Hall. One of the new mayor's central goals, consistent with best neoliberal practices, was to "break down unproductive silos" between the local foundations and City Hall. In place of the old BUR's practice of working in isolation from the local nonprofit complex, Booker wanted to "create authentic public/private partnerships to address complex challenges," noted approvingly Victoria Foundation director Irene Cooper-Basch, who served on Booker's transition team representing the "local philanthropic sector." One of the fruits of this new collaboration was the creation of the "Newark Philanthropic Liaison," a position "embedded in City Hall and included in most high-level meetings, but paid for by a cohort of private funders through the Council of New Jersey Grantmakers."[21] The liaison, as Nina Stack, the director of the Council of New Jersey Grantmakers, explains, would strengthen the public–private philanthropy partnership by operating at

> the cabinet level, sitting in on cabinet meetings, to understand what's going on, what the city is trying to achieve, the opportunities that might be coming up, and many of those require private investment, local investments . . . so being able to leverage what's happening from both angles, there might be private funders who are looking, and we've got some of them.[22]

The idea for the liaison office came from the council's sister organization, the Michigan Council of Foundations, which had created a cabinet-level position in the administration of Democratic governor Granholm. Stack explained that even before the transition report, she and a group of funders had "pitched the idea" to Booker and "some of the key people on his team . . . who completely embraced it, got it, understood it, completely embraced what the philanthropic liaison could be."[23] Jeremy Johnson, a black professional from the nonprofit art world,

94 || BOOKER IN POWER

was tapped as philanthropy's representative in the Booker administration.[24] To paraphrase former mayor Kenneth Gibson, Newark's initiation of the liaison office, while not the first, was clearly where American cities were headed. Indeed, Newark has stood out as part of this cutting-edge advance in neoliberal governance. In 2012, the U.S. Conference of Mayors recognized the Newark office as a role model for collaboration between government and its "foundation partners."[25]

Booker's embrace of a greater role in governance for philanthropy provided an impetus for a turn toward a "collective impact" approach to funding among New Jersey's foundations.[26] As part of this effort, Nina Stack helped organize various foundation "affinity groups" based on geography (Newark, Patterson, Trenton, etc.) and policy area (educations, arts, environment, etc.). The Newark affinity group, in addition to funding the liaison position, created an education subcommittee headed by Dale Englin, an officer at Victoria and formerly with the Ford Foundation, and Nicole Butler, of the Nicholson Foundation (and later a NCSF staffer). This became, as one foundation officer explained, the "most active subcommittee absolutely" of the Newark funders group, playing a central role in supporting the school reform efforts of the Booker administration.[27]

A further organizational expression of the collective impact philosophy was the formation in 2007 of another nonprofit in the neoliberal school reform efforts, the Newark Trust for Education (NTE). Shané Harris, vice president of the powerful Prudential Foundation, headquartered in Newark, was the prime mover behind the establishment of the NTE.[28] To help provide the NTE with an air of nonpolitical civic-mindedness, the new entity in the privatization-promoting nonprofit complex was chaired by the African American Rutgers University historian and Newark booster Clement Price. The state-appointed superintendent, Marion Bolden, was named an "ex officio" board member. In addition, representatives of a few nonprofits, including the executive director of the Ironbound Community Corporation (ICC), which was funded by local corporate titans like Prudential, also joined the new NTE board.[29]

Despite the ecumenicism, NTE's aim was to promote the neoliberal school reform agenda. This became clearer after the appointment of Ross Danis, a former teacher, program director of education at the Geraldine R. Dodge Foundation, and proponent of the "no-excuses" charter movement ideology. His diagnosis for poor school performance was not lack of funding or poverty but rather the incompetent teachers protected by archaic Keynesian labor laws and practices, such as seniority, collective bargaining contracts, and tenure. In 2011, the NTE, with Danis at the helm, formed the "Newark public schools funders collaborative for high quality school options" to fund the neoliberal reforms being rolled out by the new superintendent, Cami Anderson.[30]

Booker's incorporation of philanthropy into the local state, along with his administration's promotion of an array of nonprofits that refashioned education policy, has been a core feature of neoliberal state structuring. The transition "from formal government to informal 'governance' arrangements," as geographer Mark Purcell argues, "increases the flexibility of policy making" for elites pursuing core elements of the neoliberal agenda, such as privatizing public education. Through the lens of critical social movement theory, we can see this state restructuring as the movement from above using its superior control of the state to strengthen coordination among elite movement actors, in this case, between and among neoliberal state officials and philanthropy. Simultaneously, this restructuring weakened challenges from below by moving governance "out of the routinize[d] channels of the formal state," where opportunities for popular pressure are greater.[31]

KEYNESIAN VERSUS NEOLIBERAL: INTERGENERATIONAL CONFLICT AMONG THE BPMC

While the Democratic governor did not award Booker mayoral control of the schools, he did eventually intervene to ease out the state-appointed superintendent, Marion Bolden. Booker, and his ally Adubato, had backed Bolden in 2002–3 when the James administration tried to use its leverage with Governor James McGreevey to have her removed.[32] This conflict was over patronage, that is, managing, not challenging, the Keynesian structure of the school system. Yet now Booker and Wright considered Bolden, who began in 1969 as a teacher and worked her way up through the system, an obstacle to realizing the neoliberal reforms they were attempting to roll out. Bolden, who was part of the BPMC, which emerged through the opening of the public sector in the wake of the civil rights movement, clearly did not embrace the neoliberal reforms. For example, in 2004, movement activist and school board member Dana Rone worked with Howard Fuller to organize a forum on vouchers that was officially sponsored by NPS. Yet, as *Star-Ledger* reporter John Mooney emphasized, the board and "Superintendent Bolden were . . . reluctant hosts, at best." Bolden, in fact, made her opposition clear, explaining, "I don't have a whole lot of time to spend on this issue."[33]

Further marking Bolden as a problem from the perspective of movement implementers was the strong bonds she had cultivated with rank-and-file teachers and with parents and her accommodating relationship with the local AFT union bureaucracy. "I always loved," elementary school teacher Freda Barrow reminisced, "how Ms. Bolden . . . would always have convocation [a faculty gathering at beginning of the school year] with every teacher in the district down at Symphony Hall, that was wonderful, that was wonderful." Barrow contrasted this warm, caring relationship with her successor, Clifford Janey, a neoliberal reformer brought in by Booker:

> But from the time Janey got in, [he held] only one convocation and he was rude. . . . So we find from our administrator, Dr. Jackson at the time, that Janey met with the principals and he said he was not having convocation. . . . We were like "what do you mean our illustrious leader is not going to meet with us!" . . . It was like a big reunion. . . . It's like not having a tailgate party before a game.[34]

Exemplifying Bolden's and Booker's differing relations with the union leadership was the anti-union ad campaign launched by the newly formed, D.C.-based Center for Union Facts in March 2007, the year after Booker took power. The media blast, delivered through huge billboards and bus signs, lambasted the NTU for "protecting bad teachers, discouraging good educators from coming to the city's school system and failing children." Booker refused to comment on the signs, while a spokesperson claimed that there was no coordination with the group. Yet, the ads echoed his own criticisms and those of the larger "school choice" movement. In contrast, Bolden defended the union, arguing that while at times during her eight-year tenure she had taken "an opposing position with the union," she nonetheless always found that "when a teacher is overwhelmingly incompetent they [union] don't support them."[35]

These ties and practices were not what Booker and his allies needed to carry out the hard, disruptive implantation of neoliberal school reform. First-generation BUR officials, such as Bolden, accepted—and had often benefited from—core features of the Keynesian SSA, including federally supported public schools, unions, collective bargaining, seniority, and tenure. But, from the perspective of the young turks, these were simply fetters on the advance of neoliberalism. Corzine, the Goldman Sachs alum, ended the impasse by not renewing Bolden's three-year contract and, thus, effectively siding with the ascendant BPMC. While Booker still did not have control of the district, Corzine—as Bolden pointed out in November 2006, after she announced her retirement at the end of the 2007–8 school year—would not "make this kind of a move without the mayor having some voice in this." Dana Rone, of the BPMC's neoliberal wing, confirmed that Bolden was part of the enemy camp by applauding her decision to step down as she spouted standard movement talking points: "I think it's time to move on. . . . The primary duty of the Newark public schools is not being met, and that is teaching and learning."[36]

A governor-appointed committee selected Clifford Janey, the former superintendent of Washington, D.C., schools, as Bolden's successor. Although he had been pushed out in D.C. in favor of the aggressive, nationally known charter backer Michelle Rhee, Janey was a reformer as well, enacting "more rigorous assessments" and pushing out "300 teachers who weren't deemed highly qualified under the federal No Child Left Behind law" during his three-year tenure in the nation's capital.[37] He continued this track record in Newark during his abbreviated two-and-a-half-year stint, as he successfully loosened labor contracts to allow for longer class days and greater power for principals to hire and fire teachers.[38] Some of these reforms were implemented, with NTU approval, as part of the Ford Foundation–funded Global Village Zone (GVZ) program. The GVZ was headed by New York University professor Pedro Noguera, who oversaw the expansion of charter schools in New York State and was based at Central High School, where future mayor Ras Baraka was then the principal.[39] But then a personnel change in the governor's mansion created a new opportunity for Booker and his team to implement, as Chris Cerf put it, "not incremental change," as Janey was carrying out, but rather the "big, bold ambitions" they had dreamed about.[40]

THE CHRISTIE–BOOKER BIPARTISAN ALLIANCE: UNITING THE MOVEMENT, PREPARING FOR WAR

Republican Chris Christie, a former U.S. attorney, defeated Jon Corzine, the Democratic incumbent governor, in late 2009. Once he had taken office, Christie slashed, in his first annual budget, state funding for local school districts by $820 million while providing tax breaks for the state's millionaires and billionaires.[41] This was by no means an outlier, as Republican and Democratic governors across the nation gutted education funding in the wake of the 2008 financial crisis. Between 2008 and 2015, budget cuts led to nearly three hundred thousand fewer K–12 teachers and other support workers, while the student population grew by more than eight hundred thousand during the same time period. In New Jersey, between 2008 and 2014, the state's K–12 spending for education dropped 7.5 percent.[42]

While attacking public schools and teachers, Christie made it clear that the answer was charter schools. Early in his administration, he made an appearance at the annual conference of the New Jersey Charter Schools Association to assure attendees that charter schools' budgets would not be cut and that he would expand the number of charter schools in the state. At the same time, pitting public- against private-sector workers, he bellowed that teachers unions were irresponsible for demanding pay increases while private-sector workers were facing pay cuts and layoffs.[43] Christie's blustery slamming of public school teachers and other public-sector workers, along with plugging state budget deficits by refusing to make contributions to the state retirement fund—following in the footsteps of his Democratic predecessors, and breaking his own promises made during the campaign—catapulted him into the national spotlight as a potential Republican presidential challenger and darling of the Right.

Despite, indeed because of, these assaults on public education and unions, he found an ally in Newark's Democratic mayor, Cory Booker. Booker saw in the Republican governor's election a grand opportunity, "a once in a lifetime chance to get the [school] system on track."[44] Booker met with Christie in December 2009, just after his electoral victory over Corzine, and proposed a partnership to radically and rapidly roll out a neoliberal makeover of Newark's public schools. "In the backseat of the Tahoe"—as journalist Dale Russakoff recounts the encounter between the two during a tour of the city's poor and black South Ward to ostensibly tout the mayor's crime-fighting initiatives—

> Booker turned to Christie and proposed that they work together to transform education in Newark. With Christie's legal authority and Booker's mayoral bully pulpit, they would close failing schools, greatly expand charter schools, weaken tenure protections, reward and punish teachers based on their student test scores.

Christie, whose position was "we have to grab this system by the roots and yank it out and start over," embraced Booker's offer.[45]

By summer 2010, Booker had developed the privatization blueprints—"The Newark Public Schools—A Reform Plan"—which Christie enthusiastically supported. Booker, whose main aim was to outcompete even New Orleans and "make Newark the charter school capital of the nation," realized that there would be considerable opposition from teachers, students, and parents to the plan. Thus, to overcome this opposition, Booker and his allies emphasized the need for a top-down, neoliberal authoritarian imposition of the makeover. Critical to the success would be the philanthropic sector's provision of the organizational infrastructure and money to push through the bipartisan reform initiative. Unlike government funding, philanthropy could be deployed with little or no opportunity for oversight by potential opponents.

The first major coup in this transformation effort, which received wide coverage in the national media, was the $100 million awarded by Facebook founder Mark Zuckerberg. Booker, the well-connected Stanford graduate, used his social networks in the finance and Silicon Valley worlds to make contact with Zuckerberg and pitch his plans. Like the NCSF's foundation backers, Zuckerberg was looking for a city where his investment could generate "high impact" in a short five-year span and become a model of corporate-style school reform. A top priority of Zuckerberg, typifying the philanthrocapitalism agenda, was transforming the Keynesian employment agreements that based compensation on seniority and educational levels rather than on student performance on test scores. This venture philanthropist was appalled at the current compensation system, in which, from his perspective, "teachers who transformed students' lives received the same pay as the deadwood."[46]

In September 2010, on *The Oprah Winfrey Show,* Booker, Christie, and Zuckerberg announced the $100 million grant, which coincided with the release of the pro-charter "documentary" *Waiting for Superman,* which had received financial backing from the Gates Foundation and various hedge fund investors.[47] Zuckerberg's largesse was to be distributed through his newly formed foundation—Start Up: Education. But, at Booker's urging, he assented to the establishment of a less venture philanthropy and more locally rooted sounding vehicle—the Foundation for Newark's Future (FNF)—to disburse the funds. The $100 million was a matching grant to be raised over the next five years, but to get a seat on the FNF board, donors had to kick in at least $10 million. In the end, only two others, billionaire hedge fund manager William Ackman and the Goldman Sachs Foundation, met that threshold. Local philanthropists, led by private equity pioneer Ray Chambers, were told by a Booker aide overseeing fundraising that their $1 million was "insignificant."[48]

Intraphilanthropic Conflict and Conciliation

The entrance of the behemoths of philanthrocapitalism into Newark created tensions with their junior partners. "At first I thought," the NTE's Ross Danis explained, "I got $100 million. I took it to my board look, like we got $100 million. . . . And then it was like who's that guy, what's he doing up there with Cory, what happened?" He added, "I felt competitive with the Foundation for Newark's Future frankly, because you know I didn't have that kind of money . . . my burn rate was $65,000 a month . . . you know I had a nice capacity grant from Prudential, a three-year grant that launched us, but I didn't have $100 million."[49]

Irene Cooper-Basch, the director of the Victoria Foundation, also acknowledged that, at least at first, "the relationship between FNF and the other local funders . . . [was] at times uneasy."

> Although FNF joined the local Newark Funders Group, it behaved like a large national funder. About two months after he arrived, [Greg] Taylor [the first director of FNF] arranged to fly twelve of his colleagues from large foundations supporting urban education reform into Newark for a two-day retreat to brainstorm about how

FNF should invest its funding. I had learned of the meeting from a peer in another state who assumed Victoria would be participating. I reached out to Taylor and asked for an invitation. I told him that after fifty years of supporting education initiatives in Newark, Victoria might have some insights to offer the group. He told me that I was putting him in a very difficult position, since he had not invited any local funders to the retreat and the answer was "no."[50]

Although Victoria has funded education initiatives in Newark for decades, the FNF annual funding of $40 million for five years "amounted to ten times that of Victoria."[51]

Despite these initial missteps and emotional letdowns, local and national philanthropy were able to mend fences and collaborate to push for reforms upon which they largely agreed. Danis, after the initial shock of learning his outfit would not be the local interlocutor for Zuckerberg's largesse, recognized, "I had to figure out 'how do I survive in the after burn of this supernova.' I decided that I would just gather . . . data, they had a hundred million dollars but I have all the data . . . I owned all the data." Ross explains how his organization's control of local school data—"I could tell you how many dance programs are going on, and what's not happening over here, who's doing this and who's doing that"—forced funders, including the FNF, to route much of their funding through NTE and, later, through the funders' collaborative that Danis and local foundations established. As one local foundation official explained, we "got quite a bit of money from" the FNF.

In another concession to its local brethren, the FNF modified its board rules by adding a community member. The choice was Victoria trustee Robert Johnson, the first African American dean of the New Jersey Medical School. In addition, FNF named thirteen local stakeholders to a Community Advisory Board to give the Newark community more of a voice, though board members were not given any "meaningful input into funding allocation decisions." In a further effort at indigeneity, the three voting members of the FNF agreed to appoint the NCSF's Kimberly McLain as the second director.[52]

MANUFACTURING (VERY LITTLE) CONSENT

Although the big philanthrocapitalists and their partners in city government were able to mend fences with local philanthropy, they

102 || BOOKER IN POWER

were less successful with the working-class students and parents upon whom these reforms would be imposed. The reformers did recognize that they were in a battle for ideas, what the Marxist theoretician and organizer Antonio Gramsci termed *hegemony*. As Chris Cerf—whom Christie named as education commissioner in December 2010—emphasized, the reformers needed "a communications strategy to soften the battlefield for the conflict to come, to create a counternarrative to the status quo."[53] Yet, it was difficult to garner consent to an agenda of mass closing of "failing" schools, massively expanding charters, "colocations," and weakening tenure that would cause so much havoc in the lives of teachers, parents, students, and the larger community. That is, the "shock therapy" plan of a combined "rollback and rollout" of neoliberal school reform measures, one that was informed by Facebook and philanthrocapitalism's "disruption" philosophy "that you should always take an ax to your surroundings," was inimical to popular consent.[54]

In his attempt to get buy-in, Booker again turned to the circle around Michael Bloomberg. Bradley Tusk, who had just led Bloomberg's 2009 reelection campaign as well as a successful effort to lift New York State's cap on charters, was brought in to lead a "community engagement campaign." In fall 2010, his Tusk Associates, along with a number of well-connected consultants, oversaw a major mass media campaign of TV, radio, and billboard ads. There was also a "grassroots" arm of the campaign that hired locals—at a much lower rate than Tusk and allied consultants were receiving—to perform door knocking for eleven community forums, a few of which Booker led. These forums were to create a veneer of democratic input on a thoroughly antidemocratic reform agenda imposed by "philanthropic foundations [that] are not elected by anyone, but yield tremendous power in defining social and educational policy."[55] The forums were such a flop that Booker and his aides nixed the second phase.

At the same time, while Booker was encouraging community participation in a "bottom-up" reform effort, he was simultaneously signing a lucrative, foundation-funded contract with his longtime backer Chris Cerf, to develop the real blueprints. Yes, residents could vent their frustrations at the town halls and participate in "breakout sessions," where their "input" would be written on butch paper—and then filed away. Nonetheless, the real decision makers would be Booker and philanthropy's go-to man, Chris Cerf, and his newly founded firm,

Global Education Advisors. Cerf's firm received a million-dollar-plus contract—funds raised by Booker from philanthropic sources, which, in classic neoliberal form, avoided any public accounting or democratic input—to provide the predictable plan drawn from the reformers' playbook.[56] In January 2011, after Cerf had ostensibly left the private sector and become state education commissioner, he and Booker held a meeting with their philanthropic allies on the reform plan. Cerf, who was basically calling the shots in Newark schools, although Janey was still officially superintendent, outlined the "transformation" they wanted implemented, all of which was well received by their philanthropic audience:

- Reduce size of the central school district office
- Create "portfolio" schools including traditional public, charter, and schools with varying themes
- Close "failing" public schools; "colocate" charters in existing public schools
- Business principals inform strategies—treat principals as CEOs by giving them autonomy over school budget, staffing, and instruction and hold them accountable for results defined by test scores
- Renegotiate the union contract to weaken tenure protections and facilitate the firing of what the CEO-principals consider ineffective teachers, rewarding the "best ones"[57]

Cerf assured his audience that he had commitment from the two largest national charter chains in the city to double their enrollment. Space would be acquired for the charters through "colocation" with existing public schools and by using buildings of closed public schools.[58]

The proposal—marked "Strictly Confidential Draft Work Product"—was leaked a few days before the February 22, 2011, school board meeting. Hundreds of angry parents and community activists packed the meeting and denounced the plans, as it confirmed the suspicions of many that the "reform" was a conspiracy by outsiders to destroy the public school system.[59] Echoing and giving further legitimacy to those sentiments were the remarks, cited in the chapter epigraph, of the still fiery, seventy-five-year-old Amiri Baraka. The elder Baraka's remarks, which echoed those of his son, who had become Booker's chief critic on the city council, underscored the faltering of the movement from

104 || BOOKER IN POWER

above's "civil rights movement of our day" ideology. Far from a benevolent initiative, the strengthening counternarrative portrayed the charter movement as a racist, profit-driven conspiracy to privatize the schools and gentrify the city.

More fuel was thrown on the fire the following day when the *Star-Ledger* published a front-page story exposing that Chris Cerf was the founder of Global Education Advisors, the firm that had developed the report, and records listed his Montclair home as the company's address.[60] In an effort to calm the waters, Booker called on Price, the Rutgers University historian and an unofficial city ambassador, to assemble a number of civic leaders for an invitation-only meeting. The gathering, which Booker opened, allowed Cerf to explain his side of the controversy and lay out his plans for the district. Most of the business and civic leaders assembled were sympathetic to his reforms but pleaded with Cerf to do a better job of getting buy-in. Cerf explained, accurately, that a disruptive, neoliberal makeover "is inevitably hard and deeply unpopular . . . and change has casualties."[61] The language of "casualties" when discussing children was harshly criticized by Price and Richard Cammarieri, who worked for a local CDC "fixer" that ran its own charter school. But could a change of language mask the harsh realities of top-down neoliberal reform?[62]

In his state of the city address in early March 2011, Booker made another pitch for his reform agenda. But his emphasis on "engagement and inclusion" in the reform process was contradicted by holding the address in a small hall at NJPAC. The chosen venue was, as journalist Joan Whitlow conjectured, "to control who came and how they behaved," while Booker announced yet another task force that was to be filled by the same local bourgeois faces.[63] These feeble attempts to gain consent failed to calm the waters as denunciations of the school closings and colocation plans intensified. At the March 22 school board meeting, more than a thousand people turned out—with many turned away from the overflowing Barringer High School auditorium—to denounce the plans. At the same time, the charters, spearheaded by NCSF's Mashea Ashton, did their best to rally their own mass base of parents and students to defend "choice."[64]

In the face of growing opposition, and highlighting the significance of Newark for the larger movement, Booker called on and quickly received support from the Obama administration. Education secretary Arne Duncan, himself a movement veteran who oversaw mass school

BOOKER IN POWER || 105

closures as "CEO" of Chicago schools in the 2000s, whisked himself to Newark in late April to defend Booker's—and, by extension, Obama's—imperiled initiative. Using the same language as Cerf, Duncan insisted that Newark needed, not "incremental change," but rather the "fundamental and dramatic" variety. Overseen by a "strong mayor" with a "good partnership with the state" (i.e., Republican Christie) and "outside"—read philanthrocapitalist—"support," Newark, he argued, "has the potential to be a model" for the country.[65]

THE NEW SUPERINTENDENT

A key demand of Zuckerberg, consistent with philanthrocapitalism's close oversight of its "investments," was the naming of a powerful superintendent who would oversee a disruption strategy to overhaul the public school system. Following neoliberal SSA organizational best practices, the reformers looked outside the district rather than drawing from the ranks, as had been done with Bolden. But the lack of popular support for the school reform plans, and the legitimacy gap for Booker's regime, complicated those efforts. Christie, Cerf, and Booker initially courted John King, the then deputy New York State education commissioner who had been appointed by the pro-charter governor, Democrat Andrew Cuomo. A top selling point for King was, beyond being an ardent charter supporter, racial legitimacy—he was of black and Puerto Rican ancestry, while over 90 percent of Newark's public school students were black or Latinx. Underscoring Cedric Johnson's argument regarding the skills of black political elites in "soften[ing] potential opposition" to neoliberal reforms, Booker hoped King's racial identity could counterbalance the lack of popular support for the reform initiative and his white political allies, such as Cerf and Christie. King, drawn from the same neoliberal professional class as Booker, ultimately, possibly due to a recognition of the hostile reception he would face, declined the offer.[66]

With Booker's then twenty-six-year-old multibillionaire patron becoming increasingly impatient, the mayor worked with education commissioner Chris Cerf to find another candidate. The two chose, predictably, Clement Price to select a committee and lead the search. The committee, cobbled together in early 2011, was composed of twenty-five members, but one community activist member, the late Willie Rowe, criticized it as a "stacked deck" because of the dominance of local foundations and corporate officials favorable to the reform agenda. Search committee chair Price, from Rowe's perspective, "was a shill to direct people to certain conclusions," that is, select the candidate favored by Booker and Christie.[67]

By March 2011, the committee, Booker, and Cerf had settled on Jean-Claude Brizard, the Haitian American superintendent of the Rochester, New York, public schools. Brizard was especially appealing because he relished taking on and battling the teacher unions, the bête noire of the reform movement. Yet Christie ordered the announcement to be held off until May, after school board elections, because growing popular opposition was disrupting the political calculations of Booker's neoliberal coalition.[68] The year before, in 2010, Stephen Adubato Sr., an important backer of both Booker and Christie, had successfully run a pro-charter slate, headed by Shavar Jeffries, for the advisory school board election. In spring 2011, in the face of the brewing opposition to the reform effort, councilman Ras Baraka, who had been elected in 2010, cobbled together a slate to challenge Adubato's candidates. The naming of a new, pro-charter superintendent just before the election would have been a boon for Baraka, so Adubato vetoed it.[69] At the same time, Brizard was vying to head the mayoral-controlled Chicago public school system. Former Obama chief of staff and newly elected Chicago mayor Rahm Emmanuel, who ran on a campaign attacking the teacher's union, tapped Brizard as "CEO" of Chicago Public Schools just as he assumed office.

In the end, Booker and Christie decided on Cami Anderson, drawn from the same Bloomberg–Klein school reform regime that had provided much of the personnel overseeing Newark's reform process.[70] Anderson, as discussed earlier, came with stellar reform credentials and was at the time of her appointment head of alternative high schools in the New York City system. Being the first white superintendent in Newark since 1973 meant she did not have the racial legitimacy of a John King, though she did have an African American husband and a long political relationship with Booker and Cerf. An added strength of Anderson was the authentic, antiracist zeal she brought to her work to end racial disparities through school privatization.[71]

The Anderson selection was heralded by Christie and Booker, and other officials, at a May 4 ceremony held at Science Park High School—the same school, ironically, that would become the epicenter of student opposition to the new superintendent. Anderson, most likely recognizing the opposition she would face, moved quickly to advance the movement's neoliberal SSA agenda. She proceeded along the key institutional axes of the role of government, labor relations, and organization to roll back Keynesianism and roll out neoliberalism

At the central office, Anderson brought in, consistent with neoliberal practices, an army of well-paid private consultants to assist her in the district makeover rather than drawing from within the district employment pool. With philanthrocapitalist dollars, through the FNF and other vehicles, picking up the tab, she was able, as "neoliberals prefer, to insulate [her plans from] democratic pressures."[72] A foundation officer explains how the philanthropists worked with then Commissioner Cerf to provide some of those "insulation" funds for Anderson:

> When Chris Cerf was commissioner, the funders had a meeting with him . . . and they asked what the foundation community could do to support him. And he said you could help me—he didn't use these exact words—but basically an off the books entity "so I can hire people that I need to hire in the department [to assist in Newark] without the salary restrictions that we have in the public sector." And he did that and got major funding for that.[73]

Assisted by this funding, Anderson and her consultants proceeded to move on their central goals of forging a team of CEO-principals and overhauling the teacher evaluation and compensation system along neoliberal lines.[74] Consistent with corporate school reform orthodoxy, utmost importance was placed on the principals, who reformers argued had to be converted into CEOs with the maximum amount of autonomy, particularly over personnel. By summer 2011, Anderson had hired seventeen new principals, "recruiting from all over the country," and within three years had pushed out more than half of the district's seventy principals. These new CEO-principals, in a significant rollback of Keynesian labor agreements, had the power to override seniority rights and decide who would fill teaching vacancies for their schools. This meant that the tenured teachers displaced by school closings did not have an automatic right to bump less senior ones. The upending of this long-held right resulted in a growing number of "excess" teachers who had no placement but still continued to receive a salary.[75]

108 || BOOKER IN POWER

But to make real headway on changing teachers' evaluations, reforming compensation, and weakening tenure and other labor protections, there had to be change to the state's tenure law and a renegotiation of the teachers' union contract. In these initiatives, Anderson got plenty of assistance from all levels of government—the Obama, Christie, and Booker administrations—as well as from the bureaucratic leadership of the National Education Association (NEA) and AFT unions.[76] The Obama administration, as part of its Race to the Top grant program, required states to make it easier to strip tenure from teachers to be eligible for the program's funds.[77] With the support of the two teacher union federations, in summer 2012, the state legislature passed, and the governor signed, a new tenure law. The new regime allowed tenure to be stripped from teachers with two consecutive years of poor performance and, crucially, made student test scores a "predominant" factor in evaluating teachers.[78]

The administration, with the collaboration of the NTU leadership, had been stalling on negotiating a new contract, which expired in 2009. Now, armed with the new state legislation, Anderson and Cerf moved to sign a deal that weakened tenure and tied teacher pay to "performance," a major part of which would be measured by test scores and arbitrary evaluations. A January 2012 meeting Cerf held with AFT president Randi Weingarten at the union's D.C. office paved the way for the deal. The two lawyers had developed a cooperative relationship in the early to mid-2000s when Cerf was Joel Klein's chief deputy and Weingarten, before taking the AFT helm in 2008, headed the New York City local, the most powerful within the federation. At the 2012 meeting, Cerf presented an offer she couldn't refuse—either she would agree to a contract with the neoliberal labor reforms or Cerf would ensure a New Orleans solution of full charterization. In the face of the disruption threat from above, Weingarten, following standard practice among the labor bureaucracy in the neoliberal era, agreed to cooperate rather than resisting the depredations of capital and the state.[79] Thus the neoliberal implementers did show their willingness to accept Keynesian-era collective bargaining, *as long as* it was deployed to consolidate what sociologist Michael Burawoy terms "hegemonic despotism," that is, on the condition that Weingarten and the NTU engaged in negotiations not to resist but rather to "command consent to sacrifice" from education workers to advance the neoliberal SSA.[80]

With the aid of Obama-driven state changes and a compliant union leadership, the contract included a veritable neoliberal wish list. This included a four-point rating system for teachers, with "merit" pay provided for the highest rank. The evaluation would be based on the dubious measure of standardized test scores as well as evaluations by management and a "peer" reviewer selected by management.[81] Two consecutive years of a partially effective or ineffective ratings would result in dismissal, tenured or not. To further divide the teachers, the contract instituted a two-tier pay scale, with the inferior one extending the years to reach the top pay scale, and other major pay "bumps," all of which would further encourage an exodus of junior teachers. As a sweetener, back pay—all step increases were frozen after expiration of the contract in 2009—and bonuses, covered by $48 million from the philanthropy-funded FNF, were included in the deal.[82]

The contract, in a further tiering of the system and undermining of solidarity, created a new category of "turnaround/renew schools." The agreement provided the superintendent wide latitude in making the designation, including a "variety of data points," ranging from enrollment to "proficiency over time." Once designated, with only "consultation" with the union required, the superintendent could abrogate various components of the collective bargaining agreement and implement new ones, such as longer school days, among other options. If a teacher at the targeted school objected to the superintendent's diktat, he would be forced to look for another vacancy at an NPS school. If unsuccessful, the teacher would then be placed in the "pool," while nontenured teachers could be let go altogether. In addition, Anderson, without any need even for consultation with the union, proceeded with more school closures, which received full backing from Booker.[83]

The deal was hailed by the reformers, with *Star-Ledger* editor Tom Moran saluting NTU head Joe Del Grosso for courageously taking on the "taboo" of merit pay, agreeing to longer days provided by the "turnaround schools" provisions, accepting the "harsh, real-world stuff" of merit pay, and firing those "who screwed up." Del Grosso concurred, arguing that teachers want to be treated as professionals and distinguish themselves from those who "demean the profession" by not working hard, as if this were the central problem facing public education. Moran's only lament was that the "reactionary" New Jersey Education Association (NJEA), which represents the largest bulk of teachers in the state and collaborated in the weakening of tenure at the state level, was not willing to go quite as far as the NTU and Del Grosso.

While lauded by Moran and other reformers, Del Grosso got a hostile reception from the rank and file at an October 23, 2012, mass membership meeting to discuss the provisions. There was clear unhappiness, with denunciations of the contract from the floor by the union reform insurgents, grouped in the Newark Education Workers, receiving a warm response.[84] Yet, for now, the reformers and their trade union partners could celebrate. On November 16, 2012, Christie, Booker, Cerf, and Anderson joined Democratic U.S. senator Frank Lautenberg and AFT head Randi Weingarten to celebrate the teachers' ratification of the contract by a 62 percent margin. Christie hailed it as a "model" for the rest of the state, while the AFT chief touted the merit pay as "the system of the future" and the contract as a "breakthrough."[85] The political romance between Weingarten and Christie, which had begun at an impromptu encounter at the tenth anniversary 9/11 ceremony, continued to blossom. The two later appeared together on the MSNBC *Morning Joe* show touting the deal, all of which further burnished Christie's presidential bona fides as someone able to push through neoliberal reforms in a consensual, bipartisan manner.[86]

ONE STEP FORWARD, TWO STEPS BACK

In drawing "a map of the ruling class," sociologist Stanley Aronowitz argues, "social cartographers" must be sensitive to both temporal and spatial considerations; that is, the power bloc in any social formation may vary depending on the geographical context and level of the state, such as a local apparatus of the state in the form of Newark's BUR. Furthermore, "the power bloc at any time may not correspond to its antecedents and may be displaced through struggle over the composition of ruling formations." These struggles, Aronowitz emphasizes, "are no less intense than those conducted within the formation of labor."[87]

Clearly, in the case of Newark's BUR, an intense intra-elite struggle produced not simply a new personality at City Hall but a redrawn ruling class map. Booker and his philanthrocapitalist partners, through struggle, successfully deposed former mayor Sharpe James, who eventually ended up in federal prison thanks to the work of then U.S. Attorney Chris Christie. The new regime viewed "the rules by which conflicts are resolved" that James employed to manage the city's public services and working class as a serious obstacle to their political, economic, spatial, and social restructuring plans.[88] But the new power bloc wasn't finished cleaning house once they gained control of the city's executive office. Booker and top assistants like De'Shawn Wright moved against old regime elements and their methods of governing, which presented obstacles to the neoliberal makeover of public education and other reforms. The most prominent example was school superintendent Marion Bolden, who failed to go along with the program and was eventually, with the help of the Democratic governor, cashiered early in Booker's administration.

Booker and the philanthrocapitalists were able to reconfigure the local state by incorporating the foundations in the form of the liaison office, while setting up a series of satellite, parastate apparatuses, from the NCSF to NTE, to push forward movement objectives. This restructuring, even within elements included in the new power bloc, was not bereft of conflict and struggle. The local philanthropic wing of the power bloc felt disrespected and marginalized when the Silicon Valley– and hedge fund–backed foundations launched the FNF. "The aim of" organizations like the FNF, which are essential components of social movements from above, Nilsen and Cox emphasize, "is essentially to construct unity between dominant groups—a unity that cannot be taken for granted, and which sometimes unravels."[89] However, as the history of the FNF's rollout demonstrates, new organizations themselves can create fissures. But, in a sign of the movement's resiliency and agreement on the fundamentals, the new elite were able to reconfigure the FNF through a power-sharing deal to achieve their generally agreed-upon goals for public schools. Likewise, the new mayor and movement militants drawn from the Bloomberg administration initially had tactical differences when Booker took power. But, after Christie's election, they were able to close ranks and work out a blueprint to achieve their shared neoliberal SSA agenda.

In the end, the new regime successfully consolidated a "more coherent interracial governing class" than had existed under the earlier version of the BUR. This transformation, as political scientist Adolph Reed Jr. argues, reflects broader changes in the BUR and urban capitalist politics more generally in the United States.[90] Thus, as we saw, in the latter half of the aughts, the Booker regime incorporated a new BPMC cadre into the state and parastate nonprofit apparatuses of the movement. The Jameses and Boldens were replaced by accomplished, well-compensated operators like Mashea Ashton, Kimberly McLain, De'Shawn Wright, Dale Englin, and Jeremy Johnson, among others, who had a material stake in carrying out movement goals. They were accompanied by white allies, such as Chris Cerf, Cami Anderson, Lisa Daggs, and those with longer histories in Newark, such as KIPP's Ryan Hill, who shared similar material interests and legitimated their behavior with a commonly held antiracist ideology. The centrality of their antiracist ideology and the concerted effort to include the BPMC in the ranks of the movement and power bloc highlight that the new governing regime was by no means "postracial." "Racial redistribution" among the elite, as Reed argues, "remains an important element of its [the power bloc's] interest group politics and commitment to diversity is a source of its cohesion."[91]

But, the very success of the new power bloc in deposing the old regime helped construct the very force that could overthrow it. By ousting the old regime, the Booker-led forces also discarded the forms of class conciliation that had helped maintain a demobilized populace since the rise of the BUR in the 1970s. Now, the privatization drive, despite a layer of support from some charter parents and the union bureaucracy's collaboration, ignited the biggest social movement in decades, one that encompassed rank-and-file teachers, students, parents, and community activists. In the next chapter, I turn to how that movement from below emerged and the type of challenge it generated for the philanthrocapitalist-driven movement from above.

PART III

The Movement from Below

4

Rebel City?

NEWARK'S EDUCATION MOVEMENT FROM BELOW, 2010–2013

They say they are a movement . . . but they are actually funded by a few billionaires. . . . We need to build a social movement with parents, education workers, and all working-class people that want a decent school for their children and a decent society in which their children can live.

> —Branden Rippey, Newark Education Workers activist speaking at the April 2013 Newark Board of Education meeting

Every class struggle is simultaneously an intraclass struggle. . . . The process of self-organization of a class, then, involves concrete political struggles within it.

> —Judith Stepan-Norris and Maurice Zeitlin, "'Who Gets the Bird?'; or, How the Communists Won Power and Trust in America's Unions: The Relative Autonomy of Intraclass Political Struggles"

Newark's Booker-led, philanthrocapitalist-allied regime was, by the second half of the 2000s, at the vanguard of efforts to disrupt public education and pave the way for privatization. But, by the early 2010s, this elite offensive had, in turn, sparked one of the most powerful social movements nationally challenging the dismantlement of public education. Bringing in students, teachers, parents, and other community members, the movement around public schools was the most significant social movement in the city since the rise of the BUR in the early 1970s. Although there had been large demonstrations around education and other issues, "what I haven't seen," longtime Newark resident, NPS teacher, NTU activist, and later school board member Antoinette Baskerville-Richardson noted, "is a sustained organization with the capacity of having multiple actions over a period a time."[1]

|| 115

116 || REBEL CITY?

Clearly the struggle over the public schools was at the center of remaking the city.

But was this movement a "class struggle"—a question sociologists Judith Stepan-Norris and Maurice Zeitlin argue is at the center of the "intraclass struggle"? Of course, as a former industrial center, Newark historically had plenty of struggles that pitted workers and capitalists that fit the conventional definition of class struggle. Workers and capitalists struggled over division of the surplus product, control of the labor process, and, at times, control of the means of production. These struggles involved, as well, internal, intraclass contestation over demands, ideologies, organizational forms, and leadership. But, as radical geographer David Harvey emphasizes, "the processes of urbanization, over the ways in which cities are made and remade," are about class and class struggle as well.[2] "From their very inception," Harvey argues,

> cities have arisen through the geographical and social concentration of a surplus product. Urbanization has always been, therefore, a class phenomenon . . . since surpluses have been extracted from somewhere and from somebody, while control over the use of the surplus typically lies in the hands of a few. The general situation persists under capitalism. . . . Capitalism rests, as Marx tells us, upon the perpetual search for surplus value (profit). But to produce surplus value capitalists have to produce a surplus product. This means that capitalism is perpetually producing the surplus product that urbanization requires. The reverse relation also holds. Capitalism needs urbanization to absorb the surplus product it perpetually produces.[3]

But, as Harvey emphasizes, Newark, or any city, becoming a repository of "surplus absorption" entails extensive urban restructuring through what Joseph Schumpeter euphemistically called "creative destruction."[4] The working class, its routines and sources of power, invariably becomes the target of the bourgeois-led destruction efforts, albeit creatively legitimated, and the neoliberal, urban restructuring version was no different. The public schools, because of the social attachments to place they engendered, the union and tenure protections enjoyed by workers from years of struggle, and their intertwining with the forms of rule of the old BUR, made this institution a central target for elimination. The end game, creatively justified as an antiracist crusade, was privatization of public schools, one piece of the broader neoliberal SSA agenda of opening "new fields for capital accumulation in domains hitherto regarded off-limits to the calculus of profit making."[5] "What it's really about for these reformers," insurgent Newark teacher Branden Rippey inveighed at a 2013 school board meeting, "is wanting to break teacher unions, open more charter schools, and eventually open the U.S. to for-profit schooling."[6]

Although objectively, the struggle over the public schools was a class-wide one, this did not determine the form the struggle would take. Just as with the struggles over expanded reproduction to increase surplus value, the movements around social reproduction, urbanization, and the dispossession that is at their heart are contingent. Furthermore, these struggles, as Stepan-Norris and Zeitlin emphasize, are not undertaken on a blank slate but rather are constrained by the "existing historical situation and social relations (political, economic, and cultural)" in which they operate.[7] In this chapter, I examine how, within these historically received structures, the intra- and interclass struggle over public schools unfolded. I begin this chapter, therefore, by profiling three leading teacher activists, the reform union caucus they organized, and their struggles with the NTU leadership over ideologies, organization, alliances, strategy, and tactics. As the teacher and community protests against Cami Anderson's neoliberal reforms grew, privatization leaders mobilized several influential black ministers to attack and delegitimate community opposition. But far from stifling the movement, students then entered the fray en masse in 2013 as they became the central disruptive force in the movement to defend public education. I conclude with an assessment of to what extent Newark was becoming what David Harvey calls a "rebel city." That is, were the new forces that emerged among teachers, students, parents, and community members able to forge a counterhegemonic class project to challenge the movement from above's blueprints for a remade industrial city?

MAKING REBEL TEACHERS

An important component of the movement emerged among dissident members of the NTU. A leading figure was Branden Rippey, a history teacher at the selective-admission "magnet" school Science

118 || REBEL CITY?

Park High School. Rippey, who first entered the classroom in the mid-1990s, always wanted "to teach in an urban area, in institutionalized ghettoized poverty," because, reflecting back on his life choice two decades earlier, "I knew I wanted to be part of changing that . . . in a kind of progressive . . . not radical kind of way." Rippey, who grew up in a white, middle-class, professional household in Lakewood, New Jersey, a city of seventy thousand, later became radicalized through his participation in a 2002 left-wing electoral campaign for the U.S. Senate and further engagement with labor history. Then, in the mid-2000s, after Booker's election and the attacks on teachers deepened, he decided to become active in the NTU. Rippey explains how the stepped-up movement from above against public education nationally, and in Newark in particular, led him into union activism:

> You started to see the deterioration in the morale of teachers over time, and you begin to see the beginning of an antiteacher propaganda . . . an agenda going on, it started in D.C. and Chicago this was 2005 or '06 or so. . . . Rhee was in Washington and Duncan was in Chicago, Duncan was the first one to do the renews and turnarounds. We started getting news of that and I started getting worried. In 2007 there were billboards around the city funded by the Center for Union facts, $7 million campaign by the D.C.-based antiunion group, funded by Walmart and Apple, and they came to Newark to spend money to convince people that the teachers union sucked. So the sign said "Newark teachers' union failed, failing our students, failing the public," they were on buses, on trains, they were on the major routes on McCarter Highway. It was terrible, I could see there was something brewing.

Rippey became the union representative in his school and began regularly attending union meetings. To help build a fight back, he offered to do political education on labor history and educate members on the political forces and interests behind the demonization of teachers and public education more broadly, as exemplified by the billboards, deteriorating conditions at work, and growth of charters. That is, Rippey understood the importance of "showing the coherence and purposive direction" of the movement from above's project that teachers confronted and therefore "the limits of elite tolerance for needs that contradict such projects." But calling attention to the seriousness of the attacks was not to promote fatalism but rather, as Nilsen and Cox emphasize, to highlight and educate teachers about "the socially constructed nature of these projects" and therefore how "they can be challenged and, on occasion, be defeated."[8]

Thanks, but no thanks was the response of the NTU's two main leaders, Joe Del Grosso and Pete Petino, to the offer from the young, energetic, rank-and-file NTU member. "I offered those things, we had a nice two-hour conversation, and then after that," Rippey adds with a dumbfounded facial expression, *"they systematically ignored me."*[9] Therefore, from Rippey's perspective, he "started experiencing the union bureaucrats," who were more concerned with deactivating any challenges from their rank and file than in building a fight against the anti-union assault. He encountered similar responses when he advocated, at union-wide shop steward meetings, greater union militancy in the face of the increasing attacks. Underscoring the dialectical relationship between movements from above and below, what finally led him to build a reform caucus in the union was "Christie's election . . . where it was clear he was coming after us," and yet the union leadership refused to mobilize, all of which was crystallized by a postelection union meeting in early 2010.

> NTU was packed, at least fifty or sixty reps, which was most of the buildings. . . . It was so sad, it was so sad for two reasons: the reps themselves, they were like "it's so terrible, what can we do, what can we do, what's the worst that can happen, how much can he take away from us," like it was the sky is falling attitude, *and it was falling,* but there was no sense of what do we do, it was literally "how bad is it going to be, what should I tell my members, what should we get ready for." And I listened for about an hour an hour and a half of this. . . . I was getting more and more infuriated, at some point I put my hand up and I said, "Look there has been some okay information . . . you have given out on what you have been trying to do behind the scenes, there have been some good questions, but the reality is"—and I said these exact words—"I thought this was going to be a meeting about strategy and unifying our membership and creating a plan for what we are going to do. . . . I haven't heard any of that and the leadership here needs to create some kind of plan on how our forty-two hundred members can fight back and rewin political power and regain the trust of New Jerseyans and win the

> public back over." . . . This was the second depressing part, the lead-
> ership, they just had nothing. He [Petino] said, "Look, we lost an
> election and sometimes you have to take your lumps." I'm like what
> the fuck . . . we need to do something. So we sprung into action at
> Science High School later that week.[10]

In fact, the NTU president, Del Grosso, was even more conciliatory than Petino, his loyal vice president. Rather than reluctantly resigning himself to Christie's abuse, Del Grosso lauded the new governor while receiving his—or at least the membership's—lumps. In May 2010, as Christie was rolling out a slew of neoliberal education reforms, Del Grosso told the local press, "I don't consider the governor an enemy or an enemy of public education. . . . I actually have great respect for the governor." Instead of combating Christie's agenda, Del Grosso had, for example, the NTU sign off on the state's 2010 Race to the Top grant application to the Obama administration, which required further neo-liberal reforms to qualify for the funds.[11] Thus, on one side, Christie, as a leading implementer of the corporate reform agenda, was engaging in a form of elite *disruption*—withdrawal of cooperation—of public edu-cation. This came in the form of measures to weaken tenure and defund public education, achieved through slashing state spending on public schools and further strangling school budgets by imposing a cap on local property tax increases, while, as will be discussed later, protecting charter schools from the budget axe.[12] Instead of countering this elite disruption from above with a form of their own, the NTU leadership turned their sights below to "command consent to sacrifice."[13]

Another key participant in the teacher mobilization, who would also face her own pushback from the union for attempting to activate members, came from an unlikely source. Leah Owens, an African American woman who was reared in upstate New York and graduated from Duke University, came to Newark in the mid-2000s as a TFA volunteer. The antiracist, democratic promise of "an excellent edu-cation for every child"—emblazoned on the TFA recruitment flyer posted on a Duke bulletin board—is what caught her eye. She was also "attracted to the idea," which was emphasized in its literature and trainings, "of doing two years of teaching and becoming a principal." Opening your own charter school, where a principal is "able to start from scratch and . . . set the rules," was emphasized as a career path for TFA volunteers. While the TFA's training touted charter schools, it instilled, Owens explained, "an idea about unions which is basically they are an obstruction, they are in the way of progress."[14]

But, as she began learning more about Newark's history, "about how the system came to be" and what was happening nationally with public schools—partly through educationals run by a member of the first generation of BUR apparatchiks, attorney Junius Williams, and his Rutgers University–affiliated, foundation-funded Abbot Leadership Institute (ALI)—her "ideas about charter schools in the public school system began to change." As part of her political transformation, Owens organized, in June 2008, Teachers as Leaders in Newark (TaLiN) and even obtained a small grant from the local TFA, with which she had not fully broken relations, to get it started. The aim of TaLiN was to get teachers and parents involved to improve the schools. But in these efforts to engage and mobilize rank-and-file teachers, she encountered the same hostility from the NTU that her future comrade Rippey faced.

Then, in spring 2010, just as Christie rolled out his attacks, Owens proposed the topic of "budget cuts and the politics of education" for the TFA's educational discussion series for new volunteers, of which she was a team leader. But, after submitting the request, she never heard back from the local TFA, headquartered at the same downtown office building that housed the local charter movement organizations. In fall 2010, months after her initial request, Owens sent an email asking for a response. A TFA representative responded, by email, that "'oh well we decided to go in a different direction this year,' so basically," Owens deadpanned, "they just iced me out. . . . They cut me out because I raised these issues."

Undeterred by the lack of support from her former mentors, which only furthered her growing radicalization, Owens swung into action in spring 2010. She put to use the large email list she had accumulated as part of her organizing over the previous three years to organize several rallies against the deep cuts to education Booker's new ally, Chris Christie, was imposing. In these organizing efforts, she made contact and began collaborating with Al Moussab, a young, recently arrived teacher who taught social studies at East Side High School, which had a large immigrant student body. A New Jersey native, Moussab attended Montclair State University in the early 2000s, where he became politically active in the movement against the Iraq War and in the Green Party's 2000 Ralph Nader presidential campaign. He began his teaching in the suburban Bloomfield district, where "he loved the teachers, students, parents," but, like Rippey, his goal "was always to teach in a major urban city," where he saw more opportunities to be part of struggles for radical change.[15]

The series of protests in spring 2010 that Owens spearheaded brought together students, community groups like the People's Organization for Progress, the growing ranks of NTU dissidents, and other community activists focused on education, such as parent activist Whilemena Holder, Johnny Latner with One Newark Education Coalition (ONIC), and Sharon Smith with Parents Unified for Local School Education (PULSE). Even the pro-charter advocate and lawyer Shavar Jeffries, who was then running on a Booker- and Adubato-backed school board slate, attended and spoke at a March 4 rally opposing Christie's cuts to education and to tax breaks through ending the "millionaire's tax."[16]

Through these and other protests against the budget cuts, such as morning leafletting of parents at Science High as they dropped off their children, Rippey, Moussab, and Owens began to coalesce as the core of opposition among rank-and-file teachers. The NTU leadership, in contrast, continued with their TINA—There Is No Alternative—justification for inaction. They had to, as NTU official Petino put it, "take their lumps." Among those lumps was Christie freezing wages of public-sector workers—no step increases—whose contracts had expired, including NPS employees. Despite these and other attacks, the NTU stayed away from the street protests that emerged in Newark in spring 2010.

NEW CLASS ORGANIZATION: COMMUNITY AND LABOR TOGETHER

For several years, since being rebuffed by the union leadership, Rippey had been in discussions with his teaching mentor, longtime educator, and activist in the local Puerto Rican community José Velazquez about establishing an opposition union caucus. In late 2010, after the wave of protests to Christie's cuts and the NTU's paralysis, they decided to take action.[17] But the goal was not simply to unseat president Joseph Del Grosso and top assistant Pete Petino but to forge a "social movement," "social justice," unionism.[18] They defined that form of unionism as a militant, class-conscious one that united teachers, students, and the broader working-class community in a fight against what they saw as the racist, capitalist forces bent on busting teacher unions and privatizing public education.

Rippey and Velazquez gathered, initially, a core group consisting of Owens, Moussab, and a few other teachers, including Michael Iovino, who would later switch sides and run with the NTU leadership, to found the caucus. They dubbed the new organization the NEW Caucus—Newark Education Workers—to highlight that they did not see themselves as a professional elite apart from the working class but rather as an integral component.

Though quiet in the face of the attacks from Christie, the rank-and-file insurgency that took hold in early 2011 did get the NTU leadership active. The incumbent regime sent two staffers to show up outside a school where NEW was meeting "to let us know they knew what we were doing." Nonetheless, Rippey explains, "we asked 'do you want to come in,' but they were just there for intimidation. . . . They just wanted to scare away anybody that wanted anything productive to happen." In the end, NEW was able to assemble a slate to contest sixteen out of the thirty-one seats on the union's executive council for the spring 2011 biannual union election, with Velazquez standing as NEW's presidential candidate. The incumbents averaged about 1,000 votes each, while the challengers garnered about 350, but it was still the most significant electoral challenge Del Grosso and Petino had faced since coming to power in 1995.

As discussed in chapter 3, in early 2011 and through the spring, school board meetings became a central terrain of the battle over public schools. The NEW activists, consistent with their brand of social movement unionism, joined parents and other community activists in denouncing school closings, "turnarounds," colocations, and more charter school openings that the Booker regime was rolling out. But, unlike in the previous spring, the NTU leadership now had at least to appear combative. For example, at the raucous, overflow March 2011 meeting at Barringer High School, Del Grosso encouraged turnout from NTU members and used his time at the public mic to denounce a plan to "colocate" charter schools in existing public schools. Yet, the charters, underscoring their ability to cultivate some popular support, mobilized their parent and student base for the meetings as well. They spoke in support of their disruption plan to, literally, withdraw space from the public sector and turn it over to the corporate-backed charters. Mashea Ashton, the generously compensated chief executive of the NCSF and archetype of the new BPMC, whose material interests are tied to the rollback of the public sector, led the movement charge as she vigorously backed the proposal pushed by her fellow movement allies Booker and Cerf. "This is about providing high-quality public schools to as many children as possible in Newark," she confidently asserted. "I think this is really, hopefully, a cry for action that the status quo can no longer exist in Newark."[19]

In the midst of the growing ferment around the schools and discontent over the continuing misery produced by the Great Recession, Ras Baraka, principal at Central High School, and recently elected city councilman, began to mobilize. In July 2011, he spearheaded, with the support of various labor unions—but not the NTU—and local officials, including state senator Ronald Rice Sr. and councilpersons Mildred Crump and Luis Quintana, a Mass Day of Outrage protest aimed to "force corporations to pay their fair share." Baraka, wearing a "Retired Slave" T-shirt, blasted the education and other budget cuts imposed by Christie and Booker that were "shredding community fabrics" and pitting "black versus Latino versus white." In addition, he weighed in against corporations, and the Prudential Corporation in particular, the city's most powerful, for "reaping profits at the expense of the unemployed and underemployed. . . . It's recession for us, it's not a recession for Prudential." While far fewer than the five thousand promised protestors turned out, the action did show that traditional BUR elements were riding the wave of protests to confront Booker and his newly refashioned regime.[20]

In the following 2011–12 school year, as the new superintendent, Cami Anderson, began outlining her plans—more school closings and "turnaround" plans for others, while opening smaller academies and expanding charters—the board meetings and other public hearings became even rowdier.[21] In February 2012, Rutgers University's thousand-seat Paul Robeson Cultural Center was filled with angry parents, students, and teachers as Anderson unveiled her plans, many of which were drawn from what her predecessor, Clifford Janey, had laid out in his "Great Expectations" restructuring blueprint. "Anderson," according to *Star-Ledger* reporter David Giambusso, "was all but shouted off the stage by a crowd of more than 1,000 teachers, residents and community leaders who grew increasingly hostile as she tried to explain why she wants to close seven underachieving schools."[22]

Again, a month later, in early March 2012, "furious parents, teachers and students flooded" a community meeting to unveil Anderson's revised reform plans, which still included several school closings. The growing opposition to the movement from above's disruption required local notables to weigh in to defend the increasingly beleaguered superintendent. The *Star-Ledger*'s Tom Moran, whose paper had become a veritable movement organ, came to the rescue with a March 11 editorial whose title telegraphed the message: "In Newark, a School Reformer Needs Help." Moran, an unwavering backer of corporate reform, denounced a "small group of activists" for turning public school meetings into "rowdy . . . Jerry Springer Shows." The real problem, from Moran and Anderson's perspective, was "the hesitation of civil leaders" in the face of the discord. Quoting Anderson, Moran explained that the problem was that "people are taking a wait-and-see attitude. We need more people to jump in the water and say it's time for bold action." Moran concluded his editorial by saluting two influential civic leaders for stepping up to the plate: former Ford Foundation official Bob Curvin—"one of the city's most respected elders"—for intervening at school board meetings to demand civility and Shavar Jeffries, then a school board member, for publicly defending Anderson's "courage."[23]

Five prominent ministers, representing a layer of the BPMC, which had been a crucial component of the movement from above, heeded Moran's call and stepped up to pen an editorial defending Anderson's reforms. The ministers, two of whose churches operated their own charters, denounced all the "yelling and screaming," the "dysfunctional . . . Newark Attitude" of distrust of change, and encouraged those with "other viable routes to excellent schools . . . to put them on the table now." They concluded, without much basis from Anderson's record, that "we trust that those with executive responsibility for school change will be open to incorporating them."[24] These influential pastors, along with Booker, Jeffries, and assorted local officials, joined Anderson at a March 19, 2012, press conference as she unveiled her final revised disruption plan.[25] One of the authors of the editorial and an attendee at the press conference, Reverend David Jefferson, pastor of Metropolitan Baptist Church and head of the New Jersey chapter of Al Sharpton's NAN, defended Anderson's plan,

126 || REBEL CITY?

explaining that although it was "not a perfect plan," he still supported it. "For too long we've sat on the fence. For too long we've defended failure," he said.[26] Pedro Noguera, whose GVZ operation Anderson shut down, nonetheless praised her for the "vigorous shakeup," but counseled that she "must do more to engage parents as partners in this work. It's vital to the long-term success of her reforms."[27] Despite these elite efforts to shore up support for Anderson at the end of her first full year at the helm, the crusading superintendent would soon face the most serious disruption from the very force the reforms ostensibly served: "the children."

STUDENTS ENTER THE FIGHT

Measured by Piven's concept of disruption—withdrawal of cooperation from interdependent relationships—students were the third, and most powerful, component of the movement from below. The initial wave sprang up in spring 2010 in the face of Christie's budget cuts. In March, a Facebook post by Pace University freshman Michelle Lauto—the daughter of a public school teacher and a recent graduate from a suburban Bergen County public high school—called for an April 27 statewide student walkout to protest the cuts the Christie administration was imposing. More than eighteen thousand students accepted the invitation, which witnessed walkouts across the state in what the *New York Times* called "one of the largest grass-roots demonstrations to hit New Jersey in years."[28] By far the largest was in Newark, where high school students from across the city walked out—although apparently not from any charter schools—and converged in a rally at City Hall.

Though sparked by the Facebook post, the April 27 walkout in Newark—and across the state—was far from spontaneous. Students had to build for the walkout, which faced active opposition from state and local authorities. At Science Park High School, the city's most prestigious selective-admission school, a member of the debate team, Elise Tirado, was the key leader. As Jaysen Bazile, then a Science Park freshman who would later become the first president of the NSU, explained, "it was planned about two weeks before . . . they started putting together the groundwork." Regular meetings were held in the student cafeteria, where flyers were designed, a social media presence was created, and outreach to students at Science and across the city was planned. This mirrored outreach at other schools in Newark, where "phone calls, texts, Twitter, Facebook, everything," were used to build for the walkout, according to Malcolm X Shabazz High School student leader Donald Jackson.[29]

Bazile explains that in their outreach, they emphasized the cuts to extracurricular activities, such as sports and the debate team, if Christie's budget plans were to go through. This approach underscored the argument made by Francis Fox Piven and Richard Cloward in their classic work *Poor People's Movements* that poor and working-class people "experience deprivation and oppression within a concrete setting. . . . It is the daily experience of people that shapes their grievances, establishes the measures of their demands, and points out the target of their anger."[30] The organizing, which tapped into students' daily experience, sparked, according to Bazile, a "buzz leading up to it, you could just feel everything was different, everyone just felt empowered, like we were going to take control over our own education." The walkouts, for Bazile, showed to him the power in disruption:

> The event showed me that students can organize for power and we do have power like come on, like you were shutting down traffic on Broad and Market in Newark, New Jersey, that's . . . the political statement, that students, we're not going to take just any little willy-nilly thing happening to our education.

One person who felt that power in particular was Mayor Cory Booker. The students converged on the steps of City Hall, demanding to see Booker, who was already clearly identified with the author of the cuts, Chris Christie.

Despite the impressive student mobilization, "it fizzled out," Bazile lamented, because "no organization came out" of the walkouts, "we didn't organize any type of leadership structure to take it forward . . . to say 'hey, what's our next action going to be?'" Nonetheless, important gains were made. One was a commitment from NPS not to cut the debate team: "all the extracurriculars were saved," Bazile recalls.[31] The second, and most important, fruit of this "popcorn protest" was that freshmen like Bazile gained valuable organizing lessons for the next wave of protest.[32]

CULTIVATING CRITICAL CONSCIOUSNESS

After the 2010 protests petered out, Bazile went back to debating, "which," he explains, "took up most of my high school years up to my senior year." Yet, Bazile's involvement in the debate club, along with classmates such as Thais Marquez and Flavia Borletto, would help prepare the ideological ground for a revival of student protest. The debate club created a space that nurtured an anticapitalist consciousness and recognition of their power. Marquez and Bazile, who were partners on the same debate team beginning their sophomore year, and Borletto began to identify themselves as socialists. They used the debate themes—capitalism in their sophomore year and peace in their junior year—to deploy and hone their socialist worldview and analysis. Marquez explains that in her sophomore year, she and her debate partner, Bazile, advocated "dismantling all U.S. military bases, and we made an imperialism argument and how the military furthers capitalistic ventures." Marquez notes:

> The three of us, after that [2010] walkout, like we got really into Marxist theory, we started reading Marx. After the protest, we started thinking about that stuff and applying it to our debate career. So for the three of us, the debate career were really based off of critiquing capitalism and neoliberalism.... The three of us educated ourselves to understand the structures that oppressed us.

This critical consciousness was also nurtured by the Occupy movement that broke out their junior year, in 2011, and, especially, by radical teachers. Of particular influence was, as Bazile explains, their social studies teacher, and NEW activist, Branden Rippey.

> Mr. Rippey . . . I mentioned him a lot because he was influential for me because he took a very left-wing approach into describing U.S. history. I had him for U.S. II, so the way he described the U.S. labor movement . . . I was like wow, they really stood up and they took power, like Eugene Debs right, like that guy was awesome right, and he would just like hammer in stuff like that, that's what got all of us, you know, not just me everyone who knew the man and we would just keep on filtering it out to the rest of the students. *But that's what caused I would say the climate of like resistance,*

of rebellion for it to even happen in the first place. I really do think without sentiments like that we would have just, it would have passed us over, we would have been like "what can we do about it. We're just kids."[33]

Bazile added that the "whole culture at Science and Eastside, especially, . . . some key teachers I think influenced us. . . . We saw it wasn't so hard . . . to say 'hey me and you, we don't have to just sit back and take it.'"

Thus, the debate team, the Occupy movement, and, in particular, the radical teachers helped cultivate the threefold "necessary cognitions," as Piven and Cloward described the formulation in their classic *Poor People's Movements,* for social movements to emerge. "The emergence of protest movements," Piven and Cloward argue,

> entails a transformation both of consciousness and of behavior. The change in consciousness has at least three levels. First, "the system"—or those aspects of the system that people experience— loses legitimacy. Large numbers of men and women who ordinarily accept the authority of their rulers and the legitimacy of institutional arrangements come to believe in some measure that these rulers and these arrangements are unjust and wrong. Second, people that are ordinarily fatalistic, who believe that existing arrangements are inevitable, begin to assert "rights" that imply demands for change. Third, there is a new sense of efficacy; people who ordinarily consider themselves helpless come to believe that they have the capacity to alter their lot.[34]

The budding Science Park socialists, as the Anderson regime deepened the attacks on public schools in 2012 and 2013, worked to bring their advanced consciousness to their classmates.

FROM DEBATING TO ACTION

In fall 2012, as Anderson began her second academic year with a new round of budget cuts and restructuring plans, including colocating a charter school at Science High School, the radical students in the debate club decided to put their ideas into practice. Spurring on action was a deepening contradiction, Marquez emphasizes: "the Zuckerberg money . . . like $200 million are coming in, everything is going to be great and then that wasn't the case. Because my senior year there were like huge budget cuts, and I think that motivated us." Furthermore, there were the memory and experience of 2010: "we remember that we did the walkout." Likewise, Bazile argued, rank-and-file teacher opposition to a concessionary contract that was signed in October 2012—discussed in chapter 3—and the "major uproar" at public meetings over Anderson's proposed budget and deepening restructuring plans also emboldened the budding student radicals.

Marquez, Bazile recalls, finally pushed a group of radical students into action in November 2012, during their senior year: "I was coming from debate and Thais was like 'hey, we need a union, *we need a union.*'"[35] So Bazile, Marquez, Borletto, and Kyle Cotino from the debate club, along with Israel "Izzy" Alarcon, a close friend of the group, began to huddle in the classroom of a sympathetic teacher on how they would organize.

While the memory of 2010 gave them confidence, they also recognized the limitations of the earlier mobilization. "We tried," Marquez explains, "to be more strategic . . . like we knew we had to do some type of protest, but we wanted it to be more strategic than the walkout that happened freshman year." Being more "strategic" meant forging an organization that could sustain protest long term, and they started studying the Philadelphia Students Union as a model. Thus, in contrast to 2010, they decided first to hold a general citywide student meeting to educate students about the budget cuts and form a group to fight the attacks. Using their community contacts, students were able to obtain a room at Rutgers University to hold the meeting in early December 2012. For serval weeks prior, the core group, "the vanguard," as the tight-knit leaders from Science High referred to themselves, did outreach to build for the meeting. "We went to like every school after school every day," Marquez explained.

> We had like these tons of flyers. . . . So we like stuffed lockers. I remember being at University [High School] and we put flyers in each locker, we taped flyers everywhere, we made a twitter so we like made the meeting viral.

Further underscoring Piven's insight that "political action takes form within a matrix of social relations," the vanguard drew on other preexisting social relationships to build for the meeting. One was with debate team members at the other high schools. Another strength were the neighborhood ties of several vanguard members to the Ironbound section of the city, which they used to recruit students from the local East Side High School.

Approximately two hundred students and parents turned out to the December 2012 meeting, which the organizers saw as a success, especially as "we saw a lot of kids in the room," Bazile observed, who were "motivated." The vanguard prepared a detailed PowerPoint presentation on "what the exact budget cuts were . . . and how it was going to affect different schools." They also placed a special emphasis on the cuts to sports and other extracurricular activities, which got "everybody . . . like riled up," Marquez recalled. In addition, drawing on their critical Marxist worldview, they placed their struggle in a larger context, explaining that "the privatization of public schools" was happening "across the country . . . and how Newark is like the Ground Zero." Newark was targeted "because," Marquez explained, highlighting the strong influence of the racial justice framework among the vanguard, "it's . . . an immigrant population, black and brown kids, and that really resonated with people."

The organizers then went into the "where do we go from now section" in bullet point fashion. They outlined all the "little planning steps," from meetings at different schools to walkouts, to build the movement against the cuts and larger privatization drive. They were very conscious not to repeat the mistakes of 2010. As Bazile explains:

> We were like "yo, it can't be the same way because we can't just
> have a one-off . . . because we know kids are going to want to leave
> school, but if there is no organizing it is going to fall apart again."

Thus the students developed what Piven, drawing from the late social movement scholar Charles Tilly, terms a "repertoire," that is, "a specific constellation of strategies to actualize interdependent power."[36] But of course, these strategies are not developed out of thin air; they are not, as Piven argued, developed "anew with each challenge" but rather, as the term repertoires implies, strategies are "embedded in memory and culture, in a language of resistance." The 2010 walkout was especially fresh in the memory of the vanguard because they had participated in that action. Yet, as highlighted by Bazile's emphasis on not repeating the mistakes of 2010, repertoires—that is, power strategies—are not static but can be and are reinvented in response to past experiences and new conditions.

A few more meetings were held before the holiday break, but, after the initial enthusiasm, the numbers began to dwindle. Then, in January 2013, after they returned from the holiday break, Roberto Cabañas, an organizer with the recently formed community group New Jersey Communities United (NJCU), reached out to the students with an offer of support. The NJCU was a product of discussions between leaders of a Newark-based local of the Communication Workers of America (CWA) and the Center for Popular Democracy (CPD). The latter had only then recently formed to fill the national vacuum left by the implosion of the Democratic Party–allied and foundation-funded Association of Community Organizations for Reform Now (ACORN) group a few years earlier. A former ACORN staffer, Brian Kettenring, represented the CPD—formed by ex-ACORN officials to "rebrand and reestablish the organization"—in the negotiations with CWA that led to NJCU's formation in March 2012.[37] One of the first initiatives taken by Trina Scordo, NJCU's newly named executive director, was to charge lead organizer Cabañas with "developing a public education campaign to get impacted residents front and center" in the education reforms then being aggressively imposed. Initially, Cabañas explains, "I planned to organize parents first and then along comes a . . . group of students at Science Park High called the Newark Students Union."[38]

Initially NJCU and Cabañas's offer of assistance, who reached out via Facebook, provoked suspicion, because, as Marquez points out, "like we weren't sure who Roberto was, and what NJCU was at that point." Alarcon, who had the most reservations, was concerned that people "would think that New Jersey Communities United are manipulating those kids. . . . Like these kids are not operating on their own, NJCU was pushing these kids wherever they want, their own political agenda."

Despite these concerns, Marquez, Bazile, and Alarcon agreed to meet. Cabañas, a former student body president at Newark–Rutgers whose family had roots in Newark's heavily Puerto Rican North Ward, made the case for a partnership. He argued that NJCU could help the students "sustain this movement and grow it" through assistance in how to "base build" and by providing resources, such as a place to meet. The latter was becoming an important issue, Bazile points out, since we just couldn't meet at Science Park anymore, they didn't want us to, the administration. I just remember the rules changing, the school saying that no one could be in the building unless you were part of an extracurricular activity, and that was like never like that before and we were like *whaaat*.[39]

Cabañas reassured the student leaders that NJCU would not attach strings to the support it provided. Students would set the agenda. He then proposed, and the students accepted, that they hold a March 20 protest at the NJPAC in downtown Newark, where Booker and Anderson were holding a forum on "school reform" hosted by well-known New York City public radio host Brian Lehrer, to be aired on his widely followed public affairs show.[40]

The protest turnout was small—five of the vanguard from Science High, along with two from University High and a few NEW Caucus activists. Nonetheless, the action was a turning point for the students because it solidified their relationship with Cabañas, forged a group identity, and emboldened the leaders by successfully carrying out an act of disruption. For "the first time," Bazile emphasizes, "we called ourselves the Newark Students Union," under whose banner they led a disruption of the show. Marquez emphasizes the impact of the Occupy movement on their thinking: "we wanted to be as radical as Occupy . . . we wanted to occupy stuff. . . . We did the mic checks, we took a lot from Occupy." Nonetheless, despite this militancy, "initially," Cabañas says, "the students got cold feet" after they entered the swanky NJPAC and began texting back and forth with him. "We went into NJPAC to disrupt," Marquez recounts, "but I was supernervous because I was supposed to be the one that led the chant."

> But then I just started chanting "students, parents, teachers unite same struggle, same fight," and then like all the students in there like got up and started chanting and then they kicked us out.

Following the NJPAC action, from which "they got a lot of motivation," Bazile recalls, the NSU began holding regular meetings at the NJCU/CWA offices in downtown Newark to decide their next steps. Heeding the counsel of their mentor, and NEW leader, Branden Rippey, who exhorted, "You have got to organize younger kids, . . . you've got to get younger kids active and committed to organize, organize,

134 || REBEL CITY?

organize," they successfully recruited a core group of nonseniors, including sophomore Kristen Towkanik and freshman Jose Leonardo, future presidents of the NSU. The NSU was also able to diversify its ranks beyond its base at Science, with students from East Side, Barringer, and Arts High Schools now regularly attending meetings.

THE WALKOUT

In late March 2013, at about the same time as the NJPAC protest, Cabañas learned that the New Jersey state assembly's budget committee would be holding a hearing at the Rutgers–Newark campus on April 9. The committee planned to hear testimony on Christie's proposed $1.4 billion cut to education and local governments, which would mean a $56 million hit to the NPS budget. Cabañas and NSU became ambitious and decided to step up their disruption by organizing a mass student walkout and rally at Rutgers Law School, where the session would be held. "From the beginning, before we even made NSU . . . we wanted to do a walkout," Marquez emphasizes. "That had been sticking with us until it was the right moment." Now—as state legislators gathered in Newark to discuss draconian budget cuts to the state's poorest cities—was that time.

Cabañas and the students conducted "very intense" organizing in the weeks leading up to the action, sending out groups of students to flyer "every morning before school and every afternoon after school" at various high schools.[41] Their handbill blared "IT'S TIME TO REVOLT!," with a scowling photo of Christie followed by the message "WALKOUT AGAINST: Budget Cuts, Teacher Layoffs, School Closings, Chris Christie."[42] In this outreach, they did receive some support from teachers, such as then NEW activist Michael Iovino, who encouraged participation at Technology High School, where he worked. As part of the social media outreach, the NSU, with assistance from NJCU, created a video with a "Star Wars music theme. . . . They go around the table and each kid says the reasons why they're doing this walkout and then they get a picture of all of them standing together fifty or sixty kids."[43] Cabañas also oversaw trainings for marshals on how to respond to various scenarios, including "a principal locking the door on the day of the walkout." The latter was a real threat. Indeed, because of the increasing pushback the NSU was facing from administrators, the student activists, "just before the walkout . . . hashed it out" and "decided we needed a leadership structure," with Bazile being elected the first president of the NSU. "The week leading up to the walkout was really scary," Bazile recounts, "because the district was putting out threats everywhere, saying students were going to get suspended . . . expelled if you walked out." Yet, he adds, the repression was uneven.

> Our school, Science, was really plain and clear. . . . I really respect our principal Lamont Thomas for just putting [things] out clearly to us. It was like "we understand why you guys feel the need to do this [but] it is against the district policy to do this and you will be disciplined accordingly but we will not stop you, we are not going to lock the doors."

In the end, "the only discipline we got," Bazile recalls regarding Science High, "was like school-wide detention, we stayed like fifteen minutes in the auditorium together and had Mr. Rippey give us a freaking history lesson. It was great."

Other high schools, such as Central High School, where Ras Baraka, a city councilman and recently announced mayoral candidate, was principal, "welcomed us with open arms," allowing Bazile and other NSU activists to address the weekly "Big Tuesday" meeting, where the entire student body assembled. Bazile's fighting message to the assembly, which Baraka welcomed, was "hey if you don't like what's going on in the district you don't have to just sit back and take it, you don't have to just listen to your administrators saying this is the way." He added that "we know history tells us, this is why I just love Mr. Rippey, because I was like [in his address to Central High students] history tells us that we can organize for power and we have power, we can change things, right." Bazile's comments highlight how Rippey and other insurgent educators were exemplars of what Kenneth Saltman terms a "critical pedagogy," "in which teachers . . . help students theorize their experiences of oppression to *collectively address* the systemic and structural causes of that oppression."[44]

East Side and its principal, Mario Santos, in contrast, represented the iron fist response to crush any collective attempts to challenge power. Whereas in some schools, NSU activists were able to "post flyers in the stairwells and make big abstract signs with them so you can't ignore them," at East Side, Santos barred that kind of activity. For

136 || REBEL CITY?

example, in the days leading up to the March NJPAC protest, one East Side teacher recalls, "students put up signs all along the lockers about Anderson and to come out and protest the next day." In response,

> Santos not only took them down but actually had the video cameras, the videotape of the still shots of who the students were [that put up the signs] and these were all the honor students of the junior or senior class . . . and he called them all in and really scared them.

To get around the repressive environment imposed by the Santos regime, NSU relied on the "debaters . . . to distribute in schools we couldn't reach." Then, on the day of the walkout, Santos stepped up the repression, according to Bazile.

> East Side, holy crap, he [Santos] was locking doors . . . kids were like getting thrown by security officers, beaten by security officers, when they tried to leave, it was just a different school climate. Science Park was just chilled, the staff, they trusted us more than at the more comprehensive schools.

According to a report by one East Side student, who wanted to remain anonymous for fear of reprisals, "the principal yelled at us. . . . He said that it's pointless to protest for your education when you're leaving school." When the student and ten of his classmates met in the lobby to walk out, "there was a lockdown at the time, so students were deterred and went back to class," while outside, they saw a security guard wielding a bat.[45]

Santos's hardline approach was mirrored at the historic Weequahic High School, located in the city's heavily black and poor South Ward. There a student reported a story similar to East Side: "We can't leave. They lock[ed] the doors and put us on lockdown," he wrote in an email to *Truthout* reporter Rania Khalek.[46]

Anderson, in a testament to the power of disruption, made a desperate plea to the NSU to call off the walkout, but to no avail. Despite verbal threats and physical violence, more than one thousand students, from six high schools, marched out of their schools at 10:00 A.M. and to the rally in front of Rutgers Law School. Students were joined by

REBEL CITY? || **137**

community activists and teachers, such as Freda Barrow, who took a personal day to support the students and register her opposition to the cuts.[47] At Science Park, nearly "the entire school, like five hundred kids," walked out the front doors after receiving a perfunctory warning and encouragement to stay safe by the principal. "When Central High School joined us," Bazile recalls, "it was equally impressive as Science marching down Washington Street." At the protest, the NSU organized "an inside outside operation," with several students testifying inside at the hearing, where they spoke out against the cuts and demanded that Newark get "full funding" as required by the New Jersey Supreme Court under the Abbott rulings. Bazile, the NSU president, oversaw "protest duty outside" as he "bullhorned" the overflowing crowd.[48]

The action, which was widely covered in the press, put the NSU on the map as a major political player in Newark and, indeed, New Jersey politics. "People weren't taking us seriously, just kind of dismissing us because we were students," Marquez recalls. "But once we did the walkout, I feel that changed completely." From Bazile's perspective, the "Newark Student Union had made its debut, because we had branded it, the Newark Student Union Walkout. . . . We just really felt like an organization at that point, we were like we got our chops now."

The power of the students, and the growing movement challenging Christie, Booker, Anderson, and the movement-from-above implementers, was on display at the first advisory school board meeting following the walkout, which Anderson conveniently skipped due to a "prior commitment." At the April 23 meeting, the three candidates of the Ras Baraka–backed "Children First" slate, who swept the recent board election, took their seats. Shavar Jeffries, closely allied to the charters and Anderson's strongest backer on the board, had stepped down the meeting before after his three-year term ended (2010–13) to run for mayor. Acknowledging the shifting political winds, Jeffries and Booker, unlike in previous years, failed to field a slate "since it would only help the Baraka forces by giving them a bigger target."[49] As the first order of business, the Baraka-allied board chair Antoinette Baskerville-Richardson introduced a no-confidence resolution— unanimously approved—in Anderson's leadership and policies.

The board then heard from a parade of students, teachers, and community activists who praised the board's no-confidence vote and, especially, the student walkout. Many, including NSU president Bazile, who was among the first speakers, demanded "amnesty" for the students who faced disciplinary action for participating in the walkout. Underscoring the significance of the action was the presence of longtime activist Lawrence Hamm—chairman of the People's Organization for Progress (POP) and former student activist at Arts High School during the high point of the Black Power era of the late 1960s and early 1970s—who had "not," as he explained to the audience, "spoken before a Newark Board of Education meeting for thirty-nine years." He joined the chorus of those calling for dropping all charges against the student "heroes and champions of our community."

Branden Rippey, of the NEW Caucus, saluted the students and called for "building a movement" of students, teacher unions, and the larger working class against the "billionaires" leading the charge to "destabilize" public education to justify its privatization. Del Grosso, of the NTU, who just months before had praised Anderson after negotiating a new contract, was forced, in the face of the growing movement, to join the chorus denouncing Anderson and her agenda—although he did not mention anything about the student walkout. Further underscoring the shifting winds was the intervention by Junius Williams, director of the foundation-funded ALI housed at Rutgers University and who had supported Anderson's appointment while serving on the superintendent selection committee. He passionately praised the students and called for all disciplinary actions to be dropped. At the same time, while saluting the students' activism, ALI's own student group, the Youth Media Symposium, did not join the organizing for a walkout, which highlights the political constraints that come with foundation funding.[50]

ASSESSING THE MOVEMENT

As Anderson's second full year as superintendent came to a close at the end of the 2012–13 academic year, it was clear that a major movement from below had emerged that was unleashing its own campaign of disruption. One feature of this movement was the dissident union caucus that was mounting a challenge to the NTU leadership, who had effectively become partners, collaborators, in the rollback of various Keynesian artifacts, policies, agreements, and institutions and the rollout of their neoliberal counterparts. The NTU won collective bargaining rights through the strikes—mass disruption—of 1970 and 1971, for which authorities sent Del Grosso, Petino, former president Graves, and scores of other teachers to prison. Now these same former rank-and-file teachers, who had become part of a "distinct stratum of full-time professional trade union officials," invoked TINA ideology to legitimate passivism.[51] In the face of Christie's election, the union leadership argued that rank-and-file teachers had no alternative but to "take their lumps" in the form of massive cutbacks in education funding. When education commissioner Chris Cerf threatened AFT chief Randi Weingarten with busting the union, the NTU and AFT leadership again argued that they had no alternative but to accept unprecedented concessions. In fact, Weingarten, far from signing begrudgingly, stood with Chris Christie, the teachers' tormentor, to praise the concessionary deal.[52]

In response to the movement from above, and NTU's incorporation into this agenda, the NEW Caucus organized an alternative, class-conscious, social movement unionism. The NEW activists engaged in both the inter- and intraclass struggles by uniting with students and community activists in protest against budget cuts, while educating and mobilizing members against the concessionary contract signed by the union leadership. In the streets, at school board meetings, and through internal education, NEW engaged in an intense ideological struggle. It framed its battle as a class struggle pitting the billionaire- and philanthrocapitalist-driven movement from above against the multiracial working class, of which "education workers" were an integral component.

Although the NTU was able to gain membership acquiescence to the concessionary contract, the NEW-led opposition continued to grow. In a second electoral challenge, the NEW Caucus slate took eighteen seats of the thirty-one-seat executive board in the May 2013 biennial union election, with Rippey nearly ousting—589 to 580—longtime president Del Grosso.[53] If he had won, Rippey says, "I would have been radical, I would have been openly socialist but conscious of how you get nonsocialists active in the union movement." NEW planned, through its majority on the board, to introduce several resolutions to radically change the union, including creating two full-time organizing positions; organizing fight-backs against Anderson's

140 || REBEL CITY?

neoliberal reforms; establishing a political education series; and firing or demoting John Abeigon, who was being groomed to succeed the ailing Del Grosso.[54]

The NEW Caucus was also able to jump geographical scales and connect with the growing dissident union movement among teachers across the country. NEW became a member of the newly emerging United Caucuses of Rank-and-File Educators (UCORE), a national alliance of dissident "social justice unionists." UCORE, like NEW, combined "bread-and-butter issues" with struggles "to create equity and keep public schools in the hands of communities rather than private enterprises."[55] Rippey and other NEW Caucus activists met and networked with their fellow dissident leaders and reform caucuses. These included Karen Lewis in Chicago, whose Chicago Teachers Union (CTU) had led a powerful strike in fall 2012 that energized the emerging national movement against corporate education reform, and Alex Caputo in Los Angeles, whose reform insurgents had recently taken power. In Newark, Rippey envisioned "opening a third front."

At the board meetings, parents and other community activists stepped up their denunciations of school closings, colocations with charters, and other elements of the corporate reform agenda that Anderson was overseeing. This combativeness, a Newark culture of resistance, put the neoliberal reformers on the defensive by shattering any appearance of a consensus over the reform agenda they so desperately desired. The power of the denunciations and disruptions carried out at the board meetings explains why the ministers drew from the toxic wellspring of racialized underclass ideology to smear this resistance as simply part of a "dysfunctional . . . Newark Attitude."

The NSU represented the most dramatic example of disruptive power. The mass student walkouts disrupted the "institutionally regulated cooperation" that the Anderson administration, and its political backers, needed to impose and legitimate its agenda. According to the "civil rights movement of our day" exponents, the education battle pitted, as New York City school chancellor Joel Klein put it, "a system that works pretty well for bureaucrats, politicians, and adults . . . but not kids."[56] Hundreds of students, backed by radical teachers, parents, and community activists, walking out of their classrooms to protest the reformers' disruption agenda injected cognitive dissonance into the corporate reform narrative. When ideological forms of power failed to produce the desired results, Anderson resorted to pleading

REBEL CITY? || **141**

and many of her underlings to verbal threats and physical violence to contain the activation of disruptive power. The ability of students to mount the walkouts was also aided, in many cases, by the other interdependent relations in which they were embedded, particularly sympathetic teachers and opportunistic black political challengers.

Rebel City?

Nilsen and Cox conceptualize movements as nondeterministic "processes . . . centered on a widening and deepening of the scope of collective action from below."[57] Newark's movement from below during 2010–13 clearly passed from what the authors term "militant particularism" to a full-fledged "campaign." *Militant particularism*, drawing from the works of David Harvey and Raymond Williams, refers to "forms of struggle that . . . deploy specific skills and knowledge in open confrontation with a dominant group in a particular time, in a particular conflict over a particular issue."[58] But by 2013, a *campaign*, that is, a broader, deeper, and sustained level of struggle, had been forged that united "militant particularisms across social and spatial boundaries . . . around a generalized challenge to the dominant forces."[59] Clearly the students, insurgent teachers, and community activists had congealed into an oppositional force *against* the "dominant forces" in the form of the philanthrocapitalist drivers and their implementers in and around the Booker regime. The movement from below established not only new organizations but new forms, such as NEW, which grouped teachers and community members, to fight back against the attacks.

The insurgent forces in Newark also forged ties with forces across the country—such as UCORE and the Philadelphia Student Union—involved in similar defensive struggles. Yet, the picture was uneven, with less advanced forces simultaneously engaged in episodic, militant particularism and demobilized once their immediate, localized grievance was addressed. Exemplars were the administrators, teachers, parents, and students from Camden Elementary School who chartered a bus to attend the March 2012 school board meeting to oppose their designation as a "failing school" and thus conversion into a "renew school." "Kiesha Robinson . . . [and] her 11-year-old son, Deandre, was among dozens of Camden students to," as a local reporter emphasized, "plead with the nine-member board and Anderson Tuesday to save the school and its staff." The protests forced Anderson to back off, which led Robinson and other parents and teachers to "bec[o]me more at ease."[60] Thus, once their deeply felt, particularist issue was addressed, the Camden community demobilized.

Nonetheless, despite these important advances, the movement in Newark had not reached the level of a "social movement project," or what Harvey would refer to as a "rebel city." They were still at the stage of fighting *against* various elements of the corporate reform project but had not yet put forth and begun struggling *for* an alternative political economic project that "sees the social whole as the object of challenge or transformation."[61] There had been, though, some incipient advances in that direction, spearheaded by POP, a local community group. Following a yearlong protest in 2011 and 2012 for a national jobs program, POP held, in collaboration with several other groups, including NEW, a People's Conference on Jobs, Peace, Equality, and Justice.[62] The conference was to debate and agree on a broad set of demands to unite various struggles, or "silos," and a plan of action to win them. The conference, held in Newark on October 19, 2013, agreed overwhelmingly on the central demand of "jobs for all" through a mass, direct-government-employment public works and services program, open for all, paid for by taxing the rich and slashing military spending.

The demand for a democratically controlled jobs and public services program, paid for by taxing the wealth and income of the rich and ending the war machine, was, in essence, a call for what Henri Lefebvre termed a "Right to the City." It was a demand for democratic, popular control over the "processes of urbanization, over the ways in which cities are made and remade."[63] Indeed, Harvey himself, in his work *Rebel Cities*, envisioned that the demand for "democratic control over the production and use of the surplus" would most likely come about by the "uniting of various oppositional movements" as happened, on a local, limited scale, in Newark.[64] Thus the Newark case shows the ways the working class not only resisted the imposition of the neoliberal SSA simply by defending the old reformist Keynesian predecessor but also put forth a social democratic cum socialist alternative.

Of course, assembling the various groups, and developing a radical demand, while an important advance, is not the same as beginning a united campaign of struggle to put it on the agenda, let alone winning it. This is where the movement fell short. After adopting a comprehensive "jobs and public services for all" demand, the attendees held preliminary discussions on the action component of the conference, but without agreeing on any concrete steps to take. One of the central stumbling blocks that emerged in the discussions was whether this movement should run its own candidates on the platform decided democratically at the conference. The objection to this action proposal reflected the unwillingness of some activists to break with the Democratic Party, which historically has been a key weapon of containment by movements from above. In the end, no joint action materialized over the demand the one hundred plus attendees, representing groups ranging from peace to health care, unanimously endorsed.[65]

Despite this unevenness, the varied elements of the movement from below in the early 2010s in Newark had altered the class power relations in the city. The most significant expression of movement power was forcing the early exit of Booker, the movement from above's prized political leader, before seeing through the full neoliberal makeover of the school district. In the face of growing opposition to the defining policy of his decade-and-a-half-long political career, along with defeat of his city water privatization plans and a failed effort to install a political ally on the city council, Booker announced, in December 2012, that he would not seek a third term and instead would run for the U.S. Senate. An observation made by a local supporter of Booker's school reform agenda to the *New York Times* in late 2012 highlights the outgoing mayor's increasing political isolation:

> How come you can't persuade the people who elected you twice? ... When's the last time you did a town hall? Why do we have to go to Twitter to find out what you're talking about?[66]

When the incumbent senator, Frank Lautenberg, died in June 2013, Booker won the October special election and resigned as mayor the same month.[67]

Ras Baraka, as Booker exited the scene, filled the political vacuum as he presented himself as the political voice, the electoral arm, of the movement from below. In May 2013, as the opposition to Anderson reached a crescendo at the end of the school year, Baraka introduced, and the city council passed unanimously, a resolution calling for a moratorium on all of Anderson's reforms.[68] A mayoral race then heated up, with Ras Baraka, *Star-Ledger* editor Tom Moran lamented, "as the hard-core opponent of Anderson's reforms," while Shavar Jeffries, the former school board president, remained "the best hope for education reform."[69] Clearly the movement from below had upended the Booker-led BUR, an opening that Baraka worked to fill.

How, in the face of the growing disruption from below, and without their former prized political asset, would Anderson and her allies in the school reform movement respond? Would they, as "her political support in the city collapsed," pull back and seek conciliation?[70] Or, in contrast, would they step up their own campaign of disruption as this leading reform militant began the third year of her tenure?

5

The Clash of Disruptors

WHO WOULD PREVAIL? 2013–2014

Killing a dysfunctional system and building back up for the children is messy.

> —Cami Anderson, school superintendent defending the "One Newark" enrollment system, quoted in a *Forbes* article

Closing, redesigning, reopening, all the "re"-words, are just fancy words for closing a school and destabilizing a community. . . . One Newark is a direct attack on every single resident in Newark.

> —Kristen Towkanik, Newark Student Union president speaking at the January 2014 Newark Public Schools Advisory Board meeting

The fiftieth anniversary of the 1963 March on Washington for Jobs and Freedom was obviously an important date for champions of the "civil rights struggle of our lifetime." But for these twenty-first-century anti-racist partisans of neoliberal school reform, the golden anniversary was framed in purely RD terms, shorn of march organizer A. Philip Randolph's demand for a social democratic federal jobs program. To commemorate their narrow RD interpretation of this milestone, Cami Anderson and Joel Klein held a chat with the head of a then new anti-union and pro-charter group—former CNN anchor Campbell Brown. Though the August date was consciously chosen to link school privatization with the civil rights movement, this gathering was not held at some cramped church basement or union hall. Instead, it took place at the comfortable campus confines of the Google Corporation as part of the tech industry powerhouse's "Zeitgeistmind" series of "top global thinkers and leaders."[1] Brown began the discussion by noting the contrast between the "disrupters in this room"—referring to the Silicon Valley tech world—"[who] are celebrated [while] *disruptors*

|| 145

146 || THE CLASH OF DISRUPTORS

in education are vilified." "Both of you," Brown went on, "have experienced that in a big way in trying to do your jobs. Has that been the hardest part?"[2]

Anderson, underscoring the importance of Klein and the Bloomberg regime in her own rise and the larger privatization movement, prefaced her response to the query by emphasizing what "a humbling experience" it was for her "to share the stage with this giant." From Anderson's perspective, Joel Klein—to whom she gushingly referred as a "rock star," the "Mick Jagger of school reform"—was a giant because he didn't back down in the face of resistance from the "education establishment." In contrast to the public school "bureaucrats," teacher unions, and "politicians" that make up the establishment, whom she denounced as "very wedded to the status quo that is horribly broken and willing to accept failure," Klein was a courageous fighter who "dared" to take them on. One example of Klein's maverick leadership was going outside establishment ranks and making her the first TFA alumnus to be appointed a school superintendent.

Anderson made it clear that, like her former boss, she would not back down in the face of the "establishment's" vilification. She would be as pugnacious and dogged in pursuit of the movement's missions as Klein, whom she lauded for "stepping on the gas" during his eight-year run as New York City's school superintendent. Inspired by Klein's example and the civil rights icon Dr. Martin Luther King Jr., she would not simply carry on but accelerate the campaign of disruption despite the increasingly vocal opposition. "On the anniversary of Dr. King's brilliant speech," Anderson reflected as she began her third year of imposing corporate school reform in Newark, "I find myself thinking about the fierce urgency of now on a daily basis . . . of what Dr. King called the poison, the elixir of gradualism."

"Despite the politics," she was committed to deepening the changes until all the schools became high performing as measured by the reformers. Repeating the movement's ideology, she argued that poverty was simply an excuse for poor outcomes. Experience, asserted the former head of the movement's New Leaders for New Schools teacher and administrator pipeline, shows that "we get radically different results from schools next to each other . . . and yet we still think that poor kids, and *particularly kids of color,* can't achieve academic excellence."[3] Therefore Anderson's race-reductionist solution to improving schools did not require changing political economy but rather recruiting excellent, committed teachers. To make room for what she called these new "change agents, and transformational leaders," required driving out or closing failing teachers, administrators, and schools.[4]

Thus, going into the 2013–14 school year, Anderson was committed, like her role model, to seeing through the radical "education innovations" that the stolid establishment had resisted for too long.[5] Nonetheless, despite her resoluteness to carry on, increasingly hostile forces were enveloping Anderson in the movement's Newark outpost. First, Cory Booker, her longtime comrade and defender, left City Hall in October 2013 before his term expired to take a recently vacated U.S. Senate seat. While Booker always had his eyes on higher office, the emerging mass movement against his signature policy of school privatization, as well as broad opposition to his attempt to sell off the water system, contributed to his early exit. Second, though she continued to receive unstinting support from Governor Christie, who controlled the local school district, he would begin to face his own political crisis in early 2014. Further adding to the superintendent's woes was the mayoral candidacy of Ras Baraka, who, deploying a competing racial justice ideology, would make "local control" of the schools and opposition to Anderson the centerpiece of his campaign.

The fourth, and most significant, challenge was the student movement. Anderson and her comrades legitimated and framed their movement as pitting, on one side, an uncaring, selfish, and racist "education establishment," particularly tenured teachers and their unions. Arrayed on the other side, according to the movement's racial justice narrative, were students, particularly African American and Latinx youth, who were victimized by those forces. The spectacle of thousands of students walking out of class, marching in the streets, and disrupting school board meetings, while receiving broad community support, including from rank-and-file teachers, complicated this story.

In this chapter, I address how this contest evolved over the course of the critical 2013–14 academic year as both sides prepared for war. I begin by contextualizing the conflict through an overview of the uneven development practices that funneled resources to the charters while starving the public schools, helping to create "market demand" for the former. I then turn to the rollout of Anderson's radical restructuring plan that aimed to further marginalize public schools and the firestorm of protest this generated among students, parents, and teachers, which emerged at schools, at board meetings, in churches, and in

148 || THE CLASH OF DISRUPTORS

the streets. Ras Baraka, the surging mayoral candidate, capitalized on these developments as he positioned himself, with the full backing and embrace of the NSU and NTU, as the electoral champion of the movement. The disruptive protests and unifying of the pro–public school movement horizontally frayed the pro-privatization forces as a faction among the black clergy broke off and the remaining core elite bickered over how to chart a new path. I conclude with a bloodied, politically isolated Anderson confronting an emboldened, yet contradictory, enemy in City Hall.

VOTING WITH THEIR FEET OR THROWN TO THE STREET?

In the third year of Anderson's reign, the centerpiece of her radical disruption plan was a new enrollment system. Modeled after New Orleans, where the school system underwent a mass privatization after Hurricane Katrina, parents would choose from a market-based "menu of options" among charters and traditional schools. Designed to further disrupt, to rupture, attachment to neighborhoods, families would no longer have a right to go to their neighborhood school. Public schools that faced declining enrollment and/or were designated as "failing" would be closed or restructured under various schemes. The plan, dubbed "One Newark," envisioned the charterization of nearly half the city's schools, which was the "measurable outcome" the five major philanthropies had forecasted when they made their $25 million grant in 2006.[6]

Anderson defended the government-created One Newark school market, and the expansion of charters that was at its core, as simply an effort "to align supply with demand." "Families," as a press statement issued by Anderson's office explained, "are 'voting with their feet' in search of excellence."[7] Anderson claimed she was only giving families, evidenced by charter waiting lists, what they wanted—the hallowed "freedom of choice" enshrined in neoliberal ideology. But what the superintendent did not add is how charter supporters at the local, state, and federal levels of government had, especially since the Christie–Booker pact, "systematically underfunded the public sector... [while] essentially placing its thumb on the scale for charters."[8] On the public side, as discussed in chapter 3, the Christie administration imposed deep cuts to public school funding, especially for poor districts, which openly flouted the state's school funding requirements under the Abbott court rulings.[9] In addition, Christie slashed the staff of the School Development Authority (SDA), the agency responsible for repairing and rebuilding crumbling inner-city schools, while not approving any new construction in the thirty-one districts that compose the SDA. Even in cases of an "imminent peril to the health and safety of students and staff," Christie's SDA approved few repairs.[10] Finally, Anderson used her power to continue closing public schools.

While the public sector was starved, officials, Republican and Democrat alike, opened the spigots for the charters. At the federal level, the Obama administration, which came to power a year before Christie, in 2009, helped tip the scales in favor of charters in various ways. One was the Race to the Top program that dangled grants to states and school districts—many starved for funds in the midst of the Great Recession—on the condition they establish new rules to facilitate the expansion of charters. Another important assist came through the Obama administration's interest-free Qualified School Construction Bonds (QSCBs), which were awarded to states for public school construction. Obama's education secretary, Arne Duncan, explicitly encouraged states to use the funds for charters.[11]

Christie embraced Duncan's directive, as his Economic Development Authority (EDA) directed all the QSCB awards to build charter schools, particularly in Newark. For example, in 2013 alone, the EDA allocated $125 million for charter construction, with $40 million in QSCB bonds awarded to the TEAM Academy Charter Schools in Newark, part of the KIPP chain. TEAM, and its influential board members, including Booker allies Amy Rosen and Tim Cardin and hedge fund manager Dan Adan, used complicated "creative financing" arrangements, involving various for-profit and nonprofit entities, to manage and leverage the bonds, which were not available to public schools. With the QSCB funds, and assistance of the state-controlled district, TEAM acquired the closed 18th Avenue public school, where it opened the chain's first high school. Likewise, the North Star Academy, part of the Uncommon charter chain, received $40 million to acquire and renovate two Newark public school properties.[12]

The Christie and Booker administrations also deployed $100 million in QSCB bonds and a host of other public subsidies to build the Teachers Village development in a long-disinvested section of downtown Newark. Underscoring the relationship between charters and gentrification, a NPS official touted the development as "bringing

150 || THE CLASH OF DISRUPTORS

a renaissance to the central ward."[13] The complex includes gleaming new buildings to house four charter schools, more than two hundred apartments geared ostensibly for teachers, and street-level retail.[14] Finally, the charters, and their support organizations, such as the NCSF, continued to receive generous foundation funding from which public schools were, for the most part, excluded. Although the $200 million raised through Zuckerberg's matching grant was routed through the Foundation for *Newark's* Future, most of the money went to better the future of pro-charter consultants and charter schools and to sell a concessionary union contract backed by supporters of charter, not public, schools.[15]

Thus the neoliberal reformers oversaw what Pauline Lipman terms "selective disinvestment," which, she emphasizes, is "linked to the selective devalorization and revalorization of urban space."[16] On one side, authorities either closed or starved the public schools of funds, while enrolling an increasingly larger percentage of higher-need and costlier special education and English as a second language students. On the other side, the charters, which used various strategies to dissuade or push out needier students, expanded in the city, with many of the new schools sprouting up, as Lipman would predict, in the revalorized downtown. Therefore, unsurprisingly, under Anderson's reign, the flow of students into the charters jumped considerably. By the beginning of the 2013 academic year, nearly 10 percent of Newark students were in charters, more than double the rate from 2009, when Christie was elected.[17]

The post-2009 stepped-up attack on the city's public schools built on the previous two decades of massive destabilization of the city's working-class residents wrought by mass public housing demolitions and the city's (and country's) skyrocketing home foreclosure rates preceding and during the Great Recession. The public schools, and their teachers, stood out as one stabilizing force in many Newark communities. The One Newark plan promised to rip up those remaining islands of stability, creating "huge disruptions in children's lives, adults' jobs, and long-standing community relationships with neighborhood schools."[18] But, as Marx demonstrated in his discussion of primitive accumulation in volume I of *Capital,* and Anderson's epigraph acknowledges, closing the public commons and forcing people to rely on the market for what they need and want is normally a messy, violent affair. This elite form of disruption is, Marxist economist Alan

Nasser explains, "the historic mission of capitalism . . . making people's ability to get what they need and want contingent upon their ability to strike a deal with the market, i.e. a deal that contributes directly or indirectly to the making of profit and accumulation of capital."[19] Anderson got busy with that historic mission and handling the political fallout.

RIPPING OFF THE BAND-AID

Anderson presented the general outline of the One Newark plan in a June 2013 closed-door meeting among her allies at the NJPAC. The invitees included fellow activist Mashea Ashton, the NCSF head and a comrade of Anderson from her New York City movement apprenticeship years. In an editorial in the *Star-Ledger* a few days before the NJPAC gathering, Ashton defended Anderson's reforms and denounced those who tried to "scapegoat" charter schools for the district's financial and enrollment woes. Far from pulling back, Ashton wanted to see a stepped-up effort to close "failing and underperforming schools" and acceleration of "charter growth" to "provide more high-quality school options to Newark families."[20]

Anderson, for her part, did not let Ashton and her other backers down. These included state education commissioner Chris Cerf, who encouraged her, as he introduced her at the NJPAC event, to "rip the Band-Aid off" and institute the changes they wanted to see. At the vetted, invitation-only meeting—with journalist Dale Russakoff among the invitees—Anderson announced that she would create an "online unified enrollment system for all district and charter schools," as had been done in New Orleans, the movement's model. Consistent with her denouncing of gradualism at the Google gathering, and understanding of school choice as the burning antiracist battle of our day, she committed to end the timidity of her first two years and dramatically expand the number of charters. The right of African American and Latinx parents to choose schools was paramount. "How dare we . . . say that they should be trapped in failed schools while we get our act together?"[21]

Over fall 2013, Anderson, and her well-compensated consultants, prepared the blueprints of what would be called the One Newark restructuring plan. Other than meetings with charter school executives, foundation funders, and a few select ministers, the general public was kept completely uniformed about what the Anderson team had in store. The reason, Anderson correctly surmised, was that her own campaign of disruption would be met "by political forces whose objective is to create disruption."[22] The potential, indeed likelihood, of popular resistance concerned some of her foundation backers. For example, the Victoria Foundation's Cooper-Basch thought Anderson was "one of the most talented educators and strategic thinkers that I have ever met" and shared the superintendent's assessment that "Newark parents are [voluntarily] voting with their (children's) feet" by enrolling in the city's expanding charter schools. Furthermore, she endorsed and celebrated that "Anderson was brought into Newark" to spearhead radical change as represented by One Newark. Nonetheless, she was concerned about its ambitiousness. "The sheer volume of disruption, coupled with the lack of community engagement prior to the announcement of the changes," was, Cooper-Basch wrote in her study of Victoria's philanthropic work in Newark, producing "confusion and anger throughout the city." In the end, the "foundation community . . . issued a qualified letter of support signed by nine local foundations," though other elements of the funding community, such as NTE chief Danis, were much more supportive of One Newark.[23]

In contrast to the uneasiness among the local philanthropic arm of the movement, Anderson enjoyed the full backing of Governor Christie. In September, at the beginning of the 2013–14 school year, he publicly lauded her for doing a "great job" and announced that her initial three-year contract would be renewed at the end of the year. Yet, the support from Christie, delivered in his pugnacious style, only further antagonized Anderson's opponents in Newark. "I don't care about the community criticism," Christie snarled in making his announcement to reappoint Anderson. "We run the school district in Newark, not them." The comment provided perfect fodder for the Baraka campaign, which retorted that Christie "told the truth at least. He does run the school district, not us. That's why we need to get rid of him."[24]

Anderson's team finally released its plan to the public in mid-December 2013, a timing presumably chosen with the hope that the ensuing holiday break would cool out the expected outrage. Clearly abandoning the "elixir of gradualism," the shock therapy plan called for restructuring more than one-third of the district's seventy-four schools under various rubrics.[25] Some would be closed or handed over to a charter operator, with no guaranteed right of placement for former students or staff. Others would face "colocation," a hostile private–public "partnership" takeover, in which a charter occupies—disrupts—a section of the public school's classrooms and facilities. Taking a page from the Gates smaller schools initiative pursued in New York under Klein, three high schools would be transformed into smaller academies. Another set of schools would be designated as "renews." Receiving this designation would require, as done in previous years, all staff at the targeted school to reapply; accept the new regimen, including a longer school day; and give the principal the right to decide who was rehired. Without improvement—and the schools previously renewed had their test scores decline—the next step would be closure. In addition, to make real the movement's hallowed goal of "school choice," under the new enrollment system, families would rank their choices from a list of public and charter schools (of those charters that agreed to participate).[26]

In a particularly significant development in Anderson's elite form of disruption, families would no longer have a right to attend their neighborhood school. In addition to convenience and loss of community attachments, this new policy raised safety concerns for some parents. Now they would have to send their children across the city, including crossing unmarked, yet dangerous, gang boundaries. Further adding to the disruption in people's lives, many families relied on older siblings for day care of their younger children. Yet, the restructuring, including the reduction in grade levels at certain schools, promised to disrupt this fragile safety net for poor families.[27]

Anderson's office did hold meetings at schools following the release of One Newark to explain the new plan and the fate of respective schools. Parents expressed disbelief and outrage at these gatherings, particularly at elementary schools like Hawthorne and Belmont Runyon, which were slated for a charter takeover and renewal, respectively. On the evening of December 17, at the same time Anderson sent her aides to meet with parents at local schools to explain the plan, she had to face the music at the first school board meeting since the release of One Newark. The pummeling started early. Board president Antoinette Baskerville-Richardson opened the meeting denouncing the "corrupt process" that produced the plan. Continuing on a self-determination theme that echoed Baraka, she emphasized, to wide applause, that reform "can't be imported or imposed. . . . It cannot be based on failed models from New Orleans or anywhere else" but

154 || THE CLASH OF DISRUPTORS

instead must be "indigenous." She concluded by calling for a moratorium on all changes until the community had real input through, taking another page from Baraka, an "education convention." The crowd, with its incessant booing and catcalls, then shut down Anderson's attempt to present a PowerPoint presentation on One Newark. A parade of public speakers, including NEW activist Nancy Gianni, NAACP chapter president Deborah Smith-Gregory, and Baraka and fellow city councilperson Mildred Crump, then denounced the plan.[28]

The fight-backs at the school board meeting then flowed back to the schools targeted for closing. Some began to channel their outrage into "militant particularist" struggles to keep the schools open, which in some cases also connected to the broader campaign to defend public education. On Friday, December 20, a few days after being informed that Hawthorne, a K–8 school, would be turned over to a charter operator offering only grades K–4, PTA president Grace Sergio organized a morning demonstration involving parents, children, teachers, and community activists. The action, called "Fight Back Friday," which would continue through the rest of the school year, was organized in cooperation with the NTU. The NEW activists who now served on the NTU executive board successfully pressured the union to engage in public protests against Anderson's latest campaign of elite disruption. Teachers and parents organized Fight Back Fridays at other schools as well, but Hawthorne's battle became the most sustained, thanks to Sergio's persistence and support of the NTU and NEW.

At the December 20 protest, Sergio was joined by mayoral candidate Ras Baraka. Later in the day, he organized his own rally and press conference at Weequahic High School in his South Ward district, which was targeted for closure. Consistent with his campaign theme, Baraka denounced, not the reforms themselves, but rather the lack of democratic input that amounted to a denial of self-determination. He also made clear, as in the past, that he was not opposed to charters; rather, he criticized their lack of preparedness to handle kids with special needs, as would be required under One Newark.[29]

Christie, who coasted to a November 2013 reelection victory and was preparing for a presidential bid, met with Anderson privately the day after Christmas and promised his full support regardless of how intense the pushback got. Their fates were intimately tied. Christie's ability to oversee a bipartisan-supported school privatization makeover in a majority-minority city was central to gaining the confidence

THE CLASH OF DISRUPTORS || **155**

of the Wall Street interests he would need to be a serious candidate. In a further form of assistance to Anderson, at the end of December, Christie finally released $100 million from the SDA for new school construction, the first time since taking office. Then, in his January state of the state address, he stopped to greet Anderson on his way to the podium and, in his address, saluted her "bold action" taken as superintendent. While acknowledging that "her efforts haven't always been met without skepticism," he emphasized that she was still "a true partner with Newark." Although known for his harsh attacks on teachers, he showed his softer side with his handpicked superintendent of the state's largest city, letting the crowd know that "Cami is here with us today—Cami, thank you for your commitment to our kids."[30]

THE NEWARK SPRING AND THE REPUBLIC OF FEAR

Christie's fulsome praise at his January address belied the fact that his ability to assist Anderson was already on the wane. By this time, early in his second term, the governor's Bridgegate scandal had already exploded and would occupy Christie's attention and contribute to dooming his own once-promising presidential aspirations. Furthermore, public backing from Christie simply poured more fuel on the fire in Newark and made Anderson, as the embodiment of state control, a central target of the movement. The holiday break, far from demobilizing the movement, was simply a prelude to what would be the most intense, sustained wave of disruption to date. What Anderson hoped would simply be an episodic, "December-palooza" outburst of anger would instead become a sustained, well-organized Newark Spring.[31]

By the new year, the mayoral race—which was clearly shaping up as a matchup between Baraka and Shavar Jeffries, the former school board member and pro-charter advocate—was becoming a national referendum on school reform. Baraka, who had placed the issue of local control at the center of his campaign, now further embraced the burgeoning movement, which he would ride to office. On January 15, less than a week after his father and political mentor, Amiri Baraka, died at age seventy-nine, the mayoral hopeful held a "Mass Community Meeting to Stop School Closures" at the Hopewell Baptist Church.[32] The location was a sign of the shifting winds as the pastor, Joe Carter, had backed Christie in his recent 2013 reelection bid and

156 || THE CLASH OF DISRUPTORS

praised the governor's education reforms, and Christie had attended an ecumenical service there for his second inauguration.[33]

The Baraka campaign–organized event brought together parents, teachers, alumni, and others who were mobilizing across the city against Anderson's plan. Among the speakers were four principals whose South Ward elementary schools were targeted for conversion to a KIPP-run charter school (Hawthorne and Bragaw Avenue) or an early child learning center (Maple) or were being forced into the "renew" category (Belmont Runyon). Grady James, the principal of Hawthorne Elementary School, questioned the decision because his school's test scores had not only increased under his tenure but had done so at one of the highest rates in the state. In addition, there was an active PTA, the teachers had a collaborative relationship with the principal, and all this was accomplished while resources had been stripped over the previous several years and repair requests went unheeded for the nineteenth-century-built structure.[34] The gathering further strengthened the burgeoning movement to keep schools open, with morning pickets being mounted at targeted schools, such as the Friday, January 18, action organized by emerging citywide leader Grace Sergio at Hawthorne.[35]

As the movement gained steam, Anderson struck back, but in a way that highlighted her weaknesses and those of the movement she represented. The historical Achilles' heel of the reformers was their inability to gain popular consent to their agenda. But, as long as the opposition remained latent, or limited to sporadic outbursts, the reformers could ignore them. Now, as a full-fledged, sustained movement from below began to emerge, challenging Anderson's shock therapy program, the state-imposed superintendent resorted to repressive measures to hold back the tide. At noon on Friday, January 17, two days after the forum at Hopewell Baptist Church, and the same day as Fight Back Friday morning pickets of parents, teachers, and community supporters at several of the targeted schools, Anderson's office ordered the four principals to report to the central office. There Vanessa Rodriguez, Anderson's enforcer, who carried the venture philanthropy–informed title of "chief talent officer," hand-delivered them letters explaining that that they had been suspended pending an investigation of the "incident that occurred" at the January 15 forum. A fifth principal, Lisa Brown of Ivy Hill Elementary School, was also suspended after she defended the school's PTO president, a frequent Anderson critic. In addition,

Anderson ordered the suspension of a central office clerical worker who was overheard criticizing, while in the lavatory, the suspension of the principals.[36]

This atmosphere led Bob Braun, a former *Star-Ledger* reporter who wrote a widely read education blog, to describe the increasingly repressive atmosphere in the Anderson-run district as the "Republic of Fear."[37] Braun had been a critic of teachers' unions as a longtime *Star-Ledger* education reporter and in his 1972 book *Teachers and Power*. In retirement, though, he became highly critical of the reformers and shared his views through his recently created and widely movement-read, muckraking blog. Braun's support for the movement through his reporting, which began in June 2013 in the wake of the first NSU-led walkouts, was an important asset and testament to the growing ideological influence of antiprivatization forces.

CAMI'S GOTTA GO!

Rosa Luxemburg noted, in her study of the mass strike process, that when movements are in ascendancy, when they are raising new demands and bringing larger layers into the struggle, repression by the opposing class forces tends simply to spur on the movement. This dynamic was clearly at play in Newark. The suspensions of the principals, and other forms of repression, were the equivalent of throwing fuel on a rapidly growing fire. Ominously, those flames began to engulf Anderson, who became the embodiment of the hated reform agenda and repression against the opposition. As Ross Danis, one of Anderson's chief advisors, noted in reference to his movement comrade, "as soon as an issue becomes associated with you, the quickest way you get rid of the issue is getting rid of you." This personalization was given a pictorial representation in the NSU's large, iconic portrait of Anderson (and Christie), first introduced as the movement exploded in January, with "Liar" written in red across her forehead as symbolic blood dripped down her face.

Anderson was consumed by the fires of a large, angry crowd that turned out for the January 28 school board meeting—the first since the suspensions of the five principals. Those gathered turned an ostensible school board meeting into a marathon four-hour rally of disruption against One Newark and Anderson. The disruptions began early, at the five-minute mark, as the NSU began raising the chant "Parents,

FIGURE 1. From left to right: Roberto Cabañas, Leah Owens, and Branden Rippey at a May 13, 2015, rally against Anderson's school "turnaround" plans. Photograph by Paul Chinnery Photography.

teachers, students unite, same struggle, same fight!" These and other chants, including "Cami's gotta go," which emerged early in the meeting, and even a NSU march within the auditorium, were interspersed among some seventy-five speakers who signed up to passionately denounce, as former teacher Lauren Williams called it, the "dismantling of Newark public schools."

Among those who received the loudest applause was the new NSU president, and Science High junior, Kristin Towkanik, who called the One Newark plan "a direct attack on the students, community and the teachers in the Newark public schools." With impressive poise, the sixteen-year-old lectured Anderson that "closing, redesigning, reopening, all the 're'-words, are just fancy words for closing a school and destabilizing a community." Highlighting a major concern for parents, the NSU president denounced that "there is no way for a student to achieve when he has to take two buses . . . when he has to cross gang lines to get to his school." Instead of closing public schools, she called for "fixing the public schools we have now." Reflecting the growing unity of this struggle, which was forging solidarity among immigrants and native-born, black, white, and Latinx, from all the city's five wards,

Towkanik concluded that "One Newark is a direct attack on every single resident in Newark."

Ras Baraka, the surging mayoral candidate riding the tide of protest, followed up his December board appearance by demanding a "moratorium on all school closings" and all the measures under One Newark. He, like many of the other speakers, denounced the repression, calling for "fair treatment for all Newark school employees and zero tolerance for bullying and intimidation." Rising to a climax, he demanded "the immediate removal of"—emphasizing her imposed, outsider status that was central to his self-determinationist campaign message—"*state superintendent* Cami Anderson."[38] The crowd roared its approval, as many jumped to their feet and chanted "Cami's gotta go! Cami's gotta go!" Baraka's intervention further legitimated the demand for her dismissal that was first shouted at the beginning of the meeting and would become a staple of future protests.[39]

The knockout punch came at about the three-hour mark when Natasha Allen, a parent and an activist in Baraka's "Newark Anti-Violence Coalition," made her intervention. Exemplifying Nilsen and Cox's insight that popular "resistance often draws on . . . appropriations and inversions of ideologies of dominance," Allen pointed out the contradiction between parents ostensibly offered "choice" while "annihilating our choice" to keep kids "in our neighborhood schools." Joining a growing chorus, she called on Anderson "to pack your bags and go." Then, in what would prompt Anderson to walk out—along with her team—and fail to ever return to a School board meeting, Allen delivered an RD-informed rhetorical strike directed at the self-identified anti-racist: "I'm trying to figure out, do you not want for your brown babies what we want for ours?" As Anderson and her entourage left the dais the crowd cheered and took up the chant "Whose schools? Our schools!"[40]

THE AFT BUREAUCRACY POSTURES OPPOSITIONAL

AFT president Randi Weingarten's appearance at the January school board meeting, where she declared in her address that "the nation is watching, Newark," highlighted the national significance and growing strength of the movement in New Jersey's largest city. Weingarten, of course, had never lost sight of Newark. She had worked closely with

160 || THE CLASH OF DISRUPTORS

Anderson, Cerf, and Christie, acknowledging during her intervention that "I've known Cami for a long time." Indeed, she had. As discussed in chapter 3, Weingarten personally negotiated a 2012 union contract with Anderson, Cerf, and Christie that consensually introduced merit pay and other neoliberal reforms. She even sat down with Christie on the national *Morning Joe* show thirteen months before her oppositional school board appearance to tout the concessionary contract. Now, in the face of the growing movement, Weingarten, like Baraka, whose campaign the AFT and other unions were strongly backing, began to posture combative. Nonetheless, even at this public gathering, where the lawyer turned full-time union official gave a fiery speech before the working-class crowd, she concluded by making a "plea" to her professional managerial class counterpart for cooperation with the union bureaucracy: "We are asking you, please, change your mind, work together with us, let's fix, not close, public schools."[41]

The shift in Newark was part of a national effort of containment by the AFT in the face of a burgeoning national movement against corporate school reform most dramatically represented by the 2012 Chicago school strike. In spring 2013, just months after the Chicago school strike, the AFT and the NEA, along with the Service Employees International Union and several foundation-funded community groups, held a national conference to found the Alliance to Reclaim Our Schools (AROS). Academic and fellow full-time AFT union official Michael Fabricant and his frequent coauthor Michelle Fine described the gathering as an effort by a "number of national organizations with historic commitments to public education . . . [for] coordinating and scaling up . . . emergent, scattered movements." Yet, despite Fabricant and Fine's effusive praise, AROS was hostile to including the new militant union reform caucuses emerging, such as NEW and UCORE—the national alliance of reform caucuses—or non-foundation-funded community groups that were also committed to defending public education.[42]

In December 2013, the newly formed alliance, which included NJCU's parent organization, the CPD, held a National Day of Action to Reclaim Public Education in sixty cities across the country. Again highlighting the significance of the Newark battlefield, Weingarten came to Newark as part of the national day of action. The AFT and NTU worked with the NSU and NJCU to lead a march of some two hundred to the NPS office to demand "schools should be fixed, not closed" and blasting Anderson's policies. Yet, reflecting the top-down, tightly controlled nature of their organizing efforts, the leaders refused to include NEW as one of the endorsing organizations or to allow any members to speak at the rally.[43]

THE NSU–BARAKA ALLIANCE

Following the late January 2014 board meeting, movement activity reached a frenetic pace as the campaign against One Newark and Cami Anderson merged with Baraka's electoral insurgency. The alliance became official on February 18, when NJCU and NSU held a press conference with Baraka in a packed room at the downtown Robert Treat Hotel to announce their endorsement. The race, which by then was a two-person contest between Baraka and Jeffries after Puerto Rican city councilman Anibal Ramos's withdrawal, had become a citywide, and indeed national, referendum on the corporate school reform agenda.[44] Towkanik, who spoke for the NSU, explained in her remarks the relationship the student activists had with Baraka dating back to the April 2013 walkout. Towkanik lauded Baraka for always encouraging the NSU activists when he saw them, such as at the mayoral forum the NSU held in November. Now, with the official endorsement, the relationship became formalized, as the NSU, along with the CWA and NJCU, immersed itself in Baraka's campaign.

But the NSU also continued protests, including a March 18 demonstration, in alliance with NEW, that blocked downtown traffic and marched on the Prudential headquarters. This was followed by a rally, nine days later, at the state capitol of several hundred students, teachers, and parents of the burgeoning movement to press their demands. Among the most prominent attendees was the now-clear front-runner in the mayoral race, Baraka, and the most visible face of the student movement, Towkanik.[45] A week later, on April 2, the NSU flexed its muscles again by leading a mass walkout of some one thousand students, its second act of mass disruption in two years. The administration at Malcolm X Shabazz High School, whose name change from South Side was the product of student struggle to honor the slain icon, threatened students to prevent a walkout. In contrast, the NSU got a wholly different response from the now former principal of Central High, Ras Baraka.[46] "We asked him to . . . be one of the speakers at our second walkout for 2014 and he came, he did that." Underscoring

HEGEMONY AND THE BPMC

the close bonds that had developed, Towkanik adds that "after we endorsed him, it was like the solidarity was unspoken."

HEGEMONY AND THE BPMC

The failure of the school reformers to gain popular consent was, by spring 2014 and the emergence of a sustained mass movement, now a full-blown legitimacy crisis. Of course, the reformers had recognized the problem all along and had attempted to get "buy-in." The *Star-Ledger* and its editorial page editor, Tom Moran, had recognized this problem since the Christie–Booker alliance was forged and worked to address it. Moran regularly opened the paper's editorial page to Shavar Jeffries, whom the paper touted as a "standout" while he served on the school board and advocated for the neoliberal reform agenda. Also, like the *Star-Ledger,* Jeffries consistently emphasized the need for a "community-centered approach" to garner consent.[47] In the wake of the January 28 school board meeting that activists turned into a four-hour protest against Anderson and her reforms, Moran responded with an editorial touting her accomplishments and saluting her for "answering decades of failure in Newark with an ambition and urgency that's long overdue."

The question now before the movement from above was "how can Anderson deflate this opposition and rally support for reforms?" This required, from Moran's perspective, mobilizing the movement's mass base among charter parents "to press the school committee" to support Anderson's One Newark plan. Also of crucial importance for turning the tide of public opinion was having, the *Star-Ledger* editorial page editor underscored, "civic and religious leaders to step up and be counted." As he had done two years earlier, when community outrage greeted Anderson's disruption plans during her first year at the helm, Moran called on the local black elite to stand up. He pleaded that they call for a "respectful discussion" about One Newark and "push back" against what he called "provocateurs who are *disrupting* public meetings."[48]

The importance of the clerical wing of the BPMC was long recognized by Anderson and the reformers, and their support was sought out from the beginning of her tenure. One minister of particular importance was Reverend William Howard, the pastor of a "historic institution," one of the oldest black churches in the city, Bethany Baptist

Church, "which has," Reverend Howard explained, "many civic leaders as members," such as Richard Roper and city council president Mildred Crump.[49] Howard, who took the helm at Bethany in 2000, came with an impressive résumé that included being the first black president of the New York Theological Seminary, past president of the National Council of Churches, and a member of various boards, from the National Urban League to the Children's Defense Fund.[50] During his sixteen-year tenure in Newark, Howard, as would be expected of a Bethany pastor, immersed himself in civic life, including serving as chairman of the Rutgers University governing board. Though he did not endorse any candidate, he accepted Cory Booker's invitation to chair his transition team in 2006.

Thus, when Booker began the big push for school reform in 2010, he reached out to prominent ministers like Howard, whose church had converted its private Christian Academy into a charter school in 2006.[51] While not opposing Booker's initiative, Howard counseled the ambitious Newark mayor that he should "get in a deep dialogue" with the community. Although "Cory was receptive" to his message, and thanked the minister "for [his] wise counsel," in the end, Howard concludes, "he went off and did his own thing."

Upon her appointment in 2011, Anderson immediately, presumably following Booker's advice, reached out to Howard and other prominent clergy. Howard recalls receiving a call from a representative of Anderson, the day after she was named as superintendent, that she wanted to attend the Sunday service. Howard explains that she came on Mother's Day 2011, "and of course the place was packed and . . . she was introduced and was given a warm ovation." "But," Howard emphasizes,

> it was an odd meeting because she arrived after I was in the pulpit and she left by a different exit so as I greeted people at the front door as they were leaving. . . . Naturally the word got around the media, everybody knew Cami Anderson came to Bethany and was like a buzz, so reporters on Monday morning, they called me, "Dr. Howard I heard you had the superintendent at the church, what was your impression of her?" . . . and unfortunately I had to say "well yes indeed she was there and we were delighted to have her but I never met her."

164 || THE CLASH OF DISRUPTORS

They did eventually meet and talk, and Howard shared his views on the need for consultation with the community, "and she seemed to appreciate it." But, Howard adds, he eventually came to the realization that "I . . . and other leaders . . . were being played."

> Cami would say in public spaces, you know, "I met with Reverend Beckham and I met with Reverend Jefferson, I met with, you know, Reverend Howard," and she would never say they told me that this was a good idea, but by just inferring that she had somehow consulted with us, people began to associate her behavior with us.

Another influential minister, and a former city councilperson from the heavily black West Ward originally allied with Booker, Reverend Mamie Bridgeforth, echoed Howard's criticisms:

> The South Ward ministers held a meeting and she came to meet with them, and she was not honest, she was disingenuous with them. When she would come to the meeting, and when she first got here, they were open to hearing from her. . . . She [explained] what she wanted to do . . . how it would be done, and the idea was OK, she would come, she would give us her ideas, and we will listen, but she took it to mean once she met with them they were 100 percent in support of what she wanted to do. And she would go forward doing these things knowing full well that meeting with someone does not mean they endorse your ideas.

Thus Howard and Bridgforth indict Anderson's public interventions that made it appear as though they and other ministers had approved of her initiatives. But, in fact, in March 2012, as recounted in chapter 3, Howard and four other prominent male ministers penned a *Star-Ledger* editorial publicly supporting Anderson's "revised plan for school reorganization" that had generated intense opposition after the superintendent unveiled it at a public hearing. This intervention followed a Tom Moran editorial, and personal interventions, for the ministers to stand up and be counted.[52]

But a lot had changed in two years. The influential ministers, in spring 2012, responded to the call by the *Star-Ledger* to defend Anderson and her reforms in the face of public opposition. They took heat for that from some community activists, Howard recalls, including "the head of the local NAACP, [who] wrote to the clergy signatories condemning us, meaning we were too conciliatory and not radical enough." In contrast, Moran's public call in February 2014 for "civil leaders" to rally around Anderson now fell on deaf ears. Instead of admonition from fellow elites like Moran, the clergy now "feared the destabilization" from below that Anderson's behavior and program were generating. They risked further damaging their own legitimacy if they did not speak out. In a shift mirroring that of Weingarten and the union bureaucrats, the minsters began to take an oppositional stance toward Anderson after backing her during the first two years of her reign. "You know, we had to show in a very public way," Howard emphasizes,

> look this woman is not listening to us. . . . People were contemplating mass walkouts, I mean all kinds of things, we just knew it was a very unhealthy environment and was becoming more restive each day.

Bridgeforth also points to how pressure from below and the fear of further unrest, what Pastor Joe Carter termed "civil unrest," are what pushed her and other ministers into action:[53]

> Number one, you had people who were coming to members of your church and they were telling you about how this plan was . . . not only disrupting their lives . . . [but] the lives of their children . . . and you just had various ministers who were talking to each other, and you are getting the same kind of thing that maybe *we need to get somebody in here to recognize that we are sitting on a powder keg* and so we then contacted the state.[54]

Further highlighting how the mass movement forced the hand of the clergy, Bridgeforth emphasizes that "understand something . . . the pastors played catchup, the community had been out a long time." Yet, at the same time, Bridgeforth advances what Adolph Reed Jr. calls the petty bourgeois–dominated "politics of elite-brokerage" that passes for what is understood as "black politics."[55] Bridgeforth, a minster and department chair at the local community college, emphasizes the responsibility of the BPMC, as the legitimate voice of an

166 || THE CLASH OF DISRUPTORS

undifferentiated "black community," to translate the grievances of the unwashed masses to state officials.

> Because, mind you at this time all that they were hearing was from the community, community doesn't always know how to shape issues or articulate issues. And so they dismissed that as just rabble-rousers, as political people, all that kind of thing. So we felt let's come together, let's draft a position, let's see if we can share that position with clergy throughout the city and maybe the clergy might be able to make a dent when no one else could. And that was the impetus for the letter.

Similarly, Howard's initial thinking behind a letter by the clergy was that

> we wanted to alert whoever was interested, especially in Trenton, that this was what was going on, we were not a partisan group or whatever, we wanted to say from the community, my friends, this is what we see, and if you care about this with the power that you have you need to do something.

After first contacting the new state education commissioner—David Hespe, who had taken over for Chris Cerf after his February 2014 departure—and getting no response, the ministers decided to make their opposition public.[56] In a letter written by ministers Eric Beckham and Howard—who had both composed the 2012 letter admonishing community opposition to the superintendent's reforms—along with Bridgeforth and Gloria Harris, the authors emphasize above all the dangers of mass disruption. "We are extremely concerned," the ministers announced,

> about the level of public anger we see growing in the community. . . . It is venomous and it is our view that unless we have an urgent, objective, egalitarian discussion about what is happening now in the Newark school system, the climate within the city will continue to deteriorate.

That is, in an attempt to forestall further mass disruption, the ministers pleaded with the state authorities who controlled the district to declare a "MORATORIUM on the implementation of the One Newark Public School Plan." By no means did they come out against the neoliberal reforms, as they emphasized that they were "unanimous that major change is needed in Newark Public Schools." They also waffled on the central issue of privatization, explaining that "this statement neither condemns nor endorses Charter Schools." But, forced by the disruption of the movement from below, they now switched gears and called for a halt to Anderson's disruption plans "until a process can be found to obtain meaningful and credible engagement of the Newark community." In 2012, Howard, Beckham, Carter, Jefferson, and Slaughter, leading lights of the city's ministerial wing of the BPMC, maligned community opposition to corporate school reform as an expression of a "dysfunctional attitude" endemic to Newark. Now, after a sustained social movement campaign, the church elders reassessed their earlier rash judgment as they announced, "It is unfair to characterize Newarkers opposing the current approach to change as irrational and resistant to change in any case." The problem now was Anderson for having "denied meaningful input into the decision-making process [by] . . . many voices of reason in the community." Released in late April, the letter was signed initially by seventy-seven minsters, including influential figures like Percy Simmons of the Abyssinian Baptist Church and Christie backer Joe Carter, while many others requested to be included once it had been released.[57]

The open break by a large section of the black clergy, news of which the increasingly read blog of Bob Braun helped to spread, prompted Hespe to set up a meeting with the four principal authors of the letter. The meeting, held at Howard's Bethany Baptist Church, left Bridgeforth optimistic because Hespe

> led us to believe . . . that we could look forward to perhaps a total reassessment . . . of the One Newark plan. That perhaps it could be stopped in total. . . . So we left there kind of encouraged that perhaps there would be an objective look at this One Newark plan and what were the long-term implications of this plan for the city.

But in the end, Hespe, Bridgeforth explains, "lied to us, he outright lied." The four ministers went to a follow-up meeting in which they thought Hespe would have a plan on how he would address the concerns raised in their letter. Instead, Bridgeforth recounts, they were

168 || THE CLASH OF DISRUPTORS

"sandbagged," with Hespe accompanied by Anderson and a delegation of ministers who defended the superintendent's agenda. It was clear that, at this stage, Christie and his allies were not going to budge. Later, as a concession, Hespe attempted to form a "working group" to advise Anderson, but Howard rejected participation, saying, "I wouldn't go near it with a ten-foot pole."[58]

"FUCK, WHAT ARE WE GOING TO DO? THIS IS NOT GOING WELL"

In January, as the opposition intensified rather than abating in the new year, leading allies of the besieged superintendent organized "an intervention at her house," according to NTE chief Ross Danis, a self-described "coconspirator" of Anderson "for her whole run." The small, secret gathering included Danis; Anderson and her partner, Jared; Cory Booker, the new junior U.S. senator; Shané Harris of the Prudential Foundation; Chris Cerf and his fellow Montclair resident Don Katz, CEO of the Newark-based Audible corporation; and Father Ed Leahy, headmaster of a Catholic school serving "at-risk" youth. Those gathered were deeply perplexed as they "went around the table" searching for answers. One attendee argued that to counter the opposition, "we need a media campaign," and proposed "some high-priced media company to come in" to plaster the city with billboards. Danis objected because "it was part of the problem. You can't bring in any more high-priced consultants." He added, pointing to the historic weakness of the movement to gain consent, "people now see that is disingenuous, it's being manipulative."

In the end, all they could agree on was bringing back De'Shawn Wright, who, as discussed in chapter 3, was a leading cadre of the charter movement and had a long relationship with Booker, Cerf, and Anderson. Wright, who had recently been named as New York State's assistant secretary of education under John King, was brought on for a six-month contract, with Katz picking up the tab after "pressuring" from the group. Part of their thinking must have been Wright's work in Washington, D.C. Prior to being appointed by Cuomo, Mayor Vincent Gray hired the reform veteran in 2011 as his chief education advisor. In that position, Wright, with assistance from generously compensated consultants, developed a plan, similar to One Newark, of mass closure of "failing schools," expansion of charters, and layoffs of teachers and staff. Kaya Henderson, Gray's "collaborative chancellor"—as Dale Russakoff praised her—was able to consensually introduce the reforms that the heralded author of *The Prize* wanted so badly to see replicated in Newark.[59] Anderson's backers, huddled at the superintendent's new suburban residence—recently taken up after she had to flee Newark because of the increasingly heated protests, including NSU pickets at her doorstep—were hoping Wright could replicate the D.C. "success story."[60]

Wright, for his part, was a bit skeptical of what use he could be. "Given my political connection to Booker . . . I thought it best for me not to be involved at all." But those who had gathered at the emergency meeting thought he could help turn things around by providing the diplomatic skills that Anderson lacked.

> People basically said "look you can be really helpful by getting people back in the tent, because right now everyone is sort of breaking from each other," and I basically did a lot of one-off meetings at lunches [where I] tried to say like "hey what's going on, how can I be helpful."

But Wright, who began work in mid-February as the opposition to One Newark and Anderson raged, soon "realized after having some of those early conversations, [that] . . . it was much worse than I had thought." Therefore, in addition to working on implementing One Newark, Wright spent a lot of time, with few results, working to "repair relationships . . . being an ambassador" with ministers and other influential voices in the community to get them on board. It was a hard sell.

Danis was another key player in the public relations counteroffensive, with the local philanthropic "funding community" being a major target of his fence-mending efforts. Local and national philanthropy, bedrock components of the privatization movement, had provided Anderson highly prized pots of money to institute reform without public oversight. But, in Danis's words, and highlighting the power of the students' disruptive protests, "as things got hot . . . and ugly," the foundation officials "ran." Danis was able, after much coaxing and back-and-forth with various foundation directors, to compose and "issue a joint letter signed by nine local foundations." But, reflecting

170 || THE CLASH OF DISRUPTORS

their disagreements, and their desire not to be tainted by too close an association with Anderson, it was, according to one of the signers, only "a qualified letter of support."[61]

Danis also tried to get a section of the "clergy" to back Anderson, but once they "sensed that the wind had changed, they just turned, they left her in the dust." In the end, Danis, Anderson's confidant, saw the crusading superintendent as having been betrayed by the clergy, philanthropy, and even business elites like Al Koeppe, the former utility executive and head of the Newark Alliance.[62] When Anderson arrived and was "making the rounds," Danis recounted, "people were asking 'how can I help,' she said 'it's going to get ugly . . . and I need to know when it does you are going to be there, you're going to have my back.'" They reassured Anderson, "oh, absolutely," but in her time of need, they were not there.

RETREATING TO THE BUNKER

Anderson was not alone in feeling betrayed. Jeffries, her longtime movement ally, felt the same way toward Anderson. Although Jeffries was heavily outspending Baraka, thanks to generous backing from the hedge funders and other deep-pocketed supporters of the charter movement, his mayoral bid was flailing as his opponent rode the wave of opposition to One Newark and Anderson. Jeffries desperately needed Anderson to back off parts of One Newark. Danis acted as a mediator in secret talks, held among the three at what the NTE head called "my bunker"—a secret, windowless basement office in the downtown office tower that housed his organization. Danis recounts Jeffries's plea and Anderson's response:

> You just have to let me say no schools are going to be closed. Just, you know, even if she's telling me that school is going to be reopened as another kind of school, right, I just have to be able to say no schools are going to be closed. And you know, she couldn't do that . . . and you know, they're not the closest right now.

Although Booker was officially neutral, the charter movement clearly saw the contest as a referendum on the former mayor and his privatization agenda, as it poured money into the race. Independent groups not constrained by campaign contribution limits spent $5.3 million, a

THE CLASH OF DISRUPTORS || 171

record for a municipal race in New Jersey, with most raised on Jeffries's behalf. In addition, Jeffries's campaign directly raised $2.3 million, compared to Baraka's paltry $385,000. Of the soft money, $4.2 million came from Newark First, whose funds, in turn, mainly came from an arm of DFER. Former mayor Michael Bloomberg, from whose administration Booker and Christie drew much of their talent to oversee the reform agenda, contributed $400,000 to the effort. Another pro-Jeffries group, Newark Families for Progress, chipped in $285,000, while the bulk of money spent on Baraka's behalf came either directly or indirectly from the AFT, the CWA, and other labor unions.[63]

In the May 13 nationally watched race, Baraka won convincingly with 54 percent of the vote, despite Jeffries outspending his opponent by a wide margin.[64] Baraka's supporters, including NSU leader Towkanik, gathered at the Robert Treat Hotel to celebrate their people's victory over Wall Street. The victory party concluded with a nighttime march and rally on the front steps of City Hall to symbolize Baraka's populist slogan—"When I become mayor, we all become mayor." Indeed, some took the slogan to heart, as a flurry of activity ensued in the weeks following Baraka's election. Hundreds gathered, including Baraka, at Lincoln Park on the Saturday following the election for the release of the alternative Newark Promise plan. Developed by a coalition of community, labor, and civil rights groups that backed Baraka, who would eventually operate under the banner of the Alliance for Newark Public Schools, the plan echoed the new mayor's campaign rhetoric. The planks included a moratorium on One Newark; a return of local control; and development of "community schools," modeled after the Ford Foundation's GVZ, providing additional "wraparound" social services for neighborhood public schools.[65]

On May 20, a week after the election, NEW held a rally at the NPS headquarters with two key demands: an immediate moratorium on One Newark and Anderson's resignation.[66] That same day, at the NPS's business meeting, which Anderson still attended, the NSU introduced a new form of disruption into its repertoire—an occupation of the NPS offices. Beginning with an Occupy-style mic check, a dozen or so NSU activists disrupted the meeting as the group's president, Towkanik, attempted to physically hand Anderson—she refused—their Newark Promise alternative plan. In response to Anderson walking out of the meeting, the NSU escalated its disruption by initiating an occupation, along with advisory school board president Baskerville-Richardson and local NAACP president Deborah Smith-Gregory, of the NPS offices to demand Anderson replace her One Newark with their Newark Promise plan. The NSU followed the overnight occupation with a widely covered morning press conference in front of the NPS office to broadcast its demands.[67] A week later, Hespe and Anderson met with the NSU to appear that they were giving "community stakeholders ... the opportunity to have input into important education issues," without meeting their demands. The NSU's Tanasia Brown was not impressed, as she felt "we were brushed to the side," while Towkanik promised to continue the fight until Anderson's tenure, and its One Newark plan, was ended.[68]

While still proceeding with One Newark, the protests did force Anderson to give some concessions. On June 12, the last day of school, Hawthorne Elementary School parents received a letter from Anderson informing them that "due to family demand," their K–8 school would remain open as a public school and not be handed over to the TEAM charter operator. This was clearly a product of the struggle led by Grace Sergio, the elected PTA president, and the community support they were able to mount.[69] In contrast, the PULSE group, which focused on legal strategies encased in a racial justice framework, rather than protest, was unsuccessful in saving Bragaw Avenue Elementary School, as it became KIPP's first "turnaround charter school" in Newark.[70] Unlike the regular pickets at Hawthorne, PULSE's filing of civil rights complaints with the Department of Education, charging NPS with targeting schools with predominantly African American enrollment for closure, did not sway Anderson from carrying out her disruption plans at Bragaw and other schools.[71]

THE CHANGING OF THE GUARD

Anderson started out the 2013–14 academic year intent on moving beyond the "gradualism" of her first two years and finally implementing the radical, disruptive change she and the rest of the reform movement saw as necessary. The shock therapy program backfired on Anderson as the movement expanded and many of her allies among the clergy, philanthropy, and even business began openly to oppose her or to run for cover. Of course, Christie, at least publicly, maintained his ardent support, as he renewed her three-year contract in June.[72] In addition, other elements of the reform movement, such as David Weisberg of the New Teacher Project, urged her to continue "making tough decisions" and to keep pushing her "ambitious agenda through." In a testament to the national significance of the Newark fight, he added that "she's got a lot of people in Newark and around the country rooting her on."[73]

Nonetheless, despite Anderson's tough-upper-lip posturing, as she and her militant supporters vowed to carry on, whatever the costs, it was clear that the movement from below now had the upper hand. The most influential face, and main beneficiary, of that movement was clearly Ras Baraka, the city's newly elected forty-three-year-old mayor. He was able to ride the mass opposition to Anderson and the corporate school reform to the mayor's office. At the same time, Baraka carefully wrapped his campaign in a racial justice, self-determinationist packaging, rather than in a clear-cut, class-conscious one opposing the privatization of public education. Indeed, in his pronouncements and literature, he made clear that he was not against charter schools and in fact was a "strong supporter."[74] The real issue was the "lack of respect" by "outsiders" who were determining the fate of Newark without any input from those upon whom the reforms were being made. Adding insult to injury, the mercenary reformers, as he denounced at his father's memorial service, deployed a faux, opportunistic black empowerment rhetoric of invoking "Frederick Douglass' words to close public schools."

Indeed, the reformers did invoke Douglass, King, and other African American icons and symbols to legitimate their agenda. But was Baraka's "self-determination for Black and Brown communities" ideology a real challenge to the neoliberal antiracist, school choice creed? Or would it simply be a more effective way of managing the contradictions of the BUR?

PART IV

Containing the Movement

6

Ras Baraka's Self-Determination Politics

THE FIRST TIME AS TRAGEDY, SECOND TIME AS FARCE, SUMMER–FALL 2014

> There's a mythology that's out here around who I am and my family. . . . I'm not green. I don't have horns coming out of my head. I don't breathe fire. I'm not going to shut downtown down. I'm not going to close all the charter schools.
>
> —Ras Baraka, August 2013 campaign address to a gathering of Newark's largest corporations, property owners, and lawyers

> The dilemma . . . was how to appear to be progressive in addressing the needs of the black community and yet meet the needs of the major business interests.
>
> —Robert Whelan, Alma Young, and Mickey Lauria, "Urban Regimes and Racial Politics in New Orleans"

Liberal and radical voices heralded the election of Ras Baraka as part of a new urban progressive movement. Bob and Mary Dreyfuss of *The Nation* portrayed Baraka's win as a major defeat of the state's right-wing Democrats and Wall Street interests bent on privatizing public education. With Baraka's election, Mayor Bill De Blasio—the other rising progressive star elected the year before "across the Hudson" in New York City—now had, they declared, "a partner in rebuilding America's urban core." Radical voices at *Counterpunch* also touted the election as a major victory against the "education reformers' criminal activities" and their "educolonial apparatus." Max Blumenthal's coverage with the Real News Network explained, correctly, how Baraka rode the mass movement to defend public education to office. His report concluded with Baraka leading a march from the election-night party at the Robert Treat Hotel

|| 177

178 || RAS BARAKA'S SELF-DETERMINATION POLITICS

to Newark City Hall, with a marcher echoing Baraka's populist message that "as the people, we became mayor."[1]

Baraka concurred with these assessments. At the January 2014 public memorial service commemorating his father, he argued that his rise signaled the "beginning of a progressive period." In his emotional speech, Baraka passionately argued that the same progressive coalition that "united to elect President Obama"—whose administration applauded and assisted Booker's education reforms—"was coming together locally . . . [to] elect local leadership and push for change in cities across America." In an obvious reference to Booker, Jeffries, and other well-compensated black professionals overseeing the privatization drive, he denounced that "they"—referring to the Wall Street backers behind the reform drive—

> take a few of us, teach them privilege and give them degrees
> in exchange for their humanity, and send them back to further
> dismantle all that is left in our community, and the opportunists
> [*long applause*] and mercenaries that have turned our [Black Liberation] struggle into profit-making ventures.[2]

Baraka's denunciation of the neoliberal BPMC overseeing the privatization drive on behalf of their Wall Street backers, which they cynically legitimated as the "civil rights movement of our day," had echoes of his father's criticisms of the city's first generation of black leaders. The elder Baraka launched this broadside on the pages of *Monthly Review* in the wake of his bitter 1974 political divorce from the Gibson administration:

> Newark, New Jersey, is a classic neo-colonial creation where a
> Black United Front of blacks and Puerto Ricans moved through
> the late sixties to elect Kenneth Gibson black mayor of the first
> major northeastern city. Now some of the fruits borne [*sic*] of the
> struggles of the sixties can be tasted in their bitterest aspect. Those
> black faces in high places are simply objective agents of the rule
> of monopoly capitalism, as cold and cynical as they have to be,
> whether in Zaire or Newark.[3]

"The people," Ras Baraka declared at the memorial service of the city's most famous radical, "are tired of the lies" coming from the inauthentic BPMC, what his father derisively referred to as "black faces in high places" in the service of monopoly capital. What the people wanted, and he would deliver, is self-determination, "to *control their own schools* and . . . improve them themselves."[4]

Six months later, at his July 2014 inauguration, the only explicit mention of the issue that catapulted him to power was pointing out the obvious: "we have a bitter struggle over our schools." But, at the heart of the conflict, according to Baraka, was not privatization of schools but rather "who should lead them," with the current leadership siding with "expediency over democracy."[5]

Thus Baraka's solution to the "struggle over our schools" was deeply contradictory. On one hand, he demanded "self-determination" through the return of local control. On the other, he refused to call for and mobilize against privatization—the quickly expanding charterization of the district led by the same Wall Street and black comprador interests he railed against—that made a mockery of any pretense of substantively regaining local control. The inability of Baraka to mobilize against privatization was due to the constraints and responsibilities of managing the neoliberal city and his acceptance, indeed, his embrace, of them. He was committed, just as were his Newark predecessors and counterparts in other cities, to make his hometown as favorable an investment environment as possible. School privatization, with its connection to real estate, was central to the postindustrial revival he was committed to leading. While this class contradiction also confronted his predecessors, and is the centerpiece of urban capitalist politics, it was especially sharp for Baraka because he was dealing not with a mute "electoral coalition" but with an energized mass movement that was expecting results. How would the son of Amiri Baraka, who declared at his inauguration that "yeah, we need a mayor that's radical!," manage these contradictory commitments as he took the reins of power?

To answer that question, I begin the chapter by analyzing the centrality that "self-determination" played in the politics of Amiri Baraka and how the concept could be deployed to obscure the real material stakes involved in political struggles. I then turn to the elder Baraka's influence on his son's political trajectory, the eventual loyalty oath the latter would take before the city's corporate elite to support rent-intensification development, and, as I document, the centrality of charter schools to that agenda. This context sets the stage for the first school year with Baraka at the helm, as he draws on his father's

180 || RAS BARAKA'S SELF-DETERMINATION POLITICS

past political organizing feats and ideology to straddle and manage the competing movements he confronted.

LIKE FATHER, LIKE SON?

To understand Ras Baraka's self-determinationist politics, and its contradictions and limits, we need to examine the politics of his father and mentor, and one of the most influential theorists and practitioners of post–civil rights black politics. The influence of the elder Baraka extended to the campaign and continued even after his death in January 2014, a few months before his son's election. Author and singer Sister Souljah, one of the many prominent eulogists at Amiri Baraka's funeral, described the timing of his death as a final political intervention on behalf of his son: "your father was a man of action, and if he laid down now it's because he's a political strategist . . . he laid down, he made a path for you to walk on." Indeed, as the *New York Times* described it, the funeral was a veritable "political rally" for his son.[6] For its part, the *Star-Ledger,* which enthusiastically backed Shavar Jeffries, described the junior Baraka as being "raised by a well-known activist" and derided him as a propagator of an "old-school black nationalism that seems inspired by his father, but outdated."[7] Baraka, far from distancing himself, situated his campaign as part of a continuation of the struggle his father had begun. Underscoring that debt, the first words at his election-night victory speech saluted his father: "I know my father's spirit is in this room . . . that he is here with us . . . and I want to say thanks to him."

What was this "spirit" that inspired his son and the "old-school black nationalism" the *Star-Ledger* abhorred? Amiri Baraka, whom political scientist Cedric Johnson calls "arguably the most significant African American intellectual of the late twentieth century," rose to political prominence in the wake of the civil rights movement's success in dismantling the Jim Crow system and its simultaneous incapacity to address the continuing plight of wide swaths of the African American community.[8] The movement in the mid-1960s was at a crossroads, and various political tendencies emerged to point a way forward. One road was, as Adolph Reed Jr. argues, a "black-labor-left" rooted movement advocating a transformative social democratic program outlined in Bayard Rustin and A. Philip Randolph's 1966 Freedom Budget, calling for a mass, direct-government-employment public works and service program.[9] Baraka's answer was a "Black Power politics" that, in the end, Reed argues, consolidated as a "less potentially transformative, class-skewed alternative" to the Rustin–Randolph project. In essence, Baraka's Black Power politics evolved, despite the at times "overheated rhetoric about self-determination," into, as Cedric Johnson argues, a black version of "ethnic politics" as outlined by Stokely Carmichael and Charles Hamilton in their 1967 book *Black Power: The Politics of Liberation in America*.

Black Americans, the Carmichael–Hamilton thesis held, must unite as a group—a strategy that, allegedly, other ethnic groups had successfully deployed—to ascend the American stratification ladder. "Before a group can enter the open society, it must first close ranks," the authors argued, adding that "group solidarity is necessary before a group can operate effectively from a bargaining position of strength in a pluralistic society."[10] Owing to deep, pervasive institutional racism, interracial coalitions were futile, and therefore a political program that united the entire race—across class, gender, geographic, and ideological and other differences—was the only realistic strategy to improve the material conditions of Black America. Despite these differences among blacks, the real bond was the "linked fate" of the entire Black "nation" created by the pervasive racism that confronted the entire community. Thus, under the Black Power strategy of group advancement, race becomes "the paramount basis of political organizing and mobilization."[11] Although presented as a radical "anticolonial" struggle for "national liberation," Baraka's politics, Johnson argues, was in the end, despite his intensions, a black version of ethnic politics that privileged more affluent layers of African Americans.[12]

Baraka, at the local level in Newark and nationally, played the most influential role "to operationalize Black Power via the construction of local and national political institutions."[13] At the national level, Baraka was the moving force behind most of the national Black Power gatherings between the mid-1960s and mid-1970s designed to forge a common Black Agenda. As Cedric Johnson points out in his study of the Black Power movement, the central themes of the manifestos issued by these gatherings centered around "self-determination" and "Black indigenous control."[14] Although electing a black mayor, as Newark did in 1970, was important, it was only one element of realizing Black Power

182 || RAS BARAKA'S SELF-DETERMINATION POLITICS

at the local level. To achieve "nationalist hegemony" in black communities across the country, Baraka admonished activists that

> you must control everything in the community that needs to be controlled. Anything of value: any kind of anti-poverty program, politicians, celebrities, anything that brings in money, resources, into your community, you should control it.[15]

As discussed in chapter 2, of preeminent importance for constructing Black Power and achieving self-determination was gaining control of the existing public education system, as well as building new independent schools. "Formal education," Baraka and other Black Power theoreticians argued, was crucial as a "means of creating a vanguard of young activists devoted to the struggle for black political sovereignty throughout the world."[16]

Thus the idea of black control—of local, indigenous control—was a central component of the Baraka worldview. But, as Cedric Johnson perceptively points out in a critique with much relevance for the struggle over public schools, the "rhetoric of black control" can be easily deployed to obscure the real material, substantive issues and stakes at play. To highlight this problem, Johnson points to a debate at the 1969 Black Power Conference in Philadelphia over union organization and leadership legitimacy. One speaker praised the Jewish president of the 1199 union, Leon Davis, as "John Brown–like" for his committed fight against class inequality and racial oppression. But others in the audience critiqued interracialism, arguing "With white leadership at the top, how can a Black organization progress?" while another interjected, "How do you expect to build the power of Black people if the power you use is other than Black?" For Johnson, this exchange underscored the "double-edged nature of the indigenous control rhetoric." "More precisely," Johnson adds,

> *it illuminates the fashion in which the rhetoric of black control might obscure the necessarily issue based nature of political organizing.* Serious consideration of the equality of the union's programs, its organizational activities and campaigns, and the implications for the material well-being and social mobility of its black members were overshadowed by concerns over whether blacks controlled the organization's head post.[17]

Likewise, in Newark, the calls for "local control" and "self-determination" for "Black and Brown people" played a similar role. Baraka's framing of the conflict, both during the campaign and after taking office, drew attention away from, and obscured the material impacts of, the school reform agenda. The discourse suppressed a discussion of how charters affected black and other working-class people and communities through weakening labor unions, defunding and destabilizing public schools, fueling rent-intensification development, *and* how that agenda could be challenged.

Despite Amiri Baraka's impressive, herculean efforts, his attempt to forge a "Black Nationality" and political movement ran aground, both nationally and in his hometown, on the shoals of the class, ideological, party allegiance, and other differences that increasingly divided a putative "Black community."[18] By the mid-1970s, as Cedric Johnson explains, "the limits of race unity as a political strategy" had been revealed.[19] Baraka, after his abandonment in 1974 by Gibson and other black officials in his attempt to build an Afrocentric housing development in Newark's North Ward, renounced Black Nationalism and embraced a Maoist ideology. Nonetheless, despite this apparent ideological break, the commitment to the ideology of self-determination and the centrality of racism in American society and politics would continue.[20]

RAS J. BARAKA: THE POLITICS OF SELF-DETERMINATION UNDER NEOLIBERALISM

Ras J. Baraka, born in 1970 and raised in Newark as the second of five children of Amina and Amiri Baraka, was literally brought up in the movement by his activist parents.[21] After graduating from a local magnet high school, Baraka attended the famed, historically black Howard University in the late 1980s and early 1990s, where he founded the student group Black Nia FORCE. The group gained national attention in 1989 for its occupation of the university's administration building, with its principal demand being removal of Lee Atwater from the board of trustees. As campaign manager for George H. W. Bush's 1988 presidential run, Atwater had orchestrated the racist "Willie Horton" ad.

After graduation, Baraka returned to Newark, where he became a public school teacher and, later, a high school principal, while simultaneously organizing and engaging with antipolice brutality and other

184 || RAS BARAKA'S SELF-DETERMINATION POLITICS

local protests. Baraka first ran for mayor in 1994 against Sharpe James, arguing that the city needed young voices like his, but was soundly defeated by the incumbent.[22] After his loss, he continued organizing protests, with many targeting James, the black police chief, and other black officials for being part of the machinery behind the "'National Oppression' of Black People," calling for their removal.[23] In 2002, Baraka, after nearly winning an at-large council seat, was appointed by Mayor James—who had just staved off a challenge from Booker, the other youthful challenger—as deputy mayor, and in 2005, he filled the uncompleted term of an at-large councilman who died in office. After several failed attempts, he won the South Ward city council seat in 2010.[24] While in office, he continued to work as a high school principal while also mounting, in a step back from the confrontational anti-police brutality initiatives of his earlier years, "antiviolence" organizing efforts. As part of this turn, Baraka, in 2009, during the midst of his council race, was one of the founders of the Newark Anti-Violence Coalition to address, in particular, "black-on-black crime."[25]

Baraka, earlier in his career, had collaborated with Cory Booker in initiatives that took aim at Mayor James. For example, in 1999, Baraka and Booker, then a city councilman, along with Ronald Rice Jr. and Larry Crump—progeny of two longtime Newark elected officials—organized a Youth March under the aegis of the newly formed Newark Youth Coalition. The march was clearly directed at then mayor James and his failure to address the employment and other needs of the city's youths.[26] But by the time of the 2002 James–Booker contest, and increasingly after Booker's election in 2006, Baraka positioned himself as *the* challenger to the inauthentic transplant from Yale and suburban New Jersey. After his 2006 city council election defeat, Baraka organized various "antiviolence" protests criticizing Booker's failure to control crime, and homicides in particular. He demanded the firing of the police commissioner, Garry McCarthy, who had been brought over from Michael Bloomberg's New York City.[27]

Baraka, in his successful 2010 run for the South Ward city council seat, ran on a slate opposing Booker.[28] He challenged the Booker-backed incumbent, Oscar James II (no relation to the mayor), in what Clement Price called a "proxy war" with the incumbent mayor. Indeed, Baraka portrayed his opponent as a surrogate of the mayor who, following an authenticity trope that Sharpe James had used, does not "do much good for the people who were raised and live in Newark."[29]

The newly installed city councilman, as I have shown, embraced the public school movement that began to take off as he took office. Baraka's message, that Booker was more concerned about powerful interests outside the city than he was with the city's residents, echoed that of the emerging movement from below. But by spring 2013, after a Baraka-backed and -organized slate gained the dominant position on the Advisory Board, his "Children First"–backed candidates now called for a "truce with charters" as they struck an even more "conciliatory tone." Ariagna Perello, after clearly having caucused with Baraka, who was now in the midst of a mayoral bid, emphasized that "we should stop the street fighting between charter and public schools. If a charter school works, guess what? Let's share the practices." His other board allies echoed similar pro (or at least conciliatory messaging) on charters. Baraka, for his part, emphasized that the main problem was not charters per se but their "proliferation," which he argued was designed to "decentralize and destabilize our school system while creating a two-tier system of schools." He inveighed against efforts to create "false divisions" among parents, "who clearly want the same thing for their children."[30] To understand that conciliatory turn, especially as he geared up for a mayoral run, requires grasping the centrality of charters to driving up land values.

REAL ESTATE AND SCHOOL PRIVATIZATION: WHAT'S THE CONNECTION?

In the post-1970s era, cities like Newark faced continued federal government retrenchment, with the lone exception being infusion of funds for policing and prisons, while deindustrialization continued apace. In this context, the Democrats that run most U.S. cities, including the particularly vulnerable BUR formations, increasingly turned to an "entrepreneurial model of urban governance that prioritizes attracting private investment, tourism, and real estate investment."[31] Along with public housing demolition, privatizing public education has become a vital component of reviving, in particular, local real estate markets. The connection is particularly clear in Newark, where the construction of a charter school complex—Teachers Village—has played a central role in the revival of the downtown real estate market.

The development project was led by developer Ron Beit, who, between 2005 and 2012, with backing from several large investors, chief among these the billionaire private investor Nicolas Berggruen, acquired seventy-nine parcels, encompassing twenty-three acres, in downtown Newark. As Beit explained to journalist Jason Nark in a 2015 *Politico* article titled "Is Newark the Next Brooklyn?," he gave Berggruen a tour in 2005 of downtown Newark to highlight the development potential of a long-disinvested area, but one that was only a twenty-minute train ride to New York City. Berggruen, according to Beit, said "'buy it all' . . . he immediately got it." What the sharp investor "got" was the potential for cashing in on what the late urban geographer Neil Smith termed the "rent gap"—the difference between current and potential land values.[32] Beit's RBH Group, with cash supplied by Berggruen and other investors, such as financier Warren Lichtenstein, bought up properties at approximately $20 a square foot, while "comparable property sells for $175 to $250 per square foot . . . [and] Manhattan, property is anywhere from $400 to $600 a square foot."[33]

The question is how Beit and his fellow investors would realize those potentials, that is, how they would carry out a "revalorization of the area."[34] Beit's Teachers Village charter school complex, for which the city gave final approval in 2012 and which includes investors such as Goldman Sachs's Urban Investment Group and the Newark-headquartered Prudential Corporation, was a central part of solving the challenge. Envisioned as "the first phase of a larger plan to transform Newark's downtown," the "mixed-use" project, the first component of which opened in 2013, includes space for four charter schools, more than two hundred apartments marketed to educators, and street-level retail.[35] The residential space was particularly important for attracting what Beit calls the "Creative class," a term urban theorist Richard Florida has helped to popularize.[36] In addition to Teachers Village, a host of other charters, including KIPP's new high school located in the former *Star-Ledger* building, have clustered in the downtown area that has been the focus of the local state's rent-intensification agenda, as Map 6.1 demonstrates.

Teachers Village and other such efforts were by no means free market initiatives but were dependent on a variety of subsidies provided by the state, particularly the local and regional apparatuses. These included, in addition to the various zoning changes, federal and state tax credits and special subsidies provided for the building of charter schools.[37] Booker's deputy mayor for economic development, Stefan

RAS BARAKA'S SELF-DETERMINATION POLITICS || 187

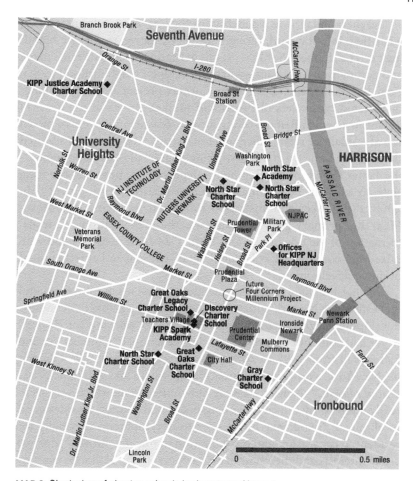

MAP 2. Clustering of charter schools in downtown Newark.

Pryor, worked closely with Governor Christie "to guide legislation and pushed state agencies" to help bring the project to fruition. This included changing the state's Urban Hub tax credit program to include residential projects, which developers lauded.[38] Christie, as discussed in chapter 4, also personally assisted by steering all of the federal government's subsidized QSCBs awarded to the state for charter construction and was especially generous with Newark and the Teachers Village complex.

188 || RAS BARAKA'S SELF-DETERMINATION POLITICS

Teachers Village was an anchor for the larger redevelopment area, what Beit, in a standard, though not very creative, real estate branding exercise dubbed "SoMa"—South of Market Street, the same name and acronym of a decades-earlier redeveloped neighborhood in San Francisco. SoMa includes a Four Corners project at the city's long-disinvested crossroads of Broad and Market Streets in the heart of downtown, which Beit envisions, as with Teachers Village, as a mixed use of residential, retail, office, and hotel space.[39] Booker, who admired Beit, calling him "the hardest-working man in all of development . . . the James Brown of development," deployed the power of the local state to assist in facilitating rent-intensification development.[40] In 2008, the Booker administration rolled out its Living Downtown Plan, the "primary goal" of which was the revitalization and transformation of the downtown area "into a '24-hour district' filled with mixed-use commercial, residential, retail, cultural and entertainment oriented development."[41]

Further highlighting the connection between school reform and real estate, the Newark initiative was overseen by Booker's economic development czar, Stefan Pryor. Previous to working for Booker, Pryor had cofounded a prominent charter school in Connecticut and had served from 1998 to 2001 as vice president for the Partnership for New York, a powerful business lobby, "where his central focus was school reform."[42] Newark's Living Downtown Plan, which was eventually adopted by the city planning board and council, was designed to eliminate "regulatory hindrances to development, especially for residential conversion and rehabilitation in the Downtown." The real estate interests and their new black partners at City Hall who oversaw the design of Newark's downtown built environment during 1970s and 1980s promoted "fortress-like architecture that kept corporate commuters off of Newark streets" because of the "real and perceived issues of safety for downtown visitors." This included building infrastructure like skybridges—demanded by the owners of the Gateway office building and paid for by the James administration—"which kept employees completely segregated from the street." This built environment was now considered an impediment to the profit-making ventures of developers like Beit, who needed "new downtown neighborhoods for people to live work and play."[43]

While deriding Booker for being beholden to powerful outside interests, Baraka himself worked assiduously, usually behind the scenes, to reassure that same investor class that he was somebody they could work with. The son of the ostensibly Marxist Amiri Baraka emphasized that he did not, as explained in the epigraph that introduced the chapter, have "green horns," that he was not some mad revolutionary hostile to business. Of course, this radical street cred was important for developing his mass base, and he used and cultivated that image to gain the support of the student, labor, and community activists defending public education. "Yeah, we need," as he proclaimed at his inauguration, "a mayor that's radical." As NEW leader Branden Rippey commented, many of the young student activists were wowed by Baraka and his radical lineage and image. But that image, including the apparent hostility to charter schools, so central to elite revitalization efforts, also presented a problem for gaining the trust of corporate interests he needed, and wanted, to govern the city. Therefore, during the campaign, Baraka combined public rallies featuring rousing, radical speeches on self-determination to his popular base with private, subdued, reassuring closed-door meetings with the city's corporate and philanthropic elite.

A prime example of Baraka managing the corporate side of the equation was an August 2013 meeting, during the heat of the campaign, with one hundred representatives from the city's largest businesses and real estate interests. They gathered at the downtown Robert Treat Hotel, owned by one of the city's most powerful real estate players, to "hear Baraka's pitch," as the *Star-Ledger* put it. He did not disappoint the well-heeled gathering. He emphasized that "they"—that is, the corporate elite gathered there—were not inauthentic elite outsiders but rather "an intricate part of what we want to do in the city." He counseled that they should ignore the radical hype—"I don't breathe fire. I'm not going to shut downtown down." He added, importantly, that "I'm not going to close all the charter schools," an initiative that corporate interests saw as central to their elite-defined revitalization agenda. Despite presenting himself, to his mass base, as a radical change from his predecessor, he emphasized to this elite gathering that he wanted to continue "downtown development," but added that "commercial and residential development needed to extend to Newark's neighborhoods as well." While deriding the school-to-prison pipeline, his solution, of businesses hiring more of the city's residents, and talk of small business entrepreneurialism, stayed well within acceptable neoliberal parameters.

The message was warmly received, with Baraka receiving a standing ovation from the corporate gathering. Al Koeppe, "a prominent voice in the city's business community," who as head of the state EDA awarded the generous tax credit subsidies to the Teachers Village initiative and other ventures to bolster real estate values, gave a favorable review of the candidate. Baraka, he assessed, "has the right compass headings *for this moment* in Newark's history."[44] Koeppe, a longtime leader of the region's corporate governing class, recognized that the regional ruling elite could use someone with Baraka's skills to manage and navigate the city's sharpening class contradictions in the form of the public school movement.

Baraka also reached out, on an individual basis, to important investors in the city. Top among these was Ron Beit, the leading architect of downtown redevelopment, with whom Baraka met several times during the campaign. The mutual admiration society forged between Beit and Booker was now replicated with Baraka as they shared their similar visons for the city and respective public–private roles for realizing those dreams. This admiration became more public after the election, as Baraka exhaled at a 2015 ribbon cutting in Newark's Ironbound: "Ron inspires me to go back and become more excited about the city." Baraka, consistent with the entrepreneurial mode of governance he embraced, was eager to "go back" to City Hall to provide the public subsidies that private developers like Beit needed to cash in on the rent gap that made the latter so "excited."[45] At the top of the list were projects like Teachers Village, which were central to the downtown rent-intensification agenda. Thus, unsurprisingly, in 2017, as shown in Figure 2, Baraka eagerly joined with Beit, as well as charter school champions and now *former* nemeses Booker and Teresa Ruiz, in the ribbon cutting for the final wing of the project.

The balancing act Baraka had to negotiate was of course not unique to this big-city Democratic mayor but rather a product, as political economist Doug Henwood observes, of "the party's fundamental contradiction. . . . It's a party of business that has to pretend for electoral reasons that it's not."[46] Yet, while this class contradiction is a structural feature of all Democratic Party politics, and capitalist politics more broadly, it was particularly sharp in the Newark case. Baraka rode to power through a movement from below that he nonetheless

FIGURE 2. Mayor Baraka and developer Ron Beit, scissors in hand, surrounded by other local officials, at the 2017 ribbon cutting for the final phase of Teachers Village in downtown Newark. Photograph by the author.

had ultimately to steer in a direction that was acceptable, or at least not antagonistic, to his corporate governing partners. At the same time, the NSU and other activists in the public school movement were emboldened and expecting results now that the new "radical mayor," whom they had put in office, was in power. How would Baraka manage these contradictory forces?

WHOSE VISION? IDEOLOGICALLY POLICING THE MOVEMENT

The NSU, emboldened by installing its ally in City Hall, went to activist summer camp as it bird-dogged Christie around the state and interrupted his gatherings with Occupy-style "mic check" interventions. In the fall, it began the new academic year with a two-day walkout, with the first day involving two hundred students, not as many as had been hoped for, marching from several high schools and then converging on the Newark school board office.[47] The most prominent of banners, which students carried at the front of their march, demanded "FULL LOCAL CONTROL." This was the central message, as well, of Mayor Baraka, who addressed the student rally outside the school board headquarters. With bullhorn in hand, the recently elected mayor passionately addressed the mobilized students who had played a central role in catapulting him to office. "I'm proud of you today," he blared.

> This says a lot of what you think about, your own conditions and what should happen in this city. . . . I'm proud of the fact you are going to take things into your own hands, that you believe ultimately the schools should be in the hands of the people of the city. So continue to march and continue to fight. Thanks to the Newark Students Union for making this happen.[48]

Thus, while fully backing the walkout, Baraka at the same time worked to channel the opposition, rhetorically, within the self-determinationist framework.

In two subsequent events in fall 2014, Baraka, and other elements of the movement to defend public education, would also ideologically police and channel the movement in ways that would help manage the contradictions of the "radical mayor." On September 13, following a NSU-led street sit-in on the second day of the walkout, the New Jersey Working Families Party (NJWFP), in coordination with Baraka, held a conference titled Community Driven Education: A Vision for the Future. The NJWFP, the state arm of a nationally networked, mainly union-funded pressure group within the Democratic Party, invited Karen Lewis, the head of the CTU, to give the keynote address. Lewis had gained national attention in 2012 by leading a strike against school closures and other elements of the neoliberal school agenda that

Mayor Rahm Emanuel was carrying out. Lewis, who joined Baraka on a panel before a crowd of 150 activists at the Paul Robeson Cultural Center on the Newark campus of Rutgers University, received a standing ovation as she took the stage.

In her remarks, the sixty-one-year-old African American chemistry teacher and union leader emphasized that the movement must set its own agenda and therefore cannot—underscoring the centrality of corporate money routed through foundations for the movement from above—"leave education up to Philanthropy." The movement, she argued, cannot win if it plays "by someone else's rules" and that it instead "must fight by our own rules" and engage in the ideological battle over the "stories the winners tell losers to keep them playing" a rigged class game. She concluded that we shouldn't be afraid to name the enemy—"the ruling class"—and that we have to build a "progressive infrastructure" to challenge the powerful forces bent on dismantling public education, unions, all of which was part of a larger class offensive.[49]

The author queried the union leader about the implausibility of building that progressive infrastructure within the Democratic Party, which was the very force leading the assault on public education in Washington, D.C., under the Obama administration, as well as in Chicago, Newark, Philadelphia, and cities across the country. Lewis, who was then contemplating a run for mayor, argued that it was unrealistic to work outside the Democratic Party because the United States does not have a multiparty system. Instead, "we must make Democrats behave." The two-party system was the only game in town. Thus Lewis, a leading figure in the movement, made clear that disruption—withdrawal of support—would not extend to the Democratic Party.[50]

Baraka, who spoke following Lewis's address, emphasized, in a further iteration of his malleable self-determination ideology, that "the fight for public education is a fight for democracy," a theme that he would increasingly emphasize while in office. An undefined "they" was demanding that "*we* have to give up our rights." Racism, he emphasized, was driving the attack on Newarkers, explaining, "It's only us, because you are a poor minority." Thus the antidemocratic imposition of the corporate education reform model was, in his estimation, "fascist" because the Black and Brown communities upon which the reform was being imposed were not given a voice. The solution, therefore, was "democracy . . . that we should be able to decide about our schools, just like other Americans, in the suburbs."[51] The problem, as Baraka diagnosed, was not privatization but rather the lack of, to use Preston Smith's term, "racial democracy" for the Black and Brown communities targeted for the reforms. Baraka's framing of the conflict as a racial justice one conveniently sidestepped confronting the movement from above's multiracial alliance demanding the maintenance and expansion of privatization.

THE MULTIPLE USES OF ANTIRACIST IDEOLOGY

The November 21 and 22 Newark Community Education Convention: Reclaiming a Village gathering organized by the Baraka administration demonstrated that the new mayor's self-determination politics were fully compatible, not simply with the continued existence of the charters, but with partnering with them as well. More than four hundred attendees, drawn from both sides of the barricades of the fight over public education—from the NSU and PULSE on one side to the NCSF and KIPP on the other—were invited and in attendance.[52] Baraka dubbing the gathering a *convention*—which clearly drew inspiration from the National Black Political Conventions that his father led in the early 1970s, aimed at forging Black Americans into a unified political force—underscored the RD politics of the affair. The elder Baraka, as discussed earlier, held that despite the myriad of political, class, regional, and other differences that divided this enthno-racial group—just as any other—African Americans could still forge "unity without conformity." This was because they all face, despite their differences, a similar antiblack animus that pervades U.S. society and therefore had an interest in combining in a united front.

In contrast, what united the more than four hundred attendees, drawn from both sides of the struggle over public schools, at the Education Convention organized by his son—forty-two years after the Gary Convention, the high-water mark of the Black Political Conventions of the post-1965 era—was "they are all here for our babies." That is, for Baraka, the bonds of antiracism, the attendees' love of Black and Brown children and their earnest commitment to ending racial disparities, was able to bridge the gap between these warring parties. Their antiracism overrode any other differences, including whether schools should be maintained in the public sphere or commodified.

In the welcoming speech to the two-day conference, Baraka made it clear that he would govern with charter schools, even though his election, as the *New York Times* headlined coverage of his victory emphasized, had been a "rebuke of Charter Schools . . . in Newark."[53] Charter schools, and their backers, were not part of the problem but rather part of the solution. The class battles during the election were now over, and the warring parties must now set aside their weapons and collaborate for the sake of the children.

> There is a bunch of vilification going on. . . . We vilify one another. We figure we can advance education by attacking unions, some of us, and I don't agree with that. Some people believe that everybody on the reform movement side is evil people, that came from Wall Street, are here to destroy us, *and I don't think that is right either.*[54]

Then, in a wink to his supporters, as he acknowledged that, as a candidate, he used this characterization to climb to power, he added, "Some of those people may be evil [*laughs*]. No, I'm only kidding." But he quickly returned to a serious demeanor as he deployed a favorite turn of phrase:

> At the end of the day, it's not true. I've been able to have conversations with people across the spectrum of ideas and fundamentally there are people on every side who genuinely have the best interests of our children at heart. *I know that,* I've spoken to them, I've seen them, I've seen it in their eyes, the words that they say, their actions, they believe in our kids, they want success. . . . They want to improve the lives and education of these kids.[55]

Thus antiracism, their love for "our kids," becomes the ideological glue that binds together the forces pushing charter schools and those defending public schools. In Baraka's worldview, conflicts over whether schools should remain in the public sphere or commodified were secondary, indeed, insignificant, compared to the deeper, more fundamental shared antiracist commitments.

Baraka, later in his address, goes even further in rehabilitating his—or at least the movement's—opponents by legitimating the pro-school privatization movement's self-conception as the "civil rights movement of our day."

> Some of them [the reformers] believe this *is actually a part of a larger movement,* and so we need to bring those people together, the people who agree we are here for our babies. We need to be together no matter what side of the spectrum you think you are on, we all need to be together for our children.[56]

During the mayoral race, as he rode the movement to power, Baraka skewered the privatizers for using "our struggle" to legitimate their "profit-making ventures." Now, after taking the reins of power and assuming the duties of managing the neoliberal city, he reversed gears and bestowed legitimacy on what he had formerly derided as a cynical maneuver.

This intervention by the newly elected mayor highlights the central contradictions of the BUR and the skill of the longtime activist at managing them. During the election, Baraka had to appear progressive by taking up the demands and oppositional stance of the movement from below to defend public education. Yet, once in power, owing to his commitment to an orthodox urban capitalist development model based on rent intensification, of which charter schools are a central component, he had to conciliate with the same forces he ran against. But at the same time, he could not afford to alienate his loyal movement backers. Thus, central to managing this contradiction was rehabilitating his erstwhile opponents, or at least a section of them, as antiracist. A race-reductionist RD ideology that cleaved racial inequality from the larger political economy provided the tools for the makeover.[57] Now the reformers were not an outside, mostly elite, white force denying self-determination to Black and Brown people on behalf of their Wall Street backers. Rather, with Baraka's imprimatur, they were anointed as committed antiracists deeply concerned with and committed to the city's children of color.

Yet, as was clear from the rumblings in the room, many from his electoral coalition were not ready to make peace. Thus, like a school principal scolding an unruly gathering of teenagers, he admonished those who attacked his education advisor, Lauren Wells, for inviting people from "the other side."[58] He called this criticism "ridiculous," arguing that "anybody that has influence on what happens in this city with regard to education needs to be at the table." Invoking black cultural icon and close friend of his father Maya Angelou, whose funeral he had recently attended, he argued that those in the struggle over schools had to have the courage to defend their views as the late poet, author, actor, and friend of Malcom X had. "Courage is what allows you to hold steadfast to the things you believe in, and some of us lack the courage, so we run at every opportunity we are challenged."

Like his conception of courage, Baraka promoted an understanding of democracy that encouraged channeling the movement away from disruption and toward tolerance and collaboration with their opponents.

> Democracy is important. . . . I know some of us believe that democracy is only relevant when it pertains to the things we want to say, or the ideas we agree with. We support democracy as long as it supports what we believe . . . which is not what democracy is about. We cannot exchange democracy for efficiency. . . . At the end of the day we have to applaud people's rights to have a voice and a say-so in what's going on in their lives, even if you don't agree with it.

He further elaborated in his address that Newark needed "a space," such as the convention, where opposing sides could debate the issue around education reforms. The entire community, just as with the Black conventions of the early 1970s, could benefit by hearing different viewpoints. "The people in this city," Baraka emphasized, "need to see this debate." The danger, he warned, was that by not engaging the opposition, we become "inflexible . . . fundamentalist about our position."

But the election, concluded just a few months before, had provided a democratic debate on this important public policy. Indeed, the fate of the public schools was the primary issue upon which Baraka had based his campaign. In the election, Newarkers, through decisive support for Baraka, who was heavily outspent by his Wall Street–backed opponent, clearly voiced their opposition to privatization and the other market solutions to improving public education. But, of course, the democratic will of the majority clashed with the interests of a wealthy minority the mayor needed—or decided he needed—to rule the city. Thus Baraka, in the name of democracy, was in fact advocating and defending his regime's antidemocratic, "thin" neoliberal version—a "democracy" that allows elections, but not policies produced by those elections that threaten privatization and antidemocratic governance structures that have nurtured and allowed its proliferation.[59] Or, in Preston Smith II's terms, Baraka led a thin RD implementing local control and "self-determination," while vetoing a substantive SD of returning schools to the public sphere.

While preaching conciliation with the charters, Baraka simultaneously, to maintain his populist credentials, doubled down on his demand for local control and the firing of Cami Anderson, who was conspicuously *not* in attendance at the convention. Baraka penned an October 20, 2014, *New York Times* editorial in which he forcefully demanded that "local control must be returned to Newark's public schools immediately." He took aim at Governor Chris Christie, whom the Baraka electoral campaign had targeted as epitomizing outside control of the district. The RD framing of the battle was given a pictorial representation in a widely distributed campaign flyer of Christie arrayed against an arm-folded Baraka surrounded by his local black and Latinx backers. In the editorial, the newly installed mayor called on Christie—"[who] likes to say that he is 'the decider' of what happens in Newark public schools," referencing a widely reported and locally reviled statement by the Republican governor—"and his appointees [i.e., Anderson] to relinquish their hold over our schools." He went on to recount various experiments, such as Anderson's One Newark enrollment system, that "had plunged the system into more

FIGURE 3. Racial democracy messaging in a 2014 Baraka campaign flyer.

chaos." The solution to all these and other problems, which he emphasized "advocates of both traditional and charter schools" agreed upon, was a return to local control. Self-determination, that is, RD, not reversing privatization, was the solution.[60]

The city's public education movement, in tandem and consistent with Baraka's agenda, stepped up its confrontation with Anderson, the personification of state control. If Anderson would not show up at school board meetings, the movement would confront her where she did appear in public. NJCU's Cabañas, working with the NSU, PULSE, and POP, clandestinely organized a bus trip of forty activists to Washington, D.C., to disrupt a November 14 address by Anderson at the American Enterprise Institute, a conservative think tank, on her "successes and triumphs" in Newark.[61]

MANAGING CONTRADICTIONS:
A SIX-MONTH REPORT CARD

Ras Baraka entered office in summer 2014 with a significant challenge. For the first time since the emergence of Kenneth Gibson as the city's first black mayor in 1970, a new local head of state was riding to power on the élan of a mass movement. Furthermore, this movement was leading a campaign of disruption targeting a core feature of the neoliberal agenda, backed by the most powerful, ascendant wings of the capitalist class: the privatization of public schools. At the same time, Baraka was committed to a rent-intensification development agenda in which the privatization of schools was an integral component. How would the new mayor manage these competing agendas? Would Baraka have what Al Koeppe, a key part of the corporate governing elite, called the "right compass" to navigate these treacherous class currents?

At least for the first six months of his term, Baraka clearly demonstrated that he did indeed have the skills to manage what urban scholars Whelan, Young, and Lauria identified as the central "dilemma" facing the BUR. The longtime activist put his skills to work as he successfully "*appear*[*ed*] to be progressive in addressing the needs of the black community," while, at the same time, concretely meeting "the needs of the major business interests."[62] Central to constructing the appearance was the deployment of a self-determinationist ideology and political practice—an RD variant that outwardly combated racial oppression

200 || RAS BARAKA'S SELF-DETERMINATION POLITICS

but substantively undergirded class domination. His skillful wielding of this ideology helped him take the "grassroot concerns" around the privatization of public education that he had championed and "convert those concerns into forms that fit into—or at least pose no threat to—the imperatives of . . . [the] larger pro-business, pro-growth priorities" that informed his governing agenda.[63] Through the alchemy of antiracism, the fight became one of "self-determination" achieved by obtaining "local control," not stopping, let alone reversing, privatization. Under Baraka's conception, supporters of charters and public schools were now bound together by their antiracist commitments, which transcended any difference over minor details like privatization. The real enemy was the antidemocratic, "fascist"—as he denounced at the gathering with Karen Lewis—and by extension racist practices and forces denying self-determination to Newark.

In addition to his own impressive skills, Baraka received assistance from other quarters that helped him manage Newark's sharpened class contradictions. One of the most important was, ironically, the white, rotund Christie himself. His trademark bullying and flaunting of the formal power he exercised over Newark's public schools—"I am the decider"—provided the perfect foil for Baraka's efforts to channel the movement into an antifascist, antiracist struggle for "self-determination." Christie's thinly veiled racist attacks served a bourgeois agenda to displace white suburban class anxieties *toward* resentment against hard-fought education equity funding gains for New Jersey's urban centers and *away* from the bipartisan capitalist policies that have fueled runaway inequality. Christie's bourgeois-rule-serving racism simultaneously strengthened the power of Baraka's own bourgeois antiracism to steer the movement toward a manageable "self-determination" struggle and away from an anticapitalist defense of the commons.

A second form of assistance came from developments in the movement from below at the national level. As Colin Barker argues, a defining feature of social movements are as "fields of argument." Important questions and debates that arise within a movement include "who are its opponents?" and "how should it define and pursue its objectives?"[64] The role of the Democratic Party has historically been a contentious one in what Zeitlin and Stepan-Norris term "the intra-class struggle" in the United States. The answer from Lewis, then head of the CTU, who enjoyed enormous prestige in movement ranks nationally at the time, was that the Democratic Party apparatus could be harnessed to achieve movement objectives. Although "corporate Democrats" were at the center of the assault on public education, the movement could still, Lewis argued, "make Democrats behave" and reconfigure the party as part of "the progressive infrastructure." Baraka, whose radical credentials were burnished by sharing the stage with Lewis, was the unspoken evidence for her thesis. Thus Lewis and the CTU helped legitimate Baraka as a vehicle for pursuing movement objectives.

A third factor that strengthened Baraka's hand was a shared embrace, among the NSU leadership, of "racism . . . as the most consequential force impeding black Americans" and other people of color.[65] The NSU emerged in the wake of the 2012 murder of black youth Trayvon Martin by white vigilante George Zimmerman and the rise of the Black Lives Matter (BLM) race-centric framing of police murder. Racism, particularly antiblack racism, abstracted from political economy, was seen as the driving force behind the killing and other forms of violence and injustice facing the entire black community. Indeed, a July 2013 *Star-Ledger* editorial by NSU founders Jaysen Bazile and Thais Marquez, penned after Zimmerman's acquittal, identified racism as the driving force behind a host of problems faced by blacks and Latinos, from the criminal justice system to home foreclosures and underfunded schools.[66] Within the group, "antiblackness," and the way it pervades American life, was the focus of numerous in-group discussions. Thus the general intellectual milieu, of which the rise of the "race first politics" of the lionized writer Ta-Nehisi Coates was also a part, helped foment what Cedric Johnson calls a "nostalgia for Black Power Militancy." As in the past, this politics inevitably congeals, Johnson argues, into a black ethnic politics that "facilitates elite brokerage dynamics rather than building effective counterpower."[67] The experience of the first six months of Ras Baraka's mayorship provides further confirmatory evidence for Johnson's thesis.

Finally, Baraka also received an assist from the NTU bureaucracy, which was able to stave off a challenge from the NEW insurgency. Although the reform caucus had won a majority of the board, it was unable to convert that power into implementing its plans, such as firing or demoting acting president Abeigon and hiring Leah Owens as a full-time organizer. Most significantly, NEW was unable to mobilize the teachers, along with other education workers, to join en masse the walkouts the students were leading in a student–worker strike.

Keeping the teachers on the sidelines eased Baraka's task of class conciliation.

Thus, by the end of 2014, in part because of Baraka's skill, the struggle had become one for "self-determination" that required the removal of Anderson. Nonetheless, Anderson, a committed, ideologically steeled movement militant, still had important backers and gave no indication that she was ready to throw in the towel. Could Baraka engineer her displacement without unrest extending to the broader privatization drive he was unwilling and unable to oppose? Would the movement from below, for its part, allow a deal that removed the reviled superintendent while retaining her equally despised reform agenda? We now turn to the second half of the tumultuous 2014–15 school year for our answer.

7

We All Become Mayor?

MOVEMENT REINVENTION AND THE OUSTING OF CAMI ANDERSON, SPRING–SUMMER 2015

> The interest-group model depends on a form of elite brokerage, centered on a relation between governing elites and entities or individuals recognized as representatives of designated groups. The heart of the relation is negotiation of policies . . . that presumably protect and advance the interests of the pertinent groups, but safely—in ways that harmonize them with governing elite's priorities.
>
> —Adolph Reed Jr., *Class Notes: Posing as Politics and Other Thoughts on the American Scene*

By the beginning of 2015, after nearly four years, Cami Anderson had implemented many "radical changes"—as she termed her efforts to "raise the bar for our kids"—to disrupt Newark's public schools and advance the neoliberal SSA.[1] She had closed, or threatened to close, "turn around," "colocate," or "renew" scores of public schools—what NSU leader Towkanik called all "the 're'-words that are just fancy words for closing a school and destabilizing a community." Under her stewardship, Newark more than doubled the percentage of its students in charters, increasing from 6.4 percent in 2011, her first year, to 13.8 percent by 2015.[2] Correspondingly, disruption through the charters' cannibalization of the NPS budget climbed from $125 million, or nearly 15 percent in the 2011–12 fiscal year, to $181 million, nearly 21 percent, by 2014–15.[3] She also, as explained in chapter 5, successfully imposed the One Newark district-wide enrollment system that denied the right to attend neighborhood schools and instead provided families with a "menu of options" among charter, magnet, and "traditional" public schools. Newark's new enrollment system, which had first been imposed on post-Katrina New Orleans, was a

|| 203

204 || WE ALL BECOME MAYOR?

new lethal weapon added to the growing arsenal deployed to disrupt public education.

On the labor front, the Anderson regime imposed, with cooperation from AFT chief Weingarten, a collective bargaining agreement designed to increase employment insecurity and undermine solidarity. The central office, the big government "behemoth" long a target of the reformers, was slashed by 164 full-time employees in the 2013–14 fiscal year alone, with Anderson's budget czar promising a "larger number of cuts for FY2014."[4] Anderson's dismantlement of the central office was, in classic neoliberal form, aimed at moving "governance out of the routinized channels of the formal state," where opportunities for popular oversight and input are greater.[5] In the place of longtime civil servants, she surrounded herself with well-compensated, movement-aligned contractors and consultants, funded by philanthropy, to plot and carry out their disruption plans free of public oversight. This arrangement was a prime example of creating, as David Harvey outlined in his work *Rebel Cities,*

> new systems of governance that integrate state and corporate interests and, through the application of money power, assure that control over the disbursement of the surplus through the state apparatuses favors corporate capital and the upper classes in the shaping of the urban process.[6]

All of this disruption fueled, as intended, "an exodus of people . . . out of Newark [public schools]," as NEW leader Branden Rippey observed. "It gets even worse," Rippey added.

> In 2012, 2013, 2014, once it has become clear that the union was going to bring us shit contracts, they weren't really going to fight, people went into defensive posture and were like "let's just get out, let's look for something better."

Freda Barrow, a public school teacher at George Washington Carver Elementary School in the heavily black South Ward, explains how the charter schools took advantage of the disruption from above to actively fuel an exodus of students and teachers from the public schools. "She"—referring to Barrow's former colleague who went to work for Newark's KIPP charter chain schools—

was encouraged to speak to parents of our high-achieving students [at George Washington Carver Elementary School]. So I already knew that was going down . . . they were what they call *"creaming off the top."* . . . Those were the parents who they were encouraged to speak to, to get them to put their kids into the charter school. She told me that. You know, just between friends, between co-workers, and they were asking them to try and recruit teachers who they thought were good, or would be a good fit. So there were a few summers when she would call me and see if I wanted to come over and interview, and I was like "no, I'm good where I am."[7]

Thus Anderson, in the key movement battleground of Newark, successfully deployed a campaign of *disruption,* a "power strategy that rests on withdrawing cooperation from social relations."[8] The varied, crosscutting networks of cooperation and interdependence, encompassing teachers, students, parents, families, neighborhoods, and unions, all anchored by the overarching institution of public schools, were torn apart by Anderson's reform agenda. As Pauline Lipman argues in her study of Chicago, "displacement from schools and communities is more than physical disruption. It breaks a web of human connection in which social and cultural practices of daily life are rooted, race and class identities are formed, and community is constituted."[9] These social relationships, at the heart what New Jersey governor Chris Christie and other movement militants derisively referred to as the "educational establishment," had provided important "bases of political participation" for working-class people and an island of stability in a sea of various capitalist predations.[10] But to impose the "new hegemonic political order" in which education is delivered by the market, the old social relationships and expectations that came with them had to be torn asunder.[11]

But, despite these advances, the movement from above in Newark and around the country was facing a continuing legitimacy crisis among the urban working-class communities upon whom the reforms were imposed. Many leading reform militants acknowledged and attempted to address this problem in their intramovement discussions. For example, at a spring 2014 "annual summit for the education reform movement," held under the auspices of the New Schools Venture Fund, speakers emphasized the need for generating consent, particularly by including African Americans in positions of leadership. At the gathering, Kaya Henderson, a TFA alumna and the then newly installed Washington, D.C., superintendent replacement for Michele Rhee, made a thinly veiled criticism of her predecessor and others in the movement who deployed similar methods. "The people we serve," Henderson emphasized, "have to be a part of their own liberation." Education secretary Arne Duncan, who provided unprecedented financial and ideological support for charters through Race to the Top and other initiatives, and whose Department of Education was staffed with many TFA veterans, was also distressed about the state of the movement. He pointed out the contradictions between the movement's self-conception as the "new civil rights movement" and the lack of black faces in leadership positions.

> Who in here has heard the phrase that education is the civil-rights movement of our age? . . . If we believe that, then we have to believe that the rest of the movement has to come with it.[12]

Dale Russakoff, the *Washington Post* journalist, in her highly acclaimed book on Newark's neoliberal school reform initiative, *The Prize: Who's in Charge of America's Schools?*, also pointed out the movement's legitimacy deficit. An in-house critic, Russakoff praised the reform agenda, including merit pay, weakening teacher unions, and expanding high-performing charter schools.[13] But, she argued, leading reform implementers had failed in gaining popular consent to their agenda, particularly in Newark. Movement leaders like Chris Cerf and Cami Anderson bristled at the criticism leveled by the seasoned journalist, but this was all made in the service of a movement whose ends Russakoff largely supported.[14]

Ras Baraka, for his part, had exploited this legitimacy crisis, and the mass movement that had emerged, to win the mayorship of his beloved hometown. But, as recounted in the previous chapter, he had to walk a political tightrope. Baraka had to deliver on his promises of self-determination while at the same time not threatening the larger privatization agenda. His counterpart, Anderson, despite the growing outrage, was committed to deepening the disruption agenda as she designated eight "failing" schools for a "turnaround" regimen.

How would this contest, as the city entered what everyone expected to be an explosive second half of the 2014–15 school year, end? It concluded, as I document in this chapter, with Baraka's removal of his nemesis, but *not* the legacy of disruption—the "radical measures"—Anderson had imposed. The students and teachers, who stepped up their disruption, as I recount herein, had different ideas as they demanded not only the removal of the state-imposed superintendent and return to local control but her entire neoliberal agenda. In the midst of this ferment, Baraka intervened to endorse and, indeed, urge disruption by his allies. But unlike the mobilized students and teachers, Baraka became even more emphatic in narrowing the movement's horizons and directing their energies to the removal of Anderson and a return to local control. His effective rebranding of the movement as an entirely RD one was accompanied by jettisoning his populist "we all become mayor" rhetoric as he negotiated a secret deal with Christie to remove Anderson. In a classic exercise in what Adolph Reed Jr. terms "elite brokerage" in the epigraph, Baraka managed to meet *a* RD demand of his popular allies, while not antagonizing their opponents. I conclude with the mayor's successful containing of discontent with a deal that did nothing to block the continued privatization of the district, let alone reverse the damage already inflicted.

THE EARLY SPRING OFFENSIVE

During the previous two springs, Newark's students and allies had stepped up their own disruption against the reformers' top-down version. In the third year of the insurgency, with their "radical mayor" now in office, things began to heat up beginning in January, during the northeastern city's frigid winter months. They mobilized against One Newark, the "turnaround" plan, and advocated for their alternative, Newark Promise, and, above all, Anderson's removal.[15]

For his part, Mayor Baraka, whose signature issue was regaining "local control" and "self-determination," doubled down on his calls for the superintendent's immediate removal. In a January 12 letter to Anderson, he denounced her "blatant disregard" for the Newark community and "manipulation of state control of Newark Public Schools to usurp the rights of Newark residents." He concluded by demanding her "immediate resignation as state-appointed superintendent of Newark public schools."[16] The Alliance for Newark Public Schools (ANPS) amplified Baraka's message with a February 8 press conference in front of the state education commissioner's Newark office. The gathering, overseen by Roberto Cabañas, the NSU advisor

208 || WE ALL BECOME MAYOR?

and NJCU staffer, with Baraka's press officer, the former Young Lord's leader Felipe Luciano, representing the administration, issued a unified "demand [for] Cami Anderson's resignation."[17]

The NSU then stepped up its disruption by holding its longest sit-in at board headquarters to date—four days, from February 17 to 20. The top demand was Anderson's resignation, which NSU cofounder and now NJCU organizer Thais Marquez called "nonnegotiable" as they vowed "to stay until she resigns." Their determination to hold out was strengthened by the solidarity of allies who broke through the Anderson-imposed blockade of food deliveries. After twelve hours of being denied food, the students and NJCU organizers called on ANPS members and sympathetic ministers to take direct action.[18] The response of the ministers underscored Piven's argument that "political action takes forms within a matrix of social relations," and therefore "those who mobilize disruptive power must overcome the constraints typically imposed by their multiple relations with others."[19] The black clergy, generally a conservative force, had largely sided with Anderson and the movement from above. But the student-led movement had broken off a section, and they provided crucial support that helped sustain the occupation. As Reverend Mamie Bridgeforth recounts, "when the young people took over her office, I was one of the clergy, along with about six or seven others, who went down there."

> They called us and they said would you please come . . . and we went. They refused to allow us to go upstairs to see those children. What they were trying to do technically was to starve the kids out. Not giving them any food or anything and eventually the kids would leave and once they left they would shut the door and they won't be able to get in again. We came in and brought food but they didn't want us to go upstairs to bring the food. I simply remember standing there at the elevator and I said to the Corporation counsel of the board . . . "Let me share something with you, we're going to see those children, we're going to take food upstairs and if you are foolish enough to allow these security guards to try to put hands on ministers, you are an idiot." So they stood there for a moment and left. And then we went upstairs and we did give the children their food. I really wanted to make sure that they were all right.

Although Hespe did renew Anderson's contract the week after the sit-in, the NSU's direct action had left the beleaguered superintendent further isolated from former allies. State senator Teresa Ruiz, for example, head of the Senate education committee and a former Jeffries backer, joined the chorus calling for her resignation. She denounced Anderson's reappointment as "devastating for the Newark Public Schools community" and a "terrible decision . . . when the district desperately needs to go in a new direction." Of course, for Ruiz, that new direction did not mean a move away from privatization. Rather, like Russakoff, she indicts Anderson for not "foster[ing] relationships with everyone" so as to introduce the reform movement agenda consensually. Nonetheless, despite Ruiz's continued bedrock support for privatization, the students' disruptive protests did create further splits among the movement from above.[20]

As always, various components of the public school defense movement used the school board meetings as a platform to raise their demands. Chief among these was the removal of Cami Anderson, but activists raised other issues as well. At the February meeting, for example, following the NSU sit-in, Rippey, accompanied by a delegation of his fellow NEW members, was the first speaker and began his intervention saluting the student protests. He then denounced the state's imposition of the high-stakes PARCC standardized test, another part of neoliberal reform agenda, that was a product of collaboration between the Gates Foundation and the for-profit Pierson testing company. Students in Newark—reflecting a broader national movement—would exercise another form of disruptive power with widespread boycotts of the test in the spring. Deborah Smith-Gregory, of the ANPS and NAACP, expounded on Anderson's failures, while holding a large report card placard delineating them and joining others in demanding her termination.[21]

At the April board meeting, as street protests and organizing intensified, the auditorium was filled to near capacity as a raucous crowd cheered on a stream of activists denouncing the One Newark enrollment system, school closings, turnaround school designations, and charters.[22] NEW, which was running its "New Visions" reform slate in the upcoming union election, denounced the incumbent bureaucrats and the 2012 concessionary contract and outlined its agenda to wide applause. The longest address—well beyond the allotted three

210 || WE ALL BECOME MAYOR?

minutes—and recipient of the most effusive applause came from Mayor Ras Baraka. I quote at length his intervention because it provides a masterful performance of managing the central contradiction of the BUR in the particularly difficult context of a mass movement:

> I think we need to flood the meetings until we get what we want.... It's important we show up and not just for our individual schools ... because if they're doing it to some kids in the South Ward they are going to do it to your kids in the North Ward.... So it's important for us to be at these meetings and not divide our community. We are one city together and what happens at Weequahic will happen at Shabazz, will happen at East Side ... Barringer ... Science, Arts, University, and if those folks aren't careful, it will happen at Newark Collegiate too [a charter school].
>
> I'm asking the community to be vigilant ... to flood these meetings ... because there is a commentary being told around the country that we are satisfied with what is happening in the City of Newark, and we are *not* satisfied with what is happening.
>
> I'm going to say some things I probably should not say. I think it's time for people to begin doing some actions in this city. I think the NTU, NEA, the AFT, Parents Union, the Students Union, every organization in this community needs to raise their voices until *this lady leaves our city immediately.* I want you to know that as the mayor of this city, I support immediately any organized and peaceful response ... about making sure we are getting what we need and what is right and just for our community.
>
> Unfortunately things have come to this, and we have to do this immediately, immediately.... We should not rely on the board.... The board has a job ... that they get us back to local control. Our job in this community is to raise our voices as loud as we can so that they can hear us all the way to Trenton that we don't like what is happening in our city.... We can't suffer this any longer. There is no more room for compromise.
>
> I think the wise thing to do, if you have advisors on this board, is to tell her immediately that the mayor suggests that she pack her things and leave. That sooner or later I'm going to take my detail and we're going to Two Cedar Street and we're going to walk her

out the front door. [*NSU students lead chant*: "If we don't get it? Shut it down, shut it down!"][23]

Baraka, in this intervention, skillfully solidarizes with and indeed encourages mass protest and disruption—"I think it's time for people to begin doing some actions." At the same time, he advocates safely channeling disruption in a self-determination direction against the illegitimate, outside-imposed superintendent. While calling for city-wide unity, he includes charters as part of the same besieged community that must unite "until this lady leaves our city immediately." This message echoed the one he gave at his first state of the city address the month before, when he called for an end of the "neocolonial state that Trenton has forced us into."[24]

TEACHER AND STUDENT REVOLTS AT EAST SIDE AND WEEQUAHIC HIGH SCHOOLS

The "turnaround" plans for two comprehensive high schools resulted in many teachers, for the first time, exercising disruptive power by withdrawing their cooperation from Anderson's directives. As East Side teacher Al Moussab explained, the "turnaround" designation "really got East Side going." The initiative came from rank-and-file teachers rather than from the NTU leadership, whose new interim president was John Abeigon, in place of the terminally ill Joe Del Grosso.

Anderson sent her trusted high schools administrator, Brad Haggerty—part of the "nest of educational entrepreneurs" that Anderson "imported from the New York City Department of Education"—to strong-arm the East Side teachers.[25] Haggerty ordered teachers to sign the extended work agreement (EWA), which would involve longer days, some weekends, and two weeks during the summer. The "extra" pay for the stretch-out amounted to a whopping $7.74/hour, approximately the same level as the abysmally low federal minimum wage.[26] If teachers refused, they could be forced to move to another school, while the nontenured teachers faced firing. The NTU president, who had negotiated the contract that included the turnaround provision, ostensibly told teachers not to sign the EWA. But, as Moussab points out, "the union leaders at East Side" allied with Abeigon were "telling people 'we're going to try to fight the weekends and the summer hours

212 || WE ALL BECOME MAYOR?

in this EWA contract but we're going to have to prepare ourselves to work the longer day.'" The political calculations of a NTU vice president who worked at the school, and who had met privately with Anderson's emissary to cut a deal, was that "if we can negotiate it, so it's only an extended day, I'll sign it."[27]

The rank-and-file teachers at East Side, surprisingly led by the particularly vulnerable nontenured faculty, and encouraged by Moussab and other NEW supporters, had other ideas. At a meeting of all the teachers, Moussab and other NEW activists intervened with a message of "let's fight this," which included a PowerPoint presentation developed by NEW's fellow insurgents at the CTU. "But," Moussab added, "a lot of [veteran] teachers said 'oh the nontenureds are going to sign this, if you're nontenured and don't sign this you can get fired.'" The following day, the nontenured teachers held their own meeting and decided, collectively, that they would not sign. This decision by the most vulnerable workers was, Moussab argued, "the catalyst, the turning point," because now the teachers "were like 'we can win this thing' . . . once we saw nontenured teachers saying no one will sign this, the tenured teachers were like 'fuck it, we're not going to sign it.'"

Further emboldening the teachers were the students who began mobilizing, with the NSU, against the school's designation as "failing" and therefore in need of a "turnaround." The students were further backed by many parents, who, Moussab recalls, "started calling up and asking what is going on with the school . . . coming in and meeting and trying to get more information, they were pretty supportive as well." Thais Marquez, one of the NSU founders who was now working with students through NJCU in the Ironbound neighborhood in which she grew up, explained that once students heard their school was targeted, they were "so great, like they were motivated." This motivation included regular morning leafleting at the school, where, Marquez says, "they did a bad-ass job" that bore fruit by "getting the whole school to walk out on May 1."

The growing movement even forced the hand of East Side's principal, Mario Santos, and the conservative Portuguese East Ward councilman Augusto Amador. The latter was allied, along with the Puerto Rican elite, with the pro-charter DiVincenzo–Adubato Democratic Party county grouping that had backed Jeffries and Christie in his 2013 reelection. Santos, as Marquez explained, worked, as he had in the past, to undermine any mobilization of disruptive power by students. At the same time, for his own bureaucratic interests in opposing the turnaround designation and desire to defuse the student mobilizations, Santos, along with Amador, organized his own anti-turnaround designation rally on Saturday, April 25—the week before the planned May 1 walkout.[28] Nonetheless the duo were unsuccessful in holding back the tide, as the May 1 noon walkout turned out to be the largest from East Side in the three-year-long insurgency. Teachers joined students as they marched through the neighborhood's main commercial artery and on to the federal courthouse, "where dozens of reporters had gathered to cover developments in the George Washington Bridge scandal."[29]

As East Side mobilized, another front opened at Weequahic High School, in the city's South Ward. In this case, the opposition was spearheaded by a longtime ally of Baraka, fellow teacher Bashir Akinyele, who admired Baraka as "a strong, fearless man, a fearless voice." Akinyele began "working with him when he ran for mayor back in '94" and collaborated with the future mayor in 2009 to create the Newark Anti-Violence Coalition. This strong bond clearly continued once his longtime comrade became mayor. After Haggerty, as at East Side, met with Akinyele and other Weequahic teachers to deliver the district's "turnaround" edict, the faculty, in a follow-up meeting, decided, "Nah, we're not going to sign it." Akinyele found, as did Moussab at East Side, that "the turnaround and the EWA thing sparked, just sparked something that I haven't seen in teachers in a long time, some activism." The students, Akinyele recounts, also began mounting various forms of disruptive action to block the turnaround plans:

> So they began to organize . . . during convocation in the gym. . . .
> They would stay in the gym when the principal told them to go to
> class, they just quietly stayed in the gym. And they held rallies in
> the hallway where they basically quietly blocked arms and did not
> move out of the hallways when it was time for classes, for classes
> to move. . . . And they did a walkout, they shut the entire Chancellor Avenue down.[30]

Through Leah Owens, Moussab made contact with Akinyele, who had not previously been involved with NEW. The two organized a Saturday, May 2, rally at Weequahic that brought together teachers from the two targeted high schools, along with parents, community

214 || WE ALL BECOME MAYOR?

activists, and leading black public officials, most prominently Mayor Ras Baraka. The broadening of the geographic basis of the movement linking East Side in the Ironbound/East Ward section and Weequahic in the South Ward was particularly significant. The heavily Latino, Brazilian, Portuguese, and immigrant Ironbound, which enjoyed a bustling and prosperous Ferry Street commercial district and was cordoned off by a concrete rail line and a four-lane, heavily trafficked thoroughfare, was both physically and psychologically removed from the rest of the city, particularly the predominantly black and poorer South Ward. Indeed, a fear expressed by some teachers at East Side was that if they did not sign the EWA, "they could be placed on the other side of Route 21," that is, transferred to a school outside the Ironbound.[31] Thus, from Moussab's perspective at the time, he felt this was "going to be huge not only for Weequahic and East Side but just historically for the South Ward and the Ironbound to unite."[32]

The united Weequahic–East Side action was followed up with a May 13 after-school rally at the school board headquarters in downtown Newark. The rally, which blocked traffic on the downtown's main thoroughfare, brought teachers and students from East Side as well as teachers from Weequahic and around the city, particularly from schools targeted for "turnaround." For the first time since Anderson took power and mounted her offensives, teachers at targeted schools were moving from rearguard, localist, defensive "militant particularist" struggles to defend their own schools to a citywide campaign that united all the schools under attack. Moussab, Rippey, Owens, and the rest of NEW had been trying to advance the movement along these lines for the last several years, and it now appeared their organizing was finally bearing fruit.

For many of the teachers, this was the first time they had attended a demonstration. What prompted the move to action for many was indignation over Anderson's order to work extra hours when they were already doing that on their own. As Vivian Rivera, a teacher from the targeted Elliott Street Elementary School, explained, "we were doing that"—working longer hours—"without being told we were a turnaround . . . sacrificing hours of our life for the students in our school."

Likewise, at East Side, Moussab explained, teachers became indignant over being ordered to teach extra hours—at minimum wage—when they were already doing that on their own because of their commitment to their students. "What a lot of the teachers said" they really needed, Moussab underscored, "was 'just give us the resources during the day, make the class sizes smaller, let us give more individual attention and we can do this.'" Thus the imposition of turnaround angered many teachers and pushed them into protest. Rivera from Elliott Street Elementary explains, "When I found out that Elliott was going to be one of the turnaround schools . . . that's how I became active."

Akinyele emceed the May 13 protest rally, with NEW activists Moussab and Rippey playing leading roles. NTU acting chief Abeigon did not even attend, reflecting how NEW activists had gained hegemony in the fight against the turnarounds. In their speeches, Rippey and Moussab both emphasized that the action, which brought teachers from across the district, represented a real turning point in the movement after several years of attacks by the reformers, particularly the despised turnaround designation. Instead of being cowed by the administration into acceding to the EWA designation—such as the one-on-one meetings the administration used "to pressure people to sign" at the George Washington Carver Elementary School in the South Ward—or fighting in isolation, teachers were now uniting.[33]

The mayor, who received a rousing introduction from Akinyele, also addressed the crowd. Over the preceding weeks, as the pace of events

FIGURE 4. Ras Baraka speaking at the May 13, 2015, rally in downtown Newark, called by NEW to oppose Anderson's plans. Photograph by Freda Barrow.

216 || WE ALL BECOME MAYOR?

accelerated, Baraka increasingly personalized his attacks on Anderson and called for more protest against her imperiled reign. At the May 13 outdoor rally, he encouraged further protests while denouncing Anderson "for trying to get people to speak against me and claiming that I am promoting violence be taken against her. . . . Having people go into her office and escorting her out is not violent." He ended with chants backing the teachers' grievances and demands—"No to turnarounds . . . No EWA . . . Hands off Weequahic, East Side . . . All our schools"—while concluding his speech with the demand of his allies in the ANPS: "Our choice is community schools, God bless you."[34]

THE KNOCKOUT PUNCH

As the teachers began to go into motion, the NSU, as president Kristin Towkanik explained, "went all-out organizing."

> We were organizing every single day before and after school, on the weekends, we would be at schools during events . . . at school board meetings, we would be on social media. . . . We were also able to use other people in other schools who were just friends, even though they were not members, we were able to . . . organize [them] for the walkout.

The NSU had been organizing walkouts since spring 2013, but leaders promised May 22 would be their largest, most powerful rollout of disruptive power. They delivered. More than two thousand high school students walked out midday from their classrooms and converged on the steps of City Hall. These included students from the longtime stronghold of Science High, who marched under a large banner demanding "FULL LOCAL CONTROL," and other magnet schools, but also included large continents from East Side and Weequahic, the two comprehensive neighborhood high schools targeted for turnaround, as well as, appropriately, Malcolm X Shabazz High. There were even defectors from the charter schools, including a student who faced disciplinary action for her participation.[35] It was truly a citywide movement, and one with national ramifications, which Towkanik made clear in her address. At the festive-like gathering, the impressive, seasoned, now eighteen-year-old activist let Chris Christie and Arne Duncan, whom she called out by name, know that

FIGURE 5. Students rally in front of Newark City Hall as part of a mass student walkout organized by the Newark Students Union, May 22, 2015. Photograph by Leah Z. Owens.

FIGURE 6. NSU activist Jose Leonardo, bullhorn in hand, leads students in blocking McCarter Highway and the main entrance to the New Jersey Turnpike. Photograph by Sherry Wolf.

218 || WE ALL BECOME MAYOR?

"we did not come here to play." Recognizing the source of students' power in disruption, she explained that actions like this "is how we get . . . attention." Towkanik drilled down on the central demand "to get our schools back" and that they "will keep going until we get our schools back." Thus, consistent with Baraka's self-determination framing of the struggle, the key solution to continued expansion of charters, of turnarounds, and all their other attacks was local control.[36]

Yet, while the students' messaging certainly pleased Baraka, some of the new mayor's actions were generating discontent among some of his most loyal and important supporters among the student leadership. One point of contention was the police's heavy handling of the May 22 protest. Towkanik "felt Ras and his administration did us dirty because he had put up barricades so we wouldn't be able to take over the street." Another point of friction was Baraka's failure to expend political capital to place a moratorium on charter expansion—a distancing from his commitments that would deepen in the coming year. Of course, the NSU, like Baraka, was clear that, as NSU vice president Jose Leonardo put it, "Anderson has got to go." But, he added, "We do understand that if Cami leaves, that's putting a Band-Aid on a bullet wound. Christie would just put someone that's maybe worse than Cami." Therefore, for Leonardo, and the rest of the NSU, as well as Baraka, "the biggest demand is full local control of our city," understood as not only the removal of Anderson but the restoration of power to the local school board. That was the elixir, but in a departure from Baraka, the NSU and other elements of the movement from below conceived of "reclaiming control of our schools" *as a means* to push back against privatization, the central threat to public schools. "Right now, they're taking advantage of that power"—referring to Christie and his state department of education control of Newark public schools—"to charterize the schools and take them away from the hands of the community."[37] Indeed, "local control" would be meaningless if most of the system were privatized. In contrast, Baraka's challenge was to chart a course that pitted an imposed, illegitimate school chief denying "self-determination" to a charter-inclusive defined "community."

These contradictions were highlighted in May when Anibal Ramos introduced and passed a city council resolution opposing a proposed state assembly bill placing a three-year moratorium on charter school expansion. The student-led mass movement had forced even the pro-charter county (DiVincenzo)- and Adubato-aligned and -groomed politicians like Ramos and state senator Teresa Ruiz to join the call for Anderson's resignation and oppose some of her measures, such as One Newark.[38] But these criticisms by no means signified that they had backed off their resolute backing of charter schools and their continued expansion. The resolution telegraphed that message. To the consternation of the defenders of public schools, voting in the affirmative were three black city council members—McCallum, Chaneyfield-Jenkins, and Osborne—who had run as part of the Baraka slate in the previous year's election. Baraka, who was known to demand and prioritize loyalty, nonetheless did not level any criticism at, or take any action against, his political allies for breaking ranks. Clearly blocking charter school expansion was not a priority for Baraka.[39]

BUTTRESSING CONSENT: THE NONPROFIT–UNION NEXUS

Assisting Baraka in managing his sharpening contradictions was, as discussed in chapter 5, the "community–labor" AROS coalition that the AFT had put together at the national level, and its local organizational expression.[40] In a follow-up October 2013 conference in Los Angeles—bankrolled by the Schott Foundation, AFT, and NEA— AROS members gathered to lay out their platform. The demands centered around support for public, neighborhood-based "community schools"; opposition to punitive, zero-tolerance disciplinary practices; reduced testing; and a living wage. Later, AROS added planks calling for a moratorium on charter school expansion and restoring elected school boards to districts under state receivership.[41]

AROS and their local coalition manifestations would prove useful for Baraka in Newark, de Blasio in New York, and what academics Fine and Fabricant referred to favorably as other "promising signs of new progressive voices emerging" at the local and national levels of the Democratic Party. Chief among their strengths, from the perspective of the "progressive" mayors taking power, such as Baraka, was their proven loyalty. The vetted groups that composed the invitation-only AROS coalition—particularly the unions and the foundations, who held the purse strings and, thus, real power—were all tightly bound to the Democrats. They could be counted on not to seriously challenge the Democratic mayors when they betrayed their commitments. Second, the central demand of "community schools," which basically

220 || WE ALL BECOME MAYOR?

involved adding additional "wraparound services" for schools designated as failing, often provided by nonprofits and foundation grants, were conveniently vague. The community schools designation did not require, as New York City activist Leonie Haimson pointed out in her critique of the initiative, reducing the student–teacher ratio, which voluminous research has shown improves school performance, particularly for poor children.[42]

The Newark arm of AROS, the ANPS, allowed local activists, in the words of NJCU organizer Roberto Cabañas, the major mover in the local formation, "to nationalize this fight." The first example of "nationalizing the fight" was the protest in December 2013, discussed in chapter 5, for which Weingarten came to Newark as part of a nationally coordinated day of protest. Then, in 2014, Cabañas began working with the NTU; the Service Employees International Union; school board president Baskerville-Richardson; the local NAACP head, Deborah Smith-Gregory; and Baraka's future education advisor, Lauren Wells, all loyal backers of the mayor, to develop an alternative to the Anderson restructuring plan. This effort eventually took the shape of the ANPS and its Newark Promise plan, which acted as a conveyer belt for demands and priorities established at the national level. The plan was first unveiled at a May 17, 2014, rally, following Baraka's election. Organized under the banner of "Schools our children deserve," the Newark event was part of AROS's national day of action commemorating the fiftieth anniversary of the landmark 1954 U.S. Supreme Court *Brown* school desegregation ruling.[43]

Just as the AFT's Weingarten made sure to exclude UCORE from the national coalition, the NTU chief Abeigon made sure to exclude UCORE's local affiliate, NEW, from the local alliance. As NEW president Rippey explained at the 2015 UCORE conference held in Newark, "NTU threatened to revoke money [for the ANPS] if NEW's name was even put on a flyer" or involved in any way in the ANPS. Although Cabañas was friendly with NEW, and the NSU student activists he mentored endorsed NEW in the 2015 union election, he would not buck the NTU leadership. Indeed, as Cabañas explained, "I was not in agreement with the student union endorsing [NEW] because they should've stayed out of that."

Further buttressing Cabañas's subordination to the NTU was the NJCU's own funding stream. The ACORN successor was funded by the CWA—the NTU's fellow AFL-CIO member—who would also not want to include the rank-and-file NEW insurgents. Thus the top-down antidemocratic nature of the ANPS, which contrasted with NEW welcoming community members, including non–education workers, ensured that it would remain safely in Baraka's corner.

To generate popular support for community schools, which the ANPS had really "bought in to" as an alternative to charters, Cabañas organized junkets of local activists to observe "really existing" examples of their model in various cities. In addition, working with its national allies, the ANPS hosted several local forums in spring 2015 on the community schools concept. At a March 20 gathering, a representative from the de Blasio administration touted the "daring moves" made by New York City's mayor to designate several schools in the South Bronx as community schools. Yet, at the same time, the de Blasio administration, which was promoted by the speaker as a model, failed to mobilize any opposition when fellow Democrat Governor Andrew Cuomo blocked a city-backed plan to freeze charter expansion and the practice of "colocation"—charter schools occupying existing public schools. With the veto by his nemesis in Albany, de Blasio retreated to a détente, an illusory "peaceful coexistence," with the privatizers. In this context, community schools became a nonconfrontational way to appear sympathetic to defenders of public schools without having to seriously confront the continued expansion of charters.[44]

At a subsequent community schools forum in May, Lauren Wells, Baraka's chief education officer and chair of the gathering, placed the struggle squarely in a racial justice framework. She denounced antidemocratic state takeovers that are "pushed on communities that look like us." In contrast, a "collective approach" to reform, as embodied in the community schools program, and the GVZ initiative she led with Pedro Noguera, is rooted in "our community." The guest speaker, Evy Franco from the CPD national office, singled out for special praise the New York City community schools initiative backed by its "fabulous mayor." The CPD was intimately involved in the initiative, with its New York City affiliate, the Make the Road immigrant rights group, receiving funding from the de Blasio administration for delivering "wraparound services" for community schools.[45] Franco touted cities like Baltimore as success stories, but as with New York, charter expansion has continued apace. This track record highlights that "community schools" and the racial justice framework in which they are encased presented no serious threat to the continued rollback of

222 || WE ALL BECOME MAYOR?

public schools and rollout of charters—that is, to the disruption from above. The initiative was, on the other hand, particularly effective as a legitimating and contradictions-managing mechanism for Baraka and other "progressive" mayors who rose to power on the wings of the growing movement against corporate school reform.[46]

THE DEAL

In the aftermath of the mass mobilizations and walkouts in May, the most intense since the student movement had emerged two years before, it was clear, particularly as the New Jersey governor geared up for a 2016 presidential run, that Anderson's reign was at its end. Yet, although Baraka's campaign slogan had been "When I become mayor, we become mayor," he jettisoned his much-touted commitment to popular democracy when negotiating the deal with his archnemesis Chris Christie. He and Christie, as depicted in a widely circulated photo of the duo squaring off at the negotiating table, would be the deciders as they entered into secret negotiations in early June.[47]

With rumors flying, Anderson submitted her resignation early Monday morning, June 22. Simultaneously, David Hespe, Christie's education commissioner, announced that Chris Cerf, Anderson's longtime movement ally, would be the new superintendent.[48] At the end of the week, Baraka and Christie issued a joint press release on the deal they had reached. A nine-person Newark Educational Success Board (NESB)—with a five-person majority chosen by Christie and four by Baraka—was set up as part of their negotiated agreement, with the board "charged . . . with developing a clear, specific pathway with appropriate timelines and benchmarks for the return of local control to the Newark community."[49]

The victory, mirroring Baraka's regime, was deeply contradictory. Clearly Christie would not have removed Anderson without the disruption unleashed by the movement, what he himself characterized as "full scale combat in Newark."[50] Student activists, such as NSU vice president Jose Leonardo, recognized the central role their movement's disruptive power played in driving her from power.

> Yeah Cami Anderson left and I would say that was in large part because of what we did. As far as I'm concerned no one stood up to Cami but the students, *at least in the way we did*. We blew

WE ALL BECOME MAYOR? || 223

it up. . . . The narrative that was going on in Newark, people knew about it . . . throughout the country like people were following it, we definitely brought attention to that.[51]

The students were obviously elated over the departure. "I thought I was dreaming to be honest," was Leonardo's reaction when he got the call from Cabañas that Anderson had resigned. "Here," he went on,

we were just walking out a couple weeks before . . . [and] a couple months before that we had . . . disrupted one of Christie's town hall meetings. . . . His stance was very clear, you know, "We're not going to compromise. We're not going to give local control." . . . And in a matter of weeks, a couple months . . . we have him sitting down agreeing to local control.

Yet, at the same time, "it was," for the seventeen-year-old high school junior and son of Dominican immigrants, "very fishy to me personally. . . . It felt like there was something more to it." Indeed, it was, as Leonardo's comments imply, contradictory. Baraka had promised, to the mass movement that brought him to power, that when he becomes mayor, "we all become mayor." But, when it came to deciding on a central question confronting the movement, he resorted to classic brokerage politics—I embody and speak for the movement, for a "Black and Brown community"—and did not allow any democratic input in deciding whether to accept the deal or in fashioning the settlement. The mass movement had forced Christie's hand, and the mass protests obliged Anderson to back off imposing her "turnaround" plans on East Side, Weequahic, and several other schools. But, at the same time, the vaunted "local control," that is, the restoration of full powers to the local board, would take at least two years. In addition, the power over approving new charters—a central tool of disruption—continued to reside with the state, and the Christie administration made no promise to hold back on its expansion plans. Furthermore, Cerf, the longtime movement leader who had just left running an arm of an education technology company headed by Joel Klein, as well as serving on the board of the National Alliance for Public Charter Schools, would now have control over the district.[52] Would there be anything to control after four years of Anderson's disruption and two more from Cerf? Nonetheless, despite their many misgivings, Leonardo and the NSU

224 || WE ALL BECOME MAYOR?

collaborated with the deal. "After the resignation and the talks were being made," Leonardo explains,

> a couple of us, some of the key people in the movement, were asked to come to the mayor's office and talk about this committee, the NESB. I was asked to be the student representative. I agreed, because my logic was before there was no compromise, there was no conversation, there was no clear steps to this thing, now there is. We definitely want the students' voice in that process, we definitely want to be represented, so I took that. And then I was elected president and Kristin stepped down and went to college.

In addition to Leonardo, Baraka's three other appointees to the NESB included Grace Sergio, the parent activist who led a successful grassroots campaign in 2013–14 to stop Anderson's plan to hand over her son's elementary school to the KIPP charter chain. The other two, Reverend Percy Simmons, a former school board member and pastor of the influential Abyssinian Baptist Church, and Mary Bennett, a retired school principal and member of the ANPS, were drawn from the ranks of the old BPMC.

With NSU on board, and with the local ANPS already squarely in his camp, Baraka had no worries that he would face any kind of popular pushback against the deal. On July 1, the ANPS held a meeting at the NTU office to organize a demonstration the day before the scheduled July 8 rubber-stamping of Cerf's appointment by the gubernatorial-appointed New Jersey State Board of Education. The NAACP president and close ally of Baraka Deborah Smith-Gregory chaired the meeting and made clear that the ANPS's wrath would be directed, *not* at Baraka, but safely at the new superintendent. "*The key is a return to local control,* as the mayor said, but," she added, "we don't need Cerf."[53] Smith-Gregory, clearly acting as a mouthpiece, explained that the "mayor's position is that we need to return to local control in about a year," and the deal the mayor negotiated was bringing this, her remarks implied, closer to reality. The planned protest would laud the mayor, while, on the other hand, "the message we want to deliver to Cerf is 'if you come here, this [i.e., protest] is what you will have to deal with.'" Cabañas, echoing Smith-Gregory, expressed his fealty to Baraka and shared her approach to framing the protest. "The mayor," as he referentially referred to the local head of state, "wants us to emphasize local control."[54]

Except for some catcalling from the street by a gadfly Baraka opponent, the choreographed July 7 March of Dignity rally went off as planned.[55] The speakers who addressed the two hundred or so protestors gathered on the steps of City Hall all sounded the agreed-upon themes of local control and opposition to Cerf. Smith-Gregory, who emceed the event, began with a call-and-response chant that telegraphed the message: "What do we want? Local control! When do we want it? Now!" "This march," she underscored to the gathering, "is to say no to Cerf and to return schools to full local control.... We say to the state board that will vote tomorrow, 'No to Cerf.'" Employing more radical phraseology, but still fully encased in a RD frame, Smith-Gregory declared that "Newark must have self-determination of what happens to our children."

Reverend Bridgeforth, who helped galvanize opposition among the black clergy to Anderson in spring 2014, dressed up local control as a national liberation struggle. She denounced the "colonialism of people of color" that was allowing outsiders to gain control of the school's billion-dollar budget. "Keep moving, Mr. Cerf," the minister and former city councilperson ordered, because, consistent with her inauthenticity trope, "you don't belong here."

The participation of the NSU's Jose Leonardo bestowed the all-important legitimacy of the student movement on this pro-Baraka rally. In contrast to the other speakers, Leonardo, in his remarks, emphasized opposition to the movement from above's central aim: "we don't want our schools privatized." But, like the rest, he raised the banner of "self-determination" as the solution. "We will continue marching until we get local control," the newly elected NSU president declared, as he concluded with the rhythmical chant "Get off our turf, say no to Cerf!"

Mayor Baraka received nothing but adulation, as expected, when he addressed the crowd. This was despite that he had assented to the deal that brought Cerf and had held what he described, in an interview with *NJ Spotlight* a few days before, as a "very cordial meeting" with the declared enemy of those gathered at the rally.[56] Baraka began by refuting any notion that he and state senator Ron Rice Sr., who strongly opposed Cerf's appointment, and preceded the mayor's address, were at odds.[57] Baraka then turned to salute the students, underscoring that "we are . . . here because of the work of the young people." He then quickly defined the aim of student-led struggle and why they were all gathered on this "historic day"—to continue the central, overriding fight for "local control and an elected school board." He lashed out at "crackpots" who criticized the deal, arguing that it was actually a huge victory because it laid the foundation for achieving the all-important local control. Recounting the two long decades under state subjugation, the student struggle had now gotten Newark to the point where "now we have this debate on how to get local control." The movement, he emphasized, now "must seize" the opportunity, provided by the deal he negotiated, to finally win self-determination.

> I don't want anybody to tell me who the superintendent is. . . .
> We want to decide for ourselves who is superintendent, our
> education, we want local control. . . . Don't lose sight over that. . . .
> We are fighting for full freedom. . . . We're opposed to slavery. . . .
> *This fight will always be about that.*[58]

Smith-Gregory then took the mic and reinforced Baraka's RD message, telling the crowd, "You can go back and say, what he said, not what the papers say. We are turning local control back to a city of color."

Baraka's reference to "crackpots" opposing the deal was directed, in particular, at reporter Bob Braun. His blog had provided the most consistent and sympathetic—particularly of Baraka himself—coverage of the movement and was influential among activists. Braun argued that the deal was a boon for Christie that allowed him "to quiet Newark"— that is, end disruptive protests, the power of the movement—

> as he tries to portray himself as someone who can reach agreements with opponents. The agreement indicates it will be at least a year before a date can be set for local control—and that's a year Christie can use to run for president without major controversies in the state's largest city.[59]

The deal strengthened Christie and his political brand based on pugnaciously, yet bipartisanly, busting teacher unions, privatizing public education, defunding public worker pensions, and rolling back the public sector more broadly. Conversely, Braun argued, it undermined

WE ALL BECOME MAYOR? || 227

a movement that "had been building and unified." Though Anderson was gone, she had been replaced by Cerf, who had worked with "Mayor Cory Booker [to] make Newark the charter capital of the nation."[60] Yet Braun's critique, which essentially attributes the deal to poor negotiating skills or lack of courage, misses the contradictions of the Baraka regime that would make this deal so appealing. By having the state-appointed Cerf in charge, who would be much more conciliatory than Anderson, Baraka could keep the focus safely on "self-determination" for several more years, while avoiding the thorny issue of continued expansion of charters. The arrangement nicely channeled political activity toward antiracism and away from class struggle.

The one counterweight to the agreement might have been NEW. But, at the time of Baraka's deal, Rippey had just been defeated in his bid for NTU president, and NEW was in full retreat. In part, the seeds of defeat were planted after the 2013 election, when the NEW slate won a majority of the union's executive council but was unable to convert that power into implementing any of its organizational reforms.[61] Despite the earlier defeats within the NTU, Rippey believed the stepped-up protests in spring 2015 among teachers at East Side, Weequahic, and other schools Anderson had targeted "would translate into" support at the ballot box for NEW. "We're like clearly among the leaders of this protest," referring to the big downtown rally on May 13, 2015, a month before the June election, "[which means] you guys who are at this protest are clearly coming around to where we have been the last three years, clearly this means you're going to vote for our ass in the election." But, Rippey lamented, "It didn't happen." A three-way race pitted Abeigon, Rippey heading the "NEW VISION" slate, and a third aspirant, Michael Dixon, the only black candidate, who had previously worked as a full-time NTU official under Del Grosso. The incumbent, Abeigon, won, with only one-third of the membership, 1,070 out of the 3,600 union members, participating. Rippey clearly saw the defeat "taking the sails out of" NEW.[62]

Therefore the defeat of NEW's challenge to the reigning NTU leadership helped quell any opposition to the Baraka–Christie deal. This did not mean that the NTU had been a critic of Baraka. Although NEW did not endorse Baraka, NEW activists on the NTU board enthusiastically backed the union's decision to support the insurgent candidate. Rippey, for his part, also believed NEW had "to tacitly support him," because, he argued,

228 || WE ALL BECOME MAYOR?

> Shavar Jeffries is a nightmare for teachers, so you can't let Shavar Jeffries become mayor, and you can't let Anibal Ramos become mayor . . . and let the charter schools proliferate . . . so you couldn't let these guys become mayor.

Nonetheless, NEW, and its social movement brand of unionism, would have complicated the Baraka regime's efforts to conciliate with the privatizers—all of which would deepen in the ensuing years.

REINVENTING THE MOVEMENT

In his classic collection of essays on the origins and operation of the first wave of BURs in the 1970s and early 1980s—*Stirrings in the Jug: Black Politics in the Post-Segregation Era*—Adolph Reed Jr. develops the concept of the "reinvention" mechanism. He elaborates on this useful tool of class rule in a case study of conflict over the siting of a new airport in Atlanta during the first term (1973–77) of the city's first black mayor, the late Maynard Jackson. Various factions of the Atlanta power structure were promoting competing locations—to the north and south of the city, and an expansion of the existing one—none of which involved material stakes for Jackson's black working-class electoral base. But, at the time, Jackson was facing pressure from his left flank because of his betrayal, in the face of business pressure, of a campaign promise to remove the white police chief, who oversaw a force that was particularly brutal against African Americans. Therefore, to help manage the class contradictions of his regime, he intervened in the intra-bourgeois siting debate by reinventing the south-side option as the "black position," along with some contracting opportunities for black businesses and professionals.

The reinvention mechanism, therefore, became an indispensable tool in managing the contradiction between Jackson's electoral and governing coalitions by, Reed argues, shifting

> the basis for black response to policy debate away from substantive concerns with potential outcome and toward protection of racial image and status, as embodied in the idiosyncratic agenda of the black official. *In this way it becomes possible for black officials to maintain support from their black constituents and the development elites that systematically disadvantage them.*[63]

The ability to make this shift is especially important, Reed adds, when a black administration has "associated itself with an aggressive egalitarian rhetoric . . . [and] have their roots in activist, protest politics, and therefore embody an imagery of antagonism toward entrenched elites."[64] Now, as noted in the introduction to this book, the connection with an activist background, or at least an egalitarian, movementist rhetoric challenging elites, had virtually disappeared among the second and especially third generation of black mayors exemplified by Booker, Fenty, Nutter, and others. But Baraka's activist pedigree and rise to power harkened back to the first generation of black mayors: he was closely identified with his activist father, had developed his own activist credentials at Howard and in his hometown, and, most importantly, emerged as the standard-bearer of a movement defending public schools facing an assault from Wall Street. At the same time, like Jackson, he was committed to working with his business partners to make the city as favorable an investment environment as possible, while simultaneously needing to appear progressive to a mobilized mass base with high expectations.

Thus, as with Maynard Jackson, we see that Baraka turned to the reinvention mechanism to solve the conundrum. He remade the movement from below as one, essentially, of "self-determination," of ending the "neocolonial" subjugation—now epitomized by the reviled white Republican governor—to which this overwhelmingly Black and Brown city had been subjected. Through this reinvention, with the assistance from some elements of the movement from below, he was able to safely channel, and eventually dock, the mass movement in a spot that did not challenge the privatization of public schools and the larger development model. It was, in the end, an exercise in "brokerage politics," as Reed outlines in an epigraph to this chapter. In this case, though, the brokering was between governing elites, with Christie conferring upon Baraka, and his "self-determination" demand, the authentic "voice of the people" mantle. We now turn to the final chapter of this saga—to how Baraka moved from channeling to winding down, incorporating, and dismantling the movement, while further accommodating its class opponents, all of which was indispensable to advancing the "Newark renaissance."

8

Making Newark Governable Again

MERGING MOVEMENTS THROUGH RACIAL DEMOCRACY, 2015–2018

> Democracy is not always working with people you agree with but with those who you don't agree with.
>
> —Ras Baraka, speaking at a panel on school reform in Newark, September 28, 2015

After a year in office, the *New York Times* sized up the "radical mayor" across the Hudson. Its assessment? The "radical," it concluded, "now looks more like a radical pragmatist." "Newark is still stubbornly," as it pointed out the obvious, "two cities: gleaming new glass towers downtown, block after block of abandoned plots and relentless poverty in its outer wards." But, by the one-year mark in office, the "son of Newark's most famous black radical" had dispelled, reporter Katie Zernike happily informed her readers, any lingering class fears among downtown business interests and the Christie-allied, Democratic Party county machine that had backed his opponent. He had not, to their relief, mobilized the city's dispossessed behind an "anti-business and antipolice" agenda, including blocking the continued expansion of charter schools. In fact, far from "divid[ing] the city," the United States' paper of record found, "those on both sides of the spectrum say that he has so far managed to do what his predecessors could not: make both Newarks *feel* as if he is their mayor."[1]

Baraka, to use the language of Whelan, Young, and Lauria, had successfully managed the central "dilemma" of the BUR during his first year in office. He had been able to "*appear* to be progressive in addressing the needs of the black community and yet meet the needs of the major business interests."[2] Central to creating this appearance was delivering on a key antiracist election promise to his popular base

|| 231

232 || MAKING NEWARK GOVERNABLE AGAIN

by driving Cami Anderson, the face of neocolonial rule, from office. But, on the other side of the class dyad, he had not simply to appear to meet, but actually to meet, the real material needs of his corporate governing partners. Ensuring that driving out Anderson did not extend to closing down charter schools, or even blocking their expansion, was one of those bottom-line class needs.

In this chapter, I document how Baraka, over the remainder of his first four-year term, successfully managed his Newark dilemma. The now "pragmatic mayor" achieved this fete by, on the corporate side, as I chronicle, deepening his collaboration with the pro-privatization forces to assist, or at least provide no serious obstacle to, the further charterizaton of the district. Baraka managed the political fallout of his betrayal by keeping the movement's "eyes on the prize" of RD through returning the school district to local control—this, he asserted, was all the movement was ever really about—while using his power and influence over leading activists and organizations to silence and contain any challenges to that narrow RD interpretation of movement demands and goals. In effect, through the power of RD, he merged the movement from below with its antagonists from above. This marriage, as I document, was symbolized by the joint celebration of the return of local control as popular forms of disruptive protests were brought to an end. Finally, to obscure his deepening embrace of the philanthrocapitalist-funded school privatization movement, he manufactured a RD insurgency at the Port to buttress his fraying radical credentials and legitimacy.

Dismantling and incorporating the social movement that brought Baraka to power was part of a larger challenge to removing all impediments to his rent-intensification development agenda. As property values continued their ascent in Hoboken, Jersey City, and Brooklyn, developers increasingly turned to Newark, as the long-hoped-for and elite-cultivated regeneration seemed at hand.[3] Thus removing remaining obstacles, such as public housing in the fast-developing Ironbound district, and containing any antidisplacement movements from those designated for removal were of prime importance. As with the public school movement, Baraka turned to RD to manage these contradictions as he denounced public housing and its supporters— and, by implication, the New Deal—as simply promoting racial disparities.

DEPLOYING STATE POWERS IN SERVICE OF THE MARKET

The sealing of the 2015 Christie–Baraka deal, and the embrace of Cerf as the new superintendent, cued to his erstwhile opponents that Baraka would not take any serious measures against the continued privatization of the district. He further reassured the charters that he was not their enemy by refusing—as Bob Braun, the Baraka champion turned critic, observed—"to talk about how the district is facing mass privatization and . . . dismiss[ing] the importance of a debate over the future of privately-operated charter schools." Thus the deal to remove Anderson, touted as a step forward for "local control," for "self-determination," had in fact enhanced the "political clout of charters" while, as became increasingly clear, sapping "the strength of the pro-neighborhood school forces."[4] That is, although the deal came in RD costuming, which helped Baraka appear progressive, its class essence was guaranteeing the continued march of the market demanded by his corporate governing partners.

The budding partnership was on display at the beginning of the 2015–16 school year as the mayor joined with charter supporters in a school backpack and supplies giveaway. The initiative was funded by leading national and local movement activist organizations, from the NCSF to TFA and the BAEO, among others. Baraka's embrace even extended to Education for Reform Now, headed by his former opponent Shavar Jeffries. Baraka, who denounced the group during the election for hiding the billionaire backers of his opponent, now welcomed its money for this bonding exercise with his former deep-pocketed opponents.[5]

In October, Baraka moved from public relations events to deploying powers of the local state to green-light further charter expansion. The North Star Academy, part of the hedge fund–backed national Uncommon Schools charter chain, needed city approval for converting a downtown property, formerly owned by the *Star-Ledger,* into a new campus to consolidate its growing K–12 citywide operation.[6] Although the power to approve charter expansion resided with the state, the local state was of enormous importance for legitimating the expansion, which explained the intense struggle over control of the mayor's office. In addition, local authorities had other forms of control, such as planning boards, that could block expansion or at least sharpen the contradictions between those struggling to defend public schools and those struggling to batter down any barrier to market expansion. What side would Baraka, who had enormous political influence over the city's Planning Board, including chair Wayne Richardson, the husband of school board president Antoinette Baskerville-Richardson, take?

The October 19, 2015, Newark Central Planning Board meeting was a showdown between public and charter school advocates. But by this time, the disruptive power of many elements of the pro–public schools movement had been severely sapped. Although NEW did have some activists at the hearing and preceding rally, its numbers had shrunk and spirits lowered following the demoralizing election loss. Most importantly, the NSU, the leading disruptive force, was in full retreat. Some of the ley leaders, such as Kristin Towkanik and Tanasia Brown, had graduated and, although studying at Rutgers–Newark, were much less involved. Jose Leonardo, who succeeded Towkanik as president, stepped down from the position at the beginning of the school year. Part of this disillusionment and general disorientation within the NSU appears to have been the incorporation of Leonardo, as explained in the previous chapter, into the NESB, created as part of the Christie–Baraka deal. Ostensibly, the NESB was to oversee the transition to local control. In reality, its most important role was to incorporate the movement into the regime, to transition the movement away from disruption and toward insider negotiations. The latter terrain is where, because of the imbalance of resources, Baraka and the movement from above enjoyed superiority. Further privileging the movement from above was a negotiations framework that was limited to addressing "local control," that is, RD, but not the continued dismantlement of public schools through privatization.

Thus, as Leonardo found, "the NESB . . . we're in there, and we meet once a month, but it's really hard to say if it's really going to get us what we want. My thing is, like because there is a lot of statutes, there is a lot of laws, a lot of regulatory stuff, the language in that setting is very foreign to me." The former NSU president's experience with insider negotiations echoes Frances Fox Piven's critique of advocacy planning, in which activists are "guided . . . into a narrowly circumscribed form of political actions, and precisely the form for which they are least equipped." For Leonardo, and Grace Sergio, the two movement appointees, to compete at this level would require, at minimum, as Piven argues, "powerful group support, stable organiza-

MAKING NEWARK GOVERNABLE AGAIN || 235

tion, professional staff and money—precisely those resources which the poor do not have."[7]

In the end, the Christie–Baraka deal, and the incorporation into the NESB—which Leonardo and the NSU had endorsed—led, from Leonardo's perspective, to confusion and retreat: "It's really hard to say where we are now, so like after that agreement my momentum just dissipated. The community kind of disappeared, that fire disappeared." Further adding to the confusion, and contributing to demobilization, was that the NSU's old ally, Ras Baraka, was increasingly collaborating with its opponents. "Because it's weird," Leonardo explains, "Cerf and the mayor, you know, are working together, we don't know clearly what the budget situation is in the schools, there is a lot of, there is a big blur I would say. I would describe the start of this year is a big blur and I feel like it's done intentionally to kind of confuse people."

In contrast to the blur confronting the NSU, the vision of North Star and its fellow charter supporters was crystal clear, and spirits were high, as they mobilized for the Planning Board vote. The charter movement turned out "hundreds of North Star students, teachers and other supporters" to back the deal.[8] The outnumbered NTU, NJCU, and other community activists organized, as did North Star/Uncommon, a rally outside City Hall before going into the city council chamber to voice their opposition to the proposal. Among those joining the NTU–NJCU rally—but not speaking to the Planning Board—was Baraka ally and city council president Mildred Crump. Her comments highlighted the dramatic, stark inequities produced by disruption in the form of "colocated" schools, where charters take over a portion of a public school. "On one side she found," according to the *Star-Ledger* report of her comments, "carpeting, air conditioning, up-to-date technology and books, while the other struggled to round up the most basic of resources."[9]

After impassioned speeches on both sides, the board voted 6–1, with two abstentions, in favor of zoning changes—variances—needed for construction of the North Star Academy. The lone dissenting vote came from board member—and NTU officer—Alex Jurgelevicius, who called for an "impact review" of its effect on Newark public schools before any approval would be given. This echoed the criticism of NTU chief John Abeigon, who addressed the board, along with scores of others on both sides, during the three-hour-long meeting.[10] Yet, despite patiently and politely listening to the long list of speakers, the board's vote was never in question. They had clearly received orders from Baraka to vote for approval. "I mean you know I will tell you right now, my husband [Wayne Richardson] is on the Planning Board, he's actually the chair of the Planning Board," explained Baskerville-Richardson on the regime machinations behind the vote. "So I kind of have inside information on how these things go. So absolutely the mayor, you know, gave people the wink or the nod or whatever to vote for it."

Thus, when Baraka had at his disposal state powers to block the expansion of charters, and a political opportunity to dramatize and mobilize against the attack, he did not deploy them. In fact, far from appearing, as he had at school board meetings, to drive out Anderson and achieve "self-determination," he instead stayed far away from the fray as he ordered the board to vote for the charter expansion. But, as part of managing the contradictions of his rule, he simultaneously came out publicly against an expansion application by the KIPP charter chain to the state department of education to open five new schools and add 5,440 new seats, nearly tripling its then current enrollment of 3,200.[11] Through his Twitter account over the weekend, and then in a statement issued on the same day as the Planning Board hearing, he denounced the KIPP plan, because it would "inflict more damage to the fragile education infrastructure in our school district."[12] Yet, while registering his opposition on the KIPP proposal to a state board over which he had no direct control, Baraka simultaneously ordered a board he did control to vote for charter expansion.

The contradictions were becoming clear for all to see, as even Baskerville-Richardson acknowledged:

> So I think a mixed message was probably sent with that, because yes the mayor gave the wink for the vote to go in that direction, and on the other hand, you know, I think pretty close to that same time he came out with an ad against charter schools with the expansion, *so I think that, that really confused people.*[13]

But, Baskerville-Richardson argues, Baraka could also rely on the deep roots and bonds forged from years of not only his own activism but that of his towering father. The antiracist, self-determination bona fides that pedigree and history provided were a crucial asset to manage the sharpening contradictions.

MAKING NEWARK GOVERNABLE AGAIN || 237

> I mean there are people right now that are not happy with Ras
> about a number of things, but the big difference is that Ras has
> a relationship with people . . . he's accessible, people have the
> opportunity to, you know, express how they feel, and *these are
> relationships that are intergenerational, so it's . . . a very different
> kind of relationship with the community* [compared to Booker
> and Jeffries].[14]

At the same time, recognizing the treacherous waters the administration was entering, Baskerville-Richardson emphasized the possibility of "repercussions to him politically from some of these decisions," adding, "I mean, we'll see." But unlike "Shavar [Jeffries], who doesn't have those relationships," the trump card for Baraka, the longtime public school teacher and political operative reiterated, was the deep relationships he had cultivated through his own and his family's activism. These bonds provided Baraka's electoral base "the opportunity to express basically their dissatisfaction," without requiring him to alter his policy direction. In sum, Baraka had, as corporate executive Al Koeppe observed during the mayoral campaign, the "right compass headings for this moment in Newark's history" to navigate between the Scylla of losing legitimacy with his mass base and the Charybdis of not delivering to his governing partners.

The power of these long-term "intergenerational" relationships to contain opposition was on display that November for the visit of President Barack Obama—a major backer of school privatization—to the city. Baraka used his influence with Lawrence Hamm, the head of POP, and protégé of his father, to derail the group's planned protest against policies pursued by the first black president.[15] While the relationship with Hamm was "intergenerational," Baraka was adept at further cementing his ties with a new generation of activists as well. This included NJCU organizer Roberto Cabañas, on whom the mayor—days before the Planning Board meeting—bestowed an award for "devotion to the community" as part of Hispanic Heritage Month.[16] The accolade, though, did not prevent Cabañas from teaming up with the NTU's Abeigon for a rally at the October school board meeting following the North Star decision, where they led a chant of "Chris Cerf has got to go! Chris Christie has to go!"[17] But this duo, as well as other ANPS members, such as the NAACP's Deborah Smith-Gregory, would not make any criticism of Baraka's increasingly

238 || MAKING NEWARK GOVERNABLE AGAIN

chummy relationship with Cerf. For his part, Cerf, clearly taking to heart Russakoff's counsel, despite initially bristling at her criticism, was very conciliatory and adept at winning over former adversaries. His public comportment provided political cover for Baraka's budding love affair with the longtime movement militant.

PEACE THROUGH STRENGTH

Although Baraka had made it clear, even during the campaign, that his fight was for local control, not against privatization, there was still great consternation regarding his election among the national and local arms of the charter movement. As Lavar Young, who headed Newark's post-election-established BAEO chapter, explains, "the mayoral race was a referendum on education."

> So at that time Ras was running against charter schools. *So the charter schools and the ed reform community were scared that once he got elected he would push this agenda forward to eliminate charters* or [block] expanding the growth of charters. So they brought in organizations like BAEO, organizations like PC2E, and said, "Hey, we want to try to figure out the landscape here and, you know, help, you know, make some inroads and put some people to work."[18]

Thus, by the beginning of 2015, in the midst of Anderson's faltering rule and a rising tide of NSU-led mass disruption, the pro-charter movement began rolling out two new organizations—BAEO/Newark and the Parent Coalition for Excellent Education (PC2E). The primary mission, taking a page from their opponents, was to mobilize their own mass base in "militant particularist" struggles, such as at North Star, or larger, campaign-level-style insurgencies to stymie any efforts to block the continued expansion of charters. Much of the funding was routed through the NCSF, with the source being the same Wall Street, Gates, Walton, and other deep-pocketed supporters that had long bankrolled the movement.[19] PC2E was by far the largest of the two movement "start-ups," with several dozen on staff and enjoying a spacious downtown office. The operation was led by Muhammed Akil, a former aide to Jersey City mayor Steve Fulop, who had led various successful electoral campaigns for his employers' allies and came from a Black Nationalist political worldview.[20] The operation, unsurprisingly, considering the skills of the director and needs of the movement, included 501(c)3 and 4 arms, the latter of which was to mobilize for elections, particularly for the school board.

By fall 2015, PC2E was up and running and ready, as Akil explained, to "mobilize the growing number" of charter families to "weigh in heavily" on politics.[21] As the local BAEO chief noted, the movement from above identified its chief weakness as the failure to forge the deep bonds necessary to mobilize its mass base. "I just don't think our charters have done a good enough job," Young argued, "of building genuine relationships. They think they have relationships because parents have decided to go to charters, but those aren't genuine relationships." That is, Young recognized, as theorists Cox and Nilsen point out, that the "creation of a hegemonic formation" by movements from above "moves along two axes—horizontally . . . [and] vertically."[22] At the former level, the movement had been able to forge an impressive level of unity among various dominant groups, particularly the influential BPMC, which increasingly included even the "radical" wing represented by Baraka. Yet, at the vertical level, among African American and Latinx working-class families, it had far less success. Young, and especially Akil's well-funded operation, who had extensive experience in local political campaigns, worked to remedy that weakness as he brought parents into the movement. PC2E's large war chest, which allowed the organization to put parents on the payroll and provide other material perks, assisted in its recruitment efforts.

After the North Star victory, the BAEO and PC2E turned their focus to the state capitol. They aimed to kill a bill in the state legislature, then sitting in committee, that would place a statewide moratorium on charter expansion while a study was conducted to assess their impact. Again, showing the power and advantages of the movement from above, PC2E, working with the two major charter chains, KIPP and North Star, organized a December 14 Hands Off Our Future Parent Lobby Day rally and meetings with legislators to block the legislation. Demonstrating that it was literally a "movement from above," charter school administrators ordered schools closed and bussed parents and students to the state capitol for the rally. In contrast, students who had walked out in NSU-led actions faced physical intimidation

240 || MAKING NEWARK GOVERNABLE AGAIN

from principals and guards, suspensions from public school administrators, and broken arms at the hands of police. The double standards on disruption underscore Piven's insight on the class-biased nature of the rules that govern interdependent relationships, that is, "the behaviors that are permissible by different parties."

> Since . . . rules are fashioned to reflect prevailing patterns of domination made possible by concentrated wealth, force, and institutional position, they typically prohibit some people but not other people from using their leverage yielded by social interdependence.[23]

But, as the Newark case demonstrates, these class-biased rules not only sanction elite forms of disruption, such as plant lockouts and school closures. They also allow, without any repercussions, mass forms of disruption, such as administrator-ordered walkouts, called for by movements from above.

PC2E's lobbying efforts enjoyed backing from the powerful pro-charter Essex County Democratic Party machine, led by county executive and Adubato protégé Joseph DiVincenzo. State senator Teresa Ruiz, head of the Senate Education Committee, whose day job was as the assistant Essex County executive, bottled up the bill in committee. Their efforts were further bolstered by a letter penned in early January by seven Newark city councilmen—the same seven who had passed a May resolution against any cap on charters—to the education commissioner opposing legislation blocking charter expansions. Baraka, for his part, did send a December 17, 2015, letter to the commissioner urging the state *not* to approve applications submitted by existing Newark charters to expand their enrollment or approve new charters. He based his opposition on the NPS budget crisis produced by the state's flat funding of the district—a crisis intensified by spiraling budget-draining charter payments. But, at the same time, he emphasized that "there are incredible charter schools in Newark," as well as public schools, and that he was not against future expansions of charters. He only requested a freeze until the current fiscal crisis was addressed, while the real future lay in "community schools." But, as he had also made clear in a November 23 vlog message, both public and charter schools were included in his broad definition of "community schools"—contradicting how his backers in the ANPS envisioned the program.[24]

PUBLIC FEUDING AND BACK-CHANNEL NEGOTIATIONS

In his November 23 vlog address, Baraka also lambasted, in clear reference to PC2E, "the monied interests, Wall Street, wealthy individuals . . . and bankers" who were "pitting" charter and public school parents against one another in an effort to decide the direction of Newark's schools. Yet, despite these public pronouncements, behind the scenes, Baraka and his aides were engineering a political conciliation arrangement with these same forces. Lauren Wells, Baraka's chief education officer and veteran of the Ford Foundation–financed GVZ program, was part of this behind-the-scenes operation. She casually raised to Leah Owens, while sitting at a September 2015 school board meeting, the idea of the NEW cofounder running for a school board seat on a Baraka-backed ticket. A few months later, in November, Baskerville-Richardson made a formal offer to Owens, explaining that to be the Baraka nominee, she would have to run on a three-person ticket with pro-charter candidates selected by PC2E and the pro-charter, North Ward councilman Anibal Ramos.

In late January 2016, Baraka and his new partners publicly announced their partnership and agreed-upon slate, which included Owens, after some mulling over of the offer.[25] Of course, Baraka had partnered with his erstwhile opponents at the start of the 2015–16 school year with the book bag giveaway. Furthermore, behind closed doors, Baraka had developed a cordial relationship with Howard Fuller's group, as Lavar Young, the head of the BAEO's Newark operation, explains:

> One of the first things that me and Chanel [the statewide BAEO representative] did when we were both hired by BAEO was set up a meeting and meet with the mayor, and we simply told the mayor we want good schools for everybody. We're not here to push the charter agenda, we're not here to push the traditional public school agenda, we're here to see how we can best service all students throughout the city. *And he was receptive of that. And we said we want to partner with you.*[26]

But the new electoral pact took the partnership to a much deeper and public level, putting an end to any remaining public bickering between former adversaries.

The strengthening alliance was on display just a week later, as Baraka and Cerf coauthored a February 1 letter to Governor Christie, signed by all the national and local charter groups active in Newark, along with other Democratic Party officeholders. The letter, ostensibly to request extra funds to address a budget shortfall, represented a breathtaking political transformation.

First, significantly, the letter began by touting the shutting down of the movement from below: "And disagreements over complex policy issues remain the subject of spirited, *although*," the letter emphasized, "*increasingly civil* [i.e., nondisruptive] *debate*."[27] Second, the authors legitimated the charters, run by private, increasingly large corporate chains, all nonunion, as "public schools," be they "charter or district." Third, it normalized, made as common sense, the past, ongoing, and future expansion of the market and rollback of the public sector. The authors calmly explain that "as the district evolves"—as if privatization were a natural rather than a politically and coercively produced restructuring—"[it would become] one with an increasingly diverse array of magnet, traditional and charter public schools." Furthermore, as part of that rollback, the letter touted the extent to which the central office, long a target of the reformers, had been dismantled. Finally, the letter was significant in avoiding the obvious, inconvenient truth: continued charter expansion was the chief source of disruption—the withdrawal of cooperation in the form of state funding—deployed against the public schools and hence the major cause of the budget deficit.[28]

In the end, Christie increased aid to NPS by only $26 million, still well below the funding level required in the latest iteration of the Abbot agreement and insufficient to cover the estimated $70 million budget deficit. A further pro-disruption element of the Baraka-backed deal was that $22 million—82 percent of the increase—went "to hold Newark charter schools harmless from aid reductions due to declining revenue in the State-operated Newark Public Schools' (NPS) budget." Half of this went to the two large charter chains operating in the city, Uncommon and KIPP. This was the second year in a row that the charters received "hold harmless" funds to protect them from the continued cutbacks being imposed on the public sector.[29] Adding to the disruption from above, Cerf used the fiscal crisis to sell off, with full

MAKING NEWARK GOVERNABLE AGAIN | 243

support from Baraka, ten shuttered schools and two other properties to the Newark Housing Authority. Despite promises to the contrary, several of the schools were then turned over to charter operators.[30]

Fissures from Below, Sutures from Above

Baraka's public embrace of the movement from above forced even his most loyal backers among the unions, NAACP, POP, and nonprofits that comprised the ANPS to voice their objections. Even Baraka's subsequent face-saving letter to Christie condemning the administration's approval of new charters and demanding a halt until the NPS budget crisis was solved was not enough to calm the growing distress among his movement-from-below allies.[31] Therefore, in mid-March 2016, weeks after Baraka's electoral pact with the charter movement and joint letter to Christie that further legitimated charters, the ANPS released a public letter addressed to "Mayor Baraka." Significantly, the letter was signed by the group's chairperson and local NAACP president Deborah Smith-Gregory, followed by a listing of the organizational members. The ANPS's letter explained that members had become "increasingly concerned with the actions of your office in regard to protecting traditional public schools." They decried Baraka's cooperation with the "charter school industry . . . and [their] tried and true strategy . . . that on the surface promotes a so-called 'unity' strategy, but that in reality divides your base of supporters."

Baraka's alienated allies denounced what they saw as two policy betrayals. One was the October Planning Board decision in which the mayor failed to use the "many tools available that would slow or stop charter school expansion in the City of Newark." They implored Baraka "to encourage the Planning Board appointees to deny any further land use decisions that would allow for the expansion [i.e., disruption from above] of Charter schools." Second, the signatories harshly criticized concessions on the community schools front, which had been the banner under which Baraka had run and the basis of the ANPS's support. After taking power, Baraka and Cerf scaled it back from a citywide initiative anchored by a high school and surrounded by "feeder" elementary schools in each of the five wards to only one ward—the South Ward Community Schools Initiative—with only five participating schools. In a further betrayal, which the ANPS denounced in its letter, two of the participating community schools—an initiative envisioned by the AFT-aligned ANPS as the people's alternative to charters—had applied to the state to convert to charters! The schools, though ostensibly public, were administered by the charter management organization Brick Education Network, run by Dominique Lee, a former TFA comrade of Anderson and favorably profiled in Russakoff's touted study. The letter concluded with a veiled warning to Baraka: "protecting our public schools is the issue that galvanized *us* to support *your* bid to become Mayor in 2014" and—alluding to a potential rupture—"*it is the issue that will continue to divide us.*"[32]

The ANPS's letter of disgruntlement was followed, two days later, by a sharper attack by Trina Scordo, the NJCU director and Cabañas's boss. She published a scathing editorial in a local online newspaper, pointedly titled "What Has Happened to the Mayor Ras Baraka We Put into Office?," that succinctly and powerfully captured the contradictions of the Baraka regime. "Despite the organized will of the people," Scordo denounced, "Mayor Baraka has decided that cutting deals with the Wall Street–influenced charter school industry is more politically expedient than following the will of the people." The "deals" with the devil she referenced—which documented the abandonment of his electoral, movement-from-below base in favor of his new, movement-from-above governing partners—were the "Unity" slate for the school board election, the Planning Board decision, and the community schools betrayal. This record led her to conclude that "all signs point to the fact that City Hall has sold out the movement to protect Newark's public schools." Yet, Scordo, head of a foundation- and AFL-CIO-funded organization, fully ensconced in the Democratic Party, also offered a road map for repairing the frayed relationship with a mayor they had brought to power:

Mayor Baraka must recommit himself and his administration to the promises he made to Newark's parents, students, and teachers. He needs to rebuild the lines of communication with the voters and community organizations that fought to put him into office. He must join the resistance to the corporate takeover of our democracy. The mayor needs to use his power to block charter-expansion efforts; create true, locally controlled community schools; and demand that the state return local control to the people of Newark.

But, she added, if he did not heed the advice of his alienated popular base, Baraka would "join the ranks of those elected leaders who have become targets for demonstrations and protests."[33]

In a tough-love effort to steer Baraka back on a righteous path and reforge their weakened bonds, Scordo began mobilizing for an April 1 action dubbed the "Take Back Newark" protest. The protest was part of a national day of action called by the CTU for "cities around the country where there is education justice movements . . . to take a stand on whatever your issues are." Initially, the protest, which never targeted Baraka but rather focused on the pro-privatization operators with whom he was increasingly cozy, had the support of the NTU and other ANPS members. "And so initially NTU," Scordo recounts, "was like 'yeah we can do it at our space, we can do this, we'll be a part of it.' But," she adds, "in the end they decided not to be." In fact, NTU chief Abeigon ordered any connection with the protests erased. "They told us . . . their names . . . [on a] flyer for doing turnout for April 1 . . . needed to come off." NTU was not alone in retracting its initial endorsements and commitments to march. After expressing support early on, most of the ANPS members "stepped back from that action," including its influential chairperson, NAACP head Deborah Gregory-Smith. Administration pressure combined with possible sweeteners, applied through the intervention of the mayor's brother and chief of staff, Amiri "Middy" Baraka Jr., ensured the obedience of the bureaucratic elements most closely allied with the mayor.[34]

Despite the orchestrated sabotage, Scordo and the NJCU went ahead with the April 1 protest. They gathered as planned outside the NTU office—despite the AFT affiliates' refusal to participate—and ended blocks away at City Hall, despite the best efforts of the mayor's brother, his chief political enforcer, to move the destination to another location. But, even while going through with the protest in the face of the Baraka regime's efforts to squash it, the action was a step back from Scordo's confrontational editorial a few weeks earlier. The NJCU director, who led the march, denounced "finance" capital for "taking over our cities" while attacking Wall Street's local Democratic Party "puppets"—implementers in Howard Ryan's conceptualization—who assisted in the looting of the homes, schools, and pensions of working-class Newarkers. Protected, though, from any criticism was Mayor Baraka, whom Scordo had essentially denounced as another puppet in her editorial less than a month earlier. Following the same script, Cabañas extended a hand of partnership, emphasizing how activists working with the mayor "got Cami out, we got community schools, we're on the road to local control," and that they needed to keep speaking out "to support our movement and mayor."

The mobilization was unsuccessful in redirecting Baraka from his wayward path. Only weeks after the rally, Baraka, along with Baskerville-Richardson and Owens, comfortably joined hands with Akil, Matthew Frankel, Ryan Hill (CEO of KIPP NJ), Shavar Jeffries, and other hard-core charter militants to celebrate the victory of the "Unity" school board slate.[35] In a postelection vlog entry, Baraka celebrated the victory and reemphasized the need for unity to achieve "local control." What "unity," increasingly invoked by Baraka, meant in practice was further collaboration with the pro-charter forces while eliminating the movement that had brought the radical cum pragmatic mayor to power, all of which was legitimated through RD ideology. While acknowledging the opposition to the pact among his electoral base—"I know it was a highly controversial election"—he felt confident enough to abandon the direct-democracy campaign rhetoric, which his actual record had contradicted at least since the June 2015 deal with Christie. "We came together at a time," as Baraka explained the rationale behind the "Unity" slate, "*when I thought* the city needed to be together around local control and a transition to local control."[36] At the same time, against Braun and other unnamed critics of his accommodation to the charter movement, Baraka increasingly turned to antiracist-tinged criticisms of them as "outsiders," "supremacists," and "paternalists."[37]

RACIAL JUSTICE TO THE RESCUE

In May 2016, just weeks after the NJCU-led protest and celebration of the "Unity" slate election victory, Baraka manufactured a racial justice movement to shore up his legitimacy with his working-class, particularly black working-class, base. But the target was not powerful real estate developers who were driving up housing costs that disproportionately hit black and Latinx renters, with the full assistance of the Baraka-led local "real estate state." Rather, the ire of the Baraka-led movement was directed at two white-led International Longshoremen Association (ILA) locals at the Port Newark–Elizabeth Marine Terminal. Baraka indicted them for discriminatory practices that locked out black Newarkers, particularly from the higher-paying checkers and mechanics positions.

Baraka held a May rally at City Hall and then led hundreds of residents, mainly black men, to board buses for a trip to Port Newark–Elizabeth. There, surrounded by Nation of Islam members, he led a disruptive march that blocked truck traffic at the port as he delivered stacks of job applications to the shipping association. He denounced that local, qualified Newark residents were being denied work because of their race and called for the port to be "desegregated." "The only requirement they didn't pass is the fact that they were black, that they live in Newark and they weren't related to people in the ILA," Baraka bellowed to cheers from the hundreds of mainly black, male Newarkers.[38] Baraka followed up the May action with a protest in July to further press their demands to hire more local residents.[39] The fiery speeches that Baraka gave at the rallies helped burnish his populist credentials. These broadsides included denouncing ILA head Harold Daggett for posting a thinly veiled racist smear on the mayor's Twitter account that Baraka and the protestors "only wanted handouts." An added benefit of the racial justice exercise is that it allowed Baraka to bond with Kim Gaddy, the charter movement choice on the school board "Unity" slate and an environmental justice activist for her day job.[40]

The critique of Baraka's use of the protest does not imply that the racial disparities were fabricated or deny the racism of the historically conservative and mob-connected ILA leadership. One of the major disparities was the majority black and Latinx city having to bear the brunt of port emissions that contribute to the city's poor air quality and, consequently, high asthma rates and other respiratory illnesses. On the employment front, the major racial disparity was in the comparatively highly paid port mechanics and checkers positions, where blacks composed only 2.5 percent of the positions. Of the total 3,299 longshoremen employed at Port Newark–Elizabeth as of 2015, only 6.3 percent were from Newark (a proxy for black), although 787, 23 percent of all longshoremen, were black, well above the 15 percent of all New Jerseyans. Latinx, in contrast, had 12 percent of the longshore jobs, while they composed 20 percent of the state's population. The real attack on employment at the port, black or otherwise, including Newark's predominately black ILA Local 1233, was through

MAKING NEWARK GOVERNABLE AGAIN

containerization that took hold in the 1960s. The effects of mechanization more broadly are why A. Philip Randolph, as historian Touré Reed points out, insisted on a mass direct-government employment, public works program, combined with rigorous enforcement of antidiscrimination laws, to address black joblessness.[41]

Baraka could have intervened to support nonunion truckers in the face of shipping companies that designated them as "independent contractors" to block unionization. To address unemployment, he could have advocated and marched for a mass public works program, as POP and other local activists had called for at the 2013 popular assembly and as Randolph championed in the 1960s. But this approach would have required a frontal assault on the neoliberal capitalist agenda of shrinking the public sector, as well as the shipping companies' cheap labor model. The focus on racial disparities attributed to the practices of the ILA and, to a lesser extent, of the shipping companies, allowed Baraka to appear as a fearless, truth-talking, combative defender of an aggrieved "black community" that he was betraying on the school front. Conversely, the theatrics at the port, including the antiracist jabs at the nearly $700,000 a year salaried ILA chief Daggett, stayed safely away from his corporate FIRE governing partners.[42]

FLIP-FLOPPING ON ONE NEWARK

The contradictions of the Baraka regime reared their head again at the beginning of the 2016–17 school year. This time, they were expressed around the One Newark universal enrollment system in which parents select from a menu of options—public, charter, and magnet. As explained in chapter 5, a central component of Anderson's disruption of the public school system was a state-created and -sustained education market designed to rupture, through an apparent "free market" choice, attachment to neighborhood public schools and to funnel students into charters. Yet, although Anderson was gone, the reforms she imposed continued, in direct opposition to the wishes and expectations of the movement that had brought Baraka to power.

By the beginning of the school year, in what was now the third year of One Newark, many parents were frustrated with this cornerstone of the reformer's market-based education system. In the face of this, Cabañas, along with activists Yolanda Johnson and Denise Coles, or-

MAKING NEWARK GOVERNABLE AGAIN || 249

ganized a "speak-out" at the district's Family Support Center, where the enrollment system was coordinated. This was followed by an airing of grievances at the September 20 Advisory Board business meeting, where scores of parents spoke at the marathon session. Among the most moving testimonies was that of Catalina Orozco, with Cerf's response exemplifying his skillful mode of operation as superintendent: show compassion for the myriad personal troubles created by the pro-market enrollment system while simultaneously channeling the solution in an individualist direction that did not point to or threaten the structural roots of the problem. "Thank you, I feel terribly sorry for your concerns and frustrations," Cerf began after Orozco concluded her heart-wrenching story. The disabled single mother needed her son placed in a neighborhood school because of her inability to travel distances to pick him up. "I am absolutely going to," he went on, "personally look at your case. I feel tremendous empathy and concern, and I'm going to try and help." He then pointed out a staff member with whom he directed Orozco to speak, adding, "I will personally get involved. You present very special circumstances, and we will try to solve your problems."[43]

Nonetheless, despite Cerf's deft handling of the structurally induced personal troubles, popular pressure moved a majority of the Advisory Board to do away with the neoliberal One Newark enrollment system at the public board meeting held a week later. Roberto Cabañas, in his address to the board, called not only for One Newark's dismantlement but for a reassessment of the pro–public school movement's aims:

> We as a community made a mistake when we claimed victory after Cami left. Because what we have now is much, much worse. It's much better funded. And we should not be having a conversation as a board about local control if One Newark continues to proliferate the charter expansion in the district. . . . *We won't have a public school district if we're not stopping One Newark.* And the only way clearly to stop One Newark is to ask Cerf to leave as superintendent.[44]

Thus, significantly, Cabañas placed privatization, not self-determination, at the heart of the issue. There could be no real local control, no real self-determination, with privatization, or at least further charter expansion. But, while taking a few jabs at Baraka, including a mocking reference to his election "when we all supposedly became mayor," he still ended his intervention, as in the past, with a plea "to ask the mayor to stand with us on the streets to demand that Cerf leave the district immediately."[45]

After the comment period, board member Marques Lewis, a long-time Baraka ally and city employee, introduced a motion to immediately end One Newark and return to the previous neighborhood enrollment model. Owens, the movement activist, who had joined the board the previous spring, also provided support by explaining how easily and seamlessly the system could be transitioned back and the simultaneous need to protect and reopen neighborhood schools. The measure passed 6–3, with, importantly, Baskerville-Richardson, now Baraka's "chief education officer," joining Padilla and Gaddy, the two hard-core, Baraka-backed charter representatives, in opposing the measure. Baskerville-Richardson publicly criticized Lewis for violating regime protocol by not vetting the motion behind closed doors before its unveiling.[46]

Clearly the measure violated the understanding Baraka had with Cerf and Christie on their June 2015 pact and road map to "local control." Therefore Baraka, dutifully, as part of upholding his end of the elite pact, strong-armed Lewis—despite his protestations that "no one told me how to vote"—and other board members to rescind their September votes. In doing this, Baraka protected a key structural change won by the movement from above to disrupt public education. At the October 18, 2016, business meeting, amid Richardson threatening to eject opponents and a raucous crowd chanting "If we don't get it, shut it down! Whose schools? Our schools!" the board voted 6–3 to rescind the decision to end One Newark, with Owens joined by two others in opposition.[47]

In a subsequent flip-flop, the following week, the board voted 7–2 in favor of a softer resolution than in September. They now called for establishing a committee to formulate a new enrollment system that would be ready by February 2017.[48] But Cerf, with no opposition from Baraka and probable behind-the-scenes coordination, vetoed the measure and obtained the backing of Christie's education commissioner to uphold his antidemocratic maneuver. NJCU, without the participation or endorsement of the NTU or the ANPS, held a rally

MAKING NEWARK GOVERNABLE AGAIN || 251

outside the December board meeting to "demand that Chris Cerf respect the democratic will of the people and our children before Wall Street's profits!"[49] But Cerf knew he was dealing, unlike his predecessor, with a Baraka who was not interested in protests but rather in fully accommodating the charter movement and its leading agent in the local state. Cerf could, therefore, comfortably ignore the street rabble and tolerate the feigned indignation of board members. For his part, Baraka confronted a tamed opposition grouped around the ANPS who would not make him pay a political price for his betrayals.[50] Cabañas, the most combative of the ANPS members, did mobilize protests against Cerf and emphasized that privatization had to end for local control to mean anything. But even he would go no further than to plead for the "radical mayor" to live up to his billing and join them in the streets.

From Public Schools to Public Housing

Baraka also invoked the racial justice framework to legitimate the destruction of the remaining traditional public housing developments. The Terrell Homes development, located along the formerly heavily polluted Passaic River, and surrounded by toxic waste sites, was in particular peril—from real estate. Cleanup efforts of the river spearheaded by the city and the ICC, the local CDC, combined with the county's subsequent creation of a park along the river, clearly placed the low-income, predominately black tenants "in the way" of the city's rent-intensification agenda. After promising residents that he would not support demolition, Baraka then "stabbed us in the back," as the tenant council president bitterly recounted. In February 2016, Baraka signed a letter to Housing and Urban Development asserting that Terrell Homes had "outlived their useful lives . . . [and therefore] demolition of the buildings is the most cost-effective measure."[51] In any redevelopment scheme, residents would face a drastic reduction from the current 275 units of the formerly named Franklin D. Roosevelt Homes, opened in the 1940s as part of the first wave of public housing.

As the keynote speaker at the September 2016 Newark Community Development Network (NCDN) conference to celebrate their four decades of work, Baraka justified his hostility to the city's public housing.[52] After a warm introduction by NCDN head and NCC official Richard Cammarieri, Baraka gave an overview of the racially discriminatory, uneven development promoted by the New Deal–created FHA, beginning in the 1930s. The result was that while white suburbia was subsidized with single-family homes, Newark was red-lined, and "we only got public housing," as he presented this important social gain of the 1930s in one-dimensional, negative terms. He added that Newark got more public housing per capita than any city and thus "it's funny," he added, "that we fight to keep them up." Thus Baraka used an ostensibly antiracist cover—a discriminatory aspect of the New Deal, and a wholly one-sided perspective on public housing—to legitimate public housing demolition in the neoliberal era that has disproportionately impacted low-income black families nationally, and particularly so in Newark and the case of Terrell Homes.[53] Baraka went on to deride those with "privilege"—presumably wealthier and whiter advocates—who would never live there but who nonetheless defend public housing and criticize other displacement-inducing effects of his administration's rent-intensification agenda.

EMANCIPATION FROM WHAT?

In a long-anticipated decision, the state board of education voted unanimously at its September 2017 meeting to approve the return of local control to the Newark school board. Baraka's choreographed celebration of regaining "self-determination" crystallized his larger method of taming and incorporating the movement from below through RD. But, in this packaging, he received the full cooperation of the movements' remnants. The ANPS organized a bus to Trenton to cheer on, in words that evoked a national liberation struggle of an oppressed people, the victory over "twenty-one years of *occupation* by the State of New Jersey."[54] The racist yoke, epitomized in the form of vulgar, white Republican Chris Christie, enveloping this majority Black and Brown district, had finally been lifted in a united community struggle led by Mayor Baraka.[55]

Following the vote in the state capitol, Baraka held a celebration in the rotunda of Newark's impressive Beaux-Arts-style City Hall. Gathered with him were the leading NSU veterans, now college students, Kristen Towkanik, Jose Leonardo, and Tanasia Brown, along with members of the ANPS. But, importantly, the contending movement, which Baraka had first challenged and then, since the 2015 pact, increasingly solidarized with, was also included in the ceremony. They were one big happy revolutionary family united in the struggle for self-determination. Consistent with that framing, Baraka's emcee for the event, Baskerville-Richardson, recognized the contributions of the pro–charter school board members, as well as Senator Ruiz, who led the charge to block the moratorium bill. It was possible to place them all under the same tent, the pantheon of the Newark anticolonial fight, because the struggle was not about privatization but about self-determination, and always had been, as Baraka explained:

> What we are asking for is right. . . . If anyone met with me, I said it was local control. If anyone talked to me, I told them it was local control. . . . Why? Because slavery is wrong, it's always been wrong. . . . It's wrong, it's wrong, it's wrong. . . . We won't be satisfied until we get free.[56]

Baraka, consistent with the theme of liberation from foreign domination, while obscuring the internal class contradictions, concluded with the rousing chants of his reelection theme—"Forward ever, backward never!"—taken from Ghanaian independence leader Kwame Nkrumah. "Unity," Baraka emphasized, is what Newark needed above all. But what unity really meant, as the thick description of this event and the broader movement makes clear, was the rewriting of the struggle and merger of the movements into Baraka's BUR—a regime, like its openly neoliberal predecessor, that had become an arm of the movement from above through its embrace, or at least accommodation of, the charter agenda.

MOVEMENT CONCLUSION: RETAKING THE STATE

Social movement theorists and activists Alf Gunvald Nilsen and Laurence Cox emphasize that social movements from above pursue their objectives "on the basis of superior access," as compared to their challengers from below, "to economic, political and cultural power resources."[57] But, in the case of Newark's Ras Baraka–led BUR, the movement from above did not see the new head of the local state, owing to his movement origins, as a reliable source of political power to protect and advance their interests. While willing to sacrifice Anderson, the movement would not tolerate a reversal of any of the structural gains made under her reign or allow any obstacles placed on the future expansion of charters. Thus, as we have seen, in the wake of his election, the movement from above mobilized its superior financial resources to forge new organizations, mount mass mobilizations, and launch electoral initiatives to reconfigure the Baraka regime.

In its effort to regain the state, the movement from above benefited from, indeed, actively exploited, the contradictions of the Baraka-led local state. While riding the movement to power, and largely financed by organized labor, Baraka was also committed to an orthodox rent-intensification development agenda pushed by FIRE, of which charter expansion was an integral part. Leading movement intellectuals like Tom Moran sensed the regime's soft underbelly. The *Star-Ledger* editorialist prophetically wrote, just after Baraka gave the green light for the North Star charter school expansion, "My guess is Baraka might flip on this question"—regarding charter expansion—"as the politics change." Moran added, recognizing the contradictory political formation within which this "shrewd politician" was encased, "Even now, he seems careful to leave himself room to maneuver."[58]

Indeed, following the October 2015 vote, Baraka progressively maneuvered into an ever deeper embrace of the movement from above. He actively, not passively, as Moran's formulation implied, "changed the politics" as he forged a "bromance" with the movement-aligned superintendent; penned a joint letter legitimating further expansion of charters; ran a "Unity" slate in the April 2016 school board elections; and, behind the scenes, undermined board challenges to Cerf.[59] In the subsequent 2017, 2018, and 2019 races, even the school board candidates Baraka fielded were increasingly charter-friendly, while the insufficiently obedient board member Owens was, after the movement had been contained, purged from "Team Baraka" when she came up for reelection. Meanwhile, the percentage of students in charter schools continued its ascent during the first term of the "radical" mayor. In the face of objections from the remnants of the movement from below, he deployed his powers, legitimated through RD ideology, to silence, delegitimate, and contain dissent.

The reconquest of the state, and the corresponding taming of the movement to defend public schools, was symbolized and reinforced by two, seemingly unconnected ceremonies on February 1, 2018—the day the local school board retook the powers the state had usurped more than two decades earlier. At a midday press conference at City Hall, Baraka was joined by Cory Booker to announce the incumbent mayor handing in petitions to qualify for the 2018 reelection race. The appearance by New Jersey's junior U.S. senator, and the rousing endorsement he gave his successor, was *not* a marriage of ideological opposites for short-term, pragmatic electoral purposes. Rather, their physical embrace onstage underscored their programmatic alignment on the signature issue of public education—the very one Baraka had used in the 2014 campaign to distinguish himself from his inauthentic predecessor. *Now,* four years later, they both agreed on "self-determination," on the return of local control, while maintaining and expanding the further march of the market. The local state was again in safe hands.

While the midday event signaled the movement from above's reconsolidation of state power, the evening, antiracist themed Emancipation Celebration—jointly organized by the Baraka administration and the ANPS to herald the handover—highlighted the movement from below's incorporation into the regime. Chaired by Cabañas and Gregory, with prominent appearances and addresses by former NSU leaders, the event framed the movement as a heroic self-determination struggle allied with their courageous, combative grassroots activist turned mayor. NTU chief John Abeigon, whom the moderators lauded and to whom they gave a prominent speaking role while failing even to recognize NEW's contributions, boldly inserted the union's concessionary 2012 contract into the resistance narrative: "if we didn't sign that contract, they would have charterized the whole district." Former NSU president Towkanik vaguely referenced the continuing fight against "systemic issues," and Cabañas pointed out that "One Newark is still in effect, which channels kids into corporate charters."[60] But in this gathering of movement veterans, no one pointed out the inconvenient truth of Baraka's collaboration with their opponents in defense of One Newark and the other "systemic issues" that had given rise to their insurgency. The courageous, defiant Baraka, armed with his powerful self-determination, antiracist ideology, which these same activists embraced, was beyond reproach. Thus, to understand the eventual defanging of this and other movements, we need the perceptive

256 || MAKING NEWARK GOVERNABLE AGAIN

lens Adolph Reed Jr. employed in the late 1970s to explain the stalling of the forward march of the previous decade's struggles and the ensuing neoliberal counterrevolution that was then taking hold. It was not principally, Reed argued, the power from above but rather "the sources of failure within the opposition" that opened the door for the brutal, decades-long ruling-class counteroffensive. We now turn to what lessons can be drawn from the Newark experience to prevent, as Reed adds, "a reproduction of failure."[61]

Conclusion

TELL NO LIES, CLAIM NO EASY VICTORIES

> Hide nothing from the masses of our people. Tell no lies.
> Expose lies whenever they are told. Mask no difficulties,
> mistakes, failures. Claim no easy victories.
> —Amilcar Cabral, extracts from Party directive, 1965

In February 1973, just months after chairing the National Black Political "Gary" Convention and at the height of his political influence, Imamu Amiri Baraka traveled to Conakry, Guinea, in West Africa. There, among "delegates from 80 sovereign nations, guerrilla movements and supporting organizations from Europe, Asia and the United States," as the *New York Times* reported, the Black Power leader gave a stirring speech at the funeral of Amilcar Cabral, the Marxist theoretician and leader of the Guinea-Bissau and Cape Verdean anticolonial armed struggle.[1] Cabral, just a few months before his assassination, made a U.S. visit during which, among various stops, he held a meeting in New York City with more than one hundred leading Black activists from some thirty organizations. During his wide-ranging dialogue with the gathering, which most likely included a Baraka-led Newark delegation, Cabral reiterated his long-standing insistence on the need for black petty bourgeois layers in the colonies, and beyond, to "return to the source." By this he meant that the global BPMC had to commit "class suicide" and politically unite with the rural and urban working masses. This entailed not only the petty bourgeoise's "real involvement in the struggle" but "their complete and absolute identification with the hopes of the mass of the people" for complete liberation. "Otherwise," Cabral lectured in another address during his 1972 tour, "the 'return to the source' is nothing more than an attempt to find short-term benefits—knowingly or unknowingly a kind of political opportunism."[2]

|| 257

258 || CONCLUSION

Four decades later, the son of Amiri Baraka "returned to the source" in the form of the movement to defend public education in the "Black and Brown" city of Newark. Councilman and then mayor Ras Baraka used his considerable political talents and influence to step up the campaign of disruption against Cami Anderson and, by extension, her Booker, Christie, and philanthrocapitalist backers. He allied with student, labor, and community activists while denouncing, in Cabralian terms, his black, "mercenary," comprador predecessor's disruption from above that "further dismantle[d] all that is left in our community" in the form of public schools. Eventually, as he touted, Baraka wrested back "local control" over the Newark public school district—or at least what remained of it—after years of "occupation" by the colonial powers in Trenton.

Yet, despite all these contributions, Baraka at the same time, knowingly or unknowingly, operated as a political opportunist by channeling the movement to serve his class interests and responsibilities. The "radical mayor" studiously refused to use his bully pulpit and the state powers at his disposal to champion and achieve the real "hopes of the masses of people" through municipal liberation from charter schools. Rather, he engaged this working-class movement armed with the BPMC's alien ideological weaponry of RD *to ensure* that the movement's social democratic, anticapitalist aspirations were not even raised, let alone achieved. He intervened in the movement before and particularly after his election to rebrand it as one for "self-determination," of "local control," while rehabilitating his former opponents and their competing antiracist ideology. Therefore, despite the pyrotechnics, "the famous 'right of self-determination of nations'"—or, in Baraka's formulation, of a "Black and Brown city"—was "nothing but hollow, petty bourgeois phraseology and humbug." As Rosa Luxemburg, another slain socialist, further elaborated in her polemic with V. I. Lenin,

> under the rule of capitalism there is no self-determination of peoples. . . . In class society each class of the nation strives to "determine itself" in a different fashion. . . . For the bourgeois classes, the standpoint of national freedom is fully subordinated to that of class rule.[3]

Newark's struggle over neoliberal school reform, a century after Luxemburg penned her critique, featured the same class dynamics. Baraka fully subordinated his operationalization of "self-determination" to the rule of the real estate and philanthrocapitalist interests he ultimately served. In practice, the Newark mayor's RD ideology, in the form of "local control," allowed the professional managerial class implementers—black, white, and Latinx—to fulfill their responsibilities of protecting the billionaire backers of school privatization, while appearing to serve those of Newark's working class. To paraphrase Luxemburg, the BPMC mayor, and his petty bourgeois and bourgeois allies, were fine with a privatization-friendly form of "self-determination"; if not, they would protect their class interests by sticking with Trenton's "despotism."[4]

Easing this legitimation work was the union bureaucracy and nonprofit apparatuses' personal, material, and political ties to the Baraka regime, which undergirded their embrace of RD. A prime example of these benefits is the career trajectory of Lauren Wells, Baraka's former "chief education officer." After leaving the administration, she launched a lucrative, RD-informed consulting business that counts the NPS among its leading clients as she displaced the Anderson-allied contractors.[5] These structures placed a limit on how far even the NJCU's Roberto Cabañas—the most committed and principled from this milieu, who tragically died in 2021—could go in challenging Baraka's betrayals. But the influence of RD also extended to activists and organizations outside these apparatuses—including the mayor's community activist opponents. This ideological hold undermined their ability to challenge the contradictions of the Baraka regime as they played out in the fight to defend public schools.[6]

Baraka's movement interventions demonstrate how the "'class struggle,'" as the late Colin Barker argued, "does not only occur *between* movements and their antagonists" but *within* them as well. This is because "[a] movement's *opponents*"—often in the guise of "allies" like Baraka—"have good reasons to try to influence how it interprets and seeks to change the world."[7] In Baraka's case, his "good reason" was to protect his rent-intensification development agenda, and therefore he intervened in the movement from below to influence "their ideas, forms of organization and repertoires of contention." These "are all," as Barker insisted, "within their opponents 'strategic sights.'"[8] Clearly RD, particularly as it was abstracted from a social democratic or socialist class agenda, was the key weapon—and Baraka the most skillful deployer—to contain the movement from below in Newark. Thus, as

260 || CONCLUSION

Preston Smith II has insisted, to make advances, working-class movements must be savvy enough to recognize how the "class interests" of the BPMC are often cloaked by what is projected as the "race interests" of all African Americans and the antiracist commitments of their bourgeois associates.[9] This recognition is particularly important in periods, as Smith emphasized, and as we are now witnessing, of renewed working-class struggle and openness to socialism.

RACIAL DEMOCRACY: FROM NEWARK TO THE NATION

In his second term, well after fully containing the public school movement, Baraka continued to rely on RD as his go-to ideological weapon to manage the neoliberal city. This was on display in the wake of the mass protests following the gruesome summer 2020 police murder of George Floyd. Despite overseeing a rent-intensification agenda, which necessitates aggressive policing, the Newark mayor was welcomed by activists, informed by a shared RD politics, to lead the city's biggest Floyd protest.[10] Then, for his part, Baraka's major policy initiative in the wake of the nationwide protests was, in addition to a renewed push for a strengthened police civilian review board, to launch the corporate-funded $100 million Newark 40 Acres and a Mule Fund (NWK FAM Fund). This fund would materially demonstrate, in a form that corporations were taking up in the wake of the Floyd protests, that "Black Lives Matter is not rhetoric, it's a statement of action." The action component, as Baraka explained at a press conference with charter school champion Al Sharpton at his side, would address the injustice of the state's gaping "racial wealth gap" separating "New Jersey's Latinx and Black families" from their white counterparts.[11]

This RD, antidisparitarian project, ostensibly to benefit all "Latinx and Black families," was, like the rest, essentially a bourgeois-serving one. These pro-capitalist features were expressed at three levels. First, Baraka and his corporate partners framed the initiative, as reflected in the title, to address "systemic racism"—that is, racial disparities—driven primarily by the unfulfilled promises and dismantlement of Reconstruction, the subsequent Jim Crow era, and the conjunctural impact of the pandemic. This conveniently left off the hook—in addition to the elite destruction of the biracial populist movement—the post–civil rights urban African American and Latinx political classes and their corporate governing partners. These forces over the last half century have not only championed and imposed the regressive urban neoliberal agenda that has deepened inequality but constructed a carceral state to manage those class divides that led millions into the streets. The latter role hit particularly close to home considering the pivotal role former Newark mayor Sharpe James played—with a far from negligible amount of black popular support—in the passage of Clinton's 1994 crime bill.

The initiative's second class feature was its RD-informed "racial wealth gap" problematic that presumed a commonality of interest between "Latinx and Black" workers and their much wealthier racial brethren. Yet, as Matt Bruenig's research has found, over 77 percent of racial wealth disparity is explained by the gap between the wealthiest 10 percent of white and black households. Conversely, Bruenig's data show, only 3 percent of the racial gap comes from the bottom 50 percent of each group. That is, these white and black households are in nearly the same class location, wealth-wise, with little, no, or even negative wealth. What Baraka's and other such initiatives obscure, as Walter Benn Michaels and Adolph Reed Jr. emphasize in their critique of antidisparitarian efforts that surged post Floyd, is that "the wealth gap among all but the wealthiest blacks and whites is dwarfed by the class gap, the difference between the wealthiest and everyone else across the board." The political logic that flows from this problematic is a united multiracial working-class struggle against the "runaway inequality" of the neoliberal era. But, of course, the corporate and super-rich list of sponsors Baraka lined up, ranging from AT&T to Newark native Shaquille O'Neal, would obviously not be interested in such an endeavor.[12] They, and their partner in City Hall, obviously preferred a politics of RD over SD.

The third and clearest evidence that this initiative's apparent "race line" was in fact a class one was the intended recipients of the corporate cash. Baraka, consistent with RD, advertised the fund as one "creating equality and opportunity for our black and brown communities" in a capitalist economy. Nevertheless, in a typical RD sleight of hand, the corporate money to combat the racial wealth gap would be directed to only one class segment of these "communities": "Black and Latinx-owned businesses." By providing "investable capital," the fund would, the city press release explained, "empower our entrepreneurs of color so that they can compete at increasingly higher levels" with their white competitors. The result would be to "enhance the value

262 || CONCLUSION

of Black and Latinx-focused small businesses and *real estate development.*"[13] Despite being clearly geared to further rent-intensification development, the backers promised it would "drive economic wealth among Black and Latinx populations in Newark."[14] Indeed, this "Black and Brown capitalism" initiative may result in driving wealth among some of Newark's petty bourgeois "populations," while driving out more of their working-class counterparts from the city.

Baraka's intervention, far from being one of "cooptation," was wholly in line with BLM's racial unity, antidisparitarian, and "self-determination" politics.[15] Like Baraka, the movement's most visible and influential leaders came out of the BPMC, mainly from the philanthropic-funded nonprofit world, including TFA veterans DeRay McKesson and Brittney Packet. BLM leaders, mirroring Newark's mayor, welcomed the deluge, which accelerated after the Floyd protests, of corporate and philanthropic dollars into the host of 501(c)3 organizations they had assembled. Kimberlé Crenshaw, the influential intersectional and critical race theorist, pointed to the corporate largesse as evidence of the superiority of RD over SD politics. Crenshaw, who heads her own RD think tank nonprofit in addition to her two elite law school appointments, lauded the post-Floyd RD-informed interventions by "every corporation worth its salt" that directed its millions to combat "structural racism and anti-blackness." In contrast, Bernie Sanders's inferior "colorblind," social democratic class agenda "cannot help you see"—which obviously didn't cloud the vision of the United States' "woke" CEOs like Jamie Dimon or Jeff Bezos—"the specific contours of race disparity." Crenshaw's critique echoed that of BLM hashtag cofounder Alicia Garza, who dismissed Sanders's program as so much "weirdo economic determinism" unable to address Black lives.[16]

The hegemony of RD, racial unity politics, including the pitting of RD and SD agendas, was underscored by its embrace at the "grassroots" level as well. In Seattle, for example, a young black activist objected to socialist city councilperson Kshama Sawant connecting the antipolice brutality protests to the demand for a tax on Amazon. "I want to tax Amazon too, but can we," exclaimed protestor Moe'Neyah Dene Holland, "please for once focus on black lives?"[17] Family survivors of black workers and youths murdered by the police, for their part, have justifiably criticized the movement's varied BPMC non-

CONCLUSION || 263

profit officials for using their suffering to enrich themselves. Implicit in these righteous denunciations was a critique of the class biases of racial brokerage politics represented by Patrisse Cullors's BLM Global Network Foundation, Tamika Mallory's Until Freedom, and other "movement" 501(c)3 entities that became the destination of philanthropic dollars.[18]

By no means was "Barakaism"—the wielding of RD to manage neoliberalism—limited to Newark and BLM. In fact, in the aftermath of the 2008 financial crash, leading Democratic Party politicians, and their media allies, increasingly weaponized RD to attack emerging class challenges. The prime example was the Democrats' attack on Bernie Sanders's presidential campaigns that focused on growing inequality and advocated a social democratic agenda of decommodifying higher education, health care, and other vital services. Although this agenda would disproportionally benefit African Americans and Latinx, his 2016 Democratic opponent, Hillary Clinton, charged that the Vermont senator's obsession with "Wall Street" ignored minority, particularly black, concerns. The Sanders campaign was, in her words, "failing to face up to the reality of systemic racism." In a prime example of race reductionism, she asked rhetorically at another stop on the campaign trail, "If we broke up the big banks tomorrow . . . would that end racism? Would that end sexism?" This trope conveniently ignored not only how the Clinton administration's banking deregulation contributed to the housing crash that decimated, in particular, black homeowners but the former First Lady's own thinly veiled racist stereotypes and rhetoric to expand the carceral and shed the welfare states.[19]

The powerful African American congressman from South Carolina James Clyburn went further than Clinton, arguing that Sanders's free higher education plan would damage black interests. Instituting "free college at public institutions," Clyburn maintained, would lead "black, private HBCUs [historically black colleges and universities] to close down," such as Allen College, where he sits on the board of trustees. The late civil rights icon John Lewis added his authority to the crusade, arguing that free higher education and other public services would be irresponsible because "there's not anything free in America." As the embodiment of RD, opposition emanating from the "Conscience of the Congress" implied that Sanders's SD agenda was not in the interests of the "black community."[20]

IN THE CONTRADICTION LIES THE HOPE

As this study has shown, RD politics, rather than posing an alternative, instead provided neoliberals, particularly the urban wing, a powerful, indispensable tool to legitimate and contain challenges to their capitalist agenda. But if RD—embraced to varying degrees by much of what passes for progressive and left politics in the United States—is of no use, then how can neoliberalism, particularly its urban revanchist arm imposed on cities across the country and world, be challenged? What are the lessons from Newark for charting and forging that path? The first step in addressing this question is determining the current state of the neoliberal SSA. As David Kotz emphasizes, the smooth functioning of a SSA is measured by whether it is able to promote profit making and continued economic expansion and investment. On those terms, neoliberalism was a "success" for nearly three decades, though growth rates were lower and income and wealth growth concentrated at the top compared to the preceding, more robust and relatively egalitarian period of regulated capitalism. But by the time of the 2008–9 Great Recession, and especially the economic crisis precipitated by the global Covid-19 pandemic that exploded in early 2020, neoliberalism has clearly entered a structural crisis. That is, the neoliberal SSA has transformed from a promoter to an obstacle to achieving central capitalist objectives.

One manifestation of the crisis has been the anemic average annual growth rate of 2.3 percent between the end of the recession in 2009 and 2019. This contrasts with rates of 4–5 percent during the postwar boom and of 3–4 percent during the neoliberal period. The "fundamental reason" for the decline in growth, Kotz argues, has been the post-2009 "inability of the neoliberal form of capitalism to promote normal accumulation any longer." Political economist Doug Henwood documents a further deterioration since the pandemic, as investment levels in new plants and equipment are now "barely keeping ahead of decay," all of which deepens the post-2009 sluggish growth in labor productivity. In sum, "such data clearly indicate," Kotz concludes, "a condition of prolonged stagnation. Neoliberal institutions are no longer effectively promoting accumulation." Profit rates, the other measure of success of a SSA, and the raison d'être of capitalism, have remained robust in the post-2009 period. But, Kotz emphasizes, "without a normal rate of economic expansion," including investment levels that drive it, "the rate of profit cannot remain high for very long."[21]

For Robert Brenner, the Federal Reserve's unprecedented move, on March 23, 2020, to provide a no-strings-attached provision of unlimited credit to nonfinancial corporations signifies a qualitative turn in the decomposition not only of neoliberalism but of capitalism. Quoting the head of a major hedge fund, Brenner argues that the massive bailouts have turned a large chunk of U.S. corporations, and essentially U.S. capitalism, into "something akin to GSEs [government-supported entities]."[22] Likewise, Eric Lerner, informed by Luxemburg's theory of accumulation and crisis, sees a qualitative turn since the pandemic as the "the global capitalist system has itself metamorphosed into a new stage of state-financed-capitalism." Not only in the United States but across the industrialized countries, "the state," Lerner argues,

> has become the main source of capitalist investment. Instead of capitalists lending capital at interest to the state, now the state lends to the capitalists at no interest. Capital investments are poured into supporting asset prices—stocks, bonds and real estate—while real investment in infrastructure and production continues to shrink.[23]

Though in crisis, there is no inevitability that neoliberalism, let alone capitalism, will be replaced. As Kotz notes, after a brief "Keynesian moment" following the 2008 crisis, the Obama administration, and other levels of the state, returned to, and indeed deepened, the neoliberal agenda. A prime example was the stepped-up push for charter schools in Newark and beyond, combined with massive budget cuts to public education from K–12 to the university level.

From Comprehensive Program to Mass Strike

Central to neoliberalism's tenacity, even in crisis, is that it is a "coherent, mutually reinforcing system of ideas, theories, and institutions, which makes it resistant to change." "Significant and workable change," Kotz emphasizes, "would require replacing the entire social structure of accumulation"—which, obviously, could only be consummated by a mass, disruptive social movement demanding it.[24] But there are two major obstacles, or "trenches," that have blocked the emergence of a movement forging and demanding a comprehensive set of demands, an alternative *program*. One is the foundation-funded nonprofit complex, which has grown enormously during the neoliberal era. The dominant liberal foundations among the complex fund and promote single-issue "campaigns" by their nonprofit grantees, often based on age, race, gender, sexuality, immigrant status, homelessness, disability, or some combination of these identities, or those constructed as such. The result has been the proliferation of an RD politics writ large—"of fragmented 'identity groups' each embedded in narrow sets of (identity) interests totally incapable of building a national movement."[25]

Further fueling this narrow approach among the "nonprofits (and the foundations that finance them)," as Marcie Smith has masterfully shown, has been the enormous influence of the late Gene Sharp—the national security state–funded and –embedded social movement theorist—and his leading mentee, George Lakey. Sharpian-informed politics, which has near-hegemonic status within this milieu, undermines constructing a comprehensive challenge to the neoliberal project due to hostility to the cooperative, public services arm of the state and therefore of making demands on it; promotion of antidemocratic "consensus" decision-making practices; and rejection of class analysis and wariness toward working-class-centered movements. Indeed, as Smith argues, Sharpism, far from a challenge, has abetted the neoliberal agenda at home and abroad.

> In Sharp's "politics of nonviolent action," the state was not the prize, not even a terrain of struggle: it was the enemy, the object to be paralyzed and dissolved. And in this regard, Sharp fit neatly into the emerging neoliberal consensus's pathological hatred of the state, and unerring faith in the "free market."[26]

The unions, arguably the central pillar of the crisis, have also not been up to the task. Beginning with labor's ineffectual challenge to the banker's "solution" to New York City's mid-1970s fiscal crisis, the massive concessions in auto and other industries following the union-backed 1979 Chrysler bailout, the failure to solidarize with the pivotal 1981 PATCO strike, and the waves of union busting that followed, including the subsequent assault on public education in Newark and

CONCLUSION || 267

elsewhere, unions have in the main abetted rather than challenged the neoliberal onslaught. Central to this weakness is that, as San Gindin argues, "though unions emerge out of the working class, they are not class but particularist organizations, representing specific groups of workers."[27] Although this orientation was able to make, or at least preserve, gains during the postwar boom, it has been spectacularly not up to the task under neoliberalism, including in its crisis stage.

In contrast, NEW—the movement-birthed formation that grouped teachers and community members—represented an organizational form that nurtured, or at least was amenable to, forging a class-wide agenda. Service workers, especially those in the public sector, and in particular education workers, are well positioned to forge a unifying set of working-class demands. "Their organic ties to the broader community," as Jane McAlevey argues, "form the potential strategic wedge needed to leverage the kind of power American workers haven't had for decades."[28] For teachers, this organic connection to their working-class students and their families is of such an intimate nature that the living conditions of the latter *are* the working conditions of education workers. That is, what happens in the lives of students and their families, which the pandemic has further highlighted, reverberates into the teachers' classrooms and schools. And, as we saw with the move to online teaching during the pandemic, what happens in the schools rebounds in the other direction as well and into the broader capitalist production process.

This organic connection can be politically operationalized by, as Gindin further argues, "reconsidering"—or, really, violating—the current public-sector bargaining system. This institution, forged through disruptive movements of the late Keynesian years, and now either dismantled, neutered, or deployed to impose neoliberal reforms, can and must be engaged disruptively. That is, education workers must violate the current collective bargaining strictures involving participation, the "scope" of bargaining, and forms of disruption. Collective bargaining, particularly but not only in the public sector, must be wielded to unite education workers with support staff, students, their families, and the broader working class to forge a common, democratically arrived-at program—and to prepare and carry out a disruptive strike to win it. This class-wide approach to bargaining is crucial to undercutting ruling-class strategies of splitting "privileged" public-sector workers from their private-sector brethren that Christie and others skillfully wielded in the wake of the Great Recession and the savaging of education budgets. The strategy outlined here, I want to emphasize, goes far beyond that deployed by the CTU and touted by Jane McAlevey in her influential study *No Shortcuts* as an exemplar of what she terms "deep organizing." For the CTU, "mass negotiations" were a member-only affair and a unilaterally issued "policy paper" outlining its vague community bargaining goals substituted for community-worker popular assemblies to establish a program and plan of struggle.[29]

Newark's 2013 popular assembly, which included NEW activists and other social movement organizations and organizers outside the nonprofit complex, came closest to operationalizing the demand-formation component of the strategy outlined herein. Through the assembly, participants debated and agreed on a direct-government-employment mass public works program of good jobs, free public services—including creating a safe, alternative energy source—and equal rights *for all,* paid for by taxing the wealth of the billionaires and slashing military spending. This *program* of economic and political demands was an RD one as well, because it combated any accessibility obstacles faced by *all* oppressed groups to ensure implementation of the program's universal intent.[30] But, it was *not* an antiracist, antioppression program cleaved from a working-class one, which the Newark case underscores invariably ends up serving privileged layers. Nor was it a "reparations" demand to singularly address the undeniable structural and direct violence inflicted on African Americans, from slavery to neoliberal capitalism, the latter of which, as we have seen, had distinct intraracial class impacts. Proponents of this "radical" version of RD have not, as the late Bruce Dixon critiqued, engaged in a serious discussion of how to construct the "huge political project require[ed] [to gain] the support of significant constituencies other than African Americans" and thus make "reparations actually happen." But, of course, as Dixon points out, the lack of any road map is central to its allure. The now newly ascendant reparations "movement" allows the BPMC to posture "as brokers and spokespeople" for the "Black community" or "Nation," while avoiding a serious struggle to win the "reallocation of resources on a vast scale" to make it at all meaningful.[31] Indeed, as Adolph Reed Jr. has emphasized, for reparations and other such race-reductionist initiatives, "developing and advancing a popular politics is not the point at all." Rather, he argues, and the Newark case demonstrates, it is instead a "politics geared toward bending ears

CONCLUSION || 269

of and currying favor from elements of the ruling class and their gate-keeping minions."[32]

The centrality of agreeing on a concrete set of political and economic demands, an anticapitalist program, and tenaciously fighting for it, is central to the arguments of both Rosa Luxemburg and Alf Gunvald Nilsen and Laurence Cox, for advancing "movement processes." In "Opportunism and the Art of the Possible"—an important contribution to intramovement debates of the day and of continuing relevance—Luxemburg emphasized that a democratically arrived-at "programme," a coherent set of political and economic demands, is what must guide the socialist movement's "practical struggle." That movement must resolutely and uncompromisingly—most importantly in the form of disruptive social movements—fight for that program. It is in that "intransigent attitude"—expressed in words and disruptive deeds—that the movement's "whole strength" lies. Intransigence is what "earns" the movement "fear and respect of the enemy and the trust and support of the people" and therefore leads the "government and the bourgeois parties to concede . . . the few immediate successes that can be gained." In other words, movements make gains by fighting for what they want, rather than accepting what has been decided as "realistic." When movements concede on their principal demands and disruptive protests to win them, they put themselves, in Luxemburg's memorable metaphor, "in the same situation as the hunter who has not only failed to stay the deer but has also lost his gun in the process."[33]

The lethal effects of opportunism in Newark's movement played out in two stages. First, by not intransigently fighting against privatization, Baraka was able to divert the movement into "chas[ing] after what is 'possible'" in the form of self-determination.[34] The movement facilitated Baraka's diversionary maneuver by failing to place stopping and reversing privatization—rather than the empty signifier of "community schools"—as a central plank of the Newark Promise plan the ANPS had hashed out behind closed doors. Thus, although the Newark student movement employed its central disruptive weapon, it was not consciously and uncompromisingly unleashed to win—other than "local control"—the weakly defined movement objectives. Then, once Baraka announced groundbreaking on the highway to local control, the movement had still failed to stay the public school–killing "deer" of privatization, which continued to run amok. Worse still, the

270 || CONCLUSION

"gun"—an intransigent movement disrupting to meet its demands—was now lost. Why? Because there was now, according to the movement's supreme leader, a road map to realizing the movement's central objective of "local control." To finally consummate "victory" required unity—not conflict—with the now politically rehabilitated privatizers.

Luxemburg's study of the mass strike process further highlights the importance of socialists convincing workers of their common interests in a comprehensive program that unites political and economic demands. By having prepared the soil in this way, the ability of socialists to advance the mass strike process when they do appear, by intervening with "lively agitation for the extension of demands," is made much more likely.[35] The real power of mass strikes lies in this continual extension of demands and the spread of strikes to larger layers of the working class—unionized and nonunionized, employed and unemployed, in production and reproduction alike. As it unfolds, the ruling class becomes gripped with fear as they collectively ask, "Who will go out on strike next? . . . What will be shut down, what will be occupied next, what new layers of workers will go into action?"[36] This terror leads the rulers to give concessions to stop the process. Therefore the ability to instill this fear, to exercise this power, is made more likely if, through educational efforts, and earlier "militant particularistic" and "campaign"-level struggles, these demands have been popularized, uncompromisingly fought for, and thus made "commonsense."

In Newark, a movement at what Nilsen and Cox call the "campaign level" emerged that challenged an important expression of the neoliberal capitalist offensive, but then became bogged down in the ideological muck of RD. Uniting behind a coherent, democratically arrived-at set of demands is crucial for avoiding RD and other class containment traps. A movement fighting for a unified program increases the chances of it advancing to what Nilsen and Cox call a "social movement project" that challenges the "social totality" or producing a revolutionary situation when movements from above and below battle over which class will rule. Thus, for Nilsen and Cox, and echoed by Barker and Leopold, to advance movements from below, socialists must recapture Marx and Engels's conception of "the movement" rather than of separated "single-issue silos," that is, movements understood as "a whole with many parts, moving—at variable speed and with differential success—towards a condition where it might

CONCLUSION || 271

engage in capitalism's total overthrow." This contrasts with the "taken-for-granted common sense" for scholars, and activists from labor and nongovernmental organization (NGO) milieus alike, "that social movements are many, disconnected from each other and thus capable of being studied [and politically engaged] in isolation from each other." This "common sense" must be combated ideologically, as part of the intramovement "fields of argument," for that badly needed anticapitalist challenge to emerge.[37]

Democracy: From Legislative Seats to the Streets

A crucial terrain, as Luxemburg argued, for advancing movements, which the Newark case highlighted, is the electoral arena. We do not violate Cabral's dictum, we do not lie, by recognizing that Baraka's mayoral campaign clearly advanced the movement to defend public education—indeed, as the *New York Times* acknowledges, the campaign had become a veritable referendum on corporate school reform. But ultimately, Baraka's victory did not allow the movement to claim victory, easy or otherwise, because once in power, the new mayor quickly dumped the direct-democracy rhetoric as he accommodated the charter school agenda. He could do this because the movement never exercised any real democratic control over its "radical mayor." This experience underscores once again the inability of movements from below to, *by allying* with Democrats, "realign" them (Shachtman–Rustin thesis), "keep them accountable" (NGO language), "make them behave" (Karen Lewis's formulation), or "use" their "ballot line" before some promised future "dirty break" (Democratic Socialists of America theoreticians). Indeed, as Newark and many other cases demonstrate, endorsements more often than not embolden Democrats to turn on their popular base.[38] But the lesson to be drawn is not that movements should abandon the electoral field but rather that they must exercise real democratic control by fielding their own candidates. To do this, they must employ a "delegated democracy" in which "movement-party" candidates are beholden to carrying out a democratically agreed-upon set of demands and are sanctioned for any violations. Furthermore, their interventions—as both candidate and once (and if) in office—must be coordinated with the movements outside parliamentary and executive offices to make advances or defend past conquests. Ensuring, Luxemburg argues, that their "tactics are tailored

272 || CONCLUSION

not to parliament alone" but also to "the people themselves, 'in the streets,'" is what gives those legislative deputies any leverage.[39]

The crucial importance of democracy is, of course, not limited to the electoral field but must be operative throughout the movement. The movement must operate through delegated deliberative bodies who select immediately recallable leaders beholden to the demands at which the base arrives. This, in turn, would be the basis for organizing at larger scales, ranging the municipal, regional, national, and even global levels. Now, of course, Luxemburg harshly critiques "the rigid, mechanical-bureaucratic conception . . . of the struggle . . . as the product of organisation at a certain stage of its strength." Rather, she argues, in dialectical fashion, "the organisation arise[s] as a product of the struggle."[40] But, as with demands formation, the ground for the mass strike can be cultivated, the likelihood of its emergence increased, if socialist activists operate during the preceding period through a strike delegate formation in which "we are all leaders."

NEWARK'S CONTRIBUTION TO THE PLOT FOR A SOCIALIST AMERICA

Where are American cities, and (U.S.) America more broadly, going? And where, as Kenneth Gibson would have asked, is Newark located in that motion? Though not the first, Newark was clearly at the center of the struggles that emerged against the intensified assault on public education as the neoliberal model faltered in the wake of the Great Recession. Though significant, the movement, as we have documented, was not able to defeat privatization, much less transform Newark into David Harvey's "rebel city." Nonetheless, what the city's class struggles of the 2010s *did* provide are important lessons for strengthening the anticapitalist, socialist movement so urgently needed. Studying that historical experience to draw out the lessons can be, as Luxemburg emphasized, a painful exercise, because the working class's "*Via Dolorosa* to freedom is covered not only with unspeakable suffering, but with countless mistakes." But there really is no choice, because the

> final liberation depends entirely upon the proletariat, on whether it understands to learn from its own mistakes. Self-criticism, cruel, unsparing criticism, that goes to the very root of the evil is life and breath for the proletarian movement. . . . Socialism is only lost if

the international proletariat is unable to measure the depth of its catastrophe and refuses to understand the lessons it teaches.[41]

Chief among those lessons from the Newark experience is that, as Karl Marx counseled the working class after Louis Bonaparte's coup, "the social revolution of the nineteenth century"—as well as the twenty-first-century one needed today—"cannot take its poetry from the past but only from the future. It cannot begin with itself before it has stripped away all superstition about the past." Among the verses that need to be left behind, as this study has demonstrated, are the intoxicating ones of self-determination and all the "nostalgia" that surrounds it.[42]

The stakes for the working class learning its lessons are particularly high in the current national and global political conjuncture. Though neoliberal capitalism still reigns, it is clear we have entered what Nancy Fraser and others, drawing from Gramsci, have called an "interregnum": a period when the "old is dying"—in the form of neoliberal hegemony—"and the new cannot be born."[43] During this period, as Gramsci predicted, and we are clearly witnessing, many "morbid symptoms" appear. The most grotesque and threatening form, since the mid-teens, is of a growing global neofascist-authoritarian wave, extending from the United States to Brazil and from India to Italy and beyond. Blake Stewart terms this "a far-right civilizationist" capitalist project that is challenging the "neoliberal cosmopolitanism" model to managing global capitalism that took hold after the end of the Cold War. But, he argues, what has given this "new politics of the right traction is . . . less the immediacy of crisis since 2008 than," as we have emphasized in this study, "the still-unfolding consequences of fundamental capitalist restructuring since the 1970s."[44]

Therefore defeating the neofascist wave requires a working-class movement, *the* movement, putting forward a socialist alternative program that addresses the root of the problem—the capitalist-produced social, political, economic, cultural, and ecological crises confronting humanity. Far-fetched? Maybe not. Though, in the current conjuncture, David Kotz argues aiming for a social democratic rather than a socialist horizon, he acknowledges that in "a structural crisis period," as we are now in, "competing proposals for major change [can] suddenly move from the political fringes into the mainstream."[45] To exploit those possibilities requires forging a coherent, comprehensive program of political and economic demands—such as the one agreed upon in Newark, expanded to include the socialization of finance—and beginning to intransigently fight for it. The Greek tragedy of Syriza's betrayal of its electoral base and the subsequent European-wide rise of the far Right highlights the grave danger of opportunism and the necessity of democratic control over the movement's electoral arm. Only through a democratically controlled mass strike movement would capital ever concede to such a transformational program, even partially. Once granted, capital would *immediately* work to overturn the concessions. This would then place on the agenda which class would rule and what system would prevail.

In Cabralian terms, the preceding scenario is by no means an easily claimed victory. But we also tell no lies when we recognize that the return to a stable, happy, regulated "people's" capitalism is not a possibility. It really is, as Luxemburg recognized, either socialism or a continued descent into barbarism.

Acknowledgments

I owe a debt of gratitude to the many institutions, organizations, colleagues, and comrades who made this book possible. Among these are Jeannette Gabriel, who insisted I study and write on the then emerging school fight back in Newark. I am especially appreciative of my comrades in Newark, across New Jersey, and beyond who allowed me to engage in dialogue at all hours of the day and night, via text, email, and conversations, on the Newark fight. These include Al Moussab, Avram Ripps, Eric Lerner, Branden Rippey, Leah Owens, Mike Howells, Cedric Johnson, Karl Schwartz, Angeline Mountauban, Dave and Debbie Poleshuck, Ganesh Trichur, Yvette Jordan, Nancy Gianni, Betty Maloney, Chris Santiago, and everyone who attended NEW meetings. I also thank the People's Organization for Progress, including chairman Lawrence Hamm, Ingrid Hill, Larry Adams, and other members, for the wealth of knowledge I gained from attending meetings, engaging in discussions, and marching in innumerable protests. My gratitude extends to POP members who have passed on, including Greg King and Aminifu Williams. I treasure as well the conversations with, and opportunity to write on Newark for, the late editors of the *Black Agenda Report,* Bruce Dixon and Glen Ford. I am also indebted to all the nonprofit representatives; civic leaders; ministers; public officials; and teacher, student, and community activists who agreed to be interviewed for this study, including the late Wilhelmina Holder and Willie Rowe.

Another important contribution to my intellectual and political development over the past decade, and thus to this study, has been the relationships—and, yes, intense disagreements at times—with activists in the Resist the Deportation Machine Network, CUNY Struggle, the Professional Staff Congress and CSI chapter, Staten Island Against Racism and Police Brutality, International Luxemburgist Network, and the CSI Solidarity email Listserv. I also thank my students at the College of Staten Island for the support and education they have provided me. This includes Luis Zaragoza, who participated

276 || ACKNOWLEDGMENTS

in the movement to close the ICE concentration camps in New Jersey, and Karen Ponce, who put her sociological imagination to work by emerging as one of the leaders of the successful Staten Island Amazon unionization vote.

The support from the College of Staten Island, and City University New York, however limited and insufficient due to the austerity attacks faced by an increasingly less public university and the failure of our union to mount a class-wide fight fightback, is also appreciated. This includes presentations of my work at a Dean's Symposium, a grant to attend the 2016 Contested Cities to Global Urban Justice conference in Madrid, and two PSC-CUNY grants (awards 46-579 and 61619-00 49). I am also thankful for the guidance and support provided by Pieter Martin at the University of Minnesota Press and the entire production staff. In addition, I thank Julia Sass Rubin for the opportunity to present my work, and query others, at the annual "Education Policy, Communities, and Social Justice" research conference she and her colleagues organize at Rutgers University's Bloustein School.

I also thank those who gave me support, in numerous ways, over the course of my wanderings during the first two years of the pandemic, while I was completing the manuscript. These include Gustavo Rivera, Sonia Santiago Rivera, Monique Fraser, Isabel Cristina Gonzalez, Najib Siddiqui, Ivy Karamitsos, Carola at Padma House, and all my friends at San Antonio Hotel Boutique. During this time, the regular WhatsApp messages from my junior, David Wisniewski, and the pictures of his loving wife, Victoria, and adorable daughter Lucia helped keep me connected wherever I was. Finally, I recognize my mother, Jean Marie Guidone Arena, who departed us in 2013, just as I began this project. Yet, I know she is still *¡presente!* in my life, including in this book, and in the lives of so, so many people she touched over the seventy-one years that she walked this earth.

Appendix

RESEARCH METHODS

My entry into this study was through what Michael Burawoy calls a "grassroots" or "public" sociology that involved an organic connection with—and education by—local activists, organizations, and movements in Newark, New Jersey.[1] That is, the study emerged out of, as Walda Katz-Fishman and Jerome Scott explain in their study on the "paths" to public sociology, "social struggle."[2] In 2008, after more than twenty years in New Orleans as a labor and community activist, and completing a public sociology–informed dissertation on the pre- and post-Katrina destruction of the city's public housing, I accepted a tenure-track position in the Department of Sociology and Anthropology at CUNY's College of Staten Island. Relocating just at the onset of the Great Recession, I moved first to a suburb of Newark and later to the city. Along with a longtime comrade, I immersed myself in various efforts in the New York/New Jersey metropolitan area that were emerging to forge a popular, working-class response to the greatest capitalist downturn since the 1930s. As part of these efforts, I joined and began fairly regular attendance at the weekly meetings, held in Newark's central ward, of POP. The social justice community organization has a predominately African American membership, but attendance at meetings, and even more so at its regular protests, draws white people, such as I, and those from other ethnic and racial groups from Newark and around the metropolitan area. A major focus of the group is antipolice brutality protests, but it also addresses a whole host of other issues, ranging from health care to jobs.

POP, since its formation in the early 1980s, has been led by chairman Larry Hamm, whose activism dates back to the early 1970s as a NPS student leader during the teacher strikes. Listening to Hamm chair the weekly meetings, along with the remembrances and commentary of other members, many from Hamm's generation or older, provided me a rich education and insights into Newark politics,

278 || APPENDIX

popular struggles, ideologies, and important players. For example, I first heard of the influential role of Stephen Adubato Sr., and the contempt with which many held him, at a POP meeting. Through POP, I developed a friendship with the late Greg King, who, like Hamm, had been a leading member of Amiri Baraka's movement. King shared with me his unpublished memoir, and oral recollections, about his involvement in CFUN, Spirit House, and the movement's security team. In addition, local personalities, including Amiri Baraka, Ras Baraka, Junius Williams, William Payne, and Robert Curvin, periodically graced POP meetings. In addition, ordinary Newarkers bringing various grievances often attended meetings, all of which helped further familiarize me with the social and political contours of Newark.

Moving to Newark's heavily immigrant Ironbound section of the city helped educate me about another facet of the city. As part of attempts to reunify the local immigrant rights movement, which had weakened after the political mass strike of May Day 2006 and the ensuing repression, I met Rita Schneider, an activist and Brazilian nun at the mainly Portuguese-speaking St. James Church. Schneider arranged for use of the church cafeteria for meetings and helped organize parishioners, particularly Brazilians, for the May Day protests local activists held in 2009 and 2010. Schneider educated me about neighborhood political and civic leaders and the terror and harm inflicted by immigrant detention, in which she was well versed through her visitation work at the local for-profit detention center. Through frequenting St. James, I also first met Leah Owens, whose TaLin group was holding meetings in the cafeteria as well.

Later in the decade, after Trump's election, and the stepped-up attack on immigrants, I became active in a newly formed coalition dedicated to closing New Jersey's ICE detention centers—what the movement termed "concentration camps." These included a private-run detention center as well as camps run by the Democratic-controlled counties of Essex (county seat, Newark) and two others. The movement mobilized for speak-outs at the county board meetings, marches, and civil disobedience actions demanding their closure. Participation in the campaign educated me about the intimate links between Newark and Essex County politics, particularly through the machine of charter school operator Stephen Adubato Sr., as well the influence of "county bosses" (executives), like Adubato protégé Joseph DiVincenzo, in state politics. Finally, I became further acquainted with DiVincenzo when a section of the movement selected me to run a 2018 independent electoral campaign against the four-time incumbent county executive.[3]

All this engagement, including the relationships I had developed, helped prepare me for conducting an ethnographic study of Newark's public school movement that I would begin in late 2013. After working with POP leaders, NEW chair Branden Rippey, and other local activists in organizing the October 2013 popular assembly, and the failure to make any advances toward implementing demands, I began immersing myself in a study of the now burgeoning movement to defend public schools. Also making it a propitious time was that I had completed my first book, *Driven from New Orleans,* and I saw the Newark case as an extension of my long-term scholarly interests and political commitments. I took advantage of my location, and the knowledge and relationships I had developed over the previous five years, to launch the study.

The form of ethnography I employed is what Burawoy calls the "extended case study method" or what Tivory and Timmermans term a "theoretically driven ethnography" or "theorygraphy."[4] Thus, as Cox and Nilsen encourage, my study centered on a theoretically informed engagement with "the reality of popular collective action" that aimed to capture "the complexities and dilemmas of actual mobilization and strategic lessons that flow from these."[5] As part of this "theorygraphy," I immersed myself, beginning in late 2013, in the theoretical works of the Reed–Reed–Johnson–Smith school of post–civil rights politics, combined with Cox and Nilsen's Marxist approach to social movements, particularly their concept of social movements from above and below. In addition, I engaged Rosa Luxemburg's theory of the mass strike and works on the social structure of accumulation. Finally, I read a number of works on Newark's history, including those by Brad Tuttle, Kevin Mumford, Steve Golin, Robert Curvin, Julia Rabig, Paul Stellhorn, and Irene Cooper-Basch.

My first data-gathering step, begun in late 2013, was a LexisNexis search on everything related to Newark Public Schools since the 1980s. From this I created a timeline, supplemented by further readings on Newark history and schools, and continued to add to the timeline as my research progressed. Through this timeline, I was able to chart the development of the different turns of the movements, the issues involved, and major actors. Informed by my theoretical concept of movements from above and below, I used the newspaper coverage to begin assembling a list of interviewees.

Beginning in 2014 and extending through 2017, I attended scores of demonstrations, school board meetings (supplemented by video recordings), and other public hearings; meetings of student, community, and labor organizations; social gatherings; a union election debate; and several educational forums. This component of my ethnographic research was a combination of traditional participant observation and what anthropologist João Costa Vargas terms "observant participation." For Vargas, this means that "while the participant observer traditionally puts the emphasis on observation, observant participation refers to active participation in the organized group, such that observation becomes an appendage of the main activity."[6] Though active in the movement, I did not take any leadership roles and held back, early on, from speaking out at school board meetings with NEW out of concern that this would close off access to movement-from-above actors. But, overall, my "observant participation," particularly with NEW, helped me gain access, develop trust with activists, and obtain rich observational and interview data.[7]

During my sabbatical year of 2015–16, I conducted the bulk of the study's more than fifty semistructured interviews with student activists, teachers, community activists, influential ministers, nonprofit leaders, foundation officers, and public officials involved in the struggle over Newark's public schools. The list was assembled from my newspaper analysis, participant observation, and recommendations from interviewees.[8] I read up as much as possible on each interviewee from observation notes and newspaper coverage to develop a number of issues and topics I wanted addressed. For example, in my research on Rev. William Howard, I discovered that he had originally been a major backer, from among the ministerial ranks, of Cami Anderson, but later turned against her. Through this methodology, he was able to elaborate his response, without any bias interjected by the author, which helped shed light on theoretically informed questions around movements from above and below. I used the real names of the people I interviewed when I was given permission. Most people wanted to be given attribution. In addition, using people's names strengthens the ability of activists to draw out the strategic lessons of this case, a central goal of this study.

I tape recorded and transcribed the interviews. Informed by the theories, my coding involved documenting the historical unfolding of the struggle as well as emerging themes that centered on "the complexities and dilemmas of actual mobilization." It was out of this dialectal process of engagement with theory and the data generated from interviews and observations, along with a host of other data sources, ranging from pamphlets distributed by activists to participation in and study of activist email Listservs and Facebook pages and review of newspaper articles and government reports, that the study's central argument regarding the crucial containment role of antiracism emerged. This insight was crystallized in the critical juncture after the firing of Anderson and yet the continued expansion of charter schools. Consistent with Burawoy's extended case study methodology, the theoretically informed engagement with data produced new "belts of theory" regarding the relationships of antiracism, social movements, and neoliberalism.[9]

Clearly, politics, like *all* research, was embedded throughout my study, ranging from the questions I asked to the theories and methods I employed, the data on which I drew, and the aims of the research. Though all research is political, "scholarship shaped by our activism," activist-scholar John Saul argues, encourages an "impressive level of engagement" that leads researchers "to ask the hard and searching questions that a more conservative and passive scholarship would obscure."[10] Thus, in my study, I strived, as the sociologist Oliver Cromwell Cox encouraged social scientists to do, to be "accurate and objective, but not neutral." Clearly, in siding with forces working to defend public education, I followed Saul's and Cox's social science dictum of being "passionately partisan in favor of the welfare of the people and against the interests of the few when they seem to submerge that welfare."[11] At the same time, to ensure that my partisanship did not detract from the accuracy and objectivity of the study, I withdrew from the research site and, later, the city itself during 2019–22, when I was focused solely on the writing stage of the study.

Notes

INTRODUCTION

1. "Mark Zuckerberg Announces $100 Million Grant," *Oprah Winfrey Show,* August 24, 2010, http://www.oprah.com/own-oprahshow/mark-zuckerbergs-big-announcement-video.

2. The Newark segment was preceded by an interview with the director of, and showing of clips from, the charter promotional film *Waiting for Superman* (dir. David Guggenheim, 2010). Christie's purported exchange with a Newark parent echoed the sentiments of those profiled in the film. Scott Olster, "Forget Superman, Charter Schools Are Waiting for Oprah," *Fortune,* September 30, 2010, https://archive.fortune.com/2010/09/30/news/economy/waiting_for_superman.fortune/index.htm. On framing the charter movement as an antiracist one, see Elizabeth Todd-Breland, *A Political Education: Black Politics and Education Reform in Chicago since the 1960s* (Chapel Hill: University of North Carolina Press, 2018), 6; Kristen Buras, *Charter Schools, Race, and Urban Space: Where the Market Meets the Grassroots Resistance* (New York: Routledge, 2015), 3.

3. "Enrollment in Newark Schools, 1999–2019," McGrady Research, https://public.tableau.com/profile/margrady.research#!/vizhome/NJCFDashboard_15575265409500/About.

4. Bob Braun, "Has Christie Divided Newark Opposition to Cerf and State Control?," *Bob Braun's Ledger* (blog), July 3, 2015, http://www.bobbraunsledger.com/has-christie-divided-newark-opposition-to-cerf-and-state-control/.

5. See the description of my research methods in the appendix.

6. In this study, I use *Black* and *African American* interchangeably. I also generally use lowercase *black* and *white* when used as racial descriptors. At other times, I do capitalize *Black, Brown,* or *White* when quoting historical texts or to convey how in particular contexts political entrepreneurs and movements desire "to denote a distinctive, coherent political community" with common interests and goals. Cedric Johnson, *From Revolutionaries to Race Leaders: Black Power and the Making of African American Politics* (Minneapolis: University of Minnesota Press, 2007), xvii; Preston Smith II, *Racial Democracy and the Black Metropolis: Housing Policy in Postwar Chicago* (Minneapolis: University of Minnesota Press, 2012), 5.

|| 283

284 || NOTES TO INTRODUCTION

7. Walter Benn Michael and Adolph Reed Jr., "The Trouble with Disparity," *Nonsite.org,* no. 32 (September 2020), https://nonsite.org/the-trouble-with-disparity/. See interview with Adolph Reed Jr., *Katie Halper Show,* September 9, 2020, https://www.youtube.com/watch?v=wwPDTkKJVDk.

8. Smith, *Racial Democracy,* 5; Adolph Reed Jr., "Marx, Race, and Neoliberalism," *New Labor Forum* 22, no. 1 (2013): 49.

9. Smith, *Racial Democracy,* xviii, 7–11. On the historic SD consensus in black politics, see Paul Prescod, "The Emancipatory Past and Future of Black Politics," *Jacobin,* January 27, 2020.

10. Michael Dumas, "'Waiting for Superman' to Save Black People: Racial Representation and the Official Antiracism of Neoliberal School Reform," *Discourse: Studies in the Cultural Politics of Education* 34, no. 4 (2013): 42.

11. Smith, *Racial Democracy,* 10; Jodi Wilgoren, "Young Blacks Turn to School Vouchers as Civil Rights Issue," *New York Times,* October 9, 2000; Julia Sass Rubin, Ryan M. Good, and Michelle Fine, "Parental Action and Neoliberal Education Reform: Crafting a Research Agenda," *Journal of Urban Affairs* 42, no. 4 (2020): 493.

12. Lester Spence, *Knocking the Hustle: Against the Neoliberal Turn in Black Politics* (Brooklyn, N.Y.: punctum books, 2015), 25, 56–60; Kate Stein, "At Success Academy Charter Schools, High Scores and Polarizing Tactics," *New York Times,* April 6, 2015. On President Obama and other black elites' use of the culture of poverty to blame the black poor for their plight, see Touré Reed, *Toward Freedom: The Case against Race Reductionism* (New York: Verso, 2020), 131–45.

13. Adolph Reed Jr., "What Materialist Black Political History Actually Looks Like," *Nonsite.org,* January 2019, https://nonsite.org/editorial/what-materialist-black-political-history-actually-looks-like; David Harvey, *A Brief History of Neoliberalism* (Oxford: Oxford University Press, 2005).

14. Sam Stein, *Capital City: Gentrification and the Real Estate State* (New York: Verso, 2019), 5.

15. Pauline Lipman, *The New Political Economy of Urban Education: Neoliberalism, Race and the Right to the City* (New York: Routledge), 22. Adolph Reed Jr. advocates use of *rent-intensifying development* over *gentrification* because the latter concept tends to "cloud a simple, straightforward dynamic—public support of private developers' pursuit of rent-intensifying redevelopment—with cultural implications that shift critique away from the issue of using public authority to engineer upward redistribution and impose hardship on relatively vulnerable residents." Reed, "What Materialist Black Political History." Echoing Reed, Wacquant exhorts "students of gentrification [to] recognize that the primary engine behind

NOTES TO INTRODUCTION || 285

the (re)allocation of people, resources and institutions in the city is the state." Loïc Wacquant, "Relocating Gentrification: The Working Class, Science and the State in Urban Research," in *Uprooting Urban America: Multidisciplinary Perspectives on Race, Class and Gentrification,* ed. Horace Hall, Cynthia Cole Robinson, and Amor Kohli (New York: Peter Lang, 2014), 17.

16. Molly Vollman Makris and Elizabeth Brown, "School Development in Urban Gentrifying Spaces: Developers Supporting Schools or Schools Supporting Developers?," *Journal of Urban Affairs* 42, no. 4 (2020): 587.

17. Makris and Brown, 588; Molly Vollman, *Public Housing and School Choice in a Gentrified City: Youth Experiences of Uneven Opportunity* (New York: Palgrave Macmillan, 2015).

18. Reed, *Toward Freedom,* 11. On social democracy emphasizing the "political-economic foundations" of racial inequality, see Smith, *Racial Democracy,* 10.

19. David Harvey, *Rebel Cities: From the Right to the City to the Urban Revolution* (New York: Verso, 2012), 18.

20. Cedric Johnson, "Gentrifying New Orleans: Thoughts on Race and the Movement of Capital," *Souls* 17, no. 3–4 (2015): 185, emphasis added.

21. On growing intraracial inequality among African Americans, see Institute on Assets and Social Policy, "Wealth Patterns among the Top 5% of African-Americans," November 2014, https://research-doc.credit-suisse.com/docView?sourceid=em&document_id=x603305. For a distillation of the findings, see Stacy Tisdale, "The Black Elite: A Look Inside Black America's Widening Wealth Gap," *Black Enterprise,* March 8, 2016, http://www.blackenterprise.com/money/the-black-elite-a-look-inside-black-americas-widening-wealth-gap/. Antonio Moore, "The Decadent Veil: Black America's Wealth Illusion," *Huffington Post,* December 6, 2017, https://www.huffingtonpost.com/antonio-moore/the-decadent-veil-black-income-inequality_b_5646472.html; David Walsh, "The Socioeconomic Basis of Identity Politics: Inequality and the Rise of an African American Elite," August 30, 2016, http://www.wsws.org/en/articles/2016/08/30/pers-a30.html.

22. Les Leopold, *Runway Inequality* (New York: Labor Institute Press, 2013).

23. Willie Legette and Adolph Reed, "The Role of Race in Contemporary U. S. Politics: V.O. Key's Enduring Insight," *Nonsite.org,* no. 23 (February 11, 2018), https://nonsite.org/the-role-of-race-in-contemporary-u-s-politics/. On socialism as a threat to racial minorities, see Conor Friedersdorf, "Democratic Socialism Threatens Minorities," *The Atlantic,* August 9, 2018, https://www.theatlantic.com/politics/archive/2018/08/a-risk-that-democratic-socialism-poses-to-all-minorities/566528/.

286 || NOTES TO INTRODUCTION

24. Legette and Reed, "Role of Race."

25. Reed, *Toward Freedom*, 16.

26. Lipman, *New Political Economy*, 12.

27. Smith, *Racial Democracy*, 9.

28. Buras, *Charter Schools*, 3, 29–30. For a critique of "notions [that] represent whites as an unproblematically cohesive bloc committed to maintaining a regime of racial hierarchy," see Adolph Reed Jr., "Color Codes," *Dissent*, Summer 2004, 94.

29. Cedric Johnson, "The Panthers Can't Save Us Now," *Catalyst* 1, no. 1 (2017), https://catalyst-journal.com/vol1/no1/panthers-cant-save-us -cedric-johnson.

30. Bree Picower and Edwin Mayorga, eds., *What's Race Got to Do with It? How Current School Reform Policy Maintains Racial and Economic Inequality* (New York: Peter Lang, 2015), 2, 6–9. For a similar approach, see Kalervo Gulson, Zeus Leonardo, and David Gilborn, "The Edge of Race: Critical Examinations of Education and Race/Racism," *Discourse: Studies in the Cultural Politics of Education* 34, no. 4 (2013): 476. Underscoring the RD theoretical underpinnings of the Ford Foundation initiative was that Lauren Wells, one of the projects' four directors, would play a central role in the Baraka administration, as explained in chapter 5, attempting to unify the contending movements from above and below under an antiracist banner. http://kirwaninstitute.osu.edu/the-ford-secondary-education-and -racial-justice-collaborative/.

31. Howard Ryan, *Educational Justice: Teaching and Organizing against the Corporate Juggernaut* (New York: Monthly Review, 2016), 26–27.

32. Picower and Mayorga, *What's Race*, 8. Cedric G. Johnson, *After Black Lives Matter: Policing and Anti-Capitalist Struggle* (New York: Verso, forthcoming). Touré Reed has a similar critique of the "racial ontology" that informs the work of Ta-Nehsi Coates, in which a transhistorical racism inevitably dooms universal redistributive programs and multiracial social movements. This worldview obscures the complex "political economic underpinnings" of racial disparities and the contingent character of "racist attitudes and discriminatorily behavior." Reed, *Toward Freedom*, 19, 109. Likewise, Vivek Chibber critiques the ontological racism that informs the field of postcolonial studies, and the work of Edward Said in particular. Chibber, "Orientalism and Its Afterlives," *Catalyst* 4, no. 3 (2020), https:// catalyst-journal.com/2020/12/orientalism-and-its-afterlives/.

33. Picower and Mayorga, *What's Race*, 9.

34. Domingo Morel, *Takeover: Race, Education, and American Democracy* (New York: Oxford University Press, 2019), 14.

35. Morel, 13. Since Morel's RD framing of the conflict echoed that of Baraka, it made sense that the mayor and the Rutgers–Newark political

NOTES TO INTRODUCTION || 287

science professor would sit down for a cordial discussion on "Takeover: A Conversation on Race, Education, and Democracy in Urban America" in April 2018, https://www.youtube.com/watch?v=77F5XX61UOs. In a devastating critique of Alexander's thesis, James Foreman Jr. points out that there was substantial support from black officials and electorate for more aggressive policing and punishment that helped build the carceral state. Foreman emphasizes that we must pay attention to "class divisions within the black community" to grasp "African American attitudes and actions on matters of crime and punishment." Foreman, *Locking Up Our Own: Crime and Punishment in Black America* (New York: Farrar, Straus, and Giroux, 2017), 13.

36. Spence, *Knocking the Hustle*, 7.

37. Cedric Johnson, "Black Political Life and the Blue Lives Matter Presidency," *Jacobin*, February 17, 2019.

38. Adolph Reed Jr., *Stirrings in the Jug: Black Politics in the Post-Segregation Era* (Minneapolis: University of Minnesota Press, 1999).

39. Eric Blanc, *Red State Revolt: The Teachers' Strike Wave and Working-Class Politics* (New York: Verso, 2019).

40. Reed, *Stirrings in the Jug*; Smith, *Racial Democracy*, 17–20.

41. Reed, *Stirrings in the Jug*, 99; Smith, *Racial Democracy*, 17–20. On the role of the Ford Foundation incubating many of the future War on Poverty programs, see Karen Ferguson, *Top Down: The Ford Foundation, Black Power and the Reinvention of Racial Liberalism* (Philadelphia: University of Pennsylvania Press, 2013), 63–64.

42. Reed, *Stirrings in the Jug*, 109.

43. Reed, 101.

44. Cited in Jamie Peck and Adam Tickwell, "Neoliberalizing Space," *Antipode* 34, no. 3 (2002): 396.

45. Reed, *Stirrings in the Jug*, 176.

46. Cedric Johnson, "The Half-Life of the Black Urban Regime: Adolph Reed, Jr. on Race, Capitalism, and Urban Governance," *Labor Studies Journal* 41, no. 3 (2016): 253.

47. Adolph Reed Jr., "The Post-1965 Trajectory of Race, Class, and Urban Politics in the United States Reconsidered," *Labor Studies Journal* 41, no. 3 (2016): 14.

48. John Arena, *Driven from New Orleans: How Nonprofits Betray Public Housing and Promote Privatization* (Minneapolis: University of Minnesota Press, 2012).

49. Johnson, "Half-Life," 5. On third wave black mayors not being constrained by unions and other collective organizations of black working-class people, see Doug Henwood's July 2013 interview of Adolph Reed Jr. on his *Behind the News* radio show, http://shout.lbo-talk.org/lbo/RadioArchive/2013/13_07_11.mp3.

288 || NOTES TO INTRODUCTION

50. On the significant "increased rate of African American inner city development" in the 2000s, see Derek Hyra, *Race, Cass and Politics in the Cappuccino City* (Chicago: University of Chicago Press, 2017), 8.

51. Reed, *Post-1965 Trajectory*, 12.

52. See Johnson's critique of New Orleans's mayor Mitch Landrieu "for his inability to link his latest crusade against 'black on black violence,' a problem he attributes to cultural dysfunction, with the rapid upward redistribution of wealth that he has facilitated." Johnson, "Gentrifying New Orleans," 188. On the role of black elected officials and civil rights leaders reproducing underclass ideology, see Spence, *Knocking the Hustle*, 25.

53. Aaron Schneider, *Renew Orleans? Globalized Development and Workers Resistance after Katrina* (Minneapolis: University of Minnesota Press, 2018).

54. Robert Alford and Roger Friedland, *Powers of Theory: Capitalism, the State, and Democracy* (Cambridge: Cambridge University Press, 1985).

55. Michael Parenti, *Democracy for the Few*, 7th ed. (Boston: Wadsworth, 2002).

56. Michael Parenti, *Power and the Powerless* (New York: St. Martin's Press, 1978). Steven Lukes refers to hegemony, the third dimension of power, as the region of "*latent conflict,* which consists in a contradiction between the interests of those exercising power and the *real interests* of those they exclude." Lukes, *Power: A Radica View* (London: Macmillan, 1974), 24–25, emphasis original.

57. Frances Fox Piven, *Challenging Authority: How Ordinary People Change America* (New York: Roman and Littlefield, 2006), 20.

58. Piven, 20. Parenti also conceptualizes interdependent relationships as "asymmetrical power relationships," as he emphasizes that though "there is an exchange of interests . . . [this] does not mean the relationship is an equitable one." Parenti, *Power and the Powerless*, 9–10.

59. Piven, 23.

60. Piven alludes to this form of disruptive power briefly on pages 20, 24, and 31.

61. Alf Gunvald Nilsen and Laurence Cox, "What Would a Marxist Theory of Social Movements Look Like?," in *Marxism and Social Movements,* ed. Colin Barker, Laurence Cox, John Krinsky, and Alf Gunvald Nilsen (Chicago: Haymarket Books, 2013), 65–66.

62. Nilsen and Cox, 66. On the distinction between a mode of production and a social formation, based on levels of abstraction, see E. O. Wright, *Classes* (London: Verso, 1985).

63. Laurence Cox and Alf Gunvald Nilsen, *We Make Our Own History: Marxism and Social Movements in the Twilight of Neoliberalism* (London: Pluto Press, 2014), 115.

NOTES TO INTRODUCTION || **289**

64. Nilsen and Cox, "What Would a Marxist Theory," 66–71; Goran Therborne, "Why Some Classes Are More Successful than Others," *New Left Review* 138 (1983): 44.

65. Mark Purcell conceptualizes Gramsci's notion of "war of position" as the way that a "movement aims to increase the influence of their alternative way of perceiving the world." Purcell, *Recapturing Democracy: Neoliberalization and the Struggle for Alternative Futures* (New York: Routledge, 2008), 4.

66. On corporate school reform efforts as a social movement, see Ryan, *Educational Justice*, 24.

67. David Kotz, *The Rise and Fall of Neoliberal Capitalism* (Cambridge, Mass.: Harvard University Press, 2015), 3; David Kotz, Terence McDonough, and Michael Reich, *Social Structures of Accumulation: The Political Economy of Growth and Crisis* (Cambridge: Cambridge University Press, 1994).

68. Kotz, *Rise and Fall*, 11, 22.

69. Adolph Reed Jr., "Antiracism: A Neoliberal Alternative to a Left," *Dialectical Anthropology* 42 (2018): 108.

70. Reed, 108. See Richard Walker's critique of Richard Rothstein's heralded book *The Color of Law* for placing the blame for racial segregation in housing principally on "policy makers in Washington," while letting off the hook the powerful role of the real estate industry, including in the crafting of New Deal housing policies. Walker, "The New Deal Didn't Create Segregation," *Jacobin*, June 18, 2019. Frank Wilderson, *Afropessimism* (New York: Liveright, 2020).

71. Reed, "Antiracism," 109. Dylan Riley, "Faultlines: Political Logics of the US Party System," *New Left Review*, 126 (November/December 2020): 43.

72. Kotz, *Rise and Fall*, 12–31, 42.

73. Harvey, *A Brief History of Neoliberalism*, 19.

74. Peck and Tickwell, "Neoliberalizng Space," 396; Jason Hackworth, *The Neoliberal City: Governance, Ideology, and Development in American Urbanism* (Ithaca, N.Y.: Cornell University Press, 2007), 12; David Wilson, "Toward a Contingent Urban Neoliberalism," *Urban Geography* 25, no. 8 (2004): 771–83.

75. Peck and Tickwell, "Neoliberalizng Space," 381.

76. Alan Sears, "The 'Lean' State and Capitalist Restructuring: Towards a Theoretical Account," *Studies in Political Economy* 59, no. 1 (1999): 92.

77. For a critique, see James Peck and Adam Tickwell, "Local Modes of Social Regulation? Regulation Theory, Thatcherism, and Uneven Development," *Geoforum* 23, no. 3 (1992): 347–63.

78. Helga Leitner, Jamie Peck, and Eric Sheppard, eds., *Contesting Neoliberalism: Urban Frontiers* (New York: Guilford Press, 2007), 5.

NOTES TO INTRODUCTION

79. Hackworth, *Neoliberal City*, 11.

80. Cox and Nilsen, *We Make Our Own History*, 15, emphasis added.

81. Cox and Nilsen, 15.

82. Leitner et al., *Contesting Neoliberalism*, 2.

83. I avoid use of the concept of "subaltern" because of the way it has been deployed, particularly by those who operate within subaltern studies, to describe multiclass groupings. This usage lumps together, for example, those in the same racial category and thus replicates the problems of racial democracy that I critique in this study. For a critique of how Gramsci's work and concepts have been "divorced from any conception of working-class struggle," see Joe Cleffie, "Rescuing Gramsci from His Misinterpreters," *International Socialist Review*, no. 93 (Summer 2014), https://isreview .org/issue/93/rescuing-gramsci-his-misinterpreters.

84. Cited in Nilsen and Cox, "What Would a Marxist Theory," 73.

85. Wainwright, cited in Nilsen and Cox, 73.

86. C. Wright Mills, *The Sociological Imagination* (New York: Oxford University Press, 2000), 4.

87. Nilsen and Cox, "What Would a Marxist Theory," 74.

88. Antonio Gramsci, *Selections from the Prison Notebooks* (London: Lawrence and Wishar, 1998), 327–28. Robin Kelley, "'We Are Not What We Seem: Rethinking Black Working-Class Opposition in the Jim Crow South," *Journal of American History* 80, no. 1 (1993): 77.

89. Nilsen and Cox, "What Would a Marxist Theory," 74.

90. Nilsen and Cox, 76.

91. David Camfield, "Re-orienting Class Analysis: Working Classes as Historical Formations," *Science and Society* 68, no. 4 (2004): 421. On the class struggles over social reproduction, see Tithi Bhattacharya, *Social Reproduction Theory: Remapping Class, Recentering Oppression* (London: Pluto Press, 2017).

92. Nilsen and Cox, "What Would a Marxist Theory," 79.

93. Rosa Luxemburg, "The Mass Strike, the Political Party, and the Trade Unions," 1906, in *Rosa Luxemburg Speaks*, ed. M. Waters (New York: Pathfinder Press, 1970), 213.

94. Eric Lerner, "Introduction: Mass Strikes Today and the Lessons of History," *Mass Strike* 2, no. 1 (2013).

95. Luxemburg, "Mass Strike," 226.

96. Colin Barker, "Class Struggle and Social Movements," in Barker et al., *Marxism and Social Movements*, 48. Judith Stepan-Norris and Maurice Zeitlin, "'Who Gets the Bird'; or, How the Communists Won Power and Trust in America's Unions: The Relative Autonomy of Intraclass Political Struggles," *American Sociological Review* 54 (August 1989): 504.

97. Barker, "Class Struggle," 48, emphasis added.

NOTES TO CHAPTER 1

1. WHOSE SCHOOLS, WHOSE CITY?

1. Fred Cook, "Mayor Kenneth Gibson Says—'Wherever the Central Cities Are Going, Newark Is Going to Get There First,'" *New York Times,* July 25, 1971.

2. Mark Gottdiener and Ray Hutchinson, *The New Urban Sociology,* 4th ed. (Boulder, Colo.: Westview Press, 2011), 101–5.

3. Paul Stellhorn, "Depression and Decline: Newark, New Jersey, 1929–1941" (PhD diss., Rutgers University, 1982), 3. For an in-depth study of the consolidation of Newark's new industrial elite, see Raymond Ralph, "From Village to Industrial City: The Urbanization of Newark, New Jersey, 1830–1860" (PhD diss., Rutgers University, 1978).

4. Susan Hirsch, *Roots of the American Working Class: The Industrialization of Crafts in Newark, 1800–1862* (Philadelphia: University of Pennsylvania Press, 1978), 292.

5. Stellhorn, "Depression and Decline," 6.

6. Brad Tuttle, *How Newark Became Newark: The Rise, Fall, and Rebirth of an American City* (New Brunswick, N.J.: Rutgers University Press, 2009), 86; Pete Dreier, John Mollenkopf, and Todd Swanstrom, *Place Matters: Metropolitics for the Twenty-First Century* (Lawrence: University Press of Kanas, 2001), 37; Jean Anyon, *Ghetto Schooling: A Political Economy of Urban Educational Reform* (New York: Teachers College Press, 1997), 53.

7. Stellhorn, "Depression and Decline," 15–16, 27–28; Anyon, *Ghetto Schooling,* 43.

8. David Gordon, "Class Struggle and the Stages of Urban Capitalist Development," in *The Rise of Sunbelt Cities,* ed. David Perry and Alfred Watkins (Beverly Hills, Calif.: Sage, 1977), 59. For more on the decentralization of industry, see Kenneth Jackson, *Crabgrass Frontier: The Suburbanization of the United States* (Oxford: Oxford University Press, 1985), 184; Jefferson Cowie, *Capital Moves: RCA's Seventy Year Quest for Cheap Labor* (New York: New Press, 1999), 33. On Newark's exodus, see Anyon, *Ghetto Schooling,* 58.

9. Stellhorn, "Depression and Decline," 14.

10. On Raymond's background, and crafty deployment of antiracism, see Stellhorn, 16–17, 36–37.

11. On the Princeton bills, mid-1930s state legislation constraining municipalities, and business boycott of city bonds, see Stellhorn, 206–11, 212, 105–12, resp.

12. In the face of growing support for a Labor Party, the CIO "created a number of vehicles that would allow people to express third-party sentiment, yet still vote for FDR," such as the Non-Partisan League. Through the American Labor Party in New York, and the Farmer-Labor Party in

292 || NOTES TO CHAPTER 1

Minnesota, the CIO, backed by the Communist Party, "brokered arrangements where people could vote for local and statewide third parties, . . . and still support FDR for president." Michael Goldfield, *The Color of Politics: Race and the Mainsprings of American Politics* (New York: New Press, 1997), 218–20. On the Communist Party's shift from the "United Front" of 1934–36 to the Popular Front, and its role in undermining formation of a Labor Party in the latter period, see Charles Post, "The New Deal and the Popular Front: Models for Contemporary Socialists?," *International Socialist Review*, no. 108 (September 1, 2021), https://isreview.org/issue/108/new-deal-and-popular-front/index.html.

13. Stellhorn, "Depression and Decline," 315–16.

14. Harvey, *Rebel Cities*, 6–9.

15. Goldfield, *Color of Politics*, 218.

16. Cited in Goldfield, 218.

17. Goldfield, 198. On suburbanization's politically conservatizing impact on striking—"debt-encumbered homeowners don't go on strike"—and promotion of consumerism, see Harvey, *Rebel Cities*, 9, 50.

18. David Roediger, *Working toward Whiteness: How America's Immigrants Became White—The Strange Journey from Ellis Island to the Suburbs* (New York: Basic Books, 2005).

19. Jackson, *Crabgrass Frontier*, 211–12. Other federal policies that assisted suburbanization included subsidies for developers to acquire "cheap land in outlying areas" and "subsidies to develop sewage and other systems that would make the land suitable for homes." Anyon, *Ghetto Schools*, 76.

20. Dreier et al., *Place Matters*, 105–6.

21. Anyon, *Ghetto Schooling*, 77.

22. Anyon, 76.

23. Dale Russakoff, *The Prize: Who's in Charge of America's Schools?* (New York: Houghton Mifflin Harcourt, 2015), 3.

24. Steve Golin, *The Newark Teachers Strike: Hope on the Line* (New Brunswick, N.J.: Rutgers University Press, 2002), 8–15.

25. Golin, 16. For transcripts of the HUAC hearings held in Newark in May and July 1955, see "Investigation of Communist Activities in the Newark, N.J., Area," hearings, May 18, 19 and July 13, 1955, Harvard College Library Collection, https://archive.org/stream/investigationofc0255unit/investigationofc0255unit_djvu.txt.

26. John Shelton, *Teacher Strike! Public Education and the Making of a New American Political Order* (Chicago: University of Illinois Press, 2017), 14.

27. Anyon, *Ghetto Schooling*, 76; Amiri Baraka, *The Autobiography of LeRoi Jones* (Chicago: Lawrenceville Books, 1984), 368.

28. Cited in Shelton, *Teacher Strike!*, 10; for more on these conflicts, see Anyon, *Ghetto Schooling*, 91–92, 111–12.

NOTES TO CHAPTER 1 || **293**

29. Lowenstein's new position left him out of the bargaining unit. Golin, *Newark Teachers Strike,* 28.

30. Tatiana Cozzarelli, "The Origins of New York's No Strike Clause," *Left Voice,* October 24, 2017, https://www.leftvoice.org/The-Origins-of -New-York-s-No-Strike-Clause; Shelton, *Teacher Strike!,* 6.

31. Marc Gaswirth, *Teachers' Strikes in New Jersey* (Metuchen, N.J.: Scarecrow Press, 1982), 17; FAQ on NJ Strikes, AAUP-AFT, Rutgers, http://www.rutgersaaup.org/strikefaq. On varying state collective bargaining and strike policies for public-sector workers, see Milla Sanes and John Schmitt, "Regulation of Public Sector Collective Bargaining in the States," Center for Economic and Policy Research, March 2014, 5, 8.

32. Shelton, *Teachers Strike!,* 8.

33. On highways decimating urban housing values, see Dennis Judd and Todd Swanstrom, *City Politics: Private Power and Public Policy* (New York: HarperCollins, 1994), 211–12; Anyon, *Ghetto Schooling,* chaps. 5 and 6.

34. Golin, *Newark Teacher Strikes,* 67.

35. Ashley Howard, "How U.S. Urban Unrest in the 1960s Can Help Make Sense of Ferguson, Mo.," research brief, *Journalist's Resource,* November 25, 2014, https://journalistsresource.org/studies/government/criminal -justice/u-s-urban-unrest-1960s-and-ferguson-missouri-research-brief/.

36. Tuttle, *How Newark Became Newark,* 159–70; Robert Curvin, *Inside Newark: Decline, Rebellion and the Search for Transformation* (New Brunswick, N.J.: Rutgers University Press, 2014), 103–12.

37. Curvin, *Inside Newark,* 120–27.

38. Keeanga-Yamahtta Taylor, "Urban Rebellions and Social Change," *Socialist Worker,* August 11, 2011, https://socialistworker.org/2011/08/12/ urban-revolts-and-social-change; Christian Parenti, *Lockdown America: Police and Prisons in the Age of Crisis* (New York: Verso, 1999).

39. For a critique of the unrest as "equivalent to, intentional political activity," see Adolph Reed Jr., "The Kerner Commission and the Irony of Antiracist Politics," *Studies in Working-Class History* 14, no. 4 (2017): 31.

40. Unlike 1955, HUAC's 1968 hearing on Newark's rebellion was held in Washington. House Un-American Activities Committee, *Subversive Influence in Riots, Looting and Burning* (Washington, D.C.: Government Printing Office, 1968), part 4, "Subversive Influence in Riots, Looting and Burning, Newark, New Jersey, April 23, 24," http://www.aavw.org/protest/subversive_huac_abstract07_excerpt.html.

41. Reed, "Kerner Commission," 32; Barker, "Class Struggle and Social Movements," 48.

42. Dan LaBotz, "The Left and the Democratic Party: The Experience of Almost a Century," *New Politics* 17, no. 2 (2019), https://newpol.org/ issue_post/the-left-and-the-democratic-party/; James Creegan, "The

Rebel Who Came In from the Cold: The Tainted Career of Bayard Rustin," *Portside,* March 17, 2016, https://portside.org/node/11123/; Bayard Rustin, "From Protest to Politics: The Future of the Civil Rights Movement," *Commentary,* February 1965.

43. Baraka, *Autobiography,* 375. On the author's transition from Jones to Barakat to Baraka, see 376. Adolph Reed Jr. perceptively points out how, ironically, the identification of the radical wing of Black Power with "Third World anti-colonial and national liberation movements in the 1960s and 1970s played a significant role in rendering invisible the class dynamics that shaped the thrust and impact of post-segregation black politics." Reed, "Revolution as 'National Liberation' and the Origins of Neoliberal Anti-racism," *Socialist Register* 53 (2017): 311.

44. Many other future black and Puerto Rican elected officials and candidates emerged out of the UCC. Nixon advisor Daniel Patrick Moynihan, who harshly criticized the community action program for fueling local conflicts, nonetheless recognized its role in "promoting the formation of an urban Negro leadership echelon" as one of its most important contributions. Mark Krasovic, *The Newark Frontier: Community Action in the Great Society* (Chicago: University of Chicago Press, 2016), 43, 280, 351; David Milton Gerwin, "The End of Coalition: The Failure of Community Organizing in Newark in the 1960s" (PhD diss., Columbia University, 1998), 149. On the vote at the 1968 Black Power Conference in Philadelphia "for the establishment of a national black political party to lead black communities in the struggle to control their own space," see Komozi Woodard, *A Nation within a Nation* (Chapel Hill: University of North Carolina Press, 1999), 108.

45. Gerwin, "End of Coalition," 174. On SDS's realignment strategy, see the Port Huron Statement of the Students for a Democratic Society, 1962, https://web.archive.org/web/20050313094822/http://coursesa.matrix.msu.edu/~hst306/documents/huron.html; Paul Leblanc, "An 'All Hands on Deck' Moment: Sixty-Six Old New Leftists Urge Support for Joe Biden," *New Politics,* April 18, 2020, https://newpol.org/an-all-hands-on-deck-moment-sixty-six-old-new-leftists-urge-support-for-joe-biden/.

46. Reed, "Kerner Commission," 34.

47. On the central role the Ford Foundation played in promoting CDCs as part of its effort of engagement with and steering of Black Power, see Ferguson, *Top Down.* While Adubato framed his Northward Center initiative as addressing aggrieved white ethnics, particularly Italians whose needs the war on poverty were supposedly leaving out, he also received generous Ford Foundation funding and deployed some of the same discourse as Black Power. On Adubato, see Rebecca Casciano, "'By Any Means Necessary': The American Welfare State and Machine Politics in Newark's North

NOTES TO CHAPTER 1 || **295**

Ward" (PhD diss., Princeton University, 2009). On Ford Foundation funding, see Julia Rabig, *The Fixers: Devolution, Development and Civil Society in Newark, 1960–1990* (Chicago: University of Chicago Press, 2016), 200.

48. On the "mau-mauing" strategy, see Adolph Reed Jr., "Splendors and Miseries of the Antiracist 'Left,'" *Nonsite.org*, November 6, 2016, https://nonsite.org/editorial/splendors-and-miseries-of-the-antiracist-left-2. On its expression in Newark and of CDCs as precursors of neoliberalism, see Rabig, *Fixers*, 1–4, 18. On Stephen Adubato turning his operation into a hybrid neoliberal political machine, see Casciano, "By Any Means Necessary."

49. For a thorough account of post-1967 white backlash politics in Newark, see Krasovic, *Newark Frontier*, esp. 208–23. On "Italian Americans appropriate[ing] the rhetorical style of Black Power," see Golin, *Newark Teacher Strikes*, 145.

50. Stellhorn, "Depression and Decline," 305, 285–306.

51. On black appointee George Richardson's split with Addonizio, and the shifting alliances and players in Newark and Essex County politics from the 1940s to early 1960s, see Curvin, *Inside Newark*, 70–78, 84–85; Krasovic, *Newark Frontier*, 40–43. On urban renewal, see Gerwin, "End of Coalition."

52. At this time, Baraka was working closely with U.S. founder Maulana Karenga, who coined the name CFUN, seeing "United Brothers" as "too sinister for the political arena." Woodard, *A Nation Within*, 108–13. On the June 1968 Black Political Convention, see Krasovic, *Newark Frontier*, 276.

53. George Richardson and Harry Wheeler refused to participate in the convention and ran for mayor against Gibson. Krasovic, *Newark Frontier*, 351; Curvin, *Inside Newark*, 139. For a list, including photographs, of the entire seven members (no candidates were fielded for the North and West Wards) of the Community's Choice Slate, see David Wildstein, "Kenneth Gibson, First Black Mayor of Newark, Dies at 86," *New Jersey Globe*, March 29, 2019, https://newjerseyglobe.com/in-memoriam/kenneth-gibson-first-black-mayor-of-newark-dies-at-86/.

54. Curvin, *Inside Newark*, 135–44. The six Italian council members, all very hostile to Gibson, were Imperiale, Michael Bontempo, Ralph Villani, Frank Megaro, Louis Turco, and Michael Bottone. Golin, *Newark Teacher Strikes*, 124.

55. Golin, *Newark Teacher Strikes*, 24–39.

56. Gaswirth, *Teachers' Strikes in New Jersey*, 17.

57. Golin, *Newark Teacher Strikes*, 62–71. For the role CFUN played in getting Campbell, the future superintendent and ONE vice president, appointed principal of Robert Treat School, see 111, 113; "Unity in the Community," Rise Up North, http://riseupnewark.com/media-tag/eugene-campbell/.

296 || NOTES TO CHAPTER 1

58. Golin, *Newark Teacher Strikes,* 101–2.

59. For a 1971 interview in which Baraka outlines his opposition to the teacher strike based on a mostly white teacher corps residing in the suburbs and thus being out of touch with Newark's students, and his opposition to what he saw as their attempts to run the district, see NJ Speaks, https://drive.google.com/file/d/0B0bae-TY1PzXOGJCSWZCQkprd1E/.

60. Although Baraka opposed the strike, he did meet with an NTU delegation, whom he criticized for failing to unite with community groups "to make the board give in and try to improve these schools." Other prominent black opponents of the strike included ONE president Fred Means, future board member Jesse Jacobs, and board member Dr. Wyman Garrett. Golin, *Newark Teacher Strikes,* 88, 101, 110–11, 136, and inter alia 72–107; Shelton, *Teacher Strike!,* 69–70.

61. Golin, *Newark Teacher Strikes,* 124.

62. Golin, 134–38. On Garret's later work as a lobbyist garnering tax abatements for developers through payoffs to Mayor James and other local officials, see Tuttle, *How Newark Became Newark,* 230–31.

63. Robert Braun, *Teachers and Power: The Story of the American Federation of Teachers* (New York: Simon and Schuster, 1972), 246, inter alia 244–76. On Braun's work contributing to the growing national demonization of teacher unions as a threat to public education and order, see Shelton, *Teacher Strikes!,* 76.

64. Golin, *Newark Teacher Strikes,* 122.

65. Golin, 140–81.

66. Golin, 147.

67. Officers served the longest terms, with Graves enduring six months on two different stretches in 1971 after the AFT refused to bankroll further appeals. On the jail experience of teachers, with an emphasis on the gender differences, see Golin, *Newark Teachers Strike,* 182–216.

68. Piven, *Challenging Authority,* 29–30.

69. Nilsen and Cox, "What Would Marxist Theory," 77–78.

70. Michael Paris, *Framing Equal Opportunity: Law and the Politics of School Finance Reform* (Stanford, Calif.: Stanford University Press, 2010), 45, 61–92.

71. Interview with Paul Tractenberg, February 19, 2016. For more on the ELC and Ford's role in the school equity cases and the larger "public interest law movement," see Paris, *Framing Equal Opportunity,* 73–75.

72. Paris, *Framing Equal Opportunity,* 5; Education Law Center, "Mission and History," https://edlawcenter.org/about/mission-history.html.

73. Shelton, *Teacher Strike!,* 173–75.

NOTES TO CHAPTER 1 || 297

74. Ryan, *Educational Justice*, 39.

75. Kathy Emery and Susan Ohanian, *Why Is Corporate America Bashing Our Public Schools?* (Portsmouth, N.H.: Heinemann, 2004), 35; Edward Fiske, "Concerns Raised on School Quality," *New York Times*, June 6, 1989; Alyson Klein, "Historic Summit Fueled Push for K–12 Standards," *Education Week*, September 23, 2014, https://www.edweek.org/teaching -learning/historic-summit-fueled-push-for-k-12-standards/2014/09; Marisa Vinovskis, *The Road to Charlottesville: The 1989 Educational Summit* (Ann Arbor: University of Michigan, 1999), https://govinfo.library.unt .edu/negp/reports/negp30.pdf.

76. Ron Marsico, "Whitman Emphasizes High Tech in Efforts to Improve Education," *Star-Ledger*, November 21, 1996; John Mooney, "Take a Deep Breath, Group Tells Schools—Business Coalition Wonders If the State Is Requiring Too Many Tests," *Star-Ledger*, April 19, 2001.

77. Morel, *Takeover*, 27.

78. Curvin, *Inside Newark*, 284–85; "Fight over Newark Takeover Costs Big Bucks," *Star-Ledger*, April 2, 1995. In 1989, Jersey City became the first district to be taken over by the state, followed by Paterson. By 2000, fourteen states had passed takeover laws. Morel, *Takeover*, 26, 84.

79. The state Department of Education replaced the elected board with a fifteen-member "Newark Advisory Board." Nick Chiles, "State Educators Upset at 'Circus' Antics in Newark Member Blames Teacher—Union," *Star-Ledger*, October 3, 1996; Morel, *Takeover*, 29; "Newark Teachers Union Election Hits New Lows," *Star-Ledger*, May 28, 1995. Following the takeover, a new coalition, Organizations United against State Takeover, was formed. Reginald Roberts, "Fighting for Schools, Organizations Unite to Take Control from State," *Star-Ledger*, September 5, 1996.

80. Thirty-seven groups applied overall. Fifteen were scheduled to open in September 1997. Nick Chiles, "17 Charter Schools Make the State's Cut," *Star-Ledger*, January 15, 1997.

81. Nick Chiles, "Brief Sketches of State's Approved Charter Schools," *Star-Ledger*, January 15, 1997. For more on Norman Atkins, the first head of the North Star School and founder of the Uncommon Schools chain, see https://www.linkedin.com/in/norman-atkins-7939b099. In 2010, he was inducted into the Charter School Hall of Fame, https://www.publiccharters .org/about-charter-schools/charter-school-trailblazers/charter-school-hall -fame.

82. Jefferson Cowie, *Stayin' Alive: The 1970s and the Last Days of the Working Class* (New York: New Press, 2010), 70.

83. Kotz, *Rise and Fall*, 66–67.

84. Shelton, *Teacher Strike!*, 173.

298 || NOTES TO CHAPTER 2

2. REGIME CHANGE

1. George Jordan and Dawn Onley, "James Rolls to 4th Term in Newark—Incumbent Repels Two Council Rivals," *Star-Ledger,* May 13, 1998.

2. Sharpe James, *Political Prisoner: A Memoir* (Newark, N.J.: Nutany, 2013).

3. The 1970 race did not expand but rather displaced three black incumbents—Irvine Turner Jr. (Central Ward–Westbrook), Reverend Horace Sharper (South Ward–James), and Calvin West (at-large–Earl Harris). The council first reached a 5–4 black majority in 1978, increasing to 6–3 in 1982 following the election of Ronald L. Rice as West Ward councilperson. The first Puerto Rican councilperson was Luis Quintana, elected to an at-large seat in 1994, and in 2002, Hector Corchado became the first Puerto Rican councilperson from the formerly heavily Italian North Ward. Since 2006, the racial-ethnic composition has not changed, with five blacks (Central, West, and South Wards and two at-large), three Puerto Ricans (North Ward, with Anibal Ramos replacing Corchado in 2006, and two at-large), and one Portuguese American (East Ward). On the national significance of the watershed 1970 election, and the local organizing that made Gibson's election possible, including the role of Amiri Baraka in the 1969 Black and Puerto Rican Convention, see Woodard, *A Nation Within,* 114–58.

4. For attention as the "carjacking capital of the world" in the 1990s, see Tuttle, *How Newark Became Newark,* 225; as the butt of jokes by Johnny Carson and Jay Leno, and TV talk show host Phil Donahue recommending in 1983 on his show that U.S. officials not bring foreign visitors to Newark, see James, *Political Prisoner,* 37, 107. In 1982, the fashion company Christian Dior planned, but eventually scuttled, an advertising campaign whose slogan was "What would New York be without the Diors?—Newark." Michael Norman, "Dior Makes Formal Apology to Newark for Reputed Slur," *New York Times,* September 15, 1982. The January 1975 issue of *Harper's Magazine* rated the fifty largest American cities and argued that "the city of Newark stands without serious challenge as the worst city of all. . . . Newark is a city that desperately needs help." Arthur Lewis, "The Worst American City," *Harper's Magazine,* January 1975. On consistently leading in "indices of social distress," see Kevin Mumford, *Newark: A History of Race, Rights, and Riots* (New York: New York University Press, 2007), 214.

5. "The Choice for Mayor in Newark," *Star-Ledger,* May 3, 1998.

6. Jonathan Wharton, *A Post-Racial Change Is Gonna Come* (New York: Palgrave, 2013), 34. On the importance of NJPAC and the Sports Arena for downtown development, and the roles played by Governor Kean and New

NOTES TO CHAPTER 2 || 299

Jersey Nets owner Ray Chambers in their emergence, see Ana M. Alaya, "For a City of Hope Clinton Selects Newark, President to Visit School to Push Public-Private Initiatives," *Star-Ledger*, November 9, 1999. The Newark Alliance, http://www.newark-alliance.org/. For financing for NJPAC, see Tuttle, *How Newark Became Newark*, 237.

7. On Ray Chambers's role and goal of sparking a downtown revival along the lines of Baltimore and Cleveland, see George Jordan, "Boosters Name Head of Newark Campaign—Former Seton Hall Chief Will Direct Civic Alliance," *Star-Ledger*, February 22, 2001.

8. Jesse Drucker, "Business Owners Chart Course of New District—Newark Nonprofit Group Must Create Budget, Decide Which Downtown Upgrades to Fund," *Star-Ledger*, September 25, 1998. On the subsequent 2001 BID approval for the adjacent Ironbound district, see Barry Carter, "Sweeping Changes in Ironbound—Cleaner Streets Are Just the Start of Plan for Improvement District," *Star-Ledger*, August 22, 2001.

9. In his autobiography, James demonizes public housing, emphasizes homeowners as his priority, and touts public housing demolition as one of his major achievements. See James, *Political Prisoner*, 99, 108, 382. On demolition of public housing, see Rabig, *Fixers*, 143, 169. For an in-depth analysis of the Stella Wright strike, see Megan Marcelin, "HOOD-WINKED: Public Housing Struggles in Newark, N.J. 1965–1975" (unpublished manuscript). On lawsuits by the Newark Coalition for Low Income Housing over the failure to rebuild a sufficient number of units, see Newark Coalition for Low Income Housing, et al., Plaintiffs, v. Newark Redevelopment and Housing Authority, and Alphonso Jackson, Secretary of Housing and Urban Development, Defendants, Civ. No. 89-1303(DRD), U.S. District Court, D. New Jersey, December 18, 2007, https://www.courtlistener.com/opinion/2442200/newark-coalition-v-newark-redev-housing-auth/.

10. Robert Cohen, "Clinton Vows Tougher Action to Stem Tide of Violent Crime," *Star-Ledger*, December 10, 1993; "A 'Gift' of Safety," *Star-Ledger*, December 27, 1993; Scott Orr, "Newark Mayor Joins the President in Calling for Passage of Crime Bill," *Star-Ledger*, April 15, 1994; Orr, "Jersey Delegation Divided on Clinton Crime Bill," *Star-Ledger*, August 10, 1994.

11. Robert Cohen, "James Mobilizes Forces to Push Urban Agenda," *Star-Ledger*, March 15, 1994.

12. James, *Political Prisoner*, 377; Michelle Alexander, "Why Hillary Clinton Doesn't Deserve the Black Vote," *The Nation*, February 10, 2016. On the active support for the bill among other black mayors and the Congressional Black Caucus, see Keeanga-Yamahtta Taylor, *From #BlackLives-Matter to Black Liberation* (Chicago: Haymarket Books, 2016), 101–2.

13. Loïc Wacquant, *Punishing the Poor: The Neoliberal Government of*

Social Insecurity (Durham, N.C.: Duke University Press, 2009), 43; Orr, "Newark Mayor."

14. On James's other homes and amenities, see Evelyn Nieves, "Does Sharpe James Retain Common Touch as Mayor of Newark?," *Star-Ledger,* May 8, 1994. For more on his improved economic fortunes, see Tuttle, *How Newark Became Newark,* 227–28.

15. Morel, *Takeover,* 31–32.

16. Ryan, *Educational Justice,* 35.

17. Ryan, 41.

18. Kenneth Saltman, *The Gift of Education: Public Education and Venture Philanthropy* (New York: Palgrave-Macmillan, 2010), 2–3. McGoey notes that since 2000, "nearly half of the 85,000 foundations in the United States" were founded, and about 5,000 new ones are set up every year. Linsey McGoey, *No Such Thing as a Free Gift* (New York: Verso, 2016), 17.

19. On Booker's family, including housing discrimination they faced in Harrington Park, and connections to Newark, see Nikita Stewart, "A Man on a Mission—First Half," *Star-Ledger,* October 3, 2000.

20. Reed, *Post-1965 Trajectory,* 2016, 12.

21. For a prescient evaluation of Obama during his initial ascent, see Adolph Reed Jr., *Class Notes* (New York: New Press, 2000), 13.

22. https://www.skaddenfellowships.org/fellows-directory?skip=0&keyword =booker&hassearched=true.

23. The Bookers regularly visited Newark for religious—Metropolitan Baptist Church—and dental services. Nikita Stewart, "A Man on a Mission—Second Half," *Star-Ledger,* October 3, 2000. On the NCC and other CDCs as part of what Jennifer Wolch refers to as the "shadow state" that assists in neoliberal state retrenchment, see Rabig, *Fixers,* 242–43.

24. On Booker's arrival in Newark, work with the Urban Justice Center, decision to run for office, and early years on the council, see Stewart, "A Man on a Mission—Second Half"; Andrew Jacobs, "Evicted, Newark's Mayor Finds Another Blighted Street," *New York Times,* November 20, 2006.

25. On the Newark Alliance, and Chambers's influential role in the group, and in Newark more generally, see Alaya, "For a City of Hope"; Jordan, "Boosters Name Head of Newark Campaign." On Booker first meeting Chambers in 1995, at a benefit for Republican governor Christine Todd Whitman, and encouraging him to relocate to Newark, see Stewart, "A Man on a Mission—Second Half." On Chambers's pioneer role in corporate raiding—what Leopold terms "financial strip mining"—through the 1982 leveraged buyout, with partner William Simon, of Gibson Greetings, see William Cohan, "The Private Equity Party Might Be Ending. It's About Time," *New York Times,* February 28, 2021; Leopold, *Runway Inequality,* 52.

NOTES TO CHAPTER 2 || **301**

26. Interview with Richard Roper, September 21, 2016. The other funders of the task force included the Prudential Foundation, PSE&G, and Lucent Technologies Foundation. Also joining the effort were African American academics and civic leaders Robert Curvin and Clement Price, who served for decades on various boards and commissions before their deaths in the mid-2010s. George Jordan, "Task Force Aims to Make Newark's Renaissance a Reality—Group Offer Advice in City's Image, Schools, Economy, and Jobs," *Star-Ledger*, November 30, 2000; "The People Begin to Clamor for a New Newark," *Star-Ledger*, May 6, 2001.

27. George Jordan, "A New Generation on Newark Council—Leaders Bring Energy, Wide Work Experience," *Star-Ledger*, June 28, 1998. Roper also cochaired, along with Thomas O'Neil of the business-led Partnership for New Jersey, a Ford Foundation–funded initiative—Leadership Newark—in the late 1990s. The goal was to develop new leaders and revitalize the "civic culture," that is, replace the old BUR guard. Jesse Drucker, "Newark Leadership Program Plants Human Development," *Star-Ledger*, September 17, 1998.

28. Underscoring Roper's enthusiasm over Booker was the civic leader's participation, along with Booker and several from his inner circle, and media entrepreneur Bo Kemp, in the creation of the Institute for Urban Excellence in 2005, a year before Booker's election as mayor. The think tank developed neoliberal governing plans based on "best practices from other cities." Katie Wang, "Booker Nonprofit Creating a Guide on Urban Issues," *Star-Ledger*, April 21, 2006.

29. For an inside view of Adubato's electoral operation, including the role of Puerto Rican political elites, such as Anibal Ramos and Teresa Ruiz, see Casciano, "By Any Means Necessary." For more on his role as "the legendary boss of the Newark's North Ward," see Terry Golway, "In NJ, Governors Get the Praise but Political 'Bosses' Do Work," *Star-Ledger*, October 9, 2011; Ted Sherman, "Clout and Community," *Star-Ledger*, October 27, 1996. On the power of New Jersey's county party organizations, see Julia Sass Rubin, "Can Progressives Change New Jersey?," *American Prospect*, June 26, 2020.

30. Yasha Levine, "The Neocon, the Messiah, and Cory Booker," *NSFWCORP*, August 25, 2013; "Election Will Bring at Least 2 Freshmen to the City Council," *Star-Ledger*, May 7, 1998; Stewart, "A Man on a Mission—Second Half"; Russakoff, *Prize*, 10.

31. For examples, see his opposition to public subsidies for the construction of the downtown Sports Arena. Wharton, *A Post-Racial Change*, 101. On his critique of creating a downtown business district that would remove local vendors, see George Jordan, "Vote Due on 'Improvement District'—Newark Closing In on New Business Surcharge for Cleanup and Renova-

302 || NOTES TO CHAPTER 2

tion of Downtown Area," *Star-Ledger*, September 2, 1998. On his camp-out and fast outside the Garden Spires housing development to call attention to poor conditions, see Nikita Stewart, "Councilman, Mayor Find Common Ground—Camp-Out Yields Hope for Project Tenants," *Star-Ledger*, August 26, 1999.

32. On favorable national media coverage of Booker early in his career, see Russakoff, *Prize*, 11.

33. Levine, "Neocon."

34. The Bradley Foundation bankrolled Murray with a $90,000 fellowship as he wrote his tract while housed at the Manhattan Institute, and later the American Enterprise Institute. Hannah Schwarz, "Bradley Foundation Gives $250,000 to 'The Bell Curve' Co-author," *Journal Sentinel*, June 2, 2016, http://archive.jsonline.com/news/milwaukee/bradley-foundation-gives-250000-to-the-bell-curve-co-author-b99748226z1-385321251.html/.

35. John Mooney, "Voucher Advocates Focus on Educating Trenton—Group Turns Its Attention from Community to Political Support," *Star-Ledger*, October 19, 2003. Anibal Ramos, who had been groomed by Steve Adubato, ran and won on the same "For Our Kids" Booker- and Adubato- (and NTU-) backed slate. Andra Gillespie, *The New Black Politician: Cory Booker, Newark, and Post-Racial America* (New York: New York University Press, 2008), 194. The 2000 election was the first for the *advisory* school board since the 1995 state takeover. Ana Alaya, "Sharpton Urges Newarkers to Cast Votes—School Election Is the City's First since 1995," *Star-Ledger*, April 12, 2000.

36. On the BAEO's contributors, see Conservative Transparency, Donor Database of Black Alliance for Educational Options, http://conservative-transparency.org/org/black-alliance-for-educational-options/?order_by=year%20 DESC; Russakoff, *Prize*, 12; Glen Ford, "Fruit of the Poisoned Tree: The Hard Right's Plan to Capture Newark NJ," *Black Commentator*, April 5, 2002.

37. On the subsequent name changes and permutations of DeVos's groups, and overlap of board members and employees with the BAEO, see the research by Mercedes Schneider, "Black Alliance for Educational Options (BAEO) Fades into a White-Moneyed Sunset," *Mercedes Schneider's Blog: Mostly Education, with a Smattering of Politics and Pinch of Personal*, November 5, 2017, https://deutsch29.wordpress.com/2017/11/05/black-alliance-for-education-options-baeo-fades-into-a-white-moneyed-sunset/.

38. For an in-depth look at Fuller, and the broader Black Power milieu in which he was immersed, see Johnson's indispensable work *From Revolutionaries to Race Leaders*, esp. 134–47. On Amiri Baraka's political collaboration with the then Owusu Sadaukai, see Baraka, *Autobiography*, 414–16.

39. Interview with Wilhelmina Holder, January 7, 2016. On Milwaukee's

NOTES TO CHAPTER 2 || 303

school voucher program, see Juliet Williams, "Voucher Schools Taught Tough Lessons—Milwaukee's Program, a Model for Others, Is Rocked by Pair of Scandals," *Star-Ledger,* April 6, 2014.

40. Jennifer del Medico, "Black Clergy End Forum with Education Focus," *Star-Ledger,* June 30, 2001; David Gibson, "Black Ministers Set Their Agenda at 2nd Annual State Conference," *Star-Ledger,* June 27, 2001.

41. John Mooney, "Church, State, and Charter Schools," October 25, 2010, http://www.njspotlight.com/stories/10/1024/2257/. Reverend Jackson justified his endorsement of Christie's reelection bid based on the incumbent's support for antiracist school vouchers: "A quality education is a civil right, and it is sad for me to see my party, which embraced the Civil Rights movement, now in New Jersey blocking low-income and minority children from escaping the slavery of failing schools." Salvador Rizzo, "Christie Wins Endorsement of Black Ministers, Who Call for School Vouchers," *Star-Ledger,* July 8, 2013.

42. Kelly Heyboyer and John Mooney, "Education Briefs," *Star-Ledger,* December 9, 2001. Bradford left E3 to head up a national effort to generate "grassroots" support for "choice"—50CAN: The 50-State Campaign for Achievement Now. He also became a "senior visiting fellow" at the conservative, pro-privatization "education reform" think tank, and operator of several charters in Ohio, the Thomas Fordham Institute. On 50CAN, see https://50CAN.org/about-us/staff/; on his think tank position, see https://edexcellence.net/about-us/fordham-staff/derrell-bradford. On the funding E3 and Bradford received from the Robertson Foundation, see Doug Martin, "Warren Buffett and Corporate School Reformers to Gentrify/Charterize Indianapolis and Other Cities," *The Shadow,* September 19, 2011, https://shadowproof.com/2011/09/19/warren-buffett-and-corporate-school-reformers-to-gentrify-charterize-indianapolis-and-other-cities/.

43. Omar Wasow, the then twenty-nine-year-old executive director of BlackPlanet.com, emphasized that opening the market is how black freedom will be achieved. "The goal then, as now, was to give poor black children access to the same quality education as their better-off white counterparts, Mr. Wasow said; only the methods have changed. Where his civil rights forebears focused on ending legal discrimination and turned to the government for protection, Mr. Wasow sees the enemy in subtler racism and believes the savior resides in the private sector. Vouchers are his voter registration." Wilgoren, "Young Blacks Turn to School Vouchers."

44. Nancy Hass, "Scholarly Investments," *New York Times,* December 4, 2009.

45. Buras, *Charter Schools,* 3–4; J. Scott, "A Rosa Parks Moment? School Choice and the Marketization of Civil Rights," *Critical Studies in Education* 54, no. 1 (2013): 45–58.

304 || NOTES TO CHAPTER 2

46. Nancy MacLean, *Democracy in Chains: The Deep History of the Radical Right's Stealth Plan for America* (New York: Random House, 2017); Chris Bonastia, "The Racist History of the Charter School Movement," *Alternet*, January 6, 2015, http://empathyeducates.org/why-the-racist-history-of-the-charter-school-movement-is-never-discussed/.

47. Russell Rickford, *We Are an African People: Independent Education, Black Power and the Radical Imagination* (Oxford: Oxford University Press, 2017), 137, inter alia 131–67.

48. Rickford, 137–42.

49. Rickford, 139–40. Likewise, Baraka condemned public housing as irredeemably repressive "public dungeons." Woodard, *A Nation Within*, 252.

50. George W. Bush's speech to the NAACP, July 10, 2000, http://www.washingtonpost.com/wp-srv/onpolitics/elections/bushtext071000.htm.

51. Haki Madhubuti (formerly Don Lee), cited in Rickford, *We Are an African People*, 153.

52. Cited in Rickford, 153, emphasis original. On Madhubuti's "damage imagery" that presents blacks as "psychologically scarred as a consequence of slavery and racial segregation," all of which provides a privileged role for black elites to assist the damaged masses, and legitimacy for "neo-conservative explanations of poverty" that went into ascendancy in the neoliberal era, see Johnson, *From Revolutionaries to Race Leaders*, 160. As in Newark (Baraka) and New Orleans (Kalamu ya Salaam), the school was run by Madhubuti's wife, Safisha Madhubuti (formerly Carol Lee). For more on the gender dynamics of the school leadership, and the Black Power movement more broadly, see Rickford, *We Are an African People*, 152–56; Barbara Ransby and Tracye Mathews, "Black Popular Culture and the Transcendence of Patriarchal Illusions," *Race and Class* 35 (1993). Madhubuti and his wife converted their school to a charter in the late 1990s. John Eligon, "Poor Scores Leave an Afrocentric School in Chicago Vulnerable," *New York Times*, February 26, 2016. On their rationale, see Raven Moses, "Charter Schools and the Black Independent School Movement," *Black Perspectives*, October 23, 2017, https://www.aaihs.org/charter-schools-and-the-black-independent-school-movement/.

53. Rickford, *We Are An African People*, 141.

54. Peter Jacobs, "In NYC's Top Charter Schools, Students Are Reportedly So Scared to Take a Break They Wet Their Pants," *Business Insider*, April 7, 2015, http://www.businessinsider.com/students-wetting-pants-success-academy-charter-schools-2015-4.

55. Nilsen and Cox, "What Would a Marxist Theory," 66–67.

56. Harvey, *A Brief History*, 42. Kotz, *Rise and Fall of Neoliberal Capitalism*, 81.

57. John Arena, "Why Does Angela Glover Blackwell Hate Public Hous-

ing? The Ideological Foundations of Public Housing Dismantlement in the United States and New Orleans," *Nonsite.org*, no. 17 (September 4, 2015), https://nonsite.org/why-does-angela-glover-blackwell-hate-public-housing/.

58. Further highlighting Booker's "postpartisanship," Bradley and Kemp attended a fundraiser for the insurgent candidate at the home of attorney H. P. Goldfield, "a former associate counsel to President Ronald Reagan." Ted Sherman, "Newark Mayor's Race Is Run in Political Arenas in and outside the State," *Star-Ledger*, March 3, 2002; Kimberly Brown, "It's Still Mayor James," *Star-Ledger*, May 15, 2002; John Fund, "Is the Real Cory Booker Now Standing Up?," *National Review*, January 15, 2017.

59. Russakoff, *Prize*, 12.

60. Sam Roberts, "Beth Curry, Who Co-Founded Investment Firm and Philanthropy, Dies at 74," *New York Times*, November 19, 2015; Ted Sherman, "Newark Candidates Have Reserve to Tap," *Star-Ledger*, May 4, 2002; John Israel, "Bain and Financial Industry Gave over $565,000 to Newark Mayor Cory Booker for 2002 Campaign," *Think Progress*, May 21, 2012, https://thinkprogress.org/bain-and-financial-industry-gave-over-565-000-to-newark-mayor-cory-booker-for-2002-campaign-74a5aa063fe7/.

61. James's charges of inauthenticity included Booker's sexuality—"a faggot white boy"—his source of funding (Jews and the Klan), and his inability act black: "You have to learn to be black, and we don't have time to teach you." Gillespie, *New Black Politician*, 84; Jelani Cobb, "Cory Booker: The Dilemma of the New Black Politician," *New Yorker*, May 22, 2012; Wharton, *A Post-Racial Change*, 40–42. On the concept of the "black leadership family," see Adolph Reed Jr., *The Jesse Jackson Phenomenon* (New Haven, Conn.: Yale University Press, 1986), 5. For a critique of the "black authenticity" trope, rooted in underclass ideology, that promotes "commonplace stereotypes" and obscures the fact that there are a "variety of black experiences" which "precludes the existence of a singular black culture," see Tourè Reed, "'Jess La Bombalera' and the Pathologies of Racial Authenticity," *Jacobin*, September 6, 2020, https://www.jacobinmag.com/2020/09/jess-la-bombalera-and-the-pathologies-of-racial-authenticity.

62. Gordon MacLeod, "From Urban Entrepreneurialism to a Revanchist City? On the Spatial Injustices of Glasgow's Renaissance," *Antipode* 34, no. 3 (2002): 604. David Harvey, "From Managerialism to Entrepreneurialism: The Transformation of Governance in Late Capitalism," *Geografiska Annaler* 71, B (1989): 3–17.

63. For a further critique of dual development, and the interurban capitalist competition that drives it, see Jamie Peck and Adam Tickwell, "Neoliberalizing Space," *Antipode* 34, no. 3 (2002): 393.

64. Kathe Newman, "Newark, Decline and Avoidance, Renaissance and Desire: From Disinvestment to Reinvestment," *Annals of the American*

306 || NOTES TO CHAPTER 2

Academy, July, 2004, 35; Kathe Newman and Elin Wyly, "Geographies of Mortgage Market Segmentation: The Case of Essex Country, New Jersey," *Housing Studies* 19, no. 1 (2004): 53–83.

65. Peter Dreier, Saqib Bhatti, Rob Call, Alex Schwartz, and Gregory Squires, *Underwater America* (Berkeley, Calif.: Hass Institute, 2016), 23; Christopher Niedt and Stephen McFarland, *Our Homes, Our Newark: Foreclosures, Toxic Mortgages, and Blight in the City of Newark* (Hempstead, N.Y.: National Center for Suburban Studies at Hofstra University, 2016).

66. Gillespie, *New Black Politician,* 17, emphasis added.

67. On the importance of the schools for James's patronage politics, see Morel, *Takeover,* 32. A small fraction of Booker's $3 million in campaign contributions came from Newark, with one-third coming from New York. In contrast, 60 percent of James's contributions came from Newark, with one-third coming from city employees. Sherman, "Newark Candidates Have Reserve to Tap." On labor support for James, see Ted Sherman, "James Proves It's Good to Be Incumbent," *Star-Ledger,* May 15, 2002.

68. Sherman, "Newark Candidates Have Reserve to Tap"; Gillespie, *New Black Politician,* 55–83.

69. For more on the hedge funders behind DFER, see Trip Gabriel and Jennifer Medina, "Charter Schools' New Cheerleaders: Financiers," *New York Times,* May 9, 2010.

70. Naomi Nix, "Shavar Jeffries' Breakthrough: What Newark Politics Taught Him about Taking Ed Reform National," *The 74,* September 22, 2015, https://www.the74million.org/article/shavar-jeffries-breakthrough -what-newark-politics-taught-him-about-taking-ed-reform-national/. "The 74," a movement organ, was created by charter backer, and former CNN host, Campbell Brown and a former operative from Michael Bloomberg's administration. Further underscoring the reach and power of the movement, the reporter for the article, Naomi Nix, had been a reporter with the *Star-Ledger.* "Newark School Board Candidates Pitch Their Ideas to Hundreds," *Star-Ledger,* March 25, 2010.

71. Gillespie, *New Black Politician,* 87–88, 194; Damien Cave and Josh Benson, "Newark Mayoral Candidate Tries to Escape Shadows," *New York Times,* May 5, 2006.

72. Gillespie, *New Black Politician,* 17; https://www.publiccharters.org/ about-us/staff/ron-rice.

73. For annual 990 reports of the nonprofit filed with the Internal Revenue Service, see http://www.eri-nonprofit-salaries.com/index.cfm? FuseAction=NPO.Summary&EIN=030498214 &BMF=1&Cobrandid=0. Jeff Mays, "View from Booker's Office Is Straight to Future," *Star-Ledger,* December 1, 2002.

74. Russakoff, *Prize,* 68.

NOTES TO CHAPTER 3 || **307**

75. Din Suleman, "Hosting First Event in New Job, James Lauded and Applauded," *Star-Ledger*, November 19, 2006.

76. Bill Turque, "Standing Up for the Children," *Washington Post*, June 12, 2008.

77. Nick Anderson, "School Tour Has Sharpton, Gingrich Promoting Classroom Innovation," *Washington Post*, November 14, 2009; Zach Miners, "Arne Duncan, Al Sharpton, and Newt Gingrich Join Forces," *U.S. News & World Report*, August 17, 2009, https://www.usnews.com/education/blogs/on-education/2009/08/17/arne-duncan-al-sharpton-and-newt-gingrich-join-forces.

78. From 2006, 2008, and 2016 990 IRS returns for NAN, in possession of the author. Sharpton, at the time of the 2008 deal with Klein, was desperately in need of cash. In July 2008—a month after the June press conference—he agreed to pay the IRS $1 million in back taxes for himself and NAN. After the press conference, NAN received, circuitously, $500,000 from a Connecticut-based hedge fund run by an ally of Klein. The hedge fund "donated" the money to the nonprofit arm of DFER—Education Reform Now—which then transferred it to NAN. Juan Gonzalez, "Rev. Al Sharpton's $500G Link to Education Reform," *Daily News*, March 31, 2009, https://www.nydailynews.com/news/rev-al-sharpton-500g-link-education-reform-article-1.359635#ixzz0whkRph5s. On how the hedge fund's donation assisted one of its major investors, see "What the NY Post Left Out: How Sharpton Was Persuaded to Ally Himself with Joel Klein & Stay Mum on Term Limits," *NYC Public School Parents* (blog), January 4, 2015, https://nycpublicschoolparents.blogspot.com/2015/01/what-ny-post-left-out-how-sharpton-was.html.

79. Johnson, "Gentrifying New Orleans," 187.

80. Johnson, 187. Similarly, Keeanga-Yamahtta Taylor argues that "the utility of Black elected officials lies in their ability, as members of the community, to scold ordinary Black people in ways that white politicians never could get away with . . . while deftly escaping the label of 'racist.' . . . The Black political establishment . . . explains the hardship of African Americans in such a way as to rationalize the poor conditions and lack of resources that pervade working-class communities of color." Taylor, *From #BlackLivesMatter*, 79, 106.

3. BOOKER IN POWER

1. Russakoff, *Prize*, 67; Jersey Jazzman, "The Chris Cerf Story (Pre-Jersey)," *Jersey Jazzman* (blog), July 24, 2012, http://jerseyjazzman.blogspot.com/2012/07/the-chris-cerf-story-pre-jersey.html.

2. On the New York State legislature awarding the mayor power over

308 || NOTES TO CHAPTER 3

the public schools in 2002, though requiring periodical renewal, see Kate Taylor, "Does It Matter Who Runs New York City's Schools?," *New York Times,* June 23, 2017. For a list, as of 2013, of mayoral-controlled school districts, see Morel, *Takeover,* 148.

3. Russakoff, *Prize,* 68.

4. Barker, *Class Struggle,* 48.

5. For Rosen's reform résumé, see "Amy Rosen, President and CEO, the Network for Teaching Entrepreneurship (NFTE)," https://www.treasury .gov/resource-center/financial-education/Pages/rosen.aspx. On Rosen's business relationship with Cerf and her husband, Tim Carden, see Bob Braun, "The Pink Hula Hoop—Part 1: Is This the Future of Public Schools?," *Bob Braun's Ledger* (blog), January 7, 2014, http://www.bobbraunsledger .com/the-pink-hula-hoop-part-1-is-this-the-future-of-public-schools/. Cerf was deputy superintendent under Klein from 2006 to 2009. Peggy McGlone, "NJ Education Commissioner Sees no Conflict in New Private Sector Job," *Star-Ledger,* February 12, 2014. For Cerf's role with Edison Schools and in the Clinton administration, see Russakoff, *Prize,* 67–68.

6. See Amy Brown, *A Good Investment: Philanthropy and the Marketing of Race in an Urban Public School* (Minneapolis: University of Minnesota Press, 2015). Interview with De'Shawn Wright, April 28, 2016. On Wright's ascent, see Diane Ravitch, "Cuomo Appoints TFAer as Deputy Secretary of Education," *Diane Ravitch's Blog,* October 19, 2012, https://dianeravitch .net/2012/10/19/cuomo-appoints-tfa-er-as-deputy-secretary-of -education/. Also see his biography posted at the Aspen Institute, where he was a 2012 Aspen-Pahara Education Fellow and a Fellow of the Aspen Global Leadership Network, http://agln.aspeninstitute.org/fellows/ deshawn-wright.

7. Interview with Wright.

8. Interview with Wright.

9. Interview with Wright.

10. Interview with Wright; Jesse Margolis, *Moving Up: Progress in Newark's Schools 2010 to 2017* (N.p.: MarGrady Research, 2017), 7, http:// margrady.com/wp-content/uploads/2017/10/Moving-Up-Progress-in -Newarks-Schools.pdf.

11. Wright used the term repeatedly in my interview with him when referring to charters, with the corollary being "low-quality seats," that is, public ones.

12. Irene Cooper-Basch, "The Evolution of Victoria Foundation from 1924 to 2003: With a Special Focus on the Newark Years from 1964 to 2003" (PhD diss., Rutgers University–Newark, 2014), 293.

13. Jeffery Snyder and Sarah Reckhow, "Political Determinants of Philanthropic Funding for Urban Schools," *Journal of Urban Affairs* 39, no. 1

(2017): 91. On the change toward targeted foundation funding of disruptive neoliberal "jurisdictional challengers" in public education, see 95–96.

14. For more on Leschly, see Cooper-Basch, "Evolution," 293; Sharon McClosky, "Stig Leschly, Call Your Office," NEWS21, June 23, 2009, https://news21.com/columbia/2009/indexa165-p=550.html.

15. Cooper-Basch, "Evolution," 294. The NCSF was part of a "string of philanthropic organizations," as the *Star-Ledger* reported, that were created since Booker took office "to provide private funds where public funds fall short." Kasi Addison, "19 Million Pledged for Charter School Fund—Foundation Has Goal of an Additional $6 Million for Newark's 12 Facilities," *Star-Ledger*, April 25, 2008; Wharton, *A Post-Racial Change*, 138. On praise for the Booker administration's collaboration with the Trust for Public Land and its "foundation partners," which contrasted with the James administration, where TPL operated "without much support from City Hall," see Todd Wilkinson, "Newark Goes for the Green—Land&People," Trust for Public Land, https://www.tpl.org/resource/newark-goes-green 151landpeople.

16. Cooper-Basch, "Evolution," 293.

17. Wright received generous compensation from the NCSF, serving in various roles from 2008 to 2011 ($83,000 in 2008, $141,000 in 2009, $140,000 in 2010, $72,000 in 2011). A significant part of the NCSF budget was spent on consultants, with the well-connected Lisa Daggs receiving approximately $200,000 in both 2010 and 2011. In 2008 alone, the NCSF gave nearly $500,000 to New Schools for New Leaders, a movement organization formerly headed by Anderson, to train new principals for Newark charter schools and $200,000 to Building Excellent Schools "to recruit train and place aspiring principals to open a new Charter school in Newark." NCSF 990 IRS returns in possession of the author. In addition to the NCSF, Daggs has served, in various capacities, other movement organizations, including TFA, the KIPP Foundation, and the Doris and Donald Fisher Fund. https://www.newschools.org/blog/no-textbook-answers/; https://www.grantmakers.io/profiles/v0/266033047-doris-and-donald-fisher-fund/; http://www.kipp.org/team/lisa-daggs/; Addison, "$19 Million Pledged."

18. Ashton also received a handsome compensation package. Like Wright, Ashton had been a Pahara-Aspen Education Fellow at the Aspen Institute. For more on Ashton, see her biography at "Our Staff," Newark Charter School Fund, in possession of the author; Russakoff, *Prize*, 68, 107. Further contributing to movement bonding was that Schnur lived in Montclair, home to Cerf, Rosen, Cardin, Don Katz, Matthew Frankel (Anderson's press spokesperson), and other movement activists. http://americaachieves.org/staff/jon-schnur/.

19. http://www.leadershipnewark.org/board/kimberly-mclain/.

20. Kotz, *Rise and Fall*, 83, emphasis added.

21. Cooper-Basch, "Evolution," 279–80.

22. Interview with Nina Stack, March 23, 2016.

23. Interview with Stack.

24. Interview with Stack. Johnson was officially employed by the Council of New Jersey Grantmakers, the coordinating arm of philanthropy that primarily operates in the Garden State. The larger foundations, such as Ford and Gates, have their own coordinating councils.

25. See the 2012 President's Annual Report of the CNJG, https://www.cnjg.org/sites/default/files/resources/2012%20CNJG%20President%27s%20Report.PDF.

26. John Kania and Mark Kramer, "Collective Impact," *Stanford Social Innovation Review,* Winter 2011. The authors of the article—which one close observer of the third sector called "the bible in many ways" for foundation officials—argued that "large-scale social change requires broad cross-sector coordination, yet the social sector remains focused on the isolated intervention of individual organizations."

27. See the 2011 and other annual reports of the Council of New Jersey Grantmakers, https://www.cnjg.org/about/financials.

28. Newark Trust for Education, Shané Harris, http://www.newarktrust.org/shane_harris_chair.

29. The ICC, which operates out of Newark's heavily immigrant Ironbound district, studiously avoided advocating against school privatization, backed, as it was, by its foundation funders. http://ironboundcc.org/about-icc/our-community/.

30. Newark Trust for Education, Funders Collaborative, http://www.newarktrust.org/funders_collaborative.

31. Mark Purcell, *Recapturing Democracy* (London: Routledge, 2008), 12.

32. "School Chief Vote Is Postponed—Irate Bolden Supporters Disrupt Meeting of Split Newark Board," *Star-Ledger,* February 14, 2003; Barbara Kukla, "Bolden and Supporters Savor Victory, For Our Kids Team Sweeps Polls," *Star-Ledger,* April 17, 2003.

33. John Mooney, "Newark, Reluctantly, Hosts School Vouchers Forum," *Star-Ledger,* September 22, 2004.

34. Interview with Freda Barrow, February 15, 2016. On Bolden's role in the 1970 and 1971 strikes, see Golin, *Newark Teacher Strikes,* 152.

35. Kasi Addison, "Ads Target Newark Teachers Union—Billboards and Bus Signs Accuse the Group of Protecting Bad Educators," *Star-Ledger,* March 6, 2007; Bess Keller, "Union and Anti-Union Group Wage Billboard Campaigns in Newark," *Education Week,* March 14, 2007, http://www.edweek.org/ew/articles/2007/03/14/27union.h26.html. On the Center for

Union Facts and director Steve Berman's mercenary role on behalf of various corporate clients, see Mercedes Schneider, "Center for Union Facts . . . Yeah Right," *Mercedes Schneider EduBlog*, December 19, 2013, https://deutsch29 .wordpress.com/2013/12/19/center-for-union-facts-yeah-right/.

36. Kasi Addison, "Bolden to Leave as Newark Schools Chief in June '08," *Star-Ledger*, November 21, 2006.

37. Rhee, like De'Shawn Wright, entered the movement through TFA, joining in 1992 after graduating from Cornell, and served three years in Baltimore. She then went on to found, in 1997, the New Teacher Project, which major school districts used to outsource teacher recruiting and training. A decade later, in 2007, Mayor Adrian Fenty named her chancellor of D.C. public schools, a newly created office established after the D.C. school board was stripped of its decision-making powers and downgraded, as in Newark, to an advisory role. https://en.wikipedia.org/wiki/ Michelle_Rhee. Kasi Addison and John Mooney, "Ex-D.C. Schools Chief Is Top Contender in Newark," *Star-Ledger*, May 15, 2008; Kasi Addison and John Mooney, "The 3 Who Want to Lead Newark Schools—Each Candidate Brings Successes—and Question Marks—to the Table," *Star-Ledger*, May 18, 2008.

38. On Janey promoting collaboration between charter and public schools, see "Newark Educators Are Learning from One Another—Public and Charter School Officials Are Ready to Move beyond Differences," *Star-Ledger*, March 14, 2010.

39. Janey gathered with Del Grosso and AFT chief Weingarten at a press conference in September 2010 to announce the signing of a "memorandum of agreement" with NPS to allow for longer school days and other changes to the union contract for seven schools. The AFT wanted to use this brokered approach to imposing neoliberal reforms as a national model. Yet, just as the program, modeled after the hedge fund–backed Harlem Children Zone, was being unveiled, Booker and Christie were in the midst of their own reform agenda that would leave out Janey and the GVZ. Winnie Hu, "Ambitious New Model for 7 Newark Schools," *New York Times*, July 25, 2010. Ford made its last grant to the GVZ in 2011, when it became clear that Noguera's operation was no longer "in alignment" with Anderson. That same year, Ford awarded the FNF (Zuckerberg money) $1.1 million for extended school time. Owen Davis, "The Newark School Reform Wars," *The Nation*, May 28, 2014. On Noguera's role in approving charters in New York State, see Norm Scott, "Pedro Noguera Gets Schooled on Charters," *Ed Notes On Line*, October 4, 2014, https://ednotesonline.blogspot .com/2014/10/pedro-noguera-gets-schooled-on-charters.html.

40. Chris Cerf, cited in David Giambusso, "Booker: It's Time to Move on Schools," *Star-Ledger*, February 6, 2011.

NOTES TO CHAPTER 3

41. "Christie's Budget, Cut by Cut," *Star-Ledger*, March 17, 2010.

42. Michael Leachman, "Most States Have Cut School Funding, and Some Continue Cutting," Center for Budget and Policy Priorities, January 25, 2016, http://www.cbpp.org/research/state-budget-and-tax/most-states-have-cut-school-funding-and-some-continue-cutting

43. Mary Ann Spoto, "Christie Promises Backing for State's Charter Schools," *Star-Ledger*, March 19, 2010.

44. Booker, cited in Russakoff, *Prize*, 5.

45. Russakoff, 4, 5.

46. Russakoff, 28–29.

47. *The Oprah Winfrey Show*, "Mark Zuckerberg Announces $100 Million Grant," September 24, 2010, http://www.oprah.com/own-oprahshow/mark-zuckerbergs-big-announcement-video; Alan Singer, "No Longer Waiting for 'Superman,'" *The Blog*, October 12, 2010, http://www.huffingtonpost.com/alan-singer/no-longer-waiting-for-sup_b_755781.html. On the same show, Winfrey also featured *Waiting for Superman*'s director, Davis Guggenheim, and announced that her Angel Network Foundation was donating $6 million to six charter school organizations. Olster, "Forget Superman."

48. Russakoff, *Prize*, 33. On the January 2011 meeting with representatives of seven billionaires and local foundations, see Russakoff, *Prize*, 68.

49. Interview with Ross Danis, April 23, 2016.

50. Cooper-Basch, "Evolution," 297.

51. Cooper-Basch, 297.

52. Cooper-Basch, 295–97.

53. Cited in Russakoff, *Prize*, 71.

54. Farhood Monjoo, "Can Facebook Fix Its Ultimate Bug?," *New York Times Magazine*, August 30, 2017, 40.

55. Amy Brown, *A Good Investment*, 19; Russakoff, *Prize*, 58–63.

56. Curvin, *Inside Newark*, 296–97; Russakoff, *Prize*, 64; "Acting N.J. Education Chief Cerf Revises Account of Ties to Consulting Firm," *Star-Ledger*, February 24, 2011; Bob Braun, "N.J. Education Chief Cerf: 'My Very Short Involvement Occurred When I Was a Civilian,'" *Star-Ledger*, February 24, 2011. On the central role that Cerf played in preparing the report, see "Book Review: 'The Prize' by Dale Russakoff," *Jersey Jazzman* (blog), September 8, 2015, http://jerseyjazzman.blogspot.com/2015/09/book-review-prize-by-dale-russakoff.html. According to Owen Davis, by 2011, one-third of the money spent by the FNF had gone to consultants. See Own Davis, "The Newark School Reform Wars," *The Nation*, May 28, 2014, https://www.thenation.com/article/archive/newark-school-reform-wars/.

57. The Gates Foundation advocated the same goals. See McGoey, *No*

Such Thing, 138–39. For Booker's support of the same agenda, see Giambusso, "Booker"; Russakoff, *Prize,* 68–70.

58. And he had the power to deliver. That same month, Governor Christie and Cerf, as commissioner, approved twenty-three new charter schools, including the expansions in Newark, bringing the state numbers to nearly one hundred charters and approximately twenty-five thousand students. Angela Delli Santi, "Christie Administration OKs 23 Charter Schools," *Star-Ledger,* January 18, 2011.

59. Kelly Heyboer, "Plan would phase out Newark's struggling schools—Confidential proposal clears space for charter sites, shifts scores of kids," *Star-Ledger,* February 22, 2011. On American History High School parents, targeted for "colocation" by the nonprofit Youth Build, storming the stage in protest, see Jessica Calefati and David Giambusso, "Officials Deal with Fallout of Newark Schools Plan, Newark School Board Meeting," *Star-Ledger,* February 27, 2011; February 22, 2011, Newark Public Schools SAB Meeting, https://www.youtube.com/watch?v=spqpzZwsXtA; Joan Whitlow, "Too Many Left Out of the Newark Schools Loop," *Star-Ledger,* February 25, 2011.

60. David Giambusso and Jessica Calefati, "N.J. Education Boss Linked to Newark Schools Consultant," *Star-Ledger,* February 23, 2011.

61. Russakoff, *Prize,* 77.

62. Whitlow, "Too Many Left Out."

63. Joan Whitlow, "Newark Mayor Has a Plan for Better Schools," *Star-Ledger,* March 4, 2011.

64. David Giambusso, "Proposal on Charters Stirs Crowd in Newark—Hundreds Join Talk on Sharing Buildings," *Star-Ledger,* March 23, 2011. On further conflict between Adubato's forces and Jeffries, see David Giambusso, "Fingers Pointed after Newark Schools Vote—Chairman Blames Power Broker; Some Say Schools at Fault," *Star-Ledger,* April 10, 2011; Russakoff, *Prize,* 104–5.

65. *Star-Ledger* Editorial Board, "A Q&A with . . . Arne Duncan: The Eyes of America Are on Newark," *Star-Ledger,* April 3, 2011.

66. More promising career options must have also been a factor. In 2011, Cuomo promoted him to the commissioner of education, and in 2016, he succeeded Arne Duncan as secretary of education. He then became "president and CEO" of the Education Trust, a foundation-backed operation that works to get colleges and universities to promote corporate school reform efforts among K–12 schools. He was handsomely compensated, making more than $500,000 in his first year. Emery and Ohanian, *Why Is Corporate America Bashing Our Public Schools?*; Education Trust, 2017 form 990, https://pdf.guidestar.org/PDF_Images/2018/521/982/2018-521982223-1 0772c37-9.pdf.

314 || NOTES TO CHAPTER 3

67. Interview with Willie Rowe, June 10, 2017; David Giambusso, "Christie to Tap NYC Educator for Newark—Schools Chief Search Has Lasted 8 Months," *Star-Ledger,* May 4, 2011.

68. On Junius Williams's criticism of the committee's secrecy, see Giambusso, "Booker"; Jessica Calefati and David Giambusso, "2 Remain in Newark's Search for School Czar," *Star-Ledger,* April 22, 2011; Russakoff, *Prize,* 99–100.

69. Giambusso, "Fingers Pointed after Newark Schools Vote." In the 2011 race, Baraka's "Children First" slate ended up taking two of three contested seats from Adubato's opposing "For Our Kids," including a Baraka ally edging out an employee of Adubato's North Ward center operation. Adubato was still able to marshal enough votes to oust Jeffries as the board president and place two of his allies in charge of the board. David Giambusso, "Reorganization of Newark School Advisory Board Shows North Ward Power Broker's Influence," May 3, 2011, *NJ.com,* https://articles.nj.com/news/index.ssf/2011/05/reorganization_of_newark_schoo.amp.

70. Despite efforts by Booker, Cerf, and Christie to keep the process as secret as possible, an audio recording of the committee's deliberations was leaked by the "community advocate" member of the committee, Willie Rowe, which committee member Ross Danis bitterly denounced. Interview with Danis; Calefati and Giambusso, "2 Remain." Robert Curvin also criticized the release of the tape. Curvin, "The White Lady from Harlem," *Star-Ledger,* May 8, 2011.

71. On antiracism as central to her identity, see Anderson's profile for her new consulting business, Thirdway Solutions, https://camianderson.com/.

72. Harvey, *A Brief History,* 66; Russakoff, *Prize,* 124–26.

73. The official elaborated further on the contradictions of this arrangement: "So I said to him, and this was just after the governor put in a salary cap for superintendents and said they were overpaid, and he was saying you can't attract the talent you need with the salaries we're able to pay. And I raised my hand and said, 'I don't get this. Is there a contradiction here?,' and he looked at me over those glasses and said, 'Yeah, it's ironic, isn't it.'" Interview with foundation officer, May 4, 2016.

74. In addition to contracting with Global Education Advisors consultants, Anderson brought in Michelle Rhee's New Teacher Project to develop a new teacher evaluation system. The New Teacher Project was also involved in efforts to pass the tenure reform bill in the state legislature. Russakoff, *Prize,* 126; Jessica Calefati, "Student Scores Will Test Teachers—Pilot Program Retools Evaluations," *Star-Ledger,* May 20, 2011.

75. "Smart to Change—Under New Policy, Newark Students Won't Be Stuck with Terrible Teachers," *Star-Ledger,* June 25, 2011; Russakoff, *Prize,* 121. On Anderson's embrace of business practices for her handpicked CEO

principals, and the influence of business author Jim Collins, see Russakoff, *Prize*, 124–25.

76. On the "realism" of AFT leader Randi Weingarten that led to collaboration in the reform, see Bob Braun, "This Teachers Union Wants to Lead Change," *Star-Ledger*, August 13, 2011. For similar cooperation from the AFT in Washington, D.C., see Ryan, *Educational Justice*, 77–78.

77. NTU president Del Grosso supported the application, while the state NJEA did not. Kristen Alloway, "State Moves to Grab Chunk of U.S. Funds for Education but Most Unions Refuse to Join Effort," *Star-Ledger*, January 20, 2010.

78. Salvador Rizzo, "Tenure Reform Sweeps through Legislature—Christie Expected to Soon Sign Bill in Which Teachers Are to Be Evaluated Yearly," *Star-Ledger*, June 26, 2012. Nonetheless, the *Star-Ledger* wanted the bill to go further by eliminating tenure protections altogether. Editorial, "Holding On to Top Teachers—to Keep the Best, We Still Need Reform from the Legislature," *Star-Ledger*, August 10, 2012. They saw the key problem as an inability to fire teachers who were not picked up by principals under the new system. Editorial, "Lessons from Newark—Proposed Reforms Offer Fresh Perspective on Charter Schools and Tenure," *Star-Ledger*, February 5, 2012.

79. Russakoff, *Prize*, 151–52.

80. Michael Burawoy, *The Politics of Production* (London: Verso, 1985), 126.

81. For contract provisions, see NTU Collective Barging Agreement, July 1, 2010–July 1, 2015, in possession of the author. For the pay scale, see 65–69. On bonuses for a highly effective rating, and for other areas, such as working at a low-performing school or in a hard-to-staff area, see 62. Those receiving a "partially satisfactory" can receive a step increase if approved by the superintendent, while those receiving an "ineffective" one would be denied altogether; see 64. For a short summary of pay scales, see NTU, "Compensation Details: The New Universal Salary Scale and Highly Effective Teaching Rewards," in possession of the author.

82. Geoff Mulvihill, "Newark Teachers Union Not in Love with Breakthrough Contract," *Washington Times*, October 1, 2015, https://www .washingtontimes.com/news/2015/oct/1/newark-teachers-union-not-in -love-with-breakthroug/. Rhee, in Washington, D.C., used a similar bonus and back pay sweetener in 2010 to sell concessions, financed with a $64.5 million donation from the Broad, Walton, Anderson, and Robertson Foundations. Ryan, *Educational Justice*, 77–78.

83. Jessica Calefati and David Giambusso, "School-Closings Meeting Riles Up Hostile Audience," *Star-Ledger*, February 4, 2012. On the state's three-tier school designation—priority, focus, and reward—as part of the

316 || NOTES TO CHAPTER 3

NCLB, see Mark Mueller, "State Warns Troubled Schools: Accept Our Help or Else," *Star-Ledger,* April 12, 2012.

84. Jessica Calefati, "Teachers Slam Union Over New Contract—Merit Bonuses Evoke Outrage in Newark," *Star-Ledger,* October 24, 2012.

85. Josh Eidelson, "Newark Teachers Union Embraces Performance Pay, Wins Peer Review," *In These Times,* October 21, 2012, http://inthesetimes .com/working/entry/14058/newark_teachers_union_contract_ performance_pay_merit_randi_weingarten_chris; Salvador Rizzo, "Christie Heaps Rare Praise on Newark Teachers Union for Merit Pay Pact," *Star-Ledger,* November 17, 2012. The governor's web page had a separate photo category for the event, underscoring the importance of the NTU–Republican–Democratic partnership that produced the contract for defining the Christie brand.

86. On the Christie–Weingarten rapprochement, see Russakoff, *Prize,* 152–53. While in office, Christie prominently posted a photo of his 9/11 encounter with Weingarten on his governor's web page. Josh Eidelson, "Some Newark Teachers, Inspired by Chicago, Seek to Thwart Concessionary Contract," *In These Times,* October 26, 2012, https://inthesetimes.com/ article/newark-teachers-union-new-caucus-contract-vote-del-grosso -ratification-owen.

87. Stanley Aronowitz, *How Class Works: Power and Social Movement* (New Haven, Conn.: Yale University Press, 2003), 106.

88. Aronowitz, 106.

89. Nilsen and Cox, "What Would a Marxist Theory," 67.

90. Reed, *Post-1965 Trajectory,* 12.

91. Reed, 17.

4. REBEL CITY?

1. Interview with Antoinette Baskerville-Richardson, March 1, 2016.

2. Harvey, *Rebel Cities,* 5.

3. Harvey, 5. For other works that address the totality of class struggle, both at the workplace and in broader society, see Schneider, *Renew Orleans?,* 28–39; Camfield, "Re-orienting Class Analysis"; Aronowitz, *How Class Works,* 2003.

4. Harvey, *Rebel Cities,* 16.

5. Harvey, 177.

6. NPS School Advisory Board meeting, April 23, 2013, https://www .youtube.com/watch?v=TZttEHdiuhg. Rippey begins speaking at the 1:38 point.

7. Stepan-Norris and Zeitlin, "Who Gets the Bird?," 504.

NOTES TO CHAPTER 4 || 317

8. Nilsen and Cox, "What Would a Marxist Theory," 67.

9. Emphasis original.

10. Interview with Branden Rippey, October 15, 2015, emphasis original.

11. John Mooney, "NTU Sticks to Own Path on Education Reform," *NJ Spotlight News*, May 13, 2010, http://www.njspotlight.com/stories/10/0511/2048/.

12. The cuts to education, to which most income taxes are dedicated, equaled the corresponding tax breaks to the wealthy. Samantha Marcus, "Murphy's Motivation: Why the Governor Froze State Spending and Is Pushing to Increase the Sales Tax," *Star-Ledger*, June 10, 2018. The NJEA did organize a statewide rally against the cuts of four hundred teachers at the Rutgers–Newark campus on April 17, where Christie was speaking. David Giambusso, "Teachers Take to the Streets in Protest of Christie's Cuts to School Aid," *Star-Ledger*, April 17, 2010. On Christie-imposed caps on local property taxes, see Salvador Rizzo, "Property Tax Increases Hit a 21-Year Low—but Sandy Could Send Rates Soaring Again," *Star-Ledger*, January 13, 2013; Richard Pérez-Peña, "New Jersey Puts 2% Cap on Local Property Taxes," *New York Times*, July 12, 2010.

13. Burawoy, *Politics of Production*, 126.

14. Interview with Leah Owens, November 6, 2015.

15. Interview with Al Moussab, October 10, 2015.

16. On the March 4 march and rally in Military Park, see "Young Teachers Lead the Fight in Newark, NJ," *Fire on the Mountain* (blog), May 5, 2010, http://firemtn.blogspot.com/2010/03/march-4-from-other-coast-newark-nj.html. Subsequent protests on March 23, May 17, and June 23 were organized by TaLiN along with a host of other groups under the banner of the "United Front for Public Education." Flyers in possession of the author.

17. Interview with Rippey; "We Continue to Organize!," NEW Caucus, June 22, 2015, https://us8.campaign-archive.com/?u=1746ba16f98cc36943b131766&id=a21f63fc42.

18. In 1995, Del Grosso stepped down from his VP position in the NTU to lead a slate that defeated Carol Graves, the longtime union president of the NTU. Petino, who for twenty-five years was Graves's top aid as "NTU director of organization," switched to Del Grosso's "Teachers About Change" slate at the last minute. See "Challengers to NTU Chief Are Boosted," *Star-Ledger*, April 25, 1995; Reginald Roberts, "Graves Loses Helm of Newark Teachers Union after 27 Years," *Star-Ledger*, June 21, 1995.

19. David Giambusso, "Proposal on Charters Stirs Crowd in Newark—Hundreds Join Talk on Sharing Buildings," *Star-Ledger*, March 23, 2011.

20. "Mass Day of Outrage," July 21, 2011, flyer in possession of the

author; Richard Khavkine, "Dozens of Newark Residents Rally at 'Mass Day of Outrage,'" *Star-Ledger*, July 22, 2011.

21. Jessica Calefati, "Newark Superintendent's Rapid Reform Wins Allies, but Critics Say Slow Down," *Star-Ledger*, August 14, 2012; Jessica Calefati, "Schools Chief Grants Charter Leases—Move Negates Pleas of Newark Parents, District's Board," *Star-Ledger*, July 5, 2012.

22. David Giambusso, "School-Closings Meeting Riles Up Hostile Audience," *Star-Ledger*, February 4, 2012.

23. Tom Moran, "In Newark, a School Reformer Needs Help," *Star-Ledger*, March 11, 2012.

24. The five ministers were William Howard, Eric Beckham, Joe Carter, David Jefferson Sr., and Ronald Slaughter. "Newark Schools Need Your Support Now," *Star-Ledger*, March 21, 2012.

25. Eunice Lee, "Anderson Presents Final Plan for Newark Schools," *Star-Ledger*, March 20, 2012.

26. Lia Eustachewich, "Angry Parents, Students Swarm Meeting to Protest Restructure Plans," *Patch*, March 28, 2012, https://patch.com/new-jersey/newarknj/angry-parents-students-swarm-meeting-to-protest-restr7a3fbba20a; Sara Neufeld, "Newark's School Turnaround Strategy Changes Course," *Huffington Post*, November 29, 2012, http://www.huffingtonpost.com/2012/11/29/newarks-school-turnaround_n_2212296.html.

27. Calefati, "Schools Chief Grants Charter Leases." In 2012, *Time* magazine named Anderson among the world's one hundred most influential people. Booker, who wrote the profile, was hyperbolic in his praise, calling her "a modern day freedom fighter" for her school reform work in Newark. See https://content.time.com/time/specials/packages/article/0,28804,2111975_2111976_2112115,00.html.

28. Winnie Hu, "In New Jersey, a Civics Lesson in the Internet Age," *New York Times*, April 27, 2010; Kelley Heyboer, "Penalties Vary for Student Protesters Following Walkout on Tuesday, Some Get Detention While Others Get Nothing," *Star-Ledger*, April 29, 2010. On the NPS budget cut, see Joan Whitlow, "Finding Ways to Do More with Less in City Schools," *Star-Ledger*, April 9, 2010; Julie O'Connor, "Districts Begin Sending Layoff Notices to Non-Tenured Teachers," *Star-Ledger*, May 14, 2010.

29. "Thousands of N.J. High School Students Leave Class, Protest Funding Cuts," *NJ.com*, April 27, 2010, http://www.nj.com/news/index.ssf/2010/04/students_across_nj_protest_gov.html.

30. Piven and Cloward, *Poor People's Movements*, 20–21.

31. Yet, according to the head of the NPS administrators' union (CASA), NPS cut programs by 10 percent in the 2010–11 academic year. See comments at the February 2011 school board meeting, beginning at the 1:09 mark, at https://www.youtube.com/watch?v=spqpzZwsXtA.

NOTES TO CHAPTER 4 || 319

32. Cited in Patrick Bond, Ashwin Desai, and Trevor Ngwane, "Marxism and South Africa's Urban Social Movements," in Barker et al., *Marxism and Social Movements,* 238.

33. Emphasis added.

34. Piven and Cloward, *Poor People's Movements,* 3–4.

35. Emphasis original.

36. Piven, *Challenging Authority,* 2006, 31; Charles Tilly, "The Web of Contention in Eighteenth Century Cities," in *Class Conflict and Collective Action,* ed. Louise Tilly and Charles Tilly (Beverly Hills, Calif.: Sage, 1981), 27–51.

37. On the merger of the Leadership for the Common Good with the CPD, see "Center for Popular Democracy and the Leadership Center for the Common Good to Merge," November 18, 2013, https://populardemocracy .org/blog/center-popular-democracy-and-leadership-center-common-good -merge.

38. Interview with Roberto Cabañas, November 3, 2015.

39. Emphasis original.

40. "WNYC & NJPAC Present Mayor Cory Booker, Cami Anderson, and Others with Host Brian Lehrer in a Community Forum on School Reform," press release, March 12, 2013, http://www.wnyc.org/press/school -reform/032013/.

41. Interview with Cabañas.

42. John Emerson, "Newark School Walk Out," http://www.eohistory .info/2013/Schools/newarkWalkOut4-9-13.htm.

43. Interview with Rippey.

44. Saltman, *Gift of Education,* 111, emphasis added.

45. Rania Khalek, "Newark Students Defy Threats to Protest Attacks on Public Education," *Truthout,* April 11, 2013, https://truthout.org/articles/ newark-students-defy-threats-to-protest-attacks-on-public-education/.

46. Khalek.

47. "Dispatches from the US Student Movement: April 15," *The Nation,* April 15, 2013, https://www.thenation.com/article/archive/dispatches -us-student-movement-april-15/; Jessica Calefati, "Newark Students Rally, Protest Budget Cuts," *Star-Ledger,* April 10, 2013; Newark Public Schools FY2014 Budget Hearing, Newark Public Schools finance presentation, March 23, 2013, Central High School, http://www.edlawcenter.org/assets/ files/pdfs/Newsblasts/NPS%20Finance%20Presentation%203-28-13.pdf.

48. Footage of the April 9 march and rally—Bazile speaks at the two-minute mark, https://www.youtube.com/watch?v=ZwFeZ6lPMZE.

49. Russakoff, *Prize,* 95–96. Adubato backed Jeffries in 2010, but the following year, the two fell out over Adubato-controlled board members voting against Cerf's plan to open smaller academies. Giambusso, "Fingers

320 || NOTES TO CHAPTER 4

Pointed after Newark Schools Vote." In 2012, Adubato did not field a slate, while Jeffries challenged Baraka's "Children First" slate with his Booker-endorsed "Education Matters" ticket.

50. Newark Public Schools board meeting, April 23, 2013, https://www.youtube.com/watch?v=TZttEHdiuhg; John Mooney, "Newark Board Votes 'No Confidence' in Schools Chief," *NJ Spotlight*, April 24, 2013, http://www.njspotlight.com/stories/13/04/23/newark-board-votes-no-confidence-in-schools-chief/#.

51. Ralph Darlington, "The Marxist Rank-and-File/Bureaucracy Analysis of Trade Unionism," in Barker et al., *Marxism and Social Movements*, 189.

52. For a recounting of this capitulation, see chapter 3.

53. Samantha Winslow, "Newark Teacher Reformers Win Majority," *Labor Notes*, June 26, 2013, https://labornotes.org/blogs/2013/06/newark-teacher-reformers-win-majority-2.

54. Interview with Rippey; Branden Rippey, "Newark Teachers Battle Governor's School Privatization Agenda," *Labor Notes*, January 28, 2014, https://labornotes.org/2014/01/newark-teachers-battle-governor%E2%80%99s-school-privatization-agenda.

55. Michelle Gunderson, "Teachers Compare Notes," *Labor Notes*, April 21, 2015, https://www.labornotes.org/2015/04/teachers-compare-notes. The Chicago Teachers Union (CTU) spearheaded the formation of UCORE following its fall 2012 strike, spurred on by the recognition that it had "made enemies with a lot of powerful people and would be sitting ducks if they did not mobilize and get more people on their side." Telephone interview with Michelle Gunderson, June 21, 2018; Samantha Winslow, "Chicago Teacher Organizing Lessons Go National," *Labor Notes*, August 12, 2013, https://www.labornotes.org/blogs/2013/08/chicago-teacher-organizing-lessons-go-national.

56. "Challenging the Education Status Quo," https://www.zeitgeistminds.com/talk/5294595164340224/ceo-of-amplify-joel-klein-with-superintendent-of-newark-public-schools-cami-anderson.

57. Nilsen and Cox, "What Would a Marxist Theory," 74.

58. Nilsen and Cox, 76.

59. Nilsen and Cox, 77.

60. Eustachewich, "Angry Parents."

61. Nilsen and Cox, "What Would a Marxist Theory," 78.

62. Flyer in possession of the author.

63. Harvey, *Rebel Cities*, 5.

64. Harvey, 22.

65. In possession of the author. For a video of the People's Conference on Jobs, Peace, Equality, and Justice, see part I, http://www.youtube.com/

NOTES TO CHAPTER 5 || 321

watch?v=WGXo8pe2MGU; part II, http://www.youtube.com/watch?v=aBlnh7xysTY.

66. Kate Zernike, "Promise vs. Reality in Newark on Mayor's Watch," *New York Times*, December 13, 2012. On Booker still mulling a third term in fall 2012, see David Giambusso, "Even If He Doesn't Run, Booker Will Be Center of Mayor's Race," *Star-Ledger*, August 19, 2012. On Booker's efforts to privatize the city's water system, and the corruption scandal surrounding them, see Guy Sterling, "What Cory Booker Isn't Telling Us about the Newark Water Crisis," *Bob Braun's Ledger* (blog), August 28, 2019, https://www.bobbraunsledger.com/what-cory-booker-isnt-telling-us-about-the-newark-water-crisis/.

67. Eunice Lee, "See Cory Booker's Resignation Letter as He Bids Farewell to Newark City Hall, Goes to Washington," *Star-Ledger*, October 30, 2013.

68. David Giambusso, "In Newark, a Deepening Divide over Schools Chief," *Star-Ledger*, May 3, 2013. Councilman Anibal Ramos, who was then preparing to enter the mayor's race, later retracted his vote. Tom Moran, editorial, "Newark Council Hobbles School Chief and Progress," *Star-Ledger*, May 12, 2013. See the May 2013 video of Baraka on the campaign trail as the candidate situates the fight to defend public schools in an authenticity narrative. "Is Cami Anderson Trying to Intimidate Ras Baraka into Leaving Central H.S.?," https://www.youtube.com/watch?v=JZFxIpNTmDw.

69. Moran, "Newark Council Hobbles School Chief."

70. Moran.

5. THE CLASH OF DISRUPTORS

1. "Challenging the Education Status Quo." On the admiration being mutual, see Klein's 2010 *Washington Post* editorial "School Reform's New Generation," June 10, 2011.

2. Emphasis added.

3. Emphasis added.

4. On the Gates Foundation's chief education officer making the same argument in her congresional testimony, see Saltman, *Gift of Education*, 104–5.

5. Peggy McGlone, "Newark Schools Chief Gets New Pact—Reorganization Plan to Face Local Review," *Star-Ledger*, June 28, 2014. On Anderson's belief in the "powers of disruption theory," see Bob Braun, "Cami Insults Top Newark High School Principal and He Says He Is Leaving," *Bob Braun's Ledger* (blog), June 26, 2015, http://www.bobbraunsledger.com/cami-insults-top-newark-high-school-principal-and-he-says-he-is-leaving/.

6. Cooper-Basch, "Evolution," 293.

322 || NOTES TO CHAPTER 5

7. Cited in Davis, "Newark School Reform Wars."

8. Owen Davis, "Flipping Schools: The Hidden Forces behind New Jersey Education Reform," *Truthout*, August 9, 2014, https://truthout.org/articles/flipping-schools-the-hidden-forces-behind-new-jersey-education-reform/.

9. Jeannette Runquist, "Christie's Budget Cuts Left N.J. Schools Unable to Provide 'Thorough and Efficient' Education, Judge Rules," *NJ.com*, March 22, 2011, https://www.nj.com/news/index.ssf/2011/03/christies_school_aid_cuts_left.html.

10. Healthy Schools Now to Governor Christie, June 26, 2013, in possession of the author; "SDA Continues Spending Spree on Administrative Overhead," Education Law Center, January 21, 2014, http://www.edlaw center.org/news/archives/school-facilities/sda-continues-spending-spree-on-administrative-overhead.html; Davis, "Flipping Schools."

11. Arne Duncan, "Key Policy Letters from the Education Secretary or Deputy Secretary," March 29, 2009, https://www2.ed.gov/policy/gen/guid/secletter/090529.html.

12. On the elaborate financial maneuvers involved in transferring public assets to private hands, see Braun, "Pink Hula Hoop—Part 1: Is This the Future of Public Schools?," *Bob Braun's Ledger* (blog), https://www.bobbraunsledger.com/the-pink-hula-hoop-part-1-is-this-the-future-of-public-schools/; Bob Braun, "Pink Hula Hoop 2: Follow the Money," *Bob Braun's Ledger* (blog), March 10, 2014, https://www.bobbraunsledger.com/pink-hula-hoop-2-follow-the-money/. For the EDA announcement of the award to TEAM and Uncommon, see "EDA Takes Action to Launch NJ Economic Opportunity Act of 2013," press release, EDA, November 15, 2013, https://www.njeda.com/eda-takes-action-to-launch-nj-economic-opporunity-act-of-2013-on-november-18/; Davis, "Flipping Schools." On the EDA's announcement of Christie's 2013 award to charters, see "Christie Administration Announces $125 Million to Support New Jersey Charter Schools," press release, EDA, March 5, 2013, https://www.njeda.com/christie-administration-announces-125-million-to-support-new-jersey-charter-schools/. On the close connection between EDA board member Tim Carden, an ally of Christie, and the TEAM Academy, see Bob Braun, "Newark School Boss Anderson Cracks Down on Critics, Suspends Five Principals in One Day," *Bob Braun's Ledger* (blog), January 18, 2014, http://www.bobbraunsledger.com/newark-school-boss-anderson-cracks-down-on-critics-suspends-five-principals-in-one-day/.

13. Davis, "Flipping Schools."

14. Davis; Tom De Poto, "Booker, Christie Unveil Education Housing Center," *Star-Ledger*, September 26, 2013; "March 2013 Newsletter: Charter Schools and Qualified School Construction Bonds," National Charter

School Resource Center, April 4, 2013, https://charterschoolcenter.ed.gov/newsletter/march-2013-charter-schools-and-qualified-school-construction-bonds.

15. Davis, "Newark School Reform Wars."

16. Lipman, *New Political Economy,* 69.

17. Margolis, *Moving Up,* 7.

18. Russakoff, *Prize,* 198.

19. Alan Nasser, "'Saving' Social Security: A Neoliberal Recapitulation of Primitive Accumulation," *Monthly Review,* December 2000, 49.

20. Mashea Ashton, editorial, "Charters Aren't the Problem," *Star-Ledger,* May 31, 2013.

21. Russakoff, *Prize,* 199. Some reformers were unhappy with Anderson for not moving aggressively enough on charter expansion during her first two years. Dale Russakoff, "Schooled: Cory Booker, Chris Christie, and Mark Zuckerberg Had a Plan to Reform Newark's Schools. They Got an Education," *New Yorker,* May 19, 2014, http://www.newyorker.com/magazine/2014/05/19/schooled.

22. Russakoff, "Schooled."

23. Cooper-Basch, "Evolution," 300–303.

24. Jennifer Rundquist, "Christie: I Don't Care What Critics Say about School Chief—Governor to Reappoint Anderson, Saying She Has Done 'a Great Job' in Newark," *Star-Ledger,* September 5, 2013.

25. Mark Weber and Bruce Baker, "An Empirical Critique of One Newark," January 24, 2014, https://njedpolicy.files.wordpress.com/2014/03/weber-baker-onenewarkresponsefinalreview1.pdf.

26. Peggy McGlone, "Newark School Restructuring Includes Plans to Put Charters in District Buildings," *NJ.com,* December 18, 2013, https://www.nj.com/education/2013/12/newark_school_plan_restructure.html.

27. For further elaboration on these concerns, see the statement by NPS parent Veronica Branch, "The One Newark Plan: Newark's Super Storm," in possession of the author.

28. During a second attempt, Anderson was able to deliver her presentation. NPS school board meeting, December 17, 2013, https://www.youtube.com/watch?v=pSRWbQS2JNg; Peggy McGlone, "Newark Charter School Plan Sparks Fury," *Star-Ledger,* December 18, 2013; John Mooney, "'One Newark' Reform Plan Proves Divisive Even before Official Release," *NJ Spotlight,* December 18, 2013, http://www.njspotlight.com/stories/13/12/18/one-newark-reform-plan-proves-divisive-even-before-official-release/.

29. Interview with Grace Sergio, February 2, 2016; South Ward councilman and mayoral candidate Ras Baraka at Weequahic High School, December 20, 2013, https://www.youtube.com/watch?v=AIEFM4eX9Vw.

30. Russakoff, *Prize,* 205; Peggy McGlone, "Newark Schools Get $100M

324 || NOTES TO CHAPTER 5

for Repairs," *Star-Ledger,* December 22, 2013; text of 2014 Christie's state of the state address, Associated Press wire service, January 14, 2014.

31. Russakoff, *Prize,* 202.

32. Peggy McGlone, "Parents, Alumni, Others Protest to Reorganize Newark Schools," *Star-Ledger,* January 15, 2014.

33. Craig McCarthy, "Kimble Joins Essex County Democrats in Endorsing Christie," *Belleville Patch,* June 20, 2013; Bob Braun, "Pastors: Cami Must Stop!," *Bob Braun's Ledger* (blog), April 20, 2014, http://www.bobbraunsledger.com/pastors-cami-must-stop/; Kathleen O'Brien, "Chris Christie Inauguration Service Is Underway at Newark Church," *Inside New Jersey,* January 21, 2014, https://www.nj.com/politics/index.ssf/2014/01/christie_inauguation.html.

34. For a refutation of Hawthorne's failing status, see the statement by PTSA president Grace Sergio, "The Secret Success of Newark's Hawthorne Ave. School," Stand4education, https://kaleenab.wordpress.com/2014/04/07/the-secret-success-of-newarks-hawthorne-ave-school-by-grace-sergio/.

35. Peggy McGlone, "5 Newark Principals Suspended Indefinitely, Allegedly for Opposing One Newark Plan," *NJ.com,* January 20, 2014, http://www.nj.com/education/2014/01/5_newark_principals_have_been_suspended_alledgedly_for_opposing_one_newark_plan.html. On other actions mounted by Sergio and Hawthorne's PTSA to keep their school open, see Bob Braun, "Cry for Newark," *Bob Braun's Ledger* (blog), April 30, 2014, http://www.bobbraunsledger.com/cry-for-newark/. On a petition drive to stop the plan, see "Newark Residents Begin Petition Drive to Block Christie Plan for Closing City Schools," *Bob Braun's Ledger* (blog), December 27, 2013, http://www.bobbraunsledger.com/newark-residents-begin-petition-drive-to-block-christie-plan-for-closing-city-schools/.

36. McGlone, "5 Newark principals"; Braun, "Newark School Boss Anderson."

37. Bob Braun, "Newark's Schools—Where Parent Notices Are Torn Up and Bathroom Conversations Are Monitored," *Bob Braun's Ledger* (blog), January 21, 2014, http://www.bobbraunsledger.com/newarks-schools-where-parent-notices-are-torn-up-and-bathroom-conversations-are-monitored/. On "aggravated assault" charges against parent Darren Martin for the January 15 incident, see Bob Braun, "Newark Parent Leader Arrested, Jailed, after Criticizing State Plan to Close Schools," *Bob Braun's Ledger* (blog), February 4, 2014, http://www.bobbraunsledger.com/newark-parent-leader-arrested-jailed-after-criticizing-state-plan-to-close-schools/.

38. Emphasis original.

39. Newark Public Schools, School Advisory Board meeting, January 28, 2014, https://www.youtube.com/watch?v=6bXumkUfkLQ.

40. Nilsen and Cox, "What Would a Marxist Theory," 71. Anderson

would continue to attend the board's monthly business meeting, but not the fourth-Tuesday board meeting, where public comment was a prominent component. Newark Public Schools, School Advisory Board meeting, part III, https://www.youtube.com/watch?v=oksM3yzJ5kk.

41. James Trim, "Christie, Teachers Unions Agree on Merit Pay for Newark Teachers," MSNBC, November 16, 2012, http://www.msnbc.com/morning-joe/christie-teachers-unions-agree-merit-pay; Newark Public Schools School Advisory Board meeting, Part II, https://www.youtube.com/watch?v=9fRnfog x394. On Weingarten shifting from her collaborationist stance, including renouncing Gates grants, see Ryan, *Educational Justice*, 69.

42. Michelle Fine and Michael Fabricant, "What It Takes to Unite Teachers Unions and Communities of Color," *The Nation*, October 12, 2014; Alliance to Reclaim Our Schools, http://www.reclaimourschools.org/about.

43. On the national coalition, see Center for Popular Democracy, "National Day of Action to Reclaim Public Education in Over 60 Cities," press release, December 9, 2013, http://populardemocracy.org/news/national-day-action-reclaim-public-education-over-60-cities; Peggy McGlone, "Unions, Students Rally in Newark for More Local Control of Schools," *Star-Ledger*, December 10, 2013.

44. "Communities United and the Newark Students Union Endorse Ras Baraka for Mayor 2014," https://www.youtube.com/ watch?v=91dpxJ5HxC4.

45. Peggy McGlone, "Newark Parents, Teachers and Students Take Protest to Trenton," *Star-Ledger*, March 28, 2014. On activists' support for Senator Rice's bill to award state-controlled districts the power to block school closings, see Peggy McGlone, "Bill Pushes Local Control of School Closings," *Star-Ledger*, January 31, 2014.

46. Interview with Kristin Towkanik, June 30, 2016; "Newark Students Stage Walkout for Underserved Schools," Al Jazeera, April 3, 2014, http://america.aljazeera.com/watch/shows/the-stream/the-stream-officialblog/2014/4/3/newark-students-stagewalkoutforunderservedschools.html. On the police action at Shabbaz, see https://www.facebook.com/NewarkStudentsUnion/posts/ 627359434006991. Promotional video by NSU for the April 3 walkout, "Are You Walking Out?," March 30, 2014, https://www.youtube.com/watch?v=o6FzLkifmFk.

47. Jeffries's *Star-Ledger* editorials began in 2007, while he was board president of TEAM (KIPP) Academy, and continued through 2012. See "Integration and a Condescending View of Black Kids," *Star-Ledger*, September 19, 2007. In his August 2010 editorial, at the time of the Zuckerburg award and before the opposition gathered force, he pushed hard for key elements of the reform agenda, such as weakening tenure and collective

326 || NOTES TO CHAPTER 5

bargaining and expanding charters. Jeffries, "Newark Schools Need Revolutionary Reform," *Star-Ledger*, August 31, 2010; Jeffries, "Newark Schools Need to Be Back in Local Hands," *Star-Ledger*, December 21, 2010; Jeffries, "What Constitutes Meaningful Change," *Star-Ledger*, March 4, 2011; Jeffries, "After School Program Save Kids (Including Me)," *Star-Ledger*, July 8, 2012. For Moran's editorials backing the reform effort while encouraging greater effort to garner consent, see Moran, "A Valuable Lesson—Newark Shouldn't Leave the Public out of the School Reform Process," *Star-Ledger*, February 24, 2011; Moran, "Home Rule Is Ideal—but Newark School Board's Dysfunction Might Endanger Reforms of State-Run District," *Star-Ledger*, August 14, 2011; Moran, "In Newark, a School Reformer Needs Help"; Moran, "Newark Council Hobbles School Chief and Progress," *Star-Ledger*, May 12, 2013.

48. Editorial, "Newark's Turning Point—Embattled Superintendent Can Put Schools on the Right Path—with Support," *Star-Ledger*, February 9, 2014, emphasis added.

49. Interview with Reverend William Howard, October 18, 2016.

50. Barry Carter, "Newark Pastor Leaves Church with Legacy of Social Justice, Community Outreach," *NJ.com*, January 1, 2016, http://www.nj.com/essex/index.ssf/2016/01/newark_pastor_leaves_church_with_legacy_of_social.html; https://en.wikipedia.org/wiki/M._William_Howard,_Jr.

51. "Five New Charters Schools Win State's Approval," *Star-Ledger*, January 19, 2005.

52. Moran, "In Newark, a School Reformer Needs Help."

53. Russakoff, "Schooled."

54. Emphasis original.

55. Reed, "Antiracism."

56. Interview with Reverend Mamie Bridgeforth. Cerf went to head an "education technology" subsidiary of Rupert Murdoch's empire run by Joel Klein, his old boss. Leslie Brody, "N.J. Schools Chief Quits to Lead Education Firm," *Star-Ledger*, February 11, 2014. For a detailed examination of Cerf's career, including how he has financially benefited from the privatization of public education, see Jersey Jazzman, "Chris Cerf Story."

57. Julie O'Connor, "Newark's School Wars—Clergy Members Fire Latest Salvo That Shows Superintendent Has Lost Control," *Star-Ledger*, April 20, 2014; Reverend Ronald Slaughter, a signatory of the 2012 letter and head of a charter school that had just received state approval for a K–12 expansion, did not sign. For the full text of the letter, see Braun, "Pastors: Cami Must Stop!" For more on Slaughter, see Peggy McGlone, "NJ Revokes 2 Charter Schools, Renews 10 Others," *NJ.com*, https://www.nj.com/education/2014/03/nj_revokes_2_charter_schools_renews_10_others.html.

NOTES TO CHAPTER 5 || 327

58. John Mooney, "Analysis: School Chief's Rehiring Raises Questions, Reflects Broader Issues," *NJ Spotlight,* June 30, 2014, http://www.njspotlight .com/stories/14/06/29/analysis-newark-school-chief-s-rehiring-raises -questions-reflects-broader-issues/. On the *Star-Ledger* admonishing Howard for his boycott of the working group, and urging other local leaders to join, see Julie O'Connor, "Cease-Fire on Newark Schools—Local Leaders Should Step Up and Advise the Superintendent," *Star-Ledger,* July 6, 2014.

59. Russakoff, *Prize,* 211; Emma Brown, "D.C. Losing De'Shawn Wright, Deputy Mayor for Education," *Washington Post,* October 18, 2012, https:// www.washingtonpost.com/local/education/dc-losing-deshawn-wright -deputy-mayor-for-education/2012/10/18/a49cd39a-1967-11e2-bd10 -5ff056538b7c_story.html; Nikolai Barrickman, "Washington DC Schools Plan to Expand Charters, Cut Jobs," World Socialist Web Site, May 15, 2012, https://www.wsws.org/en/articles/2012/05/dcps-m15.html. While the *Washington Post* praised Henderson, school employees denounced how she "patrolled and enforced her domain with impunity," creating "a unique culture of fear." Jeffery Anderson, "Kaya Henderson's Undeserved Legacy as an Educational Empress Finally Unravels," *Washington City Paper,* June 1, 2017, http://www.washingtoncitypaper.com/news/loose-lips/article/ 20863252/kaya-hendersons-undeserved-legacy-as-an-educational-empress -finally-unravels.

60. Cooper-Basch, "Evolution," 316.

61. Cooper-Basch, 301.

62. On Koeppe's faltering faith in Anderson, see Mooney, "Analysis."

63. Max Pizarro, "Examining the Joe D. 2017 Trial Balloon," *Observer,* March 28, 2016, http://observer.com/2016/03/examining-the-joe-d-2017 -trial-balloon/; Matt Friedman, "Spending by Outside Groups on Newark's Mayoral Race Topped $5 Million," *NJ.com,* July 28, 2014, http://www.nj .com/politics/index.ssf/2014/07/spending_by_outside_groups_on_ newarks_mayoral_race_topped_5_million.html. On Democrats for Education Reform, and their allied Education Reform Now Advocacy group, see https://dfer.org/ and https://edreformnow.org/.

64. David Chen and Kate Zernike, "Newark's Voters Choose New Mayor and New Path," *New York Times,* May 14, 2014; Kate Zernike, "Rebuke of Charter Schools Is Seen in Newark Election," *New York Times,* May 15, 2014.

65. Lesli Maxwell, "Newark's New Mayor Demands Return of Schools to Local Control," *Education Week,* May 17, 2014, http://blogs.edweek.org/ edweek/District_Dossier/2014/05/newarks_new_mayor_and_teachers .html?cmp=ENL-EU-NEWS3.

66. "Rally to Stop the One Newark Plan!," May 20, 2014, NEW Caucus, flyer in possession of the author.

328 || NOTES TO CHAPTER 5

67. On the May 20 action, see "Press Locked Out of Newark Public Schools Board Meeting," May 20, 2014, https://www.youtube.com/watch?v=ZcEEwpLFmfY. On the sit-in, see "Newark Students Union Protest at NPS Board Meeting," May 20, 2014, https://www.youtube.com/watch?v=rBCi21i5tjs; "Newark Students Sit-In at 2 Cedar St. and Demand to Be Heard," May 21, 2014, https://www.youtube.com/watch?v=CZKFCfilUx8.

68. Naomi Nix, "Students Vow to Keep Fighting One Newark Plan," *Star-Ledger*, May 28, 2014.

69. Peggy McGlone, "Newark's Hawthorne Avenue to Remain Neighborhood K–8 School," *NJ.com*, June 14, 2014, https://www.nj.com/education/2014/06/newarks_hawthorne_avenue_school_to_stay_open_from_k-8.html. Cami Anderson to Hawthorne Avenue families, June 12, 2014, in possession of the author.

70. Peggy McGlone, "Residents File Legal Complaint against 'One Newark'—Parents Claim School District Reorganization Plan Promotes Racial Segregation," *Star-Ledger*, August 19, 2014. NAACP president Deborah Smith-Gregory and several other Newark residents also filed a lawsuit against One Newark for violating "the New Jersey constitution, which prohibits racial segregation in public schools." On Bragaw becoming "KIPP Life Academy," the "Network's first turnaround charter school," see http://kippnj.org/schools/kipp-life-academy/.

71. John Mooney, "Feds Investigating Whether 'One Newark' Schools Initiative Is Discriminatory," *NJ Spotlight*, July 23, 2014, http://www.njspotlight.com/stories/14/07/22/feds-investigating-whether-one-newark-plan-is-discriminatory/. On earlier efforts to combat school closures by filing civil rights complaints at the U.S. Department of Education, backed by the Schott and Annenberg Foundations, see John Mooney, "Newark Parents and Activists Take School Closure Complaint to D.C. for Civil Rights Hearing," *NJ Spotlight*, January 28, 2013, http://www.njspotlight.com/stories/13/01/27/newark-parents-and-activists-take-school-closure-complaint-to-d-c-for-civil-rights-hearing/.

72. Mooney, "Analysis."

73. Mooney.

74. Ras Baraka, "A Message from Ras Baraka to Charter School parents," Believe in Newark, 2014, in possession of the author.

6. RAS BARAKA'S SELF-DETERMINATION POLITICS

1. Bob and Barbara Dreyfuss, "Ras Baraka's Victory in Newark Could Revitalize New Jersey Progressives," *The Nation*, May 14, 2014; Seth Sandronsky and Michelle Renee Matisons, "Indicting Education Crimes," *Counterpunch*, May 19, 2014, https://www.counterpunch.org/2014/05/19/

NOTES TO CHAPTER 6 || 329

indicting-education-crimes/; Max Blumenthal, "Newark Mayoral Election: Street Fight 2014," *Truthout*, May 19, 2014, http://www.truth-out.org/news/item/23795-new-jersey-mayoral-election-street-fight-2014. For more on Baraka and the movement-driven urban progressivism wave theme, see Fine and Fabricant, "What It Takes to Unite Teachers Unions." On the contradictions of the supposed progressive wave, see Sam Stein, "Progress for Whom, toward What? Progressive Politics and New York City's Inclusionary Housing," *Journal of Urban Affairs* 40, no. 6 (2018): 770–81.

2. Ras Baraka, eulogy at the funeral of his father, Amiri Baraka, January 18, 2014, http://www.ustream.tv/recorded/42843628.

3. Imamu Amiri Baraka, "Newark Seven Years Later: ¡Unidad y Lucha!," *Monthly Review* 26, no. 8 (1975): 16.

4. Emphasis added.

5. Mayor Ras Baraka Inauguration Ceremonies, July 1, 2014, https://www.youtube.com/watch?v=mdk8hbNtkkY.

6. Annie Correal, "Remembering Amiri Baraka with Politics and Poetry," *New York Times*, January 18, 2014.

7. Editorial, "Shavar Jeffries for Newark Mayor," *Star-Ledger*, May 9, 2014.

8. Johnson, *From Revolutionaries to Race Leaders*, 42.

9. Reed, "Antiracism"; A. Philip Randolph Institute, *A "Freedom Budget" for All Americans: Budgeting Our Resources 1965–1975 to Achieve "Freedom from Want"* (New York: APRI, 1966).

10. Cited in Johnson, *From Revolutionaries to Race Leaders*, xxvii.

11. Johnson, 86.

12. On the intellectual roots and class biases of ethnic pluralism, see Reed, *Toward Freedom*, 49–76. On Amiri Baraka characterizing the struggle in Newark as an "anticolonial" one, see Baraka, "Newark Seven Years Later," 16–24.

13. Johnson, *From Revolutionaries to Race Leaders*, xxx.

14. Johnson, 63, 68.

15. Cited in Johnson, 70.

16. Rickford, *We Are an African People*. On the African Free School, see Baraka, *Autobiography*, 420–21; Woodard, *A Nation Within*, 126–28.

17. Johnson, *From Revolutionaries to Race Leaders*, 68, emphasis added.

18. On the "process of black nationality formation" being at the heart of Baraka's movement, and the rationale behind the myriad social, political, economic, and cultural groups he helped forge locally, nationally, and internationally, see Woodard, *A Nation Within*, esp. 2; Johnson, *From Revolutionaries to Race Leaders*, 220.

19. Johnson, *From Revolutionaries to Race Leaders*, 70.

20. After breaking with Gibson, and embracing Maoism, Baraka's

330 || NOTES TO CHAPTER 6

Congress of Afrikan People became the Revolutionary Communist League. The RCL later merged into the League of Revolutionary Struggle (LRS), "a POC-majority Marxist Leninist group." Brad Duncan, "Fred Ho, Presente!," *Against the Current,* September 2014, https://againstthecurrent.org/atc172/p4252/. On the continuing centrality of national self-determination following Baraka's turn to Maoism, see Amiri Baraka, "Nationalism, Self-Determination and Socialist Revolution," *Black Nation,* Fall/Winter 1982, https://www.marxists.org/history/erol/ncm-7/lrs-baraka.htm.

21. His other siblings were Obalaji (1967), Shani (1972), Amiri Jr. (1973), and Ahi (1974). http://riseupnewark.com/amina-baraka/.

22. D. Ayres, "Protest at Howard U. Brings a Surprising Review," *New York Times,* March 16, 1989; R. Smothers, "Backers of Newark Group Say Brutality Protests Spurred Raid," *New York Times,* September 3, 1997.

23. See a flyer for a 1996 demonstration calling for "Resignation of Newark's Mayor, Police Chief," in possession of the author.

24. Steve Chamber, "Protesters Want Newark Mayor and Police Director to Resign," *Star-Ledger,* February 25, 1996. On the central role Baraka played leading protests against the June 1997 police killing of Dannette "Strawberry" Daniels, see Dawn Onley, "Frustration Mounting over Cop Shootings," *Star-Ledger,* June 16, 1997. For video of a City Hall rally in the Strawberry case and a 1998 city council run, see https://www.indiegogo.com/projects/take-it-personal-the-movie#/. Baraka also ran unsuccessfully for at-large council seats in 1998, 2002, and 2006. On his efforts to restore the right to address any issue at city council meetings, which Booker supported as well, see Michael Watkins, "10 Arrested Protesting for Right to Speak Out—Activists Disrupt Meeting with Song," *Star-Ledger,* November 17, 1998; Jesse Drucker, "Citizens Demand to Address City Council—Baraka Leads Protest of Newark Restriction," *Star-Ledger,* December 17, 1998.

25. The Coalition formed following the July 2009 killing of Nakisha Allen in Newark. See "About the Newark Anti-Violence Coalition," http://www.navcoalition.org/about/. An earlier iteration of this work was a 2003 Stop the Violence march that Baraka organized with Bashir Akinyele, a longtime ally. Akinyele diagnosed "our problem" as "black-on-black crime" and the gang culture that promotes it. Barry Carter, "Stop the Violence March to Wind through City—Protestors Will Go Door-to-Door in the South Ward," *Star-Ledger,* August 29, 2003.

26. Nikita Stewart, "Newark Cops Deny Permit for Youth March," *Star-Ledger,* November 4, 1999. Further underscoring the Booker–Baraka alliance, both ran in 1998 as part of the youth candidates challenging the old guard. Amiri Baraka characterized Booker and his son as the "Insurgent candidates" challenging the "city's political establishment," who have tried

NOTES TO CHAPTER 6 || 331

to lock out "young people." Jesse Drucker and George E. Jordan, "Poll Challengers Rattle Newark's Establishment—Political Vets Lay Plans to Fend Off Newcomers," *Star-Ledger,* May 17, 1998.

27. "Raising Voices and Complaints—City Hall Protesters Take Booker to Task," *Star-Ledger,* November 16, 2006.

28. This slate, indicating a further distancing from the protests Baraka's Black Nia FORCE led in the 1990s against police brutality, included Clifford Minor, who unsuccessfully challenged Booker in his reelection bid. Minor was the Essex County prosecutor who oversaw the grand jury that failed to bring an indictment against the police officer who killed Dannette "Strawberry" Daniels, a decision Baraka's group denounced at the time. Ronald Smothers, "Newark Officer Is Cleared in Shooting during Arrest," *New York Times,* September 5, 1997.

29. David Giambusso, "Ex-Prosecutor Minor to Face Booker in Mayoral Contest, 'Newark Choice' Council Ticket Includes Ras Baraka and Sharpe James's Son, John," *Star-Ledger,* January 28, 2010.

30. David Giambusso, "Newark Candidates Call Truce with Charter Schools," *Star-Ledger,* March 31, 2013.

31. Pauline Lippman, "Neoliberal Education Restructuring," *Monthly Review,* July 1, 2011.

32. Neil Smith, *The New Urban Frontier: Gentrification and the Revanchist City* (New York: Routledge, 1996).

33. Jason Nark, "Is Newark the Next Brooklyn?," *Politico,* March 19, 2015. Beit elaborates on his consortium's land acquisition and redevelopments plans for downtown Newark in an April 6, 2015, address to an audience that included "William C. Dudley, President & CEO of New York Federal Reserve, Mayor Ras J. Baraka, and representatives from the City of Newark, Goldman Sachs, Prudential, and various press." https://www.youtube.com / watch?v=UpGSrKpc5MY.

34. Loretta Lees, Thomas Slater, and Elvin Wyly, *Gentrification* (London: Routledge, 2007), 23, 174.

35. Joshua Burd, "Beit Credits EDA, Urban Transit Hub Incentive at Newark Groundbreaking," *NJ Biz,* February 9, 2012, http://www.njbiz.com/article/20120209/NJBIZ01/120209802/Beit-credits-EDA-Urban-Transit-Hub-incentive-at-Newark-groundbreaking.

36. Tom Dallessio, "Forget the 'Next Brooklyn,' Bring on the Next Newark," https://nextcity.org/daily/entry/newark-development-ron-beit.

37. Tom De Poto, "Booker, Christie Unveil Education Housing Center," *Star-Ledger,* September 26, 2013.

38. Salvador Rizzo, "State OKs Teachers Village for Newark," *Star-Ledger,* August 26, 2011; Burd, "Beit Credits EDA."

332 || NOTES TO CHAPTER 6

39. Tom De Poto, "Newark Developers to Present Plan to Make Historic Four Corners Residential," *NJ.com*, December 19, 2012, http://www.nj.com/business/index.ssf/2012/12/newark_developers_to_present_p.html; De Poto, "State Awards $52 Million in Tax Breaks for Redevelopment at Newark's 'Four Corners,'" *NJ.com*, January 15, 2014, http://www.nj.com/business/index.ssf/2014/01/state_awards_52_million_in_tax_breaks_for_newark_project.html.

40. Burd, "Beit Credits EDA."

41. "NEWARK The Living Downtown Plan, a Redevelopment Plan for Downtown Newark, New Jersey, City of Newark," May 23, 2008, in possession of the author; Philip Read, "With Lofts in Newark, Things Are Looking Up," *Star-Ledger*, November 21, 2010.

42. Pryor left the administration in 2011 to become Connecticut's education commissioner. David Giambusso, "Newark's Deputy Mayor Leaving Administration to Become Connecticut's Education Commissioner," *NJ.com*, September 6, 2011, http://www.nj.com/news/index.ssf/2011/09/newark_mayor_cory_bookers_aide.html. For more on the Partnership for New York, see Alex Ulam, "Subsidizing Inequality: New York City's Crooked Development Agenda," *Dissent,* June 23, 2014, https://www.dissentmagazine.org/online_articles/subsidizing-inequality-new-york-citys-crooked-development-agenda.

43. "NEWARK The Living Downtown Plan."

44. David Giambusso, "Baraka Makes Pitch to Newark Business Community: 'I Don't Have Horns,'" *NJ.com*, August 25, 2013, emphasis added, https://www.nj.com/essex/2013/08/baraka_makes_a_pitch_to_newark_business_community_i_dont_have_horns.html.

45. Max Pizarro, "Guadagno Attempts to Plant Political Seeds in the Ironbound," *The Observer,* July 9, 2015, https://observer.com/2015/07/guadagno-attempts-to-plant-political-seeds-in-the-ironbound/.

46. Doug Henwood, "Why Should the Left Support Obama?," *The Nation*, September 12, 2012.

47. Naomi Nix, "Students Skip School to Protest Overhaul," *Star-Ledger*, September 10, 2014; Bob Braun, "Our Leaders, the Kids," *Bob Braun's Ledger* (blog), September 9, 2014, http://www.bobbraunsledger.com/our-leaders-the-kids/.

48. https://www.youtube.com/watch?v=mIpdWVfszAE; Baraka speaks at the 1:30 point.

49. Author's observation notes, September 13, 2014.

50. Author's observation notes.

51. Author's observation notes.

52. For the list of organizations represented at the Convention, see

pp. 2–3 of the Convention Report, http://www.ci.newark.nj.us/wp-content/uploads/2015/03/RTV_Report-2015.pdf.

53. Kate Zernike, "Rebuke of Charter Schools Is Seen in Newark Election," *New York Times,* May 14, 2014.

54. Emphasis added.

55. Newark Community Education Convention, day 1, Ras Baraka address, video 1, emphasis original, http://www.ci.newark.nj.us/government/mayor/community-education-convention/.

56. Emphasis added.

57. Reed, *Toward Freedom.*

58. The composition of the attendees reflected not only the philosophy of class collaboration but the panels as well, which brought together activists from both sides. Among funders of the convention—another parallel with many of the Black political conventions, which often relied on corporate funding—only the AFT, reflecting the imbalance of financial resources between the movements from above and below, came from the public school defense movement. Most of the other funders were firmly in the reform camp, including TFA, NCSF, NTE, FNF, Education Reform Now, and Prudential. For a list of panels, see Newark Community Education Convention, http://www.ci.newark.nj.us/government/mayor/community-education-convention/.

59. Lipman, *New Political Economy,* 63; Harvey, *A Brief History of Neoliberalism.*

60. Ras J. Baraka, editorial, "A New Start for Newark Schools," *New York Times,* October 20, 2014.

61. Lyndsey Layton, "Detractors Trail Newark School Chief to D.C.," *Star-Ledger,* November 14, 2014; Bob Braun, "Cami Anderson: A National Embarrassment," *Bob Braun's Ledger* (blog), November 14, 2014, http://www.bobbraunsledger.com/cami-anderson-a-national-embarrassment/; Cami Anderson on Newark, American Enterprise Institute, November 14, 2014, https://www.youtube.com/watch?v=nbKvYMnPRDA.

62. Whelan et al., "Urban Regimes," 15, emphasis added.

63. Reed, *Stirrings in the Jug,* 5.

64. Barker, "Class Struggle," 28.

65. Reed, "Antiracism," 1.

66. Jaysen Bazile and Thais Marquez, "Raging against the Machine: The George Zimmerman Verdict," *Star-Ledger,* July 17, 2013.

67. Cedric Johnson, "An Open Letter to Ta-Nehisi Coates and the Liberals Who Love Him," *Jacobin,* February 3, 2016; Johnson, "Panthers Can't Save Us Now."

NOTES TO CHAPTER 7

7. WE ALL BECOME MAYOR?

1. Cited in Naomi Nix, "Baraka Asks for Newark Superintendent's Resignation; Again," *NJ.com*, January 15, 2015, https://www.nj.com/essex/2015/01/baraka_asks_for_newark_superintendents_resignation.html.

2. Margolis, *Moving Up*, 7.

3. Percentages are based on the general fund revenues for a given year. Newark Public Schools, FY 2011–12 budget hearing, http://content.nps.k12.nj.us/wp-content/uploads/2014/10/2011-2012BudgetPresentation.pdf; Newark Public Schools, FY 2014 budget hearing, http://content.nps.k12.nj.us/wp-content/uploads/2014/08/SABBudgetFinal1314ReadOnly.pdf.

4. Newark Public Schools, FY 2014 budget hearing.

5. Harvey, *A Brief History*, 66. See also Purcell, *Recapturing Democracy*, 12, 27.

6. Harvey, *Rebel Cities*, 23.

7. Emphasis original.

8. Piven, *Challenging Authority*.

9. Lipman, *New Political Economy*, 34.

10. https://www.youtube.com/watch?v=dC11XV58N6U; Christie refers to the "education establishment" at the 9:10 mark.

11. Henry Veltmeyer, James Petras, and Steve Vieux, *Neoliberalism and Class Conflict in Latin America: A Comparative Perspective on the Political Economy of Structural Adjustment* (New York: Macmillan, 1997), 177.

12. For the Henderson and Duncan quotes, see Russakoff, "Schooled." Exemplifying the concerted effort by the movement to diversify the charter managerial ranks, as well as a push by the BPMC to promote its material interests as those of all African Americans, is the New Orleans–based Alliance for Diversity and Excellence, http://www.adeleadership.com/home. The New Orleans–based group Overcoming Racism is another organizational expression of the intramovement efforts to address diversity in charter schools and promote entrepreneurial opportunities for the BPMC. The group, founded by a former assistant principal at the KIPP charter in New Orleans, describes itself as dedicated "to build[ing] more equitable institutions, through comprehensive race and equity training, [w]ith a primary focus on education," especially charters. https://www.overcomeracism.com/. Jennifer Larino, "5 New Orleans Education Startups to Watch," *Nola.com*, December 1, 2016, https://www.nola.com/business/index.ssf/2016/12/new_orleans_education_startups.html.

13. Her son was a movement activist himself, having been a TFA volunteer in Texas, and then taught for two years at a New York City KIPP charter school. Russakoff, *Prize*, 220.

14. Cerf whined, according to Moran, that Russakoff unfairly "slimed the

reform movement." While Moran cheerleaded the success of the charters, measured in narrow test score terms, he concurred with Russakoff that the "reformers blew the politics of this, provoking a backlash," and with her characterization of Anderson's "political ham-handedness." Tom Moran, "Newark Students Are Better Off, Despite the Political Noise," *NJ.com*, September 6, 2015, https://www.nj.com/opinion/index.ssf/2015/09/newark_moran.html.

15. Naomi Nix, "State Renews Contract of City's Besieged Schools Chief," *Star-Ledger*, February 27, 2015; Dan Ivers, "Superintendent's Severance Pay Is a Question as She Departs," *Star-Ledger*, July 1, 2015.

16. Naomi Nix, "Baraka Again Is Seeking School Chief's Resignation," *Star-Ledger*, January 16, 2015; Mayor Ras Baraka to Cami Anderson, January 12, 2015.

17. Flyer in possession of the author; Rosi Efthim, "Mayor Ras Baraka's Office Joining Local Groups Demanding Cami Anderson's Resignation," *Blue New Jersey*, February 6, 2015, http://www.bluejersey.com/2015/02/mayor-ras-barakas-office-joining-local-groups-demanding-cami-andersons-resignation/.

18. Naomi Nix, "Newark Student Sit-In Lasted through the Night at District Headquarters," *NJ.com*, February 18, 2015, http://www.nj.com/essex/index.ssf/2015/02/newark_student_sit-in_lasted_through_the_night_at.html #incart_story_package; Nix, "Newark Student Activists 'Occupy' District Offices," *NJ.com*, February 17, 2015, http://www.nj.com/essex/index.ssf/2015/02/live_newark_student_activists_occupy_district_offi.html#incart_story_package; Nix, "Coalition Blasts Newark District's Treatment of Student Activists," *NJ.com*, February 19, 2015, http://www.nj.com/essex/index.ssf/2015/02/coaltion_blasts_newark_districts_treatment_of_tud.html#incart_story_package.

19. Piven, *Challenging Authority*, 29.

20. Nix, "State Renews Contract." On Ruiz's legislative interventions opposing any caps on charter expansion, see Laura Waters, guest editorial, "Shift in NJEA's Stance on Charter Schools Is Fraught with Tension," *Star-Ledger*, October 26, 2014. On Anderson's grilling by Senators Ronald Rice Sr. and Ruiz, see Naomi Nix, "Irate Lawmakers Question Newark Superintendent about Reform Plan," *Star-Ledger*, January 7, 2015. Bob Braun, "Sensing Cami Anderson's Weakness, Baraka Heats Up Attack," *Bob Braun's Ledger* (blog), January 16, 2015, https://www.bobbraunsledger.com/sensing-cami-andersons-weakness-baraka-heats-up-attack/.

21. Newark School Board advisory meeting, February 24, 2015, https://www.youtube.com/watch?v=9Ig357FOINo.

22. Newark School Board advisory meeting, April 28, 2015, https://www.youtube.com/watch?v=8OwJYwDe2mE.

336 || NOTES TO CHAPTER 7

23. Emphasis original.

24. Author's observation notes.

25. After four years as principal in the Klein-run New York City Department of Education, Haggerty graduated to a position with New Visons for Public Schools, part of what Braun called the "endless number of private, non-governmental organizations" with which Anderson surrounded herself. For background on other members of Anderson's team, see Bob Braun, "No $ for Newark Kids, Lots for Cami Pals," *Bob Braun's Ledger* (blog), https://www.bobbraunsledger.com/no-for-newark-kids-plenty-for-cami-pals/.

26. We Oppose the One Newark Plan, April 22, 2015, https://www.facebook.com/weoppRosetheonenewarkscandal/.

27. Interview with Moussab, October 10, 2015; NEW meeting notes, April 22, 2015.

28. #WeAreEastSide, April 25, 2015, https://www.youtube.com/watch?v=LcZoIPfAWIo.

29. Naomi Nix, "Newark HS Students Protest District Turnaround Program in Front of Bridgegate Reporters," *NJ.com,* May 1, 2015, http://www.nj.com/essex/index.ssf/2015/05/newark_hs_students_protest_district_turnaround_pro.html; video of walkout, May 1, 2015, https://www.facebook.com/NjCommunitiesUnited/videos/vb.206725559432963/668138106625037/.

30. Interview with Bashir Akinyele, February 12, 2016. On the May 5 sit-in by Weequahic students in the school gym, see https://www.facebook.com/weopposetheonenewarkscandal/.

31. Notes from April 22, 2015, NEW meeting. On ethnic, racial, and geographic tensions in Newark, see Ana Y. Ramos-Zayas, *Street Therapists: Race, Affect, and Neoliberal Personhood in Latino Newark* (Chicago: University of Chicago Press, 2012).

32. Interview with Moussab; "Mayor Ras Baraka Addresses Weequahic Rally," May 2, 2015, https://www.youtube.com/watch?v=QDBf_vh2sEU.

33. Interview with Freda Barrow, February 15, 2016; "May 13 Action East Side Teacher, Ariana Calderon, Speaks at Broad & Raymond Rally," https://www.youtube.com/watch?v=ur0h4y6Tbyw.

34. Author's observation notes, May 13, 2015.

35. The incident, initially posted on Facebook, is now unavailable. Contents in possession of the author.

36. Author's observation notes; Bill Wichert, "Latest Protest Calls Students from Classrooms to City Hall," *Star-Ledger,* May 23, 2015; NJTV News, "Students Say Record Protest Crowd Shows Strong Resistance to Superintendent's Reforms," May 22, 2015, https://www.youtube.com/watch?v=mddmug2LlUE.

NOTES TO CHAPTER 7 || **337**

37. Leonardo, cited in Rebecca Nathanson, "Newark's Chaotic Schools Mess: Why Chris Christie's New Debacle Is Mired in Protest," *Salon,* November 10, 2014, https://www.salon.com/2014/11/10/newarks_chaotic_schools_mess_why_chris_christies_new_debacle_is_mired_in_protest/.

38. On Ruiz turning against Anderson and eventually calling for her resignation, see editorial, "Moment of Truth in Newark," *Star-Ledger,* March 2, 2014; "Newark School Board Asks State to Remove Anderson," *Star-Ledger,* June 5, 2015.

39. Leah Owens, as a NJCU organizer, brought several activists to the chambers to protest the vote. Author's observation notes; "We Oppose the One Newark Plan," May 13, 2015, https://www.facebook.com/weoppose theonenewarkscandal/photos/a.504043096372639.1073741828 .504033096373639/713104322133181/; "Newark City Council Passes Resolution Opposing State Legislation Limiting Charter School Growth, Anibal Ramos Jr. North Ward Councilman," May 12, 2015, http://www .Anibalramosjr.com/newark_city_council_passes_resolution_opposing_ state_legislation_limiting_charter_school_growth.

40. Fine and Fabricant, "What It Takes to Unite Teachers Unions." The Schott Foundation funded a variety of organizations and initiatives that worked with the AFT in these national efforts, including Communities for Public Education Reform (CPER), which included funding for NJCU's initiative, http://schottfoundation.org/blog/2014/12/15/90-wins-8-years -celebrating-communities-public-education-reforms-victories, and the National Opportunity to Learn Campaign, which "unites a nationwide coalition of Schott grantees and allied organizations," http://schott foundation.org/our-work/otl-network. The Alliance for Educational Justice was another Schott-funded initiative begun in 2008 and made up of students. Funding was often routed through existing NGOs, such as Make the Road in New York. For more background, including a list of member groups, see http://schottfoundation.org/content/spotlight-alliance -educational-justice. As of 2017, the group's website, http://www .allianceforeducationaljustice.org/, was no longer functional.

41. Fine and Fabricant, "What It Takes to Unite Teachers Unions"; Alliance to Reclaim Our Schools, "Education Justice Is Racial Justice, 2016–2017" platform, http://www.reclaimourschools.org/take-action/ pledge.

42. Author's observation of Haimson's comments at the School Reform, Communities, and Social Justice: Exploring the Intersections conference, May 19, 2017, Bloustein Center, Rutgers University, New Brunswick, N.J.; "Class Size Matters," Class Size Reduction Research, https://www.class sizematters.org/research-and-links/.

43. Interview with Cabañas, November 3, 2015.

338 || NOTES TO CHAPTER 7

44. The de Blasio representative touted bank and foundation funding of the initiative, which school board president Baskerville-Richardson emphasized "our mayor" fully endorsed. Author's observation notes, March 20, 2015.

45. See 2015 990 form, Schedule O, and part III, line 4D, of Make the Road New York. They are a partner in providing "wraparound services." In possession of the author. The collection of NGOs that worked with and promoted de Blasio's education initiatives was grouped under the New York City Coalition for Educational Justice, http://www.nyccej.org/.

46. Author's observation notes, June 5, 2015.

47. The secret negotiations between Christie and Baraka to remove Anderson apparently began just after the May 22 mega-march. John Mooney, "Q&A: Newark's Mayor Talks about His Surprising Alliance with Gov. Christie," *NJ Spotlight,* July 2, 2015, http://www.njspotlight.com/ stories/15/07/01/q-a-newark-s-mayor-talks-about-surprising-alliance -with-christie/. The iconic photo of Baraka and Christie squaring off in the governor's office, surrounded by their advisors, was taken by Christie's office and provided to the press. The photo, and many other archival records from the Christie administration, was not transferred to the New Jersey State Archives, in contrast to other outgoing governors, and thus was not available for publication. Email from New Jersey State Archives, May 20, 2022, in possession of the author.

48. Karen Zernike, "Cami Anderson, Picked by Christie, Is Out as Newark Schools Superintendent," *New York Times,* June 22, 2015; Tom Moran, "After a Bitter Battle, Anderson Loses. But Do the Children of Newark Win?," *Star-Ledger,* June 23, 2015.

49. Jessica Mazzola, "Christie and Baraka Announce Plan to End State Control of Schools," *Star-Ledger,* June 27, 2015.

50. Mazzola.

51. Emphasis original.

52. Tony Wan, "One Amplify: Joel Klein's Plan to Unify News Corp.'s Education Business," *EdSurge,* April 29, 2015, https://www.edsurge.com/ news/2015-04-29-one-amplify-joel-klein-s-plan-to-unify-news-corp-s -education-business; Michelle Molnar, "News Corp. Sells Amplify to Joel Klein, Other Executives," *Education Week,* October 5, 2015; Dan Ivers, "State's Pick for Newark Superintendent Resigns from Charter School Lobbying Group," *NJ.com,* June 30, 2015.

53. Emphasis added.

54. Author's observation notes, meeting at the NTU office, Newark.

55. https://www.facebook.com/alliance4nps/photos/ pb.100070608094569.-2207520000../1640430916194753/.

NOTES TO CHAPTER 8 || 339

56. Mooney, "Q&A."

57. Rice also followed Smith-Gregory's script. Braun, "Has Christie Divided Newark Opposition?"

58. Emphasis added.

59. Braun.

60. Braun.

61. Interview with Rippey, October 15, 2015.

62. Although critical of the NTU's failure to engage in disruptive protests, Braun remained neutral in the election. Bob Braun, "Newark Teachers Union Faces Critical Election," *Bob Braun's Ledger* (blog), June 17, 2015, http://www.bobbraunsledger.com/newark-teachers-union-faces -critical-election/.

63. Reed, *Stirrings in the Jug*, 176, emphasis added.

64. Reed, 167.

8. MAKING NEWARK GOVERNABLE AGAIN

1. Kate Zernike, "Defying Expectations, Mayor Ras Baraka Is Praised in All Corners of Newark," *New York Times*, August 30, 2015, emphasis added.

2. Emphasis added.

3. Dan Ivers, "Tax Breaks Aim to Extend Development," *Star-Ledger*, January 13, 2016; Naomi Nix, "Renaissance Is around Corner, City Leaders Say," *Star-Ledger*, February 15, 2015.

4. Bob Braun, "It Doesn't Look Good for Newark's Neighborhood Schools," *Bob Braun's Ledger* (blog), September 21, 2015, https://www .bobbraunsledger.com/it-doesnt-look-good-for-newarks-neighborhood -schools/.

5. Naomi Nix, "Newark Mayoral Race: Baraka Accuses Jeffries of Keeping His Donors Secret," *Star-Ledger*, May 6, 2014. On the backpack give-away, see "Newark Mayor Ras Baraka Makes Nice with Education Group He Accused of Money Laundering: The Auditor," *NJ.com*, September 5, 2015, https://www.nj.com/politics/index.ssf/2014/09/newark_mayor_ ras_baraka_changes_tune_on_education_group_he_criticized.html. ALI director Junius Williams engaged in a parallel rehabilitation effort by naming Matthew Frankel, a former Anderson spokesperson and education reform leader, as a senior advisor to Newark's 350th anniversary commemoration. Braun, "It Doesn't Look Good."

6. North Star, which had eleven other schools at the time, constructed a six-story school on the former *Star-Ledger* property, located at 355-377 Washington Street. Dan Ivers, "Charter School Proposed for Former Star-

340 || NOTES TO CHAPTER 8

Ledger Property in Newark," *NJ.com,* October 6, 2015, https://www
.nj.com/essex/2015/10/charter_school_proposed_for_former_star
-ledger_pro.html.

7. Francis Fox Piven, "Whom Does the Advocate Planner Serve?," in
The View from Below: Urban Politics and Social Policy, ed. Susan Fainstein
and Norman Fainstein (Boston: Little, Brown, 1972), 232.

8. Tom Moran, "In Newark, Charters Beef Up for a Political Fight,"
Star-Ledger, October 25, 2015. For a photo of the council chambers during
the meeting, see the Facebook page of PC2E (the page is named Parent
Action Coalition), https://www.facebook.com/ParentAdvisoryCouncil
NewarkNJ/photos/a.1646757695607075/1650420945240750/.

9. Dan Ivers, "Newark Board Approves New Home for Charter
School on Former Star-Ledger Site," *NJ.com,* October 20, 2015, https://
www.nj.com/essex/2015/10/newark_board_approves_new_home_
for_charter_school.html. At the same time, Crump maintained cordial
ties with KIPP, receiving an award, days afterward, where she saluted
KIPP and its billionaire backer, the Fisher family. Parents Action Coalition, https://www.facebook.com/ParentAdvisoryCouncilNewarkNJ/
videos/1647979148818263/.

10. Ibid.

11. Dan Ivers, "Charter School Network Announces Plans to Expand in
Newark," *NJ.com,* October 14, 2015, https://www.nj.com/essex/2015/10/
charter_school_network_announces_plans_to_expand_i.html.

12. Dan Ivers, "Baraka Calls Potential Newark Charter School Expansion 'Highly Irresponsible,'" *NJ.com,* October 19, 2015, https://www.nj.com/
essex/2015/10/baraka_calls_potential_expansion_of_newark_charter
.html#incart_2box_essex.

13. Emphasis added.

14. Emphasis added.

15. On the belated recognition of the "limitations of his [Obama's] symbolic racial victory . . . even to African Americans who had accepted him as
role-model-in-chief," see Reed, *Toward Freedom,* 144–45. Author's observation notes, POP meeting, November 5, 2015.

16. For a photo of Cabañas receiving the award at the October 14, 2015,
Hispanic Heritage Month ceremony, see https://hiveminer.com/Tags/
hispanic%2Cnewark.

17. Author's observation notes, October 26, 2015.

18. Emphasis added.

19. Interview with Lavar Young, April 4, 2016; Patrick Wall, "Group
That Fueled Rapid Growth of Newark Charter Schools Winds Down,
Marking End of an Era," *Chalkbeat,* December 19, 2019, https://newark

NOTES TO CHAPTER 8 || 341

.chalkbeat.org/2019/12/19/21055627/group-that-fueled-rapid-growth-of
-newark-charter-schools-winds-down-marking-end-of-an-era.

20. For more on Akil, see https://njleftbehind.org/2017/11/soprano
-state-muhammed-akil-pc2e-jersey-story/; Terrance McDonald, "Jersey
City Chief of Staff Steps Down, Citing 'Distraction' of Racially Inflamma-
tory Remarks," *NJ.com*, October 16, 2014, https://www.nj.com/hudson/
2014/10/jersey_city_chief_of_staff_steps_down_said_reports_of_
racially_inflammatory_remarks_are_a_distractio.html.

21. Moran, "In Newark, Charters Beef Up."

22. Cox and Nilsen, *We Make Our Own History,* 115. Charter militants
publishing editorials, which a receptive local press facilitated, was part
of this ideological offensive. See Erica Fortenberry, "A Public School
Teacher Who's Also a Charter School Parent," published in the charter-
friendly *Star-Ledger,* May 7, 2016, and Muhammed Akil, "Scapegoating
Newark's Parents and Charter Schools Is Not the Answer," *NJ Spotlight,*
January 29, 2016, https://www.njspotlight.com/stories/16/01/28/
scapegoating-newark-s-parents-and-charter-schools-is-not-the-answer/.

23. Piven, *Challenging Authority,* 28.

24. Dan Ivers, "Baraka Decries Latest Charter School Spat as Dividing
Parents," *Star-Ledger,* January 6, 2016; Mayor Ras J. Baraka's vlog, November 23, 2015, https://www.youtube.com/watch?v=bzGJZEuK6Js; January 6, 2016, https://www.youtube.com/watch?v=NEwOoTRaT5o; Bob
Braun, "Well-Financed Charter Schools Plan Lobbying Blitz—Where Are
Public Schools' Champions?," *Bob Braun's Ledger* (blog), December 11,
2015, https://www.bobbraunsledger.com/well-financed-charter-schools
-plan-lobbying-blitz-where-are-public-schools-champions/. For photos of
parents boarding busses for, and rallying in, Trenton, see Parents Action
Coalition, https://www.facebook.com/ParentAdvisoryCouncilNewarkNJ/
photos/a.1646757695607075/1661855684097276/.

25. Dan Ivers, "Baraka Joins Forces with Rivals to Form Newark School
Board 'Unity,'" *NJ.com*, January 23, 2019, http://www.nj.com/essex/index
.ssf/2016/01/baraka_charter_backers_team_up_to_form_unity_slate
.html#incart_river_home.

26. One of the fruits of this budding relationship was Lauren Wells and
another top Baraka aide taking a trip to Minnesota with the BAEO "to look
at a charter school that was actually created in Minnesota to service disconnected youth." Interview with Young, emphasis added.

27. Emphasis added. On the importance Cerf placed on shutting
down disruption—"restoring calm"—and defusing "anger in the air"
discourse, see Cerf's comments at the September 2017 state board of
education meeting. Brenda Flanagan, "Newark Regains Local Control of

Public Schools," *NJ.TV,* September 13, 2017, https://www.youtube.com/watch?v=xmWfLBPj5n8.

28. Bob Braun, "The Cerf/Baraka Letter to Christie: Surrender, Deceit, and Betrayal," *Bob Braun's Ledger* (blog), February 20, 2016, https://www.bobbraunsledger.com/the-cerfbaraka-letter-to-christie-surrender-deceit-and-betrayal/.

29. "Governor Christie's Fy17 School Aid Budget Is Wholly Inadequate? Again," Education Law Center, February 24, 2016, http://www.edlawcenter.org/news/archives/school-funding/governor-christies-fy17-school-aid-budget-is-wholly-inadequate-again.html.

30. Despite Baraka's assurances, four of the schools were handed over to the Great Oaks Legacy charter chain. Dan Ivers, "Newark Board OKs Plan to Sell Off 12 Former School Buildings," *NJ.com,* February 24, 2016, https://www.nj.com/essex/2016/02/newark_board_oks_plan_to_sell_off_12_former_school.html; Adrian Brune, "He Built a $150 Million Village . . . for School Teachers," *OZY,* May 14, 2018, https://www.ozy.com/rising-stars/he-built-a-150-million-village-for-schoolteachers/86028.

31. On Commissioner Hespe's charter expansion approval, see John Mooney, "State Approves Only Three New Charter Schools, Gives OK to 16 Expansions," *NJ Spotlight,* March 1, 2016, https://www.njspotlightnews.org/2016/03/16-02-29-state-approves-only-three-new-charters-gives-ok-to-16-expansions/. On Baraka's letter following the expansion approval, which in this case *did* condemn the charter payments for being at the heart of NPS's fiscal crisis, see Bob Braun, "Newark Mayor Calls Charter Expansion a 'Terrible' Decision," *Bob Braun's Ledger* (blog), March 2, 2016, https://www.bobbraunsledger.com/newark-mayor-calls-charter-expansion-a-terrible-decision/.

32. Alliance for Newark Public Schools to Mayor Baraka, March 14, 2016, emphasis added, in possession of the author. Bob Braun, "Newark: Baraka's Allies Criticize the Mayor for Supporting Charters," *Bob Braun's Ledger* (blog), March 17, 2016, https://www.bobbraunsledger.com/newark-barakas-allies-criticize-the-mayor-for-supporting-charters/; Braun, "Has Newark's Community Schools Initiative Been Sold Out Already?," *Bob Braun's Ledger* (blog), February 18, 2016, https://www.bobbraunsledger.com/has-newarks-community-schools-initiative-been-sold-out-already/.

33. Trina Scordo, "What Has Happened to the Mayor Ras Baraka We Put into Office?," *NJ Spotlight,* March 3, 2016, https://www.njspotlight.com/stories/16/03/03/op-ed-what-has-happened-to-the-mayor-ras-baraka-we-put-into-office/.

34. Interview with Trina Scordo, September 26, 2016; interview with Al Moussab, April 2, 2016.

35. "Muhammed Akil (PC2E): Newark School Board Election Victory,"

NOTES TO CHAPTER 8 || 343

https://www.youtube.com/watch?v=2oDkii5lsZI. On the electoral work of Akil, see "Winners and Losers: Week of the Akil Attack," *PolitckerNJ*, April 22, 2016, https://observer.com/2016/04/winners-and-losers-week-of-the-akil-attack/.

36. Mayor Baraka's vlog, April 26, 2016, emphasis added, https://www.youtube.com/watch?v=iEj2GaLwwZA.

37. Braun, "Newark: Baraka's Allies Criticize the Mayor."

38. Marisa Iati, "Hundreds 'March for Jobs,' Claim Discrimination at Port Newark–Elizabeth," *NJ.com*, May 2, 2016, https://www.nj.com/essex/2016/05/march_for_jobs_at_port_authority_of_newark_and_eli.html; Michael Hill, "Newark Mayor, Residents Protest Port of Newark Hiring," *NJTV*, May 2, 2016. https://www.njtvonline.org/news/video/newark-mayor-residents-protest-port-of-newark-hiring/; Eric Kiefer, "Newark Activists March on Port, Demand 'Desegregation,'" *Patch*, May 4, 2016, https://patch.com/new-jersey/newarknj/newark-activists-march-port-demand-desegregation-photos-video. The call for "desegregation" was most likely in reference to the division between two locals—1233 and 1235—both comprising "deep water longshoremen." When containerization took hold in the 1970s, many displaced longshoremen from Brooklyn objected to joining the predominantly black Local 1233. Thus, the ILA leadership established a new local—1235—for them, though this appeared to violate the ILA constitution because they encompassed the same category of worker. Nonetheless, there is now significant cooperation between the two, and the largely black, and black-led, Local 1233 did not support the protests. Interview with Local 1233 member, September 29, 2020.

39. "Newark Mayor Leads Protest for More Port Jobs for Residents," AP News, July 18, 2016, https://apnews.com/a6f5ed46c2d74b49bafe95601323e8e4; "Newark Mayor Ras Baraka Holds Rally for Jobs at Port Authority," *NJ.com*, July 18, 2018, https://www.youtube.com/watch?v=PpRktv9_r-M.

40. https://www.cleanwateraction.org/about/people/kim-gaddy. Baraka asked Larry Hamm to turn out POP members for the protest, but he declined, apparently, after consulting with a member of the predominantly black Local 1233 of the ILA. Interview with Local 1233 member, February 10, 2022.

41. Reed, *Toward Freedom*, 77–100; Tom Haydon, "Longshoremen Unions Discriminate against Minorities, Newark Mayor Says," *NJ.com*, March 14, 2016, https://www.nj.com/essex/2016/03/newark_mayor_wants_federal_investigation_of_port_h.html; https://olmsapps.dol.gov/query/orgReport.do.

42. In 2016, Daggett received at least two salaries, one as "president emeritus" of Local 1804-1 ($144,316), the mechanics local, which has the power to shut down ports for safety violations, and a second as president of

344 || NOTES TO CHAPTER 8

the ILA ($533,222). See https://olmsapps.dol.gov/query/getOrgQry Result.do. By 2015, ILA Local 1233 had only 876 members, a drastic decline from the precontainerization era. On the effect of containerization on employment, see Marc Levinson, *The Box: How the Shipping Container Made the World Smaller and the World Economy Bigger* (Princeton, N.J.: Princeton University Press, 2006).

43. https://www.youtube.com/watch?v=fOn77Ll0bBU; Orozco's testimony begins at the 2:35 mark. Also contributing to Cerf's attentiveness was the press coverage Orozco's case received thanks to the intervention of Johnson and Coles. Barry Carter, "School Placements Given Failing Grades," *Star-Ledger,* September 23, 2016.

44. Emphasis added.

45. NPS regular BOE meeting, September 2016, https://www.youtube .com/watch?v=RU77W7e1-o8; Cabañas begins speaking at the 2:35 mark.

46. NPS regular BOE meeting; Lewis begins at the 2:28 mark, followed by Owens, then Richardson. Board legal counsel, Charlotte Hitchcock, channeling Cerf, denounces the vote as irresponsible and illegal.

47. NPS BOE business meeting, October 18, 2018, https://www .youtube.com/watch?v=HDhVnD07_Ks; discussion on rescinding the vote begins at about the 3:21 mark.

48. NPS regular BOE meeting, October 2016, https://www.youtube .com/watch?v=WMx68aWFkd8.

49. Flyer in possession of the author.

50. The July 12, 2017, ANPS meeting minutes recount the group appealing to the mayor and getting the run-around. In addition, the group, most likely reflecting Cabañas's thinking, recognizes its failure to "become more public in its actions and share more broadly what the critical concerns are and its recommendations." In possession of the author.

51. Interview with tenant president Rita Fortenberry, April 28, 2017; Karen Yi, "Public Housing Complex Won't Be Razed—for Now," *Star-Ledger,* April 28, 2017.

52. Richard Houston, Housing and Community Development Network of New Jersey, http://hcdnnjnetworkvoices.blogspot.com/2016/10/ guest-voice-newark-community.html.

53. For a critique of the dismissal of the New Deal as simply benefiting whites and thoroughly disadvantaging blacks, and the need to understand its limitation through political economy, rather than all-encompassing, transhistorical white racism, see Touré Reed, "Between Obama and Coates," *Catalyst* 1, no. 4 (2018). Author's observation notes, September 2016.

54. Emphasis added.

55. ANPS flyer advertising the rally in Trenton, https://www.facebook

.com/alliance4nps/photos/pb.100070608094569.-2207520000..
/1969275719976936/. In the video prepared by Cabañas for the event,
Baraka is presented as an unflinching ally of a united movement, while
waxing over the sharper disagreements that emerged after Cerf's appointment. Observation by the author.

56. September 13, 2017, celebration of local control, video by Ingrid Hill,
https://www.facebook.com/ingrid.s.hill/videos/10211980912772908/.

57. Nilsen and Cox, "What Would a Marxist Theory," 69.

58. Moran, "In Newark, Charters Beef Up."

59. Tom Moran, "Cerf's Diplomacy Protects Solid Classroom Gains,"
Star-Ledger, February 11, 2018.

60. Author's observation notes, February 9, 2018.

61. Adolph Reed Jr., "Black Particularity Reconsidered," *Telos* 39 (Spring
1979).

CONCLUSION

1. Thomas Johnson, "Cabral Buried in Guinea Amid Cry of 'Revolution,'" *New York Times,* February 2, 1973.

2. African Information Service, *Return to the Source: Selected Speeches of
Amilcar Carbal* (New York: Monthly Review, 1973), 63.

3. Rosa Luxemburg, "On the Russian Revolution" (1918), https://
www.rosalux.de/stiftung/historisches-zentrum/rosa-luxemburg/on-the
-russian-revolution.

4. Luxemburg.

5. See Wells's "CREED Strategies," https://www.creedstrategies.com/.

6. The most farcical form of RD-rooted opposition to Baraka has come
from antivax forces. In early 2022, antivax entrepreneur Kevin Jenkins and his
black activist supporters challenged the mayor to debate, on Martin Luther
King Day, the administration's vaccination mandate policies. Jenkins called
for "free[ing] Newarkers from medical racism, medical tyranny and slave
passports." https://www.facebook.com/photo/?fbid=3092820007641542.

7. Emphasis original.

8. Barker, "Class Struggle and Social Movements," 48.

9. Smith, *Racial Democracy,* xviii, 7–11. This critical class lens is also
needed by activists and scholars when engaging and analyzing movements
of gays, women, immigrants, and other oppressed groups.

10. Tracey Tully and Kevin Armstrong, "Defined by Riots, Newark
Remains Peaceful," *New York Times,* June 2, 2020; Cedric Johnson, "Black
Political Life and the Blue Lives Matter Presidency," *Jacobin,* February 17,
2019, https://www.jacobinmag.com/2019/02/black-lives-matter-power
-politics-cedric-johnson.

346 || NOTES TO CONCLUSION

11. "Mayor Baraka Puts Economic Plan in Motion to Deliver Promise of '40 Acres and a Mule' and Economic Justice for Newark Residents," *Newark News,* September 29, 2020, https://www.newarknj.gov/news/mayor-baraka-puts-economic-plan-in-motion-to-deliver-promise-of-40-acres-and-a-mule-and-economic-justice-for-newark-residents.

12. Matt Bruenig, "The Racial Wealth Gap Is about the Upper Classes," *Jacobin,* July 5, 2020, https://jacobinmag.com/2020/07/racial-wealth-gap-redistribution; Walter Benn Michaels and Adolph Reed Jr., "The Trouble with Disparity," *Nonsite,* no. 32 (September 2020), https://nonsite.org/the-trouble-with-disparity/.

13. Emphasis added.

14. "Mayor Baraka Puts Economic Plan in Motion."

15. Adolph Reed Jr., "Why Black Lives Matter Can't Be Co-opted," *Nonsite,* July 23, 2021, https://nonsite.org/why-black-lives-matter-cant-be-co-opted/.

16. Doug Williams, "Black Lives Matter and the Failure to Build a Movement," *South Lawn,* August 10, 2015, https://thesouthlawn.org/2015/08/10/black-lives-matter-and-the-failure-to-build-a-movement/; Sydney Ember, "Bernie Sanders Predicted Revolution, Just Not This One," *New York Times,* June 19, 2020. On Crenshaw's ideological influence on philanthropy, including her collaboration with the NoVo Foundation, headed by Peter Buffett, heir to the fortune of financier Warren Buffett, see Kiersten Marek, "Kimberlé Crenshaw: How to Fund Women and Girls of Color," *Philanthropy Women,* July 2017, https://philanthropywomen.org/women-of-color/intersectional-giving-driving-funding-for-women-and-girls-of-color/.

17. Margaret O'Mara, "Don't Be Fooled by Seattle's Police-Free Zone," *New York Times,* June 24, 2020.

18. John Eligon, "Black Lives Matter Has Grown More Powerful, and More Divided," *New York Times,* July 4, 2021. On the wave of post-Floyd corporate giving in the name of "racial justice," and its distribution, see Tracy Jan, Jena McGregor, and Meghan Hoyer, "Corporate America's $50 Billion Promise," *Washington Post,* August 24, 2021. For a classic example of Smith's argument that the "class interests" of affluent black Americans often remain hidden behind what is projected as the "race interests" of all African Americans, see Cullors defend her expanding real estate portfolio in "Patrice Cullors Talks Money & BLM," April 15, 2021, https://mobile.twitter.com/vanlathan/status/1382874774695600129.

19. Amanda Marcott, "Hillary Clinton Suggested Breaking Up the Big Banks Won't End Racism and Sexism. Is She Right?," *In These Times,* March 11, 2016; Monica Alba and Alex Setiz-Wald, "Hillary Clinton Calls for 'Facing Up to the Reality of Systemic Racism,'" MSNBC, http://www

.msnbc.com/msnbc/hillary-clinton-calls-facing-the-reality-systemic-racism. Liberal economist Paul Krugman launched similar attacks, arguing that Sanders and Clinton represented two "competing theories of change"—SD vs. RD—with the seventy-four-year-old veteran of the civil rights movement being stone deaf to racism and sexism. Krugman, "Plutocrats and Prejudice," *New York Times,* January 29, 2016; "Hillary and the Horizontals," *New York Times,* June 10, 2016. The charter school–supporting *Nation* columnist Joan Walsh indicted Sanders for "crafting a class-based appeal that minimizes, and sometimes even diminishes, the role that racism plays in creating American social and economic inequality." Walsh, "What's Wrong with Bernie Sanders's Strategy," *The Nation,* March 21, 2016, https://www.thenation.com/article/whats-wrong-with-bernie-sanderss-strategy/. For an overview of how "antiracism" is increasingly wielded as an ideological weapon against pro–working class measures, see Briahna Gay, "Beware of the Race Reductionist," *The Intercept,* August 26, 2018, https://theintercept.com/2018/08/26/beware-the-race-reductionist/.

20. Bradford Richardson, "Clyburn: Sanders's Plan Would Kill Black Colleges," *The Hill,* February 21, 2016, http://thehill.com/blogs/ballot-box/presidential-races/270214-clyburn-sanderss-plan-would-kill-black-colleges; wmholt, "John Lewis Speaks Out against Sanders' College for All Plan," *Daily Kos,* February 20, 2016, http://www.dailykos.com/story/2016/2/19/1488121/-John-Lewis-Speaks-Out-Against-College-for-All. Congressman Gregory Meeks defended the Congressional Black Caucus's endorsement of Clinton by arguing that Sanders's socialist agenda would not adequately address racism. Rahel Gebreyes, "CBC PAC Chairman Says Bernie Sanders' Socialism Can't 'Eradicate Racism,'" *Huffington Post,* January 4, 2017, https://www.huffingtonpost.com/entry/gregory-meeks-bernie-sanders_us_56c37479e4b0c3c55052d1a1.

21. Kotz measures investment, or capital accumulation, by the "ratio of annual net investment to the value of the capital stock." David Kotz, "Biden's Economic Constraints," *Catalyst* 4, no. 4 (2021); Kotz, *Rise and Fall,* 178; Doug Henwood, "Corporate Tax Deadbeats," *LBO News,* September 17, 2021, https://lbo-news.com/2021/09/17/corporate-tax-deadbeats/.

22. Robert Brenner, "Escalating Plunder," *New Left Review,* May–June 2020, https://newleftreview.org/issues/ii123/articles/robert-brenner-escalating-plunder.

23. Eric Lerner, "Proposal for a Teach-In Series on Socialism in the World Crisis," October 2021, in possession of the author; see also Lerner's presentation "What Is State-Financed Capitalism?," https://www.youtube.com/watch?v=miW3dlHJXXs.

24. Kotz, *Rise and Fall*, 121.

25. James Petras, "US Middle East Wars: Social Opposition and Political Impotence," *James Petras Website*, July 4, 2007, http://petras.lahaine.org/articulo.php?p=1704. Another pernicious force emanating from the academy has been, as David Imbroscio has perceptively pointed out, the hegemonic "liberal expansionism" development model for cities. Peddled most influentially by urbanists Peter Dreier, John Mollenkopf, and Todd Swanstrom, this school, Imbroscio persuasively demonstrates, has legitimated the regressive agenda carried out by urban Democrats. Yet, Imbroscio's alternative, placed-based, local development–focused "inside game" undermines constructing the needed comprehensive, national, class-based counteragenda while absolving the urban black and Latinx political leadership, as does Dreier, of their central role in urban revanchism. Imbroscio, "Shaming the Inside Game: A Critique of the Liberal Expansionist Approach to Addressing Urban Problems," *Urban Affairs Review* 42, no. 2 (2006): 237–39.

26. Marcie Smith, "Change Agent: Gene Sharp's Neoliberal Nonviolence (Part One and Two)," *Nonsite*, May 10, 2019, https://nonsite.org/change-agent-gene-sharps-neoliberal-nonviolence-part-one/. On how these Sharp-informed politics undermined the Occupy movement, see John Arena, "The Mass Strike, Occupy Wall Street, and Demanding Jobs for All," *Working USA: The Journal of Labor and Society* 19, no. 3 (2016): 321–40.

27. San Gindin, "Why Workers Don't Revolt," *Jacobin*, June 14, 2021, https://jacobinmag.com/2021/06/working-class-revolt-competition-capitalism-exploitation.

28. Jane McAlevey, *No Shortcuts: Organizing for Power in the New Gilded Age* (New York: Oxford University Press, 2016), 28.

29. McAlevey, 131–32.

30. On ensuring universality through "race-sensitive" as opposed to exclusionary, "race-specific" programs, see interview with Vivek Chibber, "The Year of Racial Reckoning," *Jacobin Show*, December 9, 2020, https://www.youtube.com/watch?v=3Zxmg5TA6II. Luxemburg made a similar argument regarding the most effective method of combating oppression against ethnic Poles in Germany and the dead end of an RD politics that relies on the bourgeoisie of the oppressed group. "In Defense of Nationality" (1900), https://www.marxists.org/archive/luxemburg/1900/nationality/index.html. Curiously, this antiracist, class-wide program encounters fierce opposition even from those on the Left who put themselves forward as proponents of—and experts on—Luxemburg's theory and politics. Tatiana Cozzarelli, a leading theoretician of *Left Voice*, which filled the ideological niche left by the implosion of the International Socialist Organization, railed against such a program as "class reductionist," one unable to address

the "particular oppression" of the classes that compose "Black folks." "Class Reductionism Is Real, and It's Coming from the Jacobin Wing of the DSA," *Left Voice,* June 16, 2020, https://www.leftvoice.org/class-reductionism-is -real-and-its-coming-from-the-jacobin-wing-of-the-dsa/.

31. Bruce Dixon, "What Would a Real Discussion on Reparations Look Like? Have We Ever Had One?," *Black Agenda Report,* January 28, 2016, https://www.blackagendareport.com/real-talk-on-reparations.

32. Adolph Reed Jr., "'Let Me Go Get My Big White Man': The Clientelist Foundation of Contemporary Antiracist Politics," *Nonsite,* no. 39 (May 11, 2022). Per Dixon and Reed's critique, the post-Floyd flurry of reparations activity in New Jersey has allowed Baraka, Booker, Payne, and other neoliberal black officials to appear as radical defenders of the "black community" as they partner with, and appeal to, corporations, foundations, and the Democratic Party. "Juneteenth March and Rally for Reparations, Justice, and Democracy to Be Held in Newark on June 17," *Insider NY,* June 13, 2022, https://www.insidernj.com/press-release/juneteenth-march -rally-for-reparations-justice-democracy-to-be-held-in-newark-on-june-17/.

33. Rosa Luxemburg, "Opportunism and the Art of the Possible" (1898), Rosa Luxemburg Internet Archive, https://www.marxists.org/ archive/luxemburg/1898/09/30.htm. In "Reform or Revolution?" (1900), Luxemburg explained that in forging a program, the socialist movement must "grope" between the "two rocks" of "abandoning the mass character of the party or abandoning its final aim, falling into bourgeois reformism or into sectarianism anarchism or opportunism." https://www.marxists.org/ archive/luxemburg/1900/reform-revolution/.

34. Luxemburg, "Opportunism and the Art of the Possible."

35. Luxemburg, *Mass Strike,* 226.

36. Lerner, "Introduction: Mass Strikes Today." Kotz also emphasizes a "growing radical mass movement [that] induces *fear* of more radical change on the part of big business" as key to generating concessions. Kotz, "Biden's Economic Constraints."

37. Barker, "Class Struggle," 49–50; Leopold, *Runway Inequality,* 300–308.

38. As exemplified by New Orleans's public housing movement; see Arena, *Driven from New Orleans,* chapter 2.

39. Rosa Luxemburg, "Social Democracy and Parliamentarism" (1904), Rosa Luxemburg Internet Archive, https://www.marxists.org/archive/ luxemburg/1904/06/05.htm.

40. Luxemburg, *Mass Strike,* 221.

41. Rosa Luxemburg, "The Crisis in the German Social-Democracy (the Junius Pamphlet)" (1915), https://archive.org/stream/crisisingerman so00luxeiala/crisisingermanso00luxeiala_djvu.txt.

42. Johnson, "Panthers Can't Save Us Now"; Karl Marx, *The Eighteenth*

350 || NOTES TO CONCLUSION

Brumaire of Louis Bonaparte (1852), https://www.marxists.org/archive/marx/works/1852/18th-brumaire/ch01.htm.

43. Nancy Fraser, *The Old Is Dying and the New Cannot Be Born* (New York: Verso, 2019).

44. Citing Geoff Eley, Blake Stewart, "The Rise of Far-Right Civilizationism," *Critical Sociology* 46 (2020): 1207.

45. Kotz, "Biden's Economic Constraints."

APPENDIX

1. Michael Burawoy, "The Critical Turn to Public Sociology," *Critical Sociology* 31, no. 3 (2005): 322.

2. Walda Katz-Fishman and Jerome Scott, "Comments on Burawoy: A View from the Bottom-Up," *Critical Sociology* 31, no. 3 (2005): 372–73.

3. Brenda Flanagan, "Essex County Sheriff's Officers Clash with Anti-ICE Protesters," *NJ Spotlight News,* June 29, 2018, https://www.njspotlightnews.org/video/essex-county-sheriffs-officers-clash-with-anti-ice-protesters/.

4. Iddo Tavory and Stefan Timmermans, "Two Cases of Ethnography: Grounded Theory and the Extended Case Method," *Ethnography* 10, no. 3 (2009): 244.

5. Cox and Nilsen, *We Make Our Own History,* 15.

6. João Costa Vargas, "Activist Scholarship: Limits and Possibilities in Times of Black Genocide," in *Engaging Contradictions,* ed. Charles Hale (Berkeley: University of California Press, 2008), 176.

7. On these tensions, see Rick Fantasia, *Cultures of Solidarity* (Berkeley: University of California Press, 1988).

8. Of course, some important data sources were closed off. Two strategically placed actors who could have provided important insights into various turning points in this drama refused to be interviewed. In addition, I was unsuccessful, through a public records request, in obtaining email exchanges from some public officials.

9. Michael Burawoy, "Two Methods in Search of Science," *Theory and Society* 18 (1989): 759–805.

10. John Saul, *Socialist Ideology and the Struggle for Southern Africa* (Trenton, N.J.: African World Press, 1990), 190.

11. Oliver Cromwell Cox, *Caste, Class, and Race: A Study in Social Dynamics* (1948; repr., New York: Monthly Review, 1959), xvi.

Index

Abbot Leadership Institute (ALI), 121, 138

Abbot v. Burke, 55, 148–49

Abeigon, John: charter school movement and, 140; NTU and, 227, 235, 237, 245, 255; public schools advocacy and, 220; teachers' protests and, 211, 215

Ackman, William, 100

Adan, Dan, 149

Addonizio, Hugh, 48–52

Adubato, Stephen, Sr., 319n49; charter school movement and, 95, 314n69; funding for education and, 294n47; Newark revitalization and, 278–79; privatization of public schools and, 71; public school reform and, 58, 91; school board elections and, 106

affinity groups, philanthrocapitalism and organization of, 94–95

affirmative action, Newark rebellion and support for, 45

African Free School, 77–78

African Liberation Day Coordinating Committee, 73

Afropessimism philosophy, 20

Akil, Muhammed, 238–41, 246

Akinyele, Bashir, 213–15, 330n25

Alarcon, Israel, 130, 132

Alexander, Michelle, 11–12, 286n35

Allen, Nakisha, 159, 330n25

Allen College, 263

Alliance for Educational Justice, 337n40

Alliance for Newark Public Schools (ANPS): Anderson ouster campaign and, 207–9; charter school expansion opposed by, 237–38, 243–46; formation of, 171; local control of schools and, 269; One Newark Plan and, 250–52, 255–56, 344n50; privatization of schools protests and, 220–22

Alliance for School Choice, 73

Alliance to Reclaim Our Schools (AROS), 160, 219–20

Amador, Augusto, 212–13

American Federation of Labor (AFL), 39–40; teachers' strikes in postwar Newark, 139

American Federation of Teachers (AFT): Anderson's ties to, 159–61, 171, 204; AROS coalition and, 219–20; Newark public school reform and, 51, 54; Newark teachers and, 39–41; privatization of public schools and, 96–97, 108–10

Anderson, Cami: AFT ties to, 159–61; antiracist politics and, 145–48; Black ministers' initial support of, 162–65; Booker and, 87–89, 318n27; campaign for removal of, 207–11; charter school movement and, 2–7, 27,

|| 351

92, 145, 203–7, 309n17, 314n74, 323n21; concessions by, 171–72; counteroffensive to protests against, 168–70; legitimacy crisis for, 162–68; mayoral race and opposition to, 170–71; One Newark plan and, 151–57; privatization of public schools and, 106–10, 117, 203–7; protests against, 124–25, 141–44, 155–59, 199; resignation of, 222–28, 232, 254; state and local power blocs and, 112; student protests against, 129–38, 171–72, 203; suspension of administrators by, 155–57

Angelou, Maya, 196–97

antiracist ideology: Ras Baraka's self-determination politics and, 194–99; Black Power movement and, 27; capitalism and, 7–9; philanthrocapitalism and BPMC alliance and, 85–86, 110–11; school reform and, 4–6, 77–79

antivax movement, 345n6

Aronowitz, Stanley, 110

Ashton, Mashea, 92, 104, 112, 124, 151, 309n18

Association of Community Organizations for Reform Now (ACORN), 132

Atwater, Lee, 183

Audible corporation, 168

authenticity trope: Booker's opponents use of, 80, 184–85, 305n61; Jeffries' use of, 82

Bain Capital, 80

banking crisis (1975), 59

Baraka, Amina, 183

Baraka, Amiri: African trip of, 257; Black nationalism advocacy of, 52–53, 77, 181–83, 329n20; Black Power movement and, 181–83, 294n43; Black urban regime and, 49, 194; Booker criticized by, 330n26; death of, 155; Newark politics and, 2, 46–47, 51–52, 54, 180–83, 296nn59–60, 298n3; Newark revitalization and, 31, 87; POP and, 278; public school reform and, 42, 51–52, 54, 57, 77–78, 183, 270–71

Baraka, Amiri (Middy), Jr., 245

Baraka, Ras J.: AFT support for, 160; alienation of supporters by, 243–46; AROS coalition and, 219–20; Black urban regime and, 83–84; Booker and, 184–85, 190–91, 330n26; campaign for Anderson's removal and, 207–11; Cerf and, 225–26, 237–38, 242–43; charter schools movement and, 27, 218–19, 233–46, 338n44; Christie and, 198–202, 207, 222–28, 233–38, 338n47; as city councilman, 184–85; criticism of Booker by, 103–4; as deputy mayor, 184; disruptive power of, 258; early life of, 183–84; education career of, 97, 183–84, 314n69; election of, 27, 82, 171–73, 177–80; labor discrimination campaign of, 246–48, 343n38; as mayoral candidate, 143–44, 147–48, 152, 154–56, 159, 170–71; mobilization against privatization by, 2–7, 11, 26, 77, 124, 184–85; Newark Educational Success Board and, 223–28; NSU alliance with, 161–62, 191–92; One Newark plan protests and, 153–54, 159; One Newark restructuring plan and, 248–52; opposition to charter school expansion and, 240–41; police reform policies of, 260–63; POP and, 278; protests of privatization of schools and, 103–5; public housing programs and, 251–52; racial democracy and, 199–202, 207, 231; real estate development projects and, 188–91; regime as mayor, 199–202; reinvention mechanism and, 229; school board elections and, 106, 137–38, 314n69; self-determination politics of, 177–202; student protests supported by, 135, 216–19; turnaround protests supported by, 214–16

Barker, Colin, 25–26, 88, 270

Barrow, Freda, 96–97, 137, 204–5

Barthelemy, Sidney, 15

Baskerville-Richardson, Antoinette: charter school expansion and, 234, 236–37, 246, 253, 338n44; One Newark plan and, 153–54, 171–72, 250; public schools advocacy and, 115, 220; school board elections and, 137–38

Bazile, Jaysen, 126–28, 130–32, 134–38, 201

Beckham, Eric, 166–67

Beit, Ron, 185–88, 190–91

Bell, Terrel, 55–56

Bell Curve, The (Murray), 72

Berggruen, Nicolas, 186

Bethany Christian Academy, 163

Bey, Maryam, 57

Bezos, Jeff, 262

Bill and Melinda Gates Foundation, 3, 83, 91, 100, 209

Black Alliance for Educational Opportunities (BAEO), 72–75, 233, 238–42

Black and Puerto Rican Political Convention (Newark, 1969), 49, 298n3

Black independent schools movement, 77–79

Black Lives Matter, 201–2, 260–63

Black ministers: local control advocacy and, 225–26; opposition to One Newark protests, 165–70; privatization of public schools supported by, 125–26, 162–65; student protests supported by, 208–11

Black Ministers Council of New Jersey, 75

Black Nationalism, Amiri Baraka's advocacy of, 52–53, 77, 181–83

Black Nia FORCE, 183, 331n28

Black organicism, 10

Black political entrepreneur, ascent of, 81–83

Black politics: Black urban regime and, 48–49; community connections of, 307n80; in Newark, 1, 3–7, 63–66, 79–86, 298n3; privatization of public schools and, 9–12; reinvention mechanism and, 228–29; self-determination and, 194–99; teachers unions and, 50; urban rebellion and rise of, 46–48

Black Power (Carmichael and Hamilton), 181

Black Power Conference (1969), 182–83

Black Power movement: antiracist ideology and, 27; Amiri Baraka and, 181–83, 294n43; philanthrocapitalism legacy of, 85–86; public school reform and, 42–44, 77–79; teachers unions versus, 49–54; urban rebellions and, 46–48

Black professional managerial class (BPMC): antiracist ideology of, 59; Ras Baraka as member of, 258–60; Black Lives Matter movement and, 261–63; Black political entrepreneurs and, 81–83; Black urban regime and, 13–16; Booker's connections to, 72–75; Cabral's criticism of, 257–58; capitalist forces and, 85–86; charter school movement and, 92–93, 124–25, 238–41, 334n12; class interests of, 84–85; corporate school reform and, 67–68; emergence of, 7–9, 26–27, 48–49; hegemony and, 162–68; intergenerational conflict in, 95–97; ministerial wing of, 162–68; power realignment and, 110–12; privatization of public schools and, 9–12, 71–77, 124–26; racialized democracy and, 258–60; reparations movement and, 268–69, 349n32; school superintendent selection and, 105–10; union alliances with, 52–53

Black urban regime (BUR): Amiri Baraka and, 49, 194; Ras Baraka and, 196–99, 210–11, 231–32, 253–56; corporate school reform and, 67–68, 80–81; decline of, 80–81, 83–85, 144; disruptive power and, 16–17; emergence and consolidation of, 26, 48–49, 64, 228–29; implementers within, 67–68; neoliberalism and, 15–16, 18–22, 65–66; in Newark, 4–7, 13–16; privatization of public schools and, 58–59, 96–97, 121–22; real estate development and, 185–91; school funding reforms and, 54–55; school privatization and, 11–12;

state and local power blocs and, 110–12; teachers unions and, 54; top-down and bottom-up social movements, 17–26

Blanco, Kathleen, 91

BLM Global Network Foundation, 263

Bloomberg, Michael, 87–89, 102, 106, 111, 146, 171, 306n70

Bolden, Marion, 94–97, 105, 111

Bonaparte, Louis, 273

Booker, Cory: Anderson and, 168; Ras Baraka and, 184–85, 190–91, 255, 258, 330n26; as Black elite exemplar, 68–70; Black ministers and, 163; as Black political entrepreneur, 81–83; Black urban regime and, 110–12; Christie and, 39, 98–101; community opposition to, 27, 143–44; local foundations and, 92–95; media coverage of, 72, 301n31; as Newark mayor, 79–81, 87–89, 110, 229; Newark Now nonprofit and, 83–85; Newark school reform movement and, 2–7, 11, 15, 26; philanthrocapitalism and, 85–86, 306n67; political career of, 71–72, 184; privatization of public schools and, 71–77, 87–93, 123–24, 170–71; real estate development and, 186–88; resignation of, 143–44, 147; school superintendent selection and, 105–10; state government and objectives of, 27, 95–97; student protests and, 127; teachers and, 96–97, 108–10; Teachers Village development and, 149–50; Wright and, 169

Borletto, Flavia, 127, 130

Bradford, Derrell, 75, 303n42

Bradley, Bill, 80, 305n58
Bradley Foundation, 72–75, 77, 302n34
Branch, George, 71
Bratton, William, 89
Braun, Bob, 3, 52, 157, 167, 226–27, 233
Brenner, Neil, 21
Brenner, Robert, 265
Breunig, Matt, 261
Brick Education Network, 244
Bridgeforth, Mamie, 164–68, 208, 225
Brizard, Jean-Claude, 106
brokerage politics, Ras Baraka engagement in, 229
Brown, Campbell, 145–46, 306n70
Brown, Elizabeth, 6
Brown, Lisa, 156–57
Brown, Tanasia, 172, 234, 252
Building Excellent Schools, 309n17
Buras, Kristen, 10
Burawoy, Michael, 108–9, 277, 279
Bush, George H. W., 56–58, 183
Bush, George W., 66, 75, 77–78, 81
Business Coalition for Educational Excellence (BCEE), 56–58
business elite: Ras Baraka alliance with, 189–91, 231–32; education reform and, 56–58; Newark development and role of, 33–36, 54–55, 63–71, 80–81. See also market forces
Business Roundtable (BRT), 56–58, 66–68
Butler, Nicole, 94
Byrne, Brendan, 75

Cabañas, Roberto, 270; Anderson ouster and, 207–8; charter school expansion and, 224–25; Newark Promise plan and, 220–21;

NJCU and, 132–34, 237, 244–46, 259; One Newark plan and, 158, 248–51, 255, 344n50
Cabral, Amilcar, 257–58, 274
Camfield, David, 23
Cammarieri, Richard, 104, 252
campaign level, in bottom-up social movements, 141–44, 270–71
Campbell, Eugene, 57
Capital (Marx), 150
capitalism: antiracist politics and, 7–9; Black social movements and power of, 85–86; BPMC and, 111–12; corporate bailouts and, 265; Newark revitalization program and, 64–66; working class politics and, 16
Caputo, Alex, 140
carceral state: Black disempowerment and rise of, 11–12; Black politics and, 65; Black support for, 286n35
Cardin, Tim, 149
Carlin, Leo, 48–49
Carmichael, Stokely, 46, 181
Carter, Joe, 155–56, 167
Cascella, Vic, 52
Center for Popular Democracy (CPD), 132, 160, 221–22
Center for Union Facts, 96–97
CEO-principals, neoliberal system of, 107–10
Cerf, Christopher: AFT and, 160; Anderson and, 168; Booker and, 87–90, 97, 112; charter school movement and, 3, 83, 223–25, 227–28, 313n58, 334n14; as Newark School Superintendent, 225–26, 237–38, 242–43, 250–51; as New Jersey Education Commissioner, 102–6, 139, 151, 167; One Newark plan and,

356 || INDEX

249–51; teachers' tenure and pay legislation and, 108–10

Chambers, Raymond, 70–71, 92, 100, 298n6, 299n7, 300n25

Chaneyfield-Jenkins, Gayle, 219

charter school movement: Ras Baraka and, 27, 218–19, 232, 238, 253–56, 338n44; bipartisan federal support for, 149–51; Black ministers support for, 117, 125, 162–64; Black political entrepreneurs and, 81–85; Black support for, 238–41; Booker and, 88–93; Christie's support for, 98–101; diversity issues in, 334n12; enrollment system for, 148–55, 203–4, 249–51; hold harmless funding exemptions for, 242–43; intraphilanthropic conflict and conciliation, 100–101; legitimacy crisis for, 162–68; neoliberal agenda in, 93–95; in Newark, 2–7, 89–93; in New York State, 97, 102; origins of, 58; popular support mobilization by, 117, 123–25; protests against, 102–5, 162–68, 209–11, 216–19; real estate development promotion of, 6–7; state funding for charter schools and, 238–46; student enrollment increases in, 150; superintendent appointment and, 105–10; in Washington, D.C., 168–69; working-class politics and, 101–5. *See also* corporate school reform; local control of schools; public schools

Chicago Teachers Union (CTU), 140, 192, 200–201, 212, 245, 268, 320n55

"Children First" campaign, 137, 185, 314n69

Christie, Chris: AFT and, 160–61; Ras Baraka and, 198–202, 207, 222–28, 233–38, 252, 258, 338n47; Black politics and, 83, 303n41; Booker alliance with, 89, 98–101; Bridgegate scandal and, 155–56; education funding cuts by, 98–101, 134, 148–49, 317n12; election as governor, 110–12; Newark development and, 2–3, 283n2; One Newark plan and, 152–55, 172–73; privatization of public schools and, 98–101, 110–12, 147, 149, 205, 313n58; student protests and criticism of, 216–18; teachers' unions and, 39–41, 110, 119–22; Teachers Village development and, 149–50; as U.S. Attorney, 110

civic boosterism revival, Newark development and, 33–35

Civil Rights Act (1964), 45

civil rights movement, privatization of public schools and, 145–48; urban rebellions and, 45–48

Civil War, Newark in, 32

class structure: authenticity trope and, 305n61; Ras Baraka and, 259–60; Black Americans and, 4–5; Black political entrepreneurs and, 82–83; Black Power and dynamics of, 54, 294n43; bottom-up social movements and, 23–25, 143–44; BPMC and, 84–85; intraclass struggle and, 25–26, 110–12, 116–17; Newark development and, 32–33; philanthrocapitalism and, 101–5; in postwar Newark, 36–41; public schools in postwar Newark and, 41–44; racial democracy and, 231–32; racial wealth gap and, 261–63; real estate development and, 37–38; teachers' role in, 267–68; urban reinvention and, 228–29. *See also* Black professional managerial class; working-class politics

Clinton, Hillary, 263

Clinton, William, 56–58, 65, 81

closure of public schools: charter school movement and, 102–4, 109–10, 123–25, 140, 313n59; protests against, 154–57, 209–11

Cloward, Richard, 22–23, 127, 129

Clyburn, James, 263

Coalition for Voting Rights, 57

Coates, Ta-Nehisi, 201, 286n32

Coles, Denise, 248–49

collective impact approach, school reform and, 94–95, 310n26

colocation of schools: in New York City, 221; privatization and practice of, 102–4, 123, 140, 153, 313n59

command consent to sacrifice ideology, teachers mobilization and, 108, 120

Committee for a Unified Newark (CFUN), 49, 51, 77, 278

common sense paradigm in public policy, 13, 23, 37, 69, 74–75, 79–80

Communication Workers of America (CWA), 132–34, 171, 220–21

Communist Party: Newark development and, 35–36; suppression of, 43–44

Communities for Public Education Reform (CPER), 337n40

community, teachers' alliance with, 122–26, 141–44

Community Advisory Board (FNF), 101

Community Choice politics, 64

community development corporations (CDCs), 47–48, 69, 294n47, 299n8

Community Driven Education: A Vision for the Future (conference), 191–92

community engagement campaign, charter school plan for, 102–5, 234–38

community schools: charter schools classified as, 240–46; proposals for, 219–22, 269

Comprehensive Compliance Investigation, 57

Condon-Wadlin Act (1947), 43

Congress of Industrial Organizations (CIO), 25, 36, 40–41, 291n12

consent: Anderson's failure to gain, 156, 168–70; Black political leadership cultivation of, 85–86; charter school movement failure to gain, 102, 104, 205–7; community-centered approach to obtaining, 162; ideological offensives for gaining, 73–74, 78–79

Cooper-Basch, Irene, 100–101, 152

Corchado, Hector, 298n3

corporate school reform: Baraka's criticism of, 193–94; business support for, 66–67, 80–81; defeat in Newark of, 2, 5–7; media support for, 125. *See also* charter school movement; privatization of public schools

Corzine, Jon, 88–90, 97–98

Cotino, Kyle, 130

Council of New Jersey Grantmakers, 93

Covid-19 pandemic, racial democracy, 264–65

Cowie, Jefferson, 58–59

358 || INDEX

Cox, Laurence, 17–18, 21–25, 63, 67, 78–79, 85, 111, 119, 141, 159, 239, 253–54, 269–70, 279
Cox, Oliver Cromwell, 281
Cozzarelli, Tatiana, 348n30
Crab Grass Frontier (Jackson), 37–38
Crenshaw, Kimberlé, 262
crime legislation, Black politics and, 65–66, 260–63
critical consciousness, student protests and cultivation and, 127–28
critical race theory, privatization of public schools and, 10–12
cross-sectional approach to social change, 310n26
Crump, Larry, 184
Crump, Mildred, 63, 124, 154, 163, 235
Cullors, Patrisse, 263
culture of poverty ideology, 5
Cuomo, Andrew, 105, 221
Curry, Marshall, 80
Curry, Ravenel Boykin, IV, 80
Curvin, Robert, 125, 278, 301n26, 314n70

Daggett, Harold, 247–48, 343n42
Daggs, Lisa, 112, 309n17
Daniels, Dannette (Strawberry), 331n28
Danis, Ross, 94–95, 100–101, 152, 157, 168–70, 314n70
Danzig, Louis, 44
Davis, Leon, 182
de Blasio, Bill, 219, 221
de jure segregation, rise of BPMC and, 68–69
Del Grosso, Joe: Anderson ouster campaign and, 211; charter school movement and, 109–10; foundations and, 311n39; NTU and, 119–20, 122–23, 138–39, 317n18; public school reform and, 57

Democratic Party: abandonment of New Deal by, 9; AROS coalition and, 219–20; Ras Baraka and, 231; Black political entrepreneurs and, 81–83; BPMC and, 7–9; class structure and, 190–91; containment of top-down management and, 143–44; intraclass struggle and, 200–201; New Jersey Working Families Party and, 192–93; parent activism for public schools and, 240–41; racial democracy and, 263
Democrats for Education Reform (DFER), 82–83, 171
Denton, Peter, 72
Department of Housing and Urban Development (HUD), 45
Devos, Betsy, 73
Dick and Betsy Devos Foundation, 73
Dimon, Jamie, 262
disruptive power: Anderson's use of, 204–7; Ras Baraka's use of, 207; Black urban regime and, 16–17; Christie's neoliberal education reforms as, 120–22; clash of disruptors, 145–73; class structure and, 239–41; of markets, 150–51; Newark Students Union as example of, 140–41; postwar suppression of, 43; privatization of public schools and, 102–5, 123–24; of student protests, 126–27, 207; of teachers, 211–16
DiVincenzo, Joseph, 71, 240, 278–79
Dixon, Bruce, 268, 349n32
Dixon, Michael, 227–28
Douglass, Frederick, 77, 173
Dreier, Peter, 38, 348n25
Driven from New Orleans (Arena), 279
drivers, in corporate school movement, 66–68

INDEX | 359

dual development model, Newark
downtown revitalization and,
71–72, 80–81
Dumas, Michael, 5
Duncan, Arne, 104–5, 149, 206,
216–17

Eagle Capital Management, 80
East Side High School, turnaround
protests at, 211–16
Economic Development Authority
(EDA), 149, 190
economic growth, neoliberalism and
slowing of, 264–65
Education Equity Project, 84
Education for Reform Now, 233
Education Law Center (ELC), 55
education reform, neoliberal campaign for, 55–58
Education Trust, 313n66
electoral politics, social movements
and, 270–71
elite brokerage, disruptive power
and, 207–8
Ellenstein, Meyer, 35–36, 48
Emancipation Celebration, 255
Emmanuel, Rahm, 106, 193
Engels, Friedrich, 270
Englin, Dale, 94, 112
ethnic politics, 181
E3 (Excellent Education for Everyone) nonprofit, 72, 74–75
extended work agreement, teachers'
protests over, 211–16

Fabricant, Michael, 160, 219
federal government programs:
bipartisan support for charter
schools and, 149–51; impact in
Newark of, 37–41; suburbanization and, 292n19
Federal Housing Administration
(FHA), 37–38, 252

Fenty, Adrian, 15, 229
50CAN Campaign, 303n42
Fight Back Friday protest, 154, 156
finance, insurance, and real estate
(FIRE), charter school move-
ment and, 6–7, 253–56
Fine, Michelle, 5, 160, 219
Fisher Foundation, 91
fixers, in community development
corporations, 47, 58, 69
Florida, Richard, 186
Floyd, George, 260–63
FOCUS-Hispanic Center for Com-
munity Development, 47–48
Ford Foundation: education funding
reform and, 54–55, 294n47;
GVZ program, 97, 311n39; Sec-
ondary Educational Racial Justice
Collaborative, 10, 286n30
Foreman, James, Jr., 286n35
Foundation for Newark's Future
(FNF), 100–101, 107, 109–12,
150, 311n39
foundation-funded nonprofit
complex, 54–55; local foundation, 92–95; neoliberalism and
role of, 266–71; unions and,
219–22
Franco, Evy, 221–22
Frankel, Matthew, 246
Fraser, Nancy, 273
Freedom Budget movement, 45–47,
180–81
Fuller, Howard, 71–75, 79, 86, 96,
241
Fulop, Steve, 238–41
funding for public schools: decline
in Newark for, 42–44; moratorium on charter expansion,
239–46; New Jersey reduction
in, 98–101, 134, 148–49, 317n12;
state oversight linked to, 54–58;
structures for, 54–55

INDEX

Gaddy, Kim, 247, 250
Garrett, Wyman (Dr.), 52, 296n60
Garza, Alicia, 262
gentrification, charter schools and, 49–50. *See also* rent-intensification development agenda
Geraldine R. Dodge Foundation, 94–95
Giambusso, David, 124
Gianni, Nancy, 154
Gibson, Kenneth: Black migration to Newark and, 63–64; Black Power movement and, 183; Black urban regime and, 48–49; BPMC and, 52–53; election as mayor, 31; Newark politics and, 46, 199, 272, 298n4; school funding reforms and, 94
Gillespie, Andra, 81, 85–86
Gindin, San, 267
Gingrich, Newt, 84–85
Glassman, Carol, 47
Global Education Advisors, 102–3, 314n74
Global Village Zone (GVZ) program, 97, 126, 171, 221–22, 241, 311n39
Goldfield, Michael, 36
Goldman Sachs, 76; Urban Investment Group, 186
Goldman Sachs Foundation, 100
Golin, Steve, 40, 50–51
Good, Ryan, 5
Google Corporation, 145–46
Gordon, David, 33
Gramsci, Antonio, 23, 74, 102, 273, 289n65
Granholm, Jennifer, 93
grassroots tactics: of Black politicians, 73–75, 303n42; promotion of privatization through, 102–5; racial democracy and, 262–63; student protests and, 126–27

Graves, Carol, 53, 57, 317n18
Gray, Vincent, 168
Great Migration, Newark and, 63–64

Hackworth, Jason, 21
Haggerty, Brad, 211, 213, 336n25
Haimson, Leonie, 220
Hall, Beverly, 58
Hamilton, Charles, 181
Hamm, Lawrence, 138, 237, 277–78, 343n40
Hands Off Our Future Parent Lobby Day rally, 239–41
Harlem Children Zone, 311n39
Harrington, Michael, 46
Harris, Gloria, 49, 166–67
Harris, Shané, 94, 168
Harvey, David, 14, 20, 23, 36, 78–79, 116–17, 141–42, 204, 272–73
hegemony: BPMC and, 162–68, 239–41; charter school movement and, 102–5
Henderson, Kaya, 169, 206
Henwood, Doug, 190–91
Hespe, David, 166–68, 172, 209
Hill, Ryan, 83, 112, 246
Hirsch, Susan, 32–33
Holder, Wilhelmina, 73–75, 122
Holland, Moe'Neyah Dene, 262–63
home mortgage insurance program, suburbanization and, 37–38
HOPE VI initiative, 65
Hopewell Baptist Church (Newark), 155–56
House Un-American Activities Committee (HUAC), 41
Housing Act of 1949, 38
housing development, Newark rebellion and funding for, 44–48
Houston, Whitney, 39
Howard, William, 162–68
Howard University, 183
Hyra, Derek, 15–16

ICE detention centers in New Jersey, 278–79

I Married a Communist (Roth), 41

Imbroscio, David, 348n25

Imperiale, Anthony, 48–49, 53

implementers: Booker as example of, 85–86; in corporate school movement, 66–68

industrial capitalism, Newark's transformation and, 32–35

inequality, Black elites and class politics over, 8–9

Institute for Political Education, 78, 304n52

Institute for Urban Excellence, 301n28

intergenerational relationships: Ras Baraka use of, 137–38; BPMC and, 95–97

International Longshoremen Association (ILA), 245–48, 343n38

International Monetary Fund (IMF), 24

intraclass struggle: bottom-up social movements and, 116–17; Democratic Party and, 200–201; social movements and, 25–26, 35–36

intramovement struggle, Newark rebellion and, 44–48

Iovino, Michael, 123, 134

Ironbound Community Corporation (ICC), 47–48, 94, 310n29

"Is Newark the Next Brooklyn?" (Nark), 186

Jackson, Donald, 127

Jackson, Jesse, 80

Jackson, Kenneth, 37–38

Jackson, Maynard, 59, 228–29

Jackson, Reginald, 75, 79, 303n41

Jacob, Jesse, 52–53, 296n60

James, Grady, 156

James, Oscar, II, 184

James, Sharpe, 184; Black urban regime and, 15, 49; crime reform and, 261; criticism of Booker, 83, 305n61; defeat and imprisonment of, 110; as Newark mayor, 63–66, 70–72, 79–81, 184, 299n9, 306n67; school reform and, 26, 59; state education system and, 95

Janey, Clifford, 96–97, 103, 124, 311n39

Jefferson, David, 125–26

Jeffries, Shavar: Adubato and, 319n49; authenticity trope and, 82; Black Power movement and, 86; charter schools support by, 246; community-centered approach of, 122, 125, 162; Education for Reform Now and, 233; as mayoral candidate, 143–44, 155, 161, 170–71, 325n47; school board elections and, 106, 137, 314n69

Jenkins, Kevin, 345n6

Jewish community, Booker's ties to, 71

job discrimination, Ras Baraka campaign against, 246–48, 343n38

Jobs, Steve, 91

jobs programs, community advocacy for, 142

Johnson, Cedric, 7, 10, 12, 14–15, 73, 86, 180–83, 201

Johnson, Jeremy, 93–94, 112, 310n24

Johnson, Robert, 101

Johnson, Yolanda, 248–49

Johnson & Johnson, 57

Jones, LeRoi. *See* Baraka, Amiri

Jurgelevicius, Alex, 235

Karenga, Maulana, 295n52

Katz, Don, 168

Katz-Fishman, Walda, 277

362 || INDEX

Kawaida Inc., 47
Kean, Tom, 75, 298n6
Kelley, Raymond, 89
Kelley, Robin, 23
Kelley, Sharon Pratt, 15
Kemp, Bo, 301n28
Kemp, Jack, 80, 305n58
Kerner Commission Report, 44, 47
Kettenring, Brian, 132
Key, V. O., 8
Keynesian economics: intergenerational conflict over, 95–97; neoliberal offensive against, 56–58, 66–68, 70, 93–95, 99–101, 108–10; social movements and, 19–22, 59
Khalek, Rania, 136
King, Greg, 278
King, John, 105–6, 168, 313n66
King, Martin Luther, Jr. (Dr.), 46, 76, 146, 173
KIPP charter school chain, 82, 90–92, 149, 156, 186, 194, 204–5, 224, 236, 242–43
Klein, Joel, 84, 87–90, 92, 106, 108, 140, 146, 153, 223, 307n78
Koeppe, Al, 170, 190, 199, 237
Kopp, Wendy, 76
Kotz, David, 19–20, 59, 92–93, 264–66, 273–74

La Casa de Don Pedro, 47–48
Lakey, George, 266
Landrieu, Mitch, 288n52
Latinx community in Newark, 247–48
Latner, Johnny, 122
Lauria, Mickey, 177, 199, 231
Lautenberg, Frank, 110, 143
Lauto, Michelle, 126
Law Enforcement Assistance Administration, 45
Leadership Newark, 301n27

Leahy, Ed (Father), 168
Lee, Dominique, 244
Lefebvre, Henri, 142
Legette, Willie, 8
Lehrer, Brian, 133
Leitner, Helga, 21
Lenni Lenape Indigenous community, 32
Leonardo, Jose, 134, 217–18, 222–23, 225, 234–35, 252
Leopold, Les, 8, 270
Lerner, Eric, 265
Leschly, Stig, 91–92
Levine, Yasha, 71
Lewis, John, 263
Lewis, Karen, 140, 192–93, 200–201
Lewis, Marques, 250
liberal expansionism, 348n25
Lichtenstein, Warren, 186
Linder, William, 69
Lipman, Pauline, 6, 9, 150, 205
Living Downtown Plan (Newark), 188
local control of schools: Anderson's dismantling of, 204; Ras Baraka campaign to regain, 207–11, 222–28, 232, 238; Black Power involvement in, 182–83; charter schools movement incorporation of, 233–38, 269–70; in Newark, 3–7; philanthrocapitalism and restructuring of, 93–95, 110–12; public feuding and back-channel negotiations over, 241–46; return to Newark of, 252–53; state power and, 57–58, 239–41, 253–56; student protests for regaining, 216–19
local philanthropies: charter schools and, 233; One Newark plan and, 151–55; philanthrocapitalism and, 100–101
Lowenstein, Bob, 41–42

Lubell, Samuel, 36–37
Luciano, Felipe, 208
Luxemburg, Rosa, 23–24, 157, 265, 269–72, 279, 348n30

Maclean, Nancy, 77
MacLeod, Gordon, 80
Madhubuti, Haki, 78, 304n52
Make the Road immigrant rights group, 221, 337n40, 338n45
Malcolm X, 76, 197
Malcolm X Liberation University, 73
Mallory, Tamika, 263
Manhattan Institute, 72, 80, 302n34
March of Dignity rally (Newark), 225
March on Washington for Jobs and Freedom (1963), 45, 145
market forces: Black achievement and, 303n43; charter school enrollment system and, 148–51; school reform and, 5; state power and, 233–38. See also business elite; philanthrocapitalism
Marquez, Thais, 127, 129–34, 137, 201, 208, 212
Martin, Trayvon, 201
Marx, Karl, 21–22, 150, 270, 273
Mass Day of Outrage protest, 124
mass strike process, Luxemburg's concept of, 23–25, 157, 270
Mayorga, Edwin, 10–11
McAlevey, Jane, 267–68
McCain, John, 84
McCallum, Joseph, 219
McCarthy, Garry, 89, 184
McCarthyism, political repression of unions by, 39–42
McGoey, Linsey, 66–68
MCJ Amelior Foundation, 92
McKesson, DeRay, 262
McLain, Kimberly, 92–93, 101, 112
Means, Fred, 296n60

media coverage of Newark: Booker and, 72, 298n4, 301n31; promotion of privatization through, 102–5; support for corporate reform in, 125; takeover of public schools and, 99–101
Melamed, Jodi, 5
Merck Corporation, 57
Meredith march (1966), 46
Michaels, Walter Benn, 261
Michigan Council of Foundations, 93
militant particularism: bottom-up social movements, 141; protests against One Newark plan and, 154–55; social movements and, 23
Minor, Clifford, 331n28
mixed-use real estate development, charter school movement and, 6–7, 186
Mollenkopf, John, 38, 348n25
Mooney, John, 96
Moran, Tom, 109–10, 125, 143–44, 162, 164–65, 254, 334n14
Morel, Domingo, 11, 286n35
mortgage foreclosures, increase in Newark of, 64–66, 150–51, 299n9
Moussab, Al, 121–23, 211–15
movement from above (top-down social movements): Black elites and, 71–75; charter schools and, 17–26, 238–46; destruction of Newark public schools and, 204–5; legitimacy crises for, 162–68, 205–7; rise and power consolidation of, 26, 110–12
movement from below (bottom-up social movements): assessment of, 138–41; Ras Baraka and containment of, 200–202, 253–56, 259–60; Booker's use of, in

privatization campaign, 102–5; charter schools and, 17–26; limitations of, 141–44; militant particularism and, 141; neoliberal school reform and, 22–23; One Newark plan and mobilization of, 155–57, 172–73; sources of, 27; student protests, 126–38

Moynihan, Daniel Patrick, 294n44

multiracial social movements, 20–22

Murray, Charles, 72, 302n34

Nagin, Ray, 15

Nark, Jason, 186

Nasser, Alan, 150–51

National Action Network (NAN) nonprofit, 84–85, 125–26, 307n78

National Alliance for Public Charter Schools, 83, 223

National Black Political Conventions, 194, 257

National Commission on Excellence in Education, 56

National Day of Action to Reclaim Public Education, 160–61

National Education Association (NEA), 108–10, 160–61, 219

National League of Cities, 65

Nation at Risk, A, 56

Nation of Islam, 247

neoliberalism: Ras Baraka and, 189–99; Black politics and, 64–66; Black urban regime and, 15–16, 18–22; bottom-up social movements and, 22–25; BPMC and, 7–9, 72–75, 95–97; drivers and implementers of, 66–68; privatization of Newark schools and, 89–95, 102–5; racial democracy and, 260–63; racial democracy and challenge to, 264–72; school choice ideology and, 148–51; school reform and influence of, 5–6, 12, 26, 72–79; selective disinvestment and, 150; as social movement, 18–22

Newark: Black politics in, 63–66, 79–86, 298n3; Black urban regime and, 13–16; corporate-driven revitalization program, 63–66, 80–81; development and transformation of, 26, 31–41, 71–72; economic downturn in 1930s and, 35–36; education movement from below and, 115–44; fiscal crises in, 43–44; as majority minority city, 42–44; media coverage of, 72, 298n4; population and racial composition table, 40; population growth in, 32–33; postwar politics in, 36–44; public schools in postwar era, 41–44; school reform in, 1–7, 25–26; state takeover of schools in, 57–58; white flight from, 39, 42–44

Newark Alliance, 64, 70, 72, 170

Newark Anti-Violence Coalition, 184, 213, 330n25

Newark Central Planning Board, 234–36

Newark Charter School Fund (NCSF), 92, 99, 101, 104, 111, 124, 150–51, 194, 233, 238, 309n17

New Ark Community Coalition, 51

Newark Community Development Network (NCDN), 251–52

Newark Community Education Convention: Reclaiming a Village, 194–99, 333n58

Newark Community Union Project (NCUP), 47

Newark Educational Success Board (NESB), 222, 234–35

Newark Education Workers (NEW) Caucus: Ras Baraka and, 201–2; community ties to, 141–44, 160–62, 221, 267; declining support for, 227–28, 234, 255; extended work agreement protests and, 211–16; formation of, 110, 123, 139–41; Newark Promise plan exclusion of, 220–21; New Visions reform agenda of, 209–11, 227–28; One Newark plan protests and, 154; political activism and, 268; protests against Anderson and, 171, 209–11; student protests supported by, 133–34

Newark Families for Progress, 171

Newark First, 171

Newark 40 Acres and a Mule Fund (NWK FAM Fund), 260–63

Newark Housing Authority, 44

Newark Now nonprofit, 83–85

Newark Philanthropic Liaison, 93–94

Newark Promise plan, 171–72, 207–11, 220, 269–70

Newark PTA, 52

"Newark Public Schools, The," 99–101

Newark Public Schools Advisory Board, 72, 82, 90–91, 185

Newark rebellion (July 12–17, 1967), 44–48

Newark Star-Ledger, 109–10, 125, 143–44, 162, 164–65, 180, 201

Newark Student Federation, 53

Newark Students Union (NSU), 2; Anderson's removal and, 222–28; Ras Baraka alliance with, 161–62, 194–99, 201, 252–53, 255; decline of, 234; disruptive

power of, 216–19; privatization protests by, 132–38, 148, 192–93; protests against Anderson by, 157–59, 171–72, 203–4, 208–11. *See also* student protests of school privatization

Newark Teachers Association (NTA), 49–54

Newark Teachers Union (NTU): Anderson's negotiations with, 211–16; Ras Baraka and, 148, 201–2; Black criticism of, 49–54; Booker and, 96–97, 108–10, 315n77, 315n81; Christie and, 39–41, 139; insurgency within, 123–24, 139–41; NEW's challenge to, 227–28; One Newark plan protests and, 154–55; protests against privatization and, 117–22, 220–22, 235, 245–46

Newark Trust for Education (NTE), 94–95, 100–101, 111, 152, 170–71

Newark Youth Coalition, 184

New Community Corporation (NCC), 47–48, 69

New Deal: Democratic party abandonment of, 9; public housing under, 38, 232, 251–52, 344n53

New Jersey Communities United (NJCU), 132–34, 160–62, 212, 220–22, 235, 237, 244–46, 250–51

New Jersey Education Association (NJEA), 109–10, 315n77

New Jersey Employer-Employee Relations Act (1968), 50

New Jersey Performing Arts Center (NJPAC), 64, 104, 155, 298n6

New Jersey Working Families Party, 192–93

New Leaders for New Schools, 92, 146–47

New Orleans, Louisiana: charter school movement in, 10, 148–49, 191; destruction of public housing in, 15–16, 277; multiracial governing elite in, 16, 288n52

New Schools for New Leaders movement, 309n17

New Schools Venture Fund, 205–7

New Teacher Project, 172–73, 314n74

New Visions for Public Schools, 336n25

New York Times, 143, 180, 195, 198, 231

Nicholson Foundation, 94

Nilsen, Alf Gunvald, 17–18, 21–25, 63, 67, 78–79, 85, 111, 119, 141, 159, 239, 253–54, 269–70, 279

Nix, Naomi, 306n70

NJ Spotlight, 225

Nkrumah, Kwame, 253

Noguera, Pedro, 97, 126, 221, 311n39

North Star Academy Charter, 58, 76–77, 90–91, 149, 233–35, 339n6

North Ward Citizens Committee, 48

North Ward Education and Cultural Center, 47–48, 58

No Shortcuts (McAlevey), 268

Nutter, Michael, 15, 229

Obama, Barack, 69, 80, 84–85, 108–10, 149, 193, 237

Occupy movement, 128–29, 133

Ocean Hill–Brownsville teachers strike (New York City), 52

One Day, All Children (Kopp), 76

O'Neil, Thomas, 301n27

One Newark Education Coalition (ONIC), 122

One Newark restructuring plan: Anderson's promotion of, 148–59, 203–4; Ras Baraka and, 248–52;

legitimacy crisis for, 162–70; mayoral race and opposition to, 170–71; protests against, 159–62, 171–72, 208–11, 219, 255

"Opportunism and the Art of the Possible" (Luxemburg), 269

Oprah Winfrey Show, The, 1, 87, 100, 283n2

Organization of Negro Educators (ONE), 50–51, 53–54

Orozco, Catalina, 249

Osborne, Eddie, 219

Overcoming Racism (New Orleans), 334n12

Owens, Leah, 120–23, 158, 213, 241, 246, 250, 254, 278

Packet, Brittney, 262

Paige, Rod, 75

PARCC standardized tests, state imposition of, 209

parent activism: BPMC engagement with, 239–41; One Newark plan and galvanization of, 153–55; protests against privatization of public schools and, 121–22; student protests and, 131–34

Parent Coalition for Excellent Education (PC2E), 238–41

Parenti, Christian, 45

Parenti, Michael, 16

Parents Unified for Local School Education (PULSE), 122, 172, 194

Partnership for New Jersey, 301n27

Payne, Donald, Jr., 83

Payne, William, 278

Peck, Jamie, 20

People's Conference on Jobs, Peace, Equality, and Justice, 142

People's Organization for Progress (POP), 122, 138, 142, 237, 248, 277–79, 343n40

Perello, Ariagna, 185
Petino, Pete, 52, 119–20, 122
Philadelphia Student Union, 130, 141–44
philanthrocapitalism: Anderson's embrace of, 204; Ras Baraka and, 232, 258–60; Booker and, 66–69, 80–81, 85–86; Christie–Booker alliance and, 98–101; intraclass struggle and, 110–12; intraphilanthropic conflict and conciliation, 100–101; local government reconfiguration and, 110–12; police reform and, 260–63; privatization of Newark schools and, 91–95, 105–10; pro–charter school superintendent appointment and, 105–10; social movement against, 115–17. *See also* market forces
Picower, Bree, 10–11
Pierson testing company, 209
Piven, Frances Fox, 16–17, 22–23, 42–44, 54, 125–26, 129–31, 208, 234, 240
police violence: Ras Baraka campaign against, 183–85, 331n28; bottom-up social movements and, 201–2; in Newark, 42; Newark rebellion and, 44–48; protests against, 260–63; student protests and, 218
Politico, 186
Poor People's Movements (Piven and Cloward), 22–23, 127, 129
power: social movements and access to, 85–86; state and local context for, 110–12; student protest strategies for, 131–32
Price, Clement, 94–95, 103, 105, 184, 301n26
privatization of public schools: antiracist politics and, 145–48;

Ras Baraka support for, 233–38, 258–60; Black political entrepreneurs and, 82–83, 303n43; Black politics and social movements and, 9–12; Black urban regime and, 58–59; Booker's involvement in, 71–77, 87–93; capital accumulation and, 117; enrollment system as part of, 148–55, 203–4; legitimacy crisis for, 162–68; neoliberal campaign for, 56–58, 76–79; in Newark, 3–7; philanthrocapitalism and, 85–86; real estate development and, 6–7, 185–91; rent-intensification development agenda linked to, 27; self-determination politics and, 194–99; teachers' protests against, 117–22
Prize, The (Roussakoff), 169, 206
property values and taxes: decline in Newark of, 43–44, 54–55, 317n12; Newark regeneration and rise in, 232; school reform and, 6
Prudential Center sports complex, 64, 80–81, 298n6, 301n31
Prudential Corporation, 33, 54, 57, 92, 124, 186
Prudential Foundation, 94
Pryor, Stefan, 186–88, 332n42
Public Employees Relations Commission (New Jersey), 50
public housing: Afrocentric development projects and, 183; Ras Baraka and, 232, 251–52; Booker's involvement in, 69–70; destruction in Newark of, 64–66, 150–51, 299n9; destruction in New Orleans of, 15–16; New Deal development of, 38
Public Private Strategy Group, 89

public schools: Black Power involvement in, 52–54, 77–79, 182–83; Black urban regime assault on, 15–16; Booker's involvement in reform of, 71–75; bottom-up social movements and reform of, 22–25, 115–17; commodification of, 9–12; elite perceptions of, 55–58; foundational and nonprofit support for, 54–55; intraclass struggle and, 116–17; in postwar Newark, 41–44. *See also* charter school movement; corporate school reform; privatization of public schools

public-sector employment: abrogation of labor rights for, 43–44, 267–68; advocacy for expansion in Newark of, 86, 142–43; Christie wage freeze for, 122, 268; white dominance in Newark of, 41–42

Puerto Ricans: migration to Newark, 39, 42; Newark politics and, 49, 71, 294n44, 298n3, 301n29; turnaround protests supported by, 212–14

Purcell, Mark, 95

Puritans, Newark settlement of, 32

Qualified School Construction Bonds (QSCBs), 149, 187

Quintana, Luis, 124, 298n3

Rabig, Julia, 47

race and racism: Black class politics and, 1, 8–9; Black Power solidarity in face of, 181–83; capitalism and, 10–12

race reductionism, 7

Race to the Top Initiative, 92, 120, 149, 206

racial democracy (RD): Ras Baraka embrace of, 199–202, 207, 258–60; Black politics and, 9–12, 52–54; Black urban regime and discourse of, 14–16, 258–60; capitalism and, 7–9; civil rights movement and, 145; education reform and, 84; future of, 264–72; merging of movements in, 231–56; neoliberal school reform and, 4–6, 76–79; One Newark plan protests and invocation of, 159; police reform and, 260–63; self-determination politics and, 194–99

racial justice framework: charter schools and, 172; community schools advocacy and, 221–22; self-determination ideology and, 173, 193–94; state takeover of public schools and, 10–11; student protests and, 131, 147; working-class politics and, 246–48

racial ontology, 286n32

Ramos, Anibal, 161, 218–19, 298n3

Randolph, A. Philip, 45–46, 145, 180–81, 248

Rawlings-Blake, Stephanie, 15

Raymond, Thomas, 34–35

RBH Group, 186

Reagan, Ronald, 8–9, 19

real estate development: corporate school reform and, 67–68, 187–91, 246–47; housing segregation and, 289n70; predatory lending in Newark and, 81; privatization of schools and, 6–7; public housing destruction and, 251–52; suburbanization in Newark and, 37–38

Rebel Cities (Harvey), 142, 204, 272–73

Reckhow, Sarah, 91
Reed, Adolph, Jr., 1, 7–9, 12–16, 69, 86, 112, 180–81, 203, 207, 228–29, 256, 261, 268–69, 284n15, 294n43
Reed, Touré, 7, 248, 286n32
Reffkin, Robert, 76
reinvention mechanism, Black politics and use of, 228–29
religious schools, vouchers for, Black elite campaign for, 72–75
rent-intensification development agenda, 27, 284n15; Ras Baraka and, 199–202, 246–47, 259–63; privatization of public schools and, 186
reparations movement, 268–69, 349n32
revitalization programs: Booker's criticism of, 71–75; corporate interests and, 64–66, 80–81; James's dual development model for, 63–66, 70–72
Rhee, Michelle, 84, 97, 206, 311n37, 314n74
Rice, Ronald, Jr., 82–83, 86, 184
Rice, Ronald, Sr., 63, 82–83, 124, 225, 298n3
Richardson, Wayne, 234, 236, 250
Rickford, Russell, 77–78
"Right to the City" ideology, 142
Riley, Dylan, 20
Rippey, Branden: bottom-up social movements and, 115, 279; community partnerships and, 122–23; NEW and, 209–11, 227–28; One Newark plan protests, 158; privatization of schools and, 117–19, 138–41, 204; student protests and, 128–29, 133–35, 189, 209; turnaround protests and, 214–16

Rivera, Vivian, 214–15
Robertson Foundation, 91
Robert Treat Academy, 91
Robinson, Cedric, 11
Robinson, Kiesha, 141–42
Robinson v. Cahill, 55
Rodriguez, Vanessa, 156–57
Romney, Mitt, 80
Rone, Dana, 72, 75, 82, 96, 97
Roosevelt, Franklin Delano, 38
Roper, Richard, 70–71, 163, 301nn27–28
Rosen, Amy, 89, 149
Roth, Philip, 41
Rowe, Willie, 105–6, 314n70
Rubin, Julia, 5
Ruiz, Teresa, 190, 209, 219, 240, 253
Russakoff, Dale, 90, 151, 169, 206, 209, 238, 244, 334n14
Rustin, Bayard, 45–46, 180–81
Ryan, Howard, 10–11, 66, 245

Sadaukai, Owusu. See Fuller, Howard
Saltman, Kenneth, 66–68
San Antonio v. Rodriguez, 54–55
Sanders, Bernie, 262–63, 346n19
Santos, Mario, 135–36, 212–13
Saunders, Don, 53
Sawant, Kshama, 262
Schneider, Aaron, 16
Schneider, Rita, 278
Schnur, Jon, 92
school board elections: candidates for, 106, 137–38, 241–42, 246, 314n69; privatization of public schools and, 106–10
school choice ideology: Black elites' promotion of, 5, 72–75, 83–85; Black Power version of, 77–79; Booker's criticism of, 96; One Newark plan and, 148–55

370 ‖ INDEX

School Development Authority (SDA), 149, 155

Schott Foundation, 219, 337n40

Schumpeter, Joseph, 116–17

Schundler, Brent, 72, 75

Scordo, Trina, 132, 244–46

Scott, James, 23

Scott, Jerome, 277

Sears, Alan, 21

selective disinvestment, in public schools, 150

self-determination: Ras Baraka's ideology of, 27, 177–202, 259–60; charter school movement and, 194–99, 233–38; local school control and, 225–26, 252–53; school reform politics and, 5–6, 73–75, 77–79, 269–71

Sergio, Grace, 154, 156, 172, 234–325

Service Employees International Union (SEIU), 160, 220

"74, The" (online journal), 306n70

Shachtman, Max, 46–47

Sharp, Gene, 266

Sharper, Horace, 298n3

Sharpton, Al, 80, 83–84, 86, 125, 260, 307n78

Shelton, Jon, 41

shock therapy privatization: One Newark plan as, 152–53, 156–57; pushback against, 27, 102–5, 172–73

Simmons, Percy, 167, 224–25

Sister Souljah, 180

60 Minutes (TV program), 72

Skadden Foundation, 69

smaller schools initiative (New York City), 153

Smith, Marcie, 266

Smith, Neil, 186

Smith, Preston, II, 4–5, 10, 84, 194, 198

Smith, Sharon, 122

Smith-Gregory, Deborah, 154, 172, 209, 220, 224–25, 237–38, 243, 245, 255–56

Snyder, Jeffrey, 91

social democracy (SD): Amiri Baraka and, 180–81; Black class politics and, 7–9; school reform and, 4–6

socialist politics, Newark and example of, 272–73

social media: pushback against charter schools and, 102–5; student protests against privatization and, 126–27, 132–33

social movements: from above and below, 17–26; access to power and, 85–86; business elites in Newark and, 35–36; community-labor partnerships in, 122–26; intraclass struggle and, 25–26; mass strike process, Luxemburg's concept of, 23–25, 157; neoliberalism and, 18–22, 59; Newark development and transformation and, 26; racial democracy and merging of, 231–56; school privatization and, 12; teachers' unions and, 39–41; urban rebellions and, 44–48

social structure of accumulation (SSA): Black urban regime and, 65–66, 97; privatization of public schools and, 19–22, 24–25, 59, 92–93, 116–17; racial democracy and challenge to, 264–72; superintendent appointment and, 105–10

SoMa development project (Newark), 188

South Ward Community Schools Initiative, 243

Spence, Lester, 5, 11–12
Spirit House, 49, 278
Stack, Nina, 93–94
Start Up: Education, 100
state control of public schools: Black disempowerment and, 11–12; BPMC and, 26–27, 239–41; charter school expansion and, 239–41; local state and, 253–56; neoliberal reforms and, 5–6, 57–58
Stayin' Alive (Cowie), 58–59
Stein, Sam, 6
Stella Wright Homes demolition, 65
Stellhorn, Paul, 33
Stepan-Norris, Judith, 25, 115–17, 200
Stewart, Blake, 273
Stirrings in the Jug (Reed), 228–29
Street Fight (film), 80
"Strictly Confidential Draft Work Product," 103
student protests of school privatization: boycotts of standardized tests by, 209; community and teachers alliance with, 141–44; corporatist framing of, 147–48; grassroots origins of, 12, 126–38; local school control campaign and, 225–28; One Newark plan protests, 157–59; turnaround protests at East Side and Weequahic high schools, 211–16. *See also* Newark Students Union
Students for a Democratic Society (SDS), 47
subaltern studies, 290n83
suburbanization: federal support for, 292n19; impact on Newark of, 37–44
Swanstrom, Todd, 38, 348n25

Taft–Hartley Act (1947), 43
"Take Back Newark" protest, 245
Tavory, Iddo, 279
Taylor, Keeanga-Yamahtta, 298n38, 299n12, 307n80
Taylor Law (New York State), 50
teachers: Black politics and attacks on, 12, 49–54; Booker's relations with, 96–97, 108–10; bottom-up social movements and, 23–25, 267–68; community partnerships with, 122–26, 141–44, 267–68; performance evaluation and compensation system for, 99–100, 107–12, 314n74, 315n81; protests against privatization by, 116–22; repression of unions for, 39–44; student protests and support from, 127–30; turnaround protests at East Side and Weequahic high schools and, 211–16
Teachers and Power (Braun), 52
Teachers as Leaders in Newark (TaLiN), 121, 278, 317n16
teachers strikes: Black opposition to, 53–54, 77; Black Power movement and, 49–54; in postwar Newark, 41–44, 139; school privatization and, 12
Teachers Village (Newark), 6–7, 149–50, 185–88, 190–91
Teach for America (TFA), 76, 89, 91, 120–22, 205–6, 233, 262
TEAM Academy Charter Schools, 82, 149, 172
tenure system for school employees, neoliberal upending of, 107–10, 211–16, 314n78
Terrell Homes development, 251–52
Theodore, Nik, 21
Therborne, Goran, 18

372 ‖ INDEX

Third World movements, Black Power and influence of, 294n43
Third World Press, 78
Tickwell, Adam, 20
Tilly, Charles, 131
Time magazine, 72
Timmermans, Stefan, 279
Tirado, Elise, 126
Torricelli, Robert, 75
Towkanik, Kristen, 134, 145, 159, 161–62, 171–72, 216–19, 234, 252
Tractenberg, Paul, 54–55
Tri-City Citizens Union for Progress, 47–48
Trump, Donald, 8
turnaround/renew schools category: creation in Newark of, 109–10, 123–24, 141–44; protests against, 156–59, 207–16
Turner, Irvine, 48, 298n3
Tusk, Bradley, 102
Tusk Associates, 102–5
21st Century task force, 72, 301n26

Uncommon Schools charter chain, 58, 77, 91, 149, 233–35, 242–43
Union Caucuses of Rank-and-File Educators (UCORE), 12, 141–42, 160, 220–21, 320n21
unions: Ras Baraka lack of support for, 248; Black politics and attacks on, 12, 51–54; Black Power movement versus, 49–54; Booker's relations with, 96–97; bottom-up social movements and, 23–25, 266–71; charter school movement, response to, 116–22; community organizations and, 122–26; mobilization against privatization by, 124–26, 138–39, 159–61; neoliberal attack on, 108–10; nonprofit

connections with, 219–22; repression of, 39–44, 266–71; support for Baraka from, 171
United Brothers, 49
United Caucuses of Rank-and-File Educators (UCORE), 140–41
United Community Corporation (UCC), 46, 294n44
Until Freedom, 263
Urban Hub tax credit program, 187
Urban League, 57
urban politics: Black Americans and, 1, 3–7; Black urban regime and, 13–16; privatization of public schools and, 9–12; real estate development links to, 6–7; school reform and, 6–7; urban rebellions and, 44–48
urban renewal, federal program for, 38
U.S. Conference Mayors, 94

Velazquez, José, 122–23
venture philanthropy, 66–68
Victoria Foundation, 92–94, 100–101, 152
vigilante patrols, 48, 53, 201
Vollman, Molly, 6
Voting Rights Act (1965), 45
vouchers for school choice: Black political promotion of, 96–97; Booker's advocacy for, 72–77, 83–85, 303n43

Wagner Act (1935), 25, 43
Waiting for Superman (pro-charter documentary), 100, 312n47
Walton Family Foundation, 73, 83, 91
war of position tactics, privatization of public schools campaign and, 74–75

INDEX || **373**

War Production Board (WPB), 38–39

Washington, D.C., 91–92

Wasow, Omar, 303n43

We Are an African People (Rickford), 77

Weequahic High School, turnaround protests at, 211–16

Weingarten, Randi, 108, 110, 138, 159–61, 165, 204, 220, 311n39

Weisberg, David, 172–73

Wells, Lauren, 196, 220–22, 241, 259, 286n30, 341n26

West, Calvin, 298n3

Westbrook, Dennis, 49

Wharton, Jonathan, 85–86

"What Has Happened to the Mayor Ras Baraka We Put into Office?" (Scordo), 244–45

What's Race Got to Do with It? (Picower and Mayorga), 10–11

Whelan, Robert, 177, 199, 231

white supremacy: Black politics and, 9–12, 47–48; resurgence in Newark of, 48

Whitlow, Joan, 104

Whitman, Christine, 57–58

Williams, Junius, 121, 138, 278

Williams, Lauren, 158

Williams, Raymond, 141

Winfrey, Oprah, 1, 87, 100, 283n2

Workers Alliance of America, 25, 36

working-class politics: Ras Baraka and, 258–60; Black Power movement and, 183; charter school movement and, 239–41; federal government programs and, 38–41; industrial capitalism in Newark and, 33–36; neoliberalism of Black elites and, 7–9, 273; philanthrocapitalism and, 101–5; racial justice movement and, 246–48; racial wealth gap and, 261–63; social movements and, 46–48; urbanization and, 116–17. *See also* class structure

Works Progress Administration (WPA), 35–36

Wright, De'Shawn, 89–93, 95–97, 111–12, 168–70, 309n17

Young, Alma, 177

Young, Andrew, 15

Young, Lavar, 238–41

"Young Blacks Turn to School Vouchers as Civil Rights Issue" (*New York Times*), 76

Youth March, 184

Youth Media Symposium, 138

Zeitgeistmind series (Google Corporation), 145–46

Zeitlin, Maurice, 25, 115–17, 200

Zernike, Katie, 231

Zimmerman, George, 201

Zuckerberg, Mark, 2, 87, 99, 101, 150

John Arena is associate professor of sociology at the City University of New York's College of Staten Island. He is author of *Driven from New Orleans: How Nonprofits Betray Public Housing and Promote Privatization* (Minnesota, 2012).